Great Chefs of the East©

great chefs of the east©

From the Television Series
Great Chefs of the East

By
Ellen Brown

GREAT CHEFS Publishing

THE LAST ONE
PEMAQUID ME

Other Great Chefs®
companion cookbooks
are available:

Great Chefs of New Orleans I
Great Chefs of San Francisco
Great Chefs of New Orleans II
Great Chefs of Chicago
Southwest Tastes
the Louisiana new Garde

All series now available on home video, including
Great Chefs of the East.

Additional home videos available,
each with recipe booklet:

Great Chefs: Appetizers	*Mexican Madness*
Great Chefs: Desserts	*Down Home Cookin'*
Great Chefs: Seafood Sampler	*Oriental Obsessions*
Great Chefs: Chocolate Edition	*Great French Fest*
Great Chefs: Chocolate Passion	*Great Chefs: Great American Inns*
Great Chefs: Chocolate Dreams	*A Southwest Thanksgiving Feast*
A New Orleans Jazz Brunch	*An International Holiday Table*
Great Chefs, Great BBQ	*Great Chefs, Great Pizza*
Great Southern Barbecue	*Great Women Chefs*
Great Outdoor Cooking	

Front cover:	Poached Salmon in White Wine;
	Yves Labbé, Le Cheval d'Or, Jeffersonville, Vermont
Back cover, top:	Smoked Roasted Capon Breasts with Sweet-Potato Fries;
	Jeffrey Buben, Vidalia, Washington, D.C.
Back cover, bottom:	Warm Salad of Asparagus and Artichokes;
	Daniel Boulud, Restaurant Daniel, New York, New York

Published by
Great Chefs Publishing
G.S.I., Inc.
P.O. Box 56757
New Orleans, LA 70156
1-800-321-1499

Printed in China
First Printing

Library of Congress Cataloging
Publication Date: January 1995

Ellen Brown
Great Chefs of the East®

Library of Congress Catalogue Card Number 94-77617
Includes index
    1. Cooking in America
        I. Great Chefs of the East
        II. Title

ISBN	Hardbound 0-929-714-65-2
	Softbound 0-929-714-66-0
UPC	Hardbound 0-4900-92-652-1
	Softbound 0-4900-92-660-1

TABLE OF CONTENTS

ACKNOWLEDGMENTS

Rather than the author of this book, I am really more of a manager of a team that made the book possible. My deepest thanks go to:

Amanda Lydon, recipe tester *extraordinaire,* tireless worker, and beloved friend, who will be joining the ranks of the Great Chefs before very long;

Executive producer John Shoup, and producer-director John Beyer, of the *Great Chefs of the East* television series, whose insistence on quality production is as strong as that of the chefs they tape;

Anna Mulrine, Dominique DuBois, Allison Brody, and Irene Spector, for their assistance with research, biographies, and a myriad of details;

David Vaughan, for sharing his vast knowledge of wine to add another dimension to this book;

Eric Futran, whose photography of the dishes and their creators enlivens these pages artistically;

Mimi Luebbermann and Carolyn Miller, for their superb production and editing of the manuscript;

Larry Escudier, for his inspired design and layout;

Linda Nix and Cybil Curtis of Great Chefs Publishing, for their aid and assistance in rounding up tardy recipes and missing chefs;

Meredith Whiting and the staff of Brown & Whiting Public Relations, for their support;

And Samantha Cat Brown, who spent hours watching us work and who ate all the mistakes.

—Ellen Brown

From Pilgrims and Plantations to World-Class Dining

*a*merican cuisine in the eastern states—from the rocky harsh coastline of Maine to the gentle Tidewater of Virginia on Chesapeake Bay—developed more from pragmatic adaptation than by grand design. The region's varied topography and temperamental, often unforgiving, climate demanded flexibility from its settler-cooks, while rewarding them with a cornucopia of foods.

The Atlantic coast was staggeringly fertile country, with rich, dark soil, thick woods, and oceans teeming with life. The seemingly unlimited resources, from the Virginia woods to the coastal waters of Maine, included a wide variety of wild game birds and animals, fish, shellfish, fruits, and vegetables.

While the climate may have been similar to that of the settlers' European homeland, the crops the land supported were not, and dishes brought from Europe were altered to make use of indigenous foods and cooking methods learned from the Native Americans.

In general, early American cooking was distinguished by a communal spirit, frugality, and the open exchange of information and techniques. The characteristically American melding of cultures that would later be labeled "the melting pot" began in colonial times as a literal blending of cuisines.

The Native Americans were life-saving teachers for the first settlers; they understood the land and weather, and centuries of experience lay behind their way of living off the bounty of the earth. The various tribes had fashioned a diet that mixed cultivated and wild foods; they caught fish, game birds, buffalo, and venison to supplement their own harvest of corn, sweet potatoes, berries, tomatoes, turkey, and squash. Although no one seems to be able to confirm whether or not turkey was on the menu at the first Thanksgiving dinner in 1621, it is known that the group consumed geese, venison, cornbread, oysters, eel, cod, watercress, leeks, plums, and sweet wine.

The influence of the Native American tribes on the East Coast settlers was far-reaching. From them, European women learned to preserve native foods such as beans and corn, and how to cook such native dishes as succotash. Farmers learned to grow the triumvirate of the Native American diet: corn, beans, and squash. When the three vegetables were planted together, the plants formed a symbiotic relationship: The corn rapidly grew a hearty stalk to form the perfect stake to support the crawling tendrils of beans, while the squash grew into a hardy bush that smothered any weeds.

The Native Americans also instructed the early settlers on alternative methods of cooking. They mounded dried beans into deer hides, for example, adding maple sugar and preserved bear fat. The hides were then closed and placed over coals in large underground pits. The beans cooked slowly for hours, in a method that evolved into the traditional dish of beans baked with salt pork and molasses over an open-hearth fire.

It was the Algonquins who introduced New England settlers to clams and lobsters and to their favorite way of cooking them: the clambake. The method essentially steamed the seafood over a fire laid in an open pit, and emphasized the flavor of the ocean by layering the food with damp seaweed. The clambake remains a favorite New England form of cooking for special gatherings.

Another Native American cooking technique was designed to make use of the shad caught in Maryland and Virginia in early spring. A long, narrow fire was set over as much as twenty-five feet of ground. When the fire was nearly reduced to ashes, boned shad fillets wrapped in bacon were nailed skin-side down to greased cedar planks, then the planks were stuck into the ground at an angle to cook the fish by the heat of the flames. Larry Forgione's recipe for Cedar-planked Salmon with Wilted Greens and Toasted Pumpkin Seed Vinaigrette is based on this native technique.

Like the Native Americans, the colonists soon learned to cook with cornmeal and maple syrup, two of the basic indigenous ingredients of American cooking. The "sugaring" of maple trees still elicits a social gathering or celebration. The selection of maple desserts in this collection of recipes only hints at the range of guises maple flavoring took in colonial times.

Corn was crucial to the settlers in the long winter months, since their European wheat grew poorly in the New World. Corn was easily dried and ground. The resulting products could be made into pies, puddings, soups, casseroles, and fritters. Cornmeal was ubiquitous, being made into johnnycakes, corn pone, corn bread, cornmeal mush, and corn muffins; coarsely ground corn became the grits so popular in Virginia and the southern states.

The influence of the Native Americans on homestead baking left its imprint in the names of many dishes. Rye 'n' Injun bread was a mixture of rye flour and cornmeal, and Indian pudding (also called hasty pudding) is a cornmeal mush sweetened with molasses and baked overnight in the hearth fire. The Red Lion Inn's recipe for Indian Pudding included here is a simplified version of this colonial standby.

Regional tastes were shaped by function and utility. Cod was so plentiful in the waters off Massachusetts that Cape Cod was named for the fish. The fish became for New Englanders what pork was to settlers in the rest of the country: the staple around which sustaining dishes were designed. Salt cod became synonymous with New England, particularly as a basis for the chowders that merchant and whaling vessels depended on for sustenance through long months at sea.

These chowders, which Herman Melville detailed so evocatively in *Moby Dick,* were originally thick stews of milk, salt pork, and clams, thickened with crumbled crackers or dried biscuits. The list of acceptable ingredients for chowder, however, has become the center of regional contentions. To many New England purists, the addition of potatoes and herbs is cause enough for disqualification, while the tomatoes found in the scorned Manhattan clam chowder are akin to heresy to some.

A Boston school of cooking sprang out of these traditions, and dishes such as New Bedford pudding or New England boiled dinner were published in recipe books such as Fannie Farmer's, helping to establish and preserve regional dishes.

For inhabitants of coastal New England, the predominance of merchant and whaling vessels ensured a steady stream of foreign seafaring cooking influences, particularly Portuguese, and made exotic seasonings available. Many dishes, including even those made from the sweetest of the regional ingredients—apples, cranberries, beach plums, and elderberries—benefitted from foreign spices.

The ocean and rivers were as prolifically fertile as the ground. Piles of lobsters up to two feet high were reported to wash up on the beaches of Plymouth, Massachusetts. Striped bass, also known as "rockfish," or "stripers," grew as large as six feet long, making them the favored catch for settlers trying to survive the winter on dried fish. On Long Island, oysters were plentiful and often prodigiously large enough to serve as a staple food for the thirteen tribes of Delaware Indians living in the region, and sturgeon were so abundant in the Hudson River that caviar was called "Albany beef" and given out free as a bar snack.

Pumpkin Soup with Fig Quenelles; Peter Platt, Wheatleigh Inn, Lenox, Massachusetts

Away from the coasts, most families lived on farms and followed agrarian eating patterns. Farming families rose before dawn and enjoyed huge breakfasts before beginning a day of often back-breaking labor. The work day was broken up by a large noontime "dinner," with the last meal of the day assuming far less importance.

Different settlement patterns around the country instilled traditions that varied wildly from those on the coast. Inland settlements ate what they raised from their harvests, while coastal settlements harvested the sea. The first and second waves of European immigrants had settled for the most part in Pennsylvania, New Jersey, and New York. The Dutch had settled New York, but the inland settlers known as the Pennsylvania Dutch were actually German; the label *Dutch* was a mishearing of *Deutsch*.

If there can be said to be a characteristically American cooking style, it was born out of Middle Atlantic farmlands, where Dutch, German, and English cuisines united over the course of the nineteenth century to create the culinary tradition of mainstream America. Hearty breakfasts of pancakes, oatmeal, waffles, doughnuts, ham, and pork sausages all derive from midland farms of pre-dominantly Germanic origin.

For farmers with uncertain crops, farm animals were highly valuable, and every attempt was made to ensure that each scrap of food, particularly meat, was used. Laura Ingalls Wilder opened her famous memoirs of life on the American prairie in the nineteenth century with an account of Butchering Time, when her father and neighbors gathered together to slaughter the family pig. After a week of intensive work by the whole family, she wrote, the pig had been divided into sections and processed into such foods as hickory-smoked hams, headcheese, sausage, lard, salt pork, and cracklings.

The best farms functioned like highly efficient factories in which every animal product was either eaten or recycled to fill a household need. Scrapple is a typically Pennsylvanian dish that evolved from this tradition of total utilization: cornmeal mush blended with fatty pork scraps, formed into a loaf shape, and fried. The entire community turned out together for periods of frantic preservation to ensure that nothing was wasted.

This emphasis on frugality did not preclude meals of abundance, however. Pennsylvania Dutch family farms in particular were the setting for meals that ushered in the American love of family-style dining. The traditional dinner centered around meat accompanied with "seven sweets and seven sours," ranging from jellies, conserves, puddings, and preserved fruits to a dazzling array of homemade pickled vegetables and tangy sauces. The sweets served with dinner did not replace dessert, however, and the meal concluded with another dizzying round of pies, both sweet and sour. The fillings exhibited the range and adaptability of regional ingredients and tastes. Apple, pumpkin, and peach may have been perennial favorites, but most farm wives learned to substitute green tomatoes if apples were unavailable, or sweet potatoes when pumpkins were out of season.

The craggy inlets of the Chesapeake Bay made Maryland's coastline welcoming to settlers. As a result, the earliest Spanish and English settlers joined the Native Americans in depending in great measure on an ocean harvest for survival.

Cedar-planked Salmon with Wilted Greens and Toasted Pumpkin Seed Vinaigrette; Larry Forgione, An American Place, New York

The substantial crab population resulted in dozens of regional dishes, ranging from crab cakes, stuffed crab, and crab imperial to soft-shells, crab boils, and crab butter. Besides its hardy shad population, the Maryland coast also harbored countless oyster beds, especially around the Chincoteague Islands off the coastal peninsula. The Chesapeake was also crowded with terrapins, a surfeit that eventually spawned the development of other regional delicacies, such as boiled diamondback terrapin and clear turtle soup.

Maryland's proximity to Virginia led to considerable overlap in the regional specialties of both states. Virginians rightfully prized local Smithfield hams, for which farmers fed their pigs a special peanut diet to give the hams their characteristically dark color and complex flavor. Maryland cooks embellished the ham further by cutting deep slits in the flesh and stuffing the hams with a mixture of spicy wild greens such as cabbage, mustard greens, or spinach. Both states served their ham with beaten biscuits, not the feathery-light biscuits of the South, but sturdy crackerlike breads made with a dough that was kneaded for hours to create gluten.

As country farms became increasingly sophisticated in their use of native ingredients, the urban centers of these eastern states were looking to Europe in an effort to gain sophistication. French influences were acknowledged, for example, in Eliza Smith's 1742 cookbook, which has a number of recipes with French titles and uses terms such as *à la mode, à la braise,* and *à la daube.*

Celery Root Soup with Shad Roe; Jean-Louis Palladin, Jean-Louis at the Watergate, Washington, D.C.

After serving as envoy to Paris, Thomas Jefferson returned to Virginia with a French cook and hundreds of foreign seeds to transplant to the lands of his Charlottesville estate, Monticello. Impressed equally by the wines and olive oil of Europe, Jefferson also brought seedlings to establish vineyards and olive groves on the grounds of his estate, and went to the extent of employing European workers to tend them. Although his vineyards did not flourish, the country's greatest gourmand would be pleased to taste the wines produced in his region today.

A visionary centuries before his time, not only did Jefferson serve wine rather than spirits, but his diet included many fresh vegetables at a time when affluence and meat were almost synonymous. Will Greenwood, the former chef at Washington's Jefferson Hotel, serves updated dishes based on Jefferson's diaries of meals in the grand dining room at Monticello.

Jefferson's continued fascination with French food captured the essence of many Americans' feelings of solidarity with France after the nearly simultaneous revolutions of the two countries, so much so that entertaining in the "French style," meaning everything from food to decor and clothing, became the height of fashion.

First lady Dolley Madison received a great deal of credit for popularizing ice cream in America, but James Parkinson was the Pennsylvania entrepreneur responsible for making ice cream available to the American public; he opened the first American commercial ice cream manufacturing dairy in Philadelphia. Despite his success, Parkinson noted that the French influence on American food was inescapable. "The admission is well nigh universal that the French 'made us,' and that we are 'The Sheep' of French pastures" wrote Parkinson. "So deeply rooted is the sentiment in the public mind that . . . when any American confectioner or caterer makes any invention to his craft, he feels that to secure its sales, and to establish its popularity, he must give it a French name."

The restaurants that capitalized on this craze for things European instilled a sense of culinary inferiority about American cuisine that would last well into the twentieth century and the birth of New American cuisine. Lorenzo, Charles, and Siro Delmonico were three Swiss brothers who took advantage of the fever for French food when they opened their namesake restaurant in New York in 1831. Delmonico's immediately set itself apart from the not very significant competition by presenting food as it had never been served before in the United States. The self-service style found in the few

*Cranberry-Walnut Crostata; Johanne Killeen,
Al Forno Restaurant, Providence, Rhode Island*

competing dining rooms couldn't compete with the luxurious surroundings the Delmonico brothers offered, with food served on elegant china and accompanied with fine silver.

By the mid-nineteenth century, Delmonico's was a harbinger of the notion of a restaurant as a place to see and be seen. Presidents dined there, famous novelists wandered through to absorb the atmosphere, and fashionable, if slightly scandalous, women dined there in the days before ladies of good breeding dined in restaurants unescorted.

The menus at Delmonico's were a study in combining French chic with American abundance and enthusiasm. John Mariani's *America Eats Out* describes the menu: a "seven-page *Carte du Restaurant Français,* printed in both French and English and offering nine soups, eight side dishes, fifteen seafood presentations, eleven beef items, twenty kinds of veal, eighteen vegetables, sixteen pastries, thirteen fruit dishes, and sixty-two imported wines."

Another simultaneous influence on the American conception of dining out was the growth of the continental railroad. The "iron horse" that dramatically altered travel, business, and shipping also ushered in revolutionary ways to eat. The chefs on the first Pullman cars improvised meals from fresh produce, fish, meats, and wines delivered for that night's dinner each day when the train stopped at a new station, so the meals they served were the first experience many Americans had with regional cooking. Traveling diners might enjoy a dinner of codfish balls and boiled lobsters the first night, a next day's lunch of Chesapeake oysters and Maryland crab cakes, and dinner based on Virginia's spoon breads and peanut-fed hams.

While fine dining in urban centers remained French in character, ethnic restaurants became popular after the waves of immigration in the late nineteenth century. Delis serving knishes and blintzes emerged on New York's Lower East Side to feed the Jewish population from Eastern Europe, and Italian trattorias with *antipasti* carts became part of the landscape in Boston's North End. Until after World War II, however, these enclaves of ethnic dining were intended primarily for immigrants. Soldiers returning from Europe and Asia brought a new sense of adventurous dining back with them, and forays into Chinatowns by Caucasian families and into Little Italys by non-Italians soon became part of the American dining scene.

*Indian Pudding; Steven Mongeon, Red Lion
Inn, Stockbridge, Massachusetts*

Another watershed event in the history of eastern restaurants was the 1948 World's Fair in New York, which brought many great chefs to this continent, some of whom remained. Chef and food writer Pierre Franey began the American phase of his career as a result of this fair.

Like the earliest form of American cooking, the cuisine celebrated in *Great Chefs of the East* is based on indigenous ingredients, seasonal foods, and flexibility of preparation. Modern chefs can draw upon the world's larder, and the lines between different ethnic cuisines have blurred and shifted so much in the past decade that American regional food remains a reassuring tradition. For chefs like Larry Forgione, Anne Rosenszweig, and Jack McDavid, rediscovering that food was the first step toward creating what has been labeled New American cuisine, a style of cooking that combines new and old dishes, cuisines, techniques, and foods from a variety of sources.

Joining these Americans are foreign-born cooks who add their own personal touches based on combining cuisines. While some, such as André Soltner at New York's Lutèce and Francesco Ricchi at Ristorante i Ricchi in Washington, retain their allegiance to authentic dishes, the Chinese food at Susanna Foo Chinese Cuisine in Philadelphia includes French accents, and the French food at Jean-Louis Palladin's Jean-Louis at the Watergate in Washington has broadened from nouvelle French to include many American ingredients.

Dishes such as Indian Pudding, Cod Cakes with Bacon and Wilted Greens, Oysters with Champagne Sauce, Pumpkin Soup with Fig Quenelles, Cranberry-Walnut Crostata, and Sautéed Soft-Shell Crabs with Hazelnuts are all based in traditional American food. Other dishes, such as Maple Crêpes Soufflées or Celery Root Soup with Shad Roe, illustrate the merging of American ingredients with French techniques.

The chefs of today have also been responsible for creating the sources for many of the ingredients listed in these recipes. The rebirth of interest in wild game, free-range poultry and meat, heirloom fruits and vegetables, wild mushrooms, and fresh greens began with chefs who demanded the same high quality of ingredients as they had found in Europe. Thanks to them, home cooks now have access to a large and amply stocked larder of superlative foods.

Oysters with Champagne Sauce; Paul Milne, 208 Talbot, St. Michaels, Maryland

Basic Techniques and Recipes

*S*ome techniques and a few basic recipes are common to many dishes in this book, and they are fully explained in this chapter. Individual recipes will refer you to the specific page that discusses the technique, or you may want to take a few moments and read through these listings as a way to augment your culinary prowess or discover another way to perform a task with which you are familiar.

Warm Valrhona Chocolate Cakes with Vanilla Ice Cream; Jean-Georges Vongerichten, JoJo/Vong, New York

Basic Techniques

Handling Bell Peppers and Chilies

Bell peppers now come in a rainbow of colors, and there are literally hundreds of varieties of chilies. Here are some general rules common to all:

Seeding and Deribbing: Either cut out the ribs and seeds with a paring knife, or cut away the flesh, leaving a skeleton of ribs and seeds to discard. For the second method, cut a slice off the bottom of the pepper or chili so that it will stand up on the cutting board. Holding the pepper or chili with your free hand, slice its natural curvature in sections. You will be left with all the flesh and none of the seeds and ribs. The flesh may now be cut as indicated in the recipe.

Roasting and Peeling: Cut a small slit near the stem end of each pepper or chili to ensure that they will not explode. Roast the peppers or chilies in one of the following ways:

• For a large number of peppers or chilies, and to retain the most texture, lower them gently into 375°F oil and fry until the skin blisters. Turn them with tongs when one side is blistered, since they will float to the surface of the oil. This method is also the most effective if the vegetables are not perfectly shaped, since it is difficult to get the heat from a broiler into the folds of peppers and some chilies.
• Place the peppers or chilies 6 inches from the preheated broiler element of the stove, turning them with tongs until all surfaces are charred.
• Place the peppers or chilies on the cooking rack of a hot charcoal or gas grill and turn them until the skin is charred.
• Place a wire cake rack over a gas or electric burner set at the highest temperature and turn the peppers with tongs until all surfaces are charred.
• Place the peppers or chilies on a rack on a baking sheet in a preheated 550°F oven until they are totally blistered. Use this method only for a sauce or any other recipe in which the peppers or chilies are to be pureed.

Cool the peppers or chilies by one of the following methods:
• Place them in ice water. This stops the cooking action immediately and cools them enough to peel them within 1 minute. The peppers or chilies will stay relatively firm.
• Place the peppers in a paper bag, close it, and let them cool. This also effectively separates the flesh from the skin, but it will be 20 minutes or longer before they are cool enough to handle, and they will soften somewhat during that time.
Finally, pull the skin off and remove the seeds.

Handling Fresh Chilies: Certain precautions should be exercised in handling fresh hot chilies, since they contain potent oils. Either wear rubber gloves, or wash your hands thoroughly with soap and hot water after handling chilies and never touch your skin until you've washed your hands. Also wash the knife and cutting board in hot, soapy water. Do not handle hot chilies under running water, since that spreads the oil vapors upward to your eyes.

Cleaning Dried Chilies: Remove the stem, then pull the chili apart lengthwise, splitting it in half. Brush the seeds from both halves and the chili is ready to cook. If it is dusty, rinse it under cold water.

Ancho-rubbed Game Hens; Bobby Flay, Mesa Grill, New York

Caramelizing Sugar

Combine 3 parts granulated sugar and 1 part water in a small, heavy saucepan. Bring to a simmer over a medium flame, swirling the pan occasionally until you see that the sugar crystals have dissolved and the liquid is clear. This should take about 3 to 4 minutes.

Cover the pan, raise the heat to medium high, and let it boil, undisturbed, for 2 minutes, or until the bubbles look thick. Remove the lid. Within a few seconds, the syrup will begin to color. Swirl the pot by its handle, since the syrup will color first directly over the heat. When the syrup is almost the desired color, remove the pan from the heat and continue to swirl. It will darken another shade or two from the residual heat of the pot.

If lining a mold, immediately pour the caramel into the center of the mold and rotate the mold to spread the caramel in an even layer.

To clean the pan in which the caramel was made, fill the pan with water to the top of the hardened caramel and place it over high heat. Stir it as the water comes to a boil, and the pan will be virtually clean.

Melting Chocolate

Chop the chocolate into small pieces with a heavy knife or in a food processor fitted with the steel blade. If using a food processor, break the chocolate into chunks with a heavy knife first.

Melt the chocolate in a double boiler placed over barely simmering water, stirring just until smooth. Or, place the chocolate in a microwave-safe bowl and microwave on 100 percent for 20 seconds, stir, and repeat as necessary; or place in a preheated 250°F oven, then turn off the heat immediately. Stir after 3 minutes and return to the warm oven if necessary.

Opening Coconuts

Puncture one of the "eyes" of the coconut with a sharp, pointed tool such as an icepick. Pour out the liquid, then crack the coconut by hitting it with a hammer in the middle, where the shell is widest. Continue around the nut until you have cracked the shell in a circle around the middle and can separate the two halves. Pry the meat out of the shell with a sharp, heavy knife. Or, heat the coconut in a preheated 350°F oven for 15 minutes, then let sit until cool enough to handle. Wrap the coconut in a kitchen towel and crack it into pieces with a hammer.

Shaving Coconut: Break the meat into small pieces, peel off the brown papery inner covering, then grate the meat with the large holes of a box grater or use a vegetable peeler to create shavings. Coconut may also be shredded in a food processor using the shredding disk or chopped finely with the steel blade.

Grinding Coconut: Break the meat into small pieces, peel off the brown inner peel, and grate the meat with the fine holes of a grater. Alternatively, cut the meat into ½-inch cubes using a heavy, sharp knife. Grind the meat in a food processor using an on-and-off pulsing action.

Toasting Coconut: To toast fresh coconut, slice the peeled meat thinly with a sharp paring knife. Arrange the slices on a baking sheet and bake in a preheated 300°F oven for 15 to 20 minutes, or until golden. To toast dried coconut, reduce the baking time to 5 to 7 minutes.

Raspberry Gratin with Caramel;
Jean-François Taquet, Restaurant Taquet,
Wayne, Pennsylvania

Handling Fresh Crabs

Like lobsters, crabs should always be lively and alive when purchased whole. Store live crabs in the refrigerator in a brown paper bag and use them the day they are purchased.

To Cook Whole Crabs: Place live crabs in boiling water, or set them on a rack and steam. They die instantly when they hit the water or the steam mounts. In about 10 to 12 minutes, when they change from their natural color to red, they are done. Be careful not to overcook crabs or the meat will become mushy.

Cleaning Soft-Shell Crabs: Some fish stores have crabs that are already cleaned; however, it is not difficult to do it yourself. Turn the crab on its back. Pull off the triangular apron. Lift up the side flaps and pull out the spongy fingerlike gills. With scissors, cut off the face just behind the eyes. Gently press above the legs and pull out the bile sac, then rinse the crab under cold running water. Soft-shell crabs are delicious cooked on a grill either marinated or brushed with butter. They are most often sautéed or pan-fried, first dusted with seasoned flour or batter, for about 3 to 5 minutes per side.

To Pick Over Crabmeat: Packaged fresh or frozen crabmeat has bits of shell and cartilage that must be removed. Spread the crabmeat out on a dark-colored plate, and many fragments will become obvious to pick out. Then carefully rub the morsels between your fingers, being careful not to break up the large lumps.

Cleaning Fresh Foie Gras

Soak the foie gras in tepid water to cover for 1 hour. Pat the liver dry and separate it into the large and small lobes. Remove and discard the connecting tube and any blood vessels or nerve tissue that are visible.

Foie Gras with Cactus Pears; Alain Borel, L'Auberge Provençale, White Post, Virginia

Roasting Garlic

Remove the excess papery skin from a whole head, or bulb, of garlic, but keep the bulb intact. Rub the head of garlic with 1 teaspoon of olive oil. Loosely wrap the bulb in aluminum foil and bake it in a preheated 375°F oven for 45 minutes. Let cool until warm enough to handle. Separate the cloves and press out pulp by pinching the top of each clove; the soft pulp will emerge from the stem end.

Grilling

Prepare the fire at least 30 minutes before you want the food to start cooking, with the vents completely opened at the bottom of the grill. Use a chimney starter with crumpled newspaper in the bottom and briquets or charcoal above. Once the coals are lit, spread them evenly to assure uniform cooking and prevent charring. Before placing the food on the grill, check the temperature of the fire. Here are the terms used to describe a fire:

• **Hot:** The coals are showing a red glow, and you can hold your hand at grill level for only 2 seconds.
• **Medium-Hot:** The coals are lightly covered with gray ash, and you can hold your hand at grill level for 3 to 5 seconds.
• **Medium:** The coals are totally covered with gray ash, and you can hold your hand at grill level for 6 to 7 seconds.

Using Wood Chips: Soak aromatic wood chips in water to cover for 30 minutes, then drain them and sprinkle them on hot or medium-hot coals just before or during grilling.

High-Altitude Baking

All batters for baked goods will need some adjustment at altitudes of 3,000 feet or more, except for low-moisture recipes such as pie crust pastry and rolled cookie dough. In high-altitude baking it is best to start with minimum adjustments, since the amount of humidity in the atmosphere may also make a difference. Here are some easy ways as well as firm rules for adjusting to high altitudes:

• Decrease the sugar slightly.
• Increase the number of eggs slightly.
• At elevations above 3,500 feet, increase the oven temperature by 25 degrees.
• Increase the amount of flour by 2.5 percent at 3,500 feet, and by up to 10 percent at 8,000 feet.
• Start by using cold ingredients rather than room-temperature ingredients.

Making Ice Cream Without a Machine

While there are a number of inexpensive ice cream machines on the market today, it is possible to make ice creams and sorbets without any sort of freezer. Here are two methods:

Food Processor Method: Freeze mixture in ice cube trays for 45 minutes to 1 hour, or until the cubes are almost frozen. Empty the ice cube trays into a food processor and process with the steel blade, using on-and-off pulsing motions, until the mixture is smooth. Put back into the ice cube trays and freeze for another 30 minutes. Process again and scrape the ice cream into a plastic container or mixing bowl. Freeze again until solid. When you are ready to serve, let sit for several minutes.

Electric Mixer Method: Freeze the mixture in a mixing bowl until the outer 2 to 3 inches is frozen. Remove from the freezer and beat with an electric mixer until smooth. Repeat 2 more times, then allow to freeze totally. When you are ready to serve, let sit for several minutes.

Handling Lobsters

Lobsters should be eaten within hours of getting them from the tank. They should be stored in the refrigerator, ideally in the crisper, wrapped in a few layers of wet newspaper. In that condition, they can stay alive for 1 day. Never store lobsters in fresh water; it will kill them.

To kill a lobster just before cooking, with the point of a knife make a small incision in the back of the shell where the chest and tail meet.

To Boil or Steam: The best liquid for boiling or steaming is fresh unpolluted sea water. If that is not available, use salted water (1 tablespoon salt per quart of water). Whether steaming or boiling, always use a pot that is larger than the volume of lobster to be cooked since a quick return to boiling is essential, as is room for the steam to circulate. For boiling, fill the pot three-quarters full. For steaming, fill the pot with 2 inches of water and put a steaming rack in place so that the lobsters are not touching the water. For either preparation, some fresh seaweed, available from the fishmonger, may be added to the pot for flavoring. For either method, make sure the water is at a rolling boil before you add the lobsters. Start counting the time once the water has come back to a boil or after the pot has filled with steam. Cook for 6 minutes for a 1 pound lobster, 9 minutes for 1½ pounds; 12 minutes for 2 pounds. Simmer lobsters that weigh 4 or more pounds; do not boil.

After cooking, punch a little hole with a knife behind the lobster's eyes to allow the water to drain from the body. This keeps the green tomalley, or liver, nice and firm and prevents a flood on the plate. Crack the claws in the kitchen before serving the lobster, and give each person a cracker to help remove the meat from the arms and claws.

To Shell a Lobster: Twist the tail to remove it from the body, then split the shell with a large, heavy knife and remove the meat. Remove the intestinal vein that runs the length of the tail. The body meat is removed simply by ripping the body open and picking out the meat. Discard the oblong sand sac, found just below and behind the eyes, and the spongy gills found along the body walls.

Break the arm from the claw, cut apart the sections, and pry the meat out with a lobster pick or seafood fork. Loosen the movable part of the claw by twisting it slowly from side to side until it snaps off. The meat should still be attached, but the shell removed.

For a small lobster, use a lobster cracker to crack the claws. For a lobster over 2 pounds, place the claw on a cutting board, with a chef's knife right below the joint. Hit it with a hammer until the knife breaks the shell but does not go into the meat. Repeat on the other side, and the claw should be open.

"Frenching" a Rack of Lamb

Ask your butcher to prepare the rack of lamb for cooking by cutting and scraping off the meat about 1½ inches from the ends of the ribs, which is called "Frenching." This allows the diners to hold onto the end of each chop more neatly. Ask the butcher to reserve all bones and meat to be used in making stock.

Cleaning Leeks

Trim the top of the leek, leaving some green or removing it altogether, depending on the recipe. Discard the outer leaves and trim the root. Split the leek in quarters or halves almost through the root, depending on size. Rinse the leek down to the root under cold running water, separating the leaves to rinse between them, and reassemble the layers for cooking.

Handling Mussels

Mussels should always be refrigerated, and should be used within 2 days of purchase or harvesting. Raw shucked mussels may be frozen in an airtight container with their natural juices. Cooked shucked mussels should be frozen separately from the liquor in which they were cooked. Use frozen mussels within 3 months.

To Clean Mussels: Rinse the mussels under cold running water. Debeard them by grasping the beard between your thumb and a dull knife blade, then pull the beard free. Scrape or pull away any beard that remains. Using a stiff brush, scrub the shell of each mussel to remove every bit of grass and mud. Scales and barnacles do not have to be removed, except when the shells are going to be served with the dish. Soak the mussels in cold water for 1 hour, changing the water 2 to 3 times.

Toasting Nuts and Pumpkin Seeds

Spread the nuts in a single layer in a shallow pan. Bake in a preheated 350°F oven, shaking the sheet occasionally, until the nuts or seeds are golden, 5 to 12 minutes, depending on size. Let cool.

Toasting Sesame Seeds

Place the sesame seeds in a small dry sauté pan or skillet over medium heat. Watch them closely and stir frequently until they reach a nutty brown color and release their fragrance.

Rack of Lamb with Persimmon Chutney and Peanut Crust; Scott Williams, Americus at the Sheraton Washington, Washington, D.C.

Halibut Enrobed in a Crisp Potato Crust; Peter Platt, Wheatleigh Inn, Lenox, Massachusetts

Shucking Fresh Oysters

Scrub the oysters thoroughly with a brush under cold running water. Never submerge oysters in plain water or they will suffocate.

There are several ways to open an oyster. For easiest shucking, use an oyster knife, a pointed can/bottle opener, or a screwdriver. Protect your hand by wearing a heavy glove or enclose the oyster in several thicknesses of a folded kitchen towel.

Shucking by Hand: Hold the shell in the palm of your hand with the deeper side down to preserve most of the oyster liquor. Locate the hinged part of the oyster (the narrow end) and, with a back-and-forth motion, gently work the tip of the oyster knife between the shell halves.

Once the knife has penetrated the shell by ¼ inch or so, make sure the oyster is firmly impaled on the blade by giving the shell a few shakes. It should remain stuck on the end of the knife. Working very carefully, twist the knife back and forth to open the shell.

Once the shell is opened, slide the knife across the top of the shell to cut the adductor muscle and run the knife under the body of the oyster. Discard the top shell.

The Microwave Method: Place the oysters in a glass casserole dish. Put them in microwave for 5 minutes on Warm (30 percent). Remove from the oven, pry open, and shuck at once. Using this method, the oysters will be still be raw, and should be placed on a bed of ice to chill well before serving.

You can completely open oysters by putting them in the microwave for 3 minutes on High (100 percent). The oysters will be thoroughly cooked.

The Oven Method: Preheat the oven to 400°F and scrub the oysters. Place the oysters on a baking sheet in middle of the oven for 5 minutes. Have ready a dish pan or sink full of ice water. Immediately dump the oysters into the chilled water. The hinges will pry open easily.

Peeling Peaches

Firm peaches may be peeled with a sharp paring knife. Place ripe peaches in boiling water for 30 seconds, remove them from the pan with a slotted spoon, and place them in ice water to stop the cooking. The skins will slip right off. Rub cut peaches with a cut lemon or toss with lemon juice to prevent discoloration.

Handling Phyllo Dough

Phyllo dough is available in 1-pound packages in the freezer section of supermarkets. A package of phyllo contains approximately 18 to 24 sheets, each sheet measuring about 12 by 20 inches. The phyllo should be defrosted completely for at least 8 hours at room temperature before opening. It can also be defrosted in a microwave oven at Medium (50 percent) power; take it from the outer carton but leave the inner plastic pouch sealed. Defrost for 3 to 5 minutes, depending on the power of the microwave.

When handling phyllo, you should try to work as quickly as possible, so it is important to have all ingredients ready. If using only part of the dough at a time, cover the remaining phyllo with a slightly damp towel or plastic wrap, or put the phyllo that you aren't immediately using in the refrigerator, tightly wrapped in plastic wrap.

Removing Silver Skin

Tenderloins and many other cuts of meat are covered with an almost iridescent membrane called the silver skin, which must be removed since it is tough and will cause the meat to curl as it cooks. To remove the silver skin, trim the meat of fat and trim away any irregular edges to form an even piece. With the blade of a sharp paring knife, scrape away at the end of the silver skin while pulling with your fingers down the length of the meat. Repeat this process, turning the meat as necessary, until all the silver skin has been scraped and pulled away. Do not try to remove silver skin in long pieces since there is a tendency to tear the meat.

Peeling and Seeding Tomatoes

Cut out the core of the tomato. With a knife, make an X on the bottom of the tomato. Plunge the tomato into boiling water for exactly 10 seconds. Remove with slotted spoon to a bowl of cold water, then drain. Peel off the skin. Cut the tomato in half crosswise. Squeeze and shake the tomato gently over a bowl or sink to remove the seeds. Any clinging seeds may be removed with the tip of a paring knife or your finger.

To Tourner Vegetables

This terms refers to the classic French technique of cutting hard vegetables such as carrots and potatoes into elegant ovals less than 1 inch in length with a sharp paring knife. To master the craft, cut a vegetable into a rectangle slightly larger than the desired size of the tournéed vegetable and then cut away at the corners to form an oval. Vegetables cut into chunks or dice of the same size will cook in the same amount of time as tournéed vegetables, of course, and are far simpler to prepare for home dining.

Apple Tarts; Dawn Rose, Olives, Charlestown, Massachusetts

Warm Apple Tarts; Stephen Johnson,
Hamersley's Bistro, Boston

Basic Recipes

Basil Oil
Makes 1 cup

In a medium bowl, combine ¾ cup minced, stemmed fresh basil with 1 cup of olive oil. Cover and let sit for a minimum of 48 hours. Pour through a fine-meshed sieve into a glass jar or bottle; cover.

Mint Oil

Replace the basil in the above recipe with ¾ cup minced fresh mint leaves and proceed as directed.

Caramel Sauce
Makes 2 cups
This is a basic caramel sauce with a thick consistency enriched by both butter and cream.

1½ cups granulated sugar
½ cup water
3 tablespoons butter
1 cup heavy (whipping) cream, heated
½ teaspoon vanilla extract

Place the sugar and water in a medium, heavy saucepan. Bring to a simmer over medium heat, swirling occasionally. Cover the pan, raise high to medium high, and cook for 2 minutes, or until the liquid gives off large, thick bubbles. Remove the cover and cook, swirling the syrup, until it turns golden brown.

   Remove the pan from heat and stir in the butter with a wooden spoon. Add the cream, stirring constantly, then add the vanilla. Return the pan to a low flame and stir constantly until any lumps have melted and the syrup is smooth. Serve warm over ice cream or cake, or pour into a jar, cover, and refrigerate for up to 1 week.

Note: *To make butterscotch, substitute light brown sugar for the granulated sugar, and add 2 teaspoons of cider vinegar to the syrup along with the vanilla.*

Clarified Butter

Melt butter over low heat, then cover and refrigerate it. Once the fat has hardened, you can scoop it off, being careful to leave the bottom layer of milk solids. Store the clarified butter covered in the refrigerator for up to 2 weeks.

   If you don't have time to let the butter chill, melt the butter gently so that the milk solids settle on the bottom of the pan, forming a creamy white sediment. Carefully and slowly pour off the clear yellow butter and discard the milk solids or add them to soup or sauce.

Crème Anglaise
Makes 2 cups

This basic custard sauce is the perfect consistency to serve with everything from rich chocolate cake to simple baked apples.

4 egg yolks
⅓ cup sugar
1½ cups milk, heated
2 teaspoons vanilla extract
1 tablespoon butter at room temperature (optional)

Plum Soufflé with Cinnamon; Nitzi Rabin,
Chillingsworth, Brewster, Massachusestts

Place the egg yolks in a medium, heavy saucepan and whisk them over low heat until they are pale in color. Add the sugar 1 tablespoon at a time, beating well between each addition. Beat until the mixture reaches the consistency of cake batter.

Whisk in the milk, then stir continuously with a wooden spoon until the custard coats the spoon and a line drawn down the back of the spoon remains visible. Remove from heat and stir in the vanilla.

If the custard is to be chilled, press a sheet of plastic wrap directly onto the surface to prevent a skin from forming, or dot the top with bits of the optional butter. Chill the custard for up to 2 days.

Note: If the custard begins to overheat and the egg yolks are forming lumps, remove it immediately from the heat and whisk briskly to cool the mixture. Push the custard through a fine-meshed sieve with the back of a spoon to remove the lumps. If it has not sufficiently thickened, return it to heat to complete cooking.

Crème Fraîche

Crème fraîche is now widely available in specialty foods stores; however, it is also easy to make by combining 1 cup of heavy (whipping) cream (preferably not ultra-pasteurized) with 1 tablespoon of buttermilk in a small saucepan. Slowly heat the cream to 105°F.

Pour the mixture into a clean glass container and cover it loosely. Set in warm place (70° to 80°F) until thickened, about 24 to 36 hours. Cover tightly and refrigerate for 1 more day to develop the tangy flavor.

Chicken Stock
Makes 12 cups

6 quarts water
5 pounds chicken bones, skin, and trimmings
2 carrots, peeled and cut into chunks
1 large onion, halved
3 garlic cloves, halved
3 celery stalks, halved
3 fresh thyme sprigs, or 1 teaspoon dried thyme
6 fresh parsley sprigs
3 bay leaves
12 black peppercorns

Place the water and chicken bones and scraps in a large stockpot over medium-high heat. Bring to a boil, then reduce heat to a simmer, skimming off the foam that rises for the first 10 or 15 minutes. Cook for 1 hour, then add the remaining ingredients. Raise the heat to bring the liquid to a boil, reduce heat to low, and simmer the stock for 3 hours.

Strain the stock through a fine-meshed sieve and let cool. Cover and refrigerate. Remove and discard the congealed layer of fat on the surface. Store in the refrigerator up to 3 days. To keep longer, bring the stock to a boil every 3 days, or freeze it for up to 3 months.

Roasted Red Pepper Ravioli with Braised Duck; Lynne Aronson and Toni D'Onofrio, Lola, New York

Veal or Beef Stock

Makes 3 quarts

8 pounds veal or beef bones and trimmings
2 onions, halved
2 carrots, peeled and halved
2 celery stalks, halved
3 garlic cloves, halved
8 quarts water
3 fresh thyme sprigs, or 1 teaspoon dried thyme
6 fresh parsley sprigs
2 bay leaves
12 peppercorns

Preheat the oven to 400°F. Place the bones and trimmings in a roasting pan and roast in the center of the oven until they are brown, about 45 minutes, turning occasionally. Add the vegetables to the pan and roast 20 minutes longer, or until the vegetables are brown.

Place the bones and vegetables in a deep stockpot and pour off any accumulated fat. Add 1 quart of the water to the pan and place on the stove over high heat. Stir to scrape up the brown bits clinging to the bottom of the pan. Pour this liquid into the stockpot with the remaining 7 quarts water and the herbs and spices, and bring to a boil over medium-high heat. Reduce the heat so that the stock is barely simmering, and skim the surface of the scum that will rise for the first 10 or 15 minutes. Simmer the stock for 5 to 6 hours, strain through a fine-meshed sieve, and discard the solids. Let cool, then cover and refrigerate. Remove and discard the congealed layer of fat on the surface. Store in the refrigerator for up to 3 days. To keep longer, bring the stock to a boil every 3 days, or freeze it for up to 3 months.

Fish Stock

Makes 12 cups

4 quarts water
1 cup dry white wine
4 pounds fish trimmings (such as skin, bones, heads, shellfish shells)
2 tablespoons fresh lemon juice
1 onion, halved
2 celery stalks, halved
4 fresh parsley sprigs
2 fresh thyme sprigs, or 1 teaspoon dried thyme
6 peppercorns

In a large stockpot, bring the water and wine to a boil over high heat. Rinse all the fish trimmings under cold running water, add to the stockpot, and bring to a boil. Reduce heat to a simmer and cook for 1 hour.

Add the remaining ingredients to the pot. When the water returns to a boil, reduce heat to a simmer and cook for 1½ to 2 hours. Strain the stock through a fine-meshed sieve, pressing on the solids with the back of a large spoon. Discard the solids and let the stock cool. Cover and refrigerate for up to 3 days. To keep longer, bring the stock to a boil every 3 days, or freeze it for up to 3 months.

Vegetable Stock

Makes 3 quarts

4 large leeks, carefully washed
2 large carrots, peeled and sliced
4 large celery stalks, sliced
4 large yellow onions, sliced
5 garlic cloves

Lobster Crisp in Water Chestnut Flour; Lydia Shire and Susan Regis, Biba, Boston

6 fresh parsley sprigs
4 fresh thyme sprigs, or 1 teaspoon dried thyme
2 bay leaves
4 quarts water
½ teaspoon white peppercorns
1 teaspoon black peppercorns
Salt to taste

Place all the ingredients except for the salt in a large stockpot. Slowly bring the liquid to a boil over medium heat, reduce heat to a simmer and cook, partially covered, for 1½ hours. Strain through a fine-meshed sieve, pressing liquid from the solids with the back of a large spoon. Let cool, then cover and refrigerate for up to 3 days. To keep longer, bring to a boil every 3 days, or freeze for up to 3 months.

Rich Stock

Pour 1½ times the amount of stock specified into a small saucepan and bring to a boil over high heat. Cook the stock to reduce it by one third. If the stock is not unsalted, add a few slices of raw potato or some uncooked rice as the stock is reducing to absorb much of the salt.

Veal Demi-Glace
Makes 2 cups

Traditional demi-glace is thickened with flour and must simmer gently with much tending, but this quick version is much lighter and can be made more quickly because it is thickened at the end with arrowroot or cornstarch.

2 tablespoons vegetable oil
1 large onion, diced
2 celery stalks, diced
1 carrot, peeled and sliced
½ cup diced ham
3 tablespoons tomato paste
1 thyme sprig
1 bay leaf
6 peppercorns
10 cups veal stock (see page 21)
½ cup Madeira
2 to 3 teaspoons arrowroot or cornstarch mixed with
    2 tablespoons cold water
Salt and freshly ground black pepper to taste
1 tablespoon unsalted butter

Heat the oil in a large saucepan over medium heat. Add the onion, celery, carrot, and ham, stir, and cover. Cook over low heat for 10 minutes. Uncover the pan and stir the tomato paste, thyme, bay leaf, and peppercorns. Whisk in the stock and Madeira, and bring to a boil over high heat.

Once the mixture has started to boil, reduce heat to medium high and cook the sauce until only 2 cups of liquid remain. Depending on the rate at which the liquid is boiling, this may take anywhere from 30 minutes to 1 hour. Strain the liquid through a fine-meshed sieve into a 2-cup measuring cup. If it has not reduced enough, pour the liquid back into the pan and keep boiling. If it has reduced too much, add enough water to make 2 cups.

Pour the liquid back into the pan and bring it back to a simmer. Whisk in the arrowroot or cornstarch mixture 1 teaspoon at a time, returning the sauce to a simmer after each addition, until the sauce reaches the desired consistency. If using the sauce immediately, swirl in the butter. If not serving immediately, do not whisk in the butter, but remove the pan from heat and place dots of the butter on the surface of the sauce to prevent a skin from forming. Whisk the butter in when reheating the sauce.

Venison Loin Chop, Andrew Wilkinson, The Rainbow Room, New York

Part III: The Recipes

*t*he nineteenth-century French gastronome Brillat-Savarin once wrote that "the discovery of a new dish brings more joy to mankind than the discovery of a new star."

By analogy, the recipes in these next chapters are like a new galaxy. The chefs profiled on these pages include some of the most venerable names in American cooking. Some of them are American-born and are practitioners of New American cuisine or have adopted the cuisine of another country, while others have adopted the region from Maine to Virginia as their home and were originally born in locales from Tuscany to Taiwan.

Viewers are able to get a sense of the chefs' personalities as well as their diverse dishes while watching the *Great Chefs of the East* television series. The purpose of this book is to allow replication of their food in the home kitchen by providing exact amounts of ingredients and detailed instructions that can't be included in a fast-paced video.

For decades the common wisdom was that "chefs' recipes don't work." Some cooks believed that chefs intentionally omitted an ingredient when asked for a recipe, while other cooks feared that since many chefs do not measure, their "guess-timates" about quantities were frequently wrong.

This is not the case. Most chefs are more than willing to part with recipes; however, the equipment in the professional kitchen is not equivalent to that of the home kitchen. Even if a chef measures accurately, the amount of time needed to reduce a liquid by half on a powerful commercial stove, for example, is far shorter than on a home stove.

All of the recipes in this book have been tested in a home kitchen and include detailed instructions on creating the dishes. The "Basic Techniques and Recipes" chapter is a primer for basic preparations used in the recipes.

Some of these recipes are sure to become part of your everyday repertoire; others are special dishes to prepare for special meals. Notes following each recipe discuss advance preparation whenever possible, so that you can spend more time with your guests when entertaining.

Menu Planning

When a chef orchestrates a "tasting" menu, now a popular offering in many restaurants, he or she is making the same kind of choices for the diner that the home cook must make at every meal. Decisions on how to combine colors, textures, forms and flavors are an integral part of the process.

In every meal one food is the "star," and the most important decision in menu planning is its selection; this is as true for a multi-course dinner party as for a one-course family dinner that includes different foods on the same plate. The guiding principle is that there should be only one "star" on a plate, and the other foods are selected to glorify it with complementary flavors and contrasting colors and textures. Once the "star" has been chosen, then its color and texture determines that of the supporting players. Spicy should be balanced by mild, dark tones should be complemented by light, and soft should be contrasted with crunchy.

For a multi-course meal, the equation becomes extended to include not only the "star" of the entree, but which courses become "stars" for the meal. Some must be prominent, and others become subservient. An elaborate soup should be followed by a less complex entree, leading to a show-stopper dessert. Conversely, if the entree is the

focus of the meal, then the starter should be simple—anything from smoked salmon to a simple soup or salad.

The courses should be balanced in terms of color, flavor, and texture in the same way that the entree plate is balanced. But additional factors are the spirit of the meal, the cuisine or cuisines from which it is drawn, and the elegance of the table setting and occasion. The "Menus for Entertaining" section presents a variety of complete menus based on these principles.

Organizing Your Cooking

Once the menu is planned, the shopping and cooking follow suit, and here one of the organizing principles of a professional kitchen is equally valid for the home cook: the *mise en place,* which begins with a pad and paper rather than a knife and chopping board.

Gather all the recipes that you will be preparing for the meal and lay them out side by side in front of you. Read each recipe through from top to bottom so that instructions such as "marinate overnight" are not overlooked. Note the cooking times, and then calculate the preparation times. Subtract the cooking times from the time the meal is to be served. Add up the preparation times to determine when the cooking must begin. At the same time, check to see how each dish is cooked. Most home cooks have only one oven, and if two dishes need to be baked at different temperatures, one must be a dish that can be made ahead and reheated.

Now the recipes must be integrated so that the cook knows which step of which recipe to complete in what order, and at what time the preparation must be completed so that the dishes will be ready at the same time.

Yet another list made in advance will save time when cooking: Add up the common ingredients to the recipes and do them all at once. For example, if the total meal requires 4 cups of chopped onions, chop them at the same time and then use them as needed.

The food processor is to the home cook what a team of cooks are to the professional chef. It does a lot of the work for the cook who then puts the pieces together. When preparing ingredients to be used later, you can save the step of washing the processor constantly if you start with the foods that will cling to it the least. For example, if the foods needed for a dish are chopped onion, minced carrots, and grated Cheddar cheese, begin with the onions and carrots and do the cheese last.

The recipes in *Great Chefs of the East* may be followed verbatim or used as road maps. Feel free to substitute as you see fit. Omitting garlic from a recipe, for example, will not change the fundamental taste of the dish, unless it is a key to the recipe and used in great quantity. Changing an herb from basil to oregano because that is what is growing in your garden is not a problem, nor is substituting one species of fish for another as long as the flesh is similar in texture and the cooking time is altered according to its thickness.

Baking is far more scientific than general cooking, however, and for baked goods recipes should be followed strictly, allowing substitutions only for added ingredients, such as walnuts for pecans or Grand Marnier for brandy.

In the way that musicians can look at a musical score and hear the notes in their head, food professionals can read a recipe and taste it in their mouth. The recipes in *Great Chefs of the East* are virtuoso performances, and while reading them gives a clue to the chef's genius, the real proof is in the eating.

Hot Appetizers and Soups

*t*he dishes in this chapter were prepared as appetizers or first courses by the chefs on episodes of *Great Chefs of the East.* Combine several of them to make a meal, or augment them with dishes from the Cold Appetizers and Salads chapter.

The recipes in this chapter are reflective of the diversity throughout the book; the only factor that unites the dishes is the creativity of the chefs. There are comforting dishes such as Porcini Broth with Soft Polenta, a creamy cornmeal pudding surrounded by a fragrant broth and topped with cheese and a poached egg, and Roasted Garlic Custards with Mushrooms and Green Onions, savory flans that are equally easy to make.

There are luxurious dishes, such as Fresh Burgers of Duck Foie Gras with Apples, and Smoked Lobster and Wild Mushroom Pancakes with Crème Fraîche and a Trio of American Caviars. And there are quick-and-easy dishes such as Steamed Mussels, and Risotto with Wild Mushrooms, a dish that sets the standard for the genre.

Steamed Mussels; Georges Perrier, Le Bec-Fin, Philadelphia

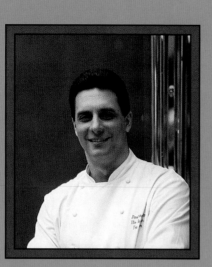

PAUL INGENITO
The Russian Tea Room, New York, New York

New York City is the land of the "restaurant rabbits," who hop to each new spot as soon as it opens. Yet as long as there are performances at Carnegie Hall, the venerable Russian Tea Room will greet the throngs after the last "Bravo!" is shouted.

As the music played next door has changed with the times, so has the fare served at The Russian Tea Room, now with Paul Ingenito as chef. A 1984 graduate of the Culinary Institute of America, Ingenito worked with Larry Forgione at An American Place in New York. Besides being able to work with the innovative Forgione, Ingenito accompanied his mentor to charity dinners and other appearances on nationwide tours, where he also learned from notable chefs such as Wolfgang Puck, Jonathan Waxman, and Dean Fearing. In 1989, Ingenito became executive sous-chef at the historic Russian Tea Room and was promoted to executive chef less than a year later.

Ingenito describes his style as "refined country cooking," citing the influence of his grandmother's Italian country stews and soups, plus ethnic influences from all over the world "from bistro to grand brasserie," he says. The mainstays on his menu are the Russian classics—blini, zakuska, karsky shashlik, and borscht—but he has developed such signature dishes as Borscht with Braised Duck, and Grilled Sea Scallops with Silver Dollar Blini, Osetra Caviar, and Lemon Vodka Mignonette.

Borscht with Braised Duck

Paul Ingenito, The Russian Tea Room
New York, New York

Serves 6 to 8

Brilliant red beet borscht, laden with cabbage and other vegetables, is the essence of Russian cuisine. The addition of succulent braised duck and baby vegetables makes this a sophisticated dish for a winter supper. Serve with a loaf of crusty bread.

Braised Duck
3 duck legs
6 cups rich duck stock or chicken stock
  (see page 20)

Borscht
2 tablespoons bacon fat, or 2 tablespoons
  oil plus ¼ teaspoon salt
1 onion, thinly sliced
1 carrot, cut into ¹⁄₁₆-inch julienne
½ head cabbage, shredded
1 tablespoon tomato puree
5 beets, cut into ¹⁄₁₆-inch julienne
4 tablespoons red wine vinegar
2 tablespoons potato starch, or
  2 teaspoons cornstarch
Salt and freshly ground black pepper
  to taste

Garnish
12 small Yukon Gold potatoes, peeled
6 baby turnips, peeled
6 baby golden beets, trimmed of all but
  1 inch of the tops
6 baby red beets, trimmed of all but
  1 inch of the tops
24 leaves red Swiss chard
½ cup sour cream
Leaves from 1 bunch fresh dill, minced

To braise the duck legs: Preheat the oven to 325°F. Place a Dutch oven over medium heat. Add the duck legs, skin-side down, and cook them, turning them frequently, for about 10 to 15 minutes, or until evenly brown. Remove the duck legs to a platter and add the stock to the pan over medium heat, stirring to scrape up the brown bits clinging to the bottom of the pan. Return the duck legs to the pan, cover tightly, and transfer to the preheated oven. Cook for 1 to 1½ hours, or until the duck meat is so tender it virtually falls off the bone. Remove the pan from the oven, remove the duck with a slotted spoon, and strain the remaining stock or broth; set aside.

To make the borscht: Heat the bacon fat in a large saucepan or stockpot. Add the onion and sauté for 3 minutes, or until the onion is translucent. Add the carrot and cook until tender, about 3 minutes. Stir in the shredded cabbage and cook until wilted, about 4 minutes. Measure 4 cups of the reserved stock and add it to the vegetable mixture. Add the tomato puree, then lower heat and bring the soup to a simmer over medium heat, skimming off any fat that rises to the surface.

Place the beets in a small saucepan, add water to cover, and bring to a boil over medium-high heat. Add 1 tablespoon of the red wine vinegar and reduce heat to low. Continue to cook until the beets are tender, about 15 to 20 minutes. Drain the beets, reserving the cooking liquid. Measure the beets in a measuring cup and add an equal amount of the cooking liquid to the soup pot. Add the remaining 3 tablespoons red wine vinegar and bring the borscht back to a simmer. Dissolve the potato starch in 2 tablespoons of the cooled beet juice and add to the simmering borscht. Cook gently for an additional 2 minutes, or until the liquid is slightly thickened. Adjust the seasoning with salt and pepper. Set aside.

To make the garnish: Fill 1 large saucepan and 2 small saucepans with lightly salted water. Add the potatoes and turnips to the large pan and place the gently washed baby beets in the other 2 pans; do not cook the beets in the same pan or the red beets will "bleed" into the golden ones. Bring all 3 pots to a boil over medium-high heat and boil the potatoes and turnips for 20 minutes, or until tender; boil each pot of beets, covered, for 30 to 35 minutes, or until tender. Drain all the vegetables and let cool. When the beets are cool enough to handle, slip off the skins and trim the tops.

To serve: Place the borscht over low heat. Bring a large saucepan of lightly salted water to a boil and add the Swiss chard leaves. Cook until they are wilted, about 3 minutes. Remove the leaves with a slotted spoon and blot them dry with paper towels. Add the blanched baby vegetables to the boiling water and cook for 45 seconds. Remove with a slotted spoon. Arrange 3 to 4 leaves around the border of each soup plate. In the center of each bowl, arrange the julienne of carrots, onion, cabbage, and beets that cooked in the soup. Cut the blanched baby vegetables in half and place them on top of the cabbage mixture. Pull the meat off the braised duck legs and divide among the soup bowls. Pour the hot borscht broth into the bowls. Garnish with dollops of sour cream and sprinkle liberally with dill.

Note: Every part of this dish, with the exception of the blanched Swiss chard leaves, may be prepared 2 days in advance and refrigerated. Cover and refrigerate the borscht with the vegetables in it; cover and refrigerate all of the garnish vegetables and the duck meat separately.

Borscht with Braised Duck; Paul Ingenito, The Russian Tea Room, New York

Fresh Burgers of Duck Foie Gras with Apples

Christian Delouvrier, Lés Célébrités
New York, New York

Serves 2

These "burgers" are made of sautéed buttery foie gras sandwiched between two sautéed tart apple slices that balance its richness. An elegant appetizer, the dish is easy to make, but it must be cooked at the last minute.

Foie Gras Burgers

2 Granny Smith or other tart green apples
Salt and freshly ground black pepper to taste
2 tablespoons duck fat or olive oil
2 teaspoons confectioners' sugar
½ cup sliced porcini mushrooms
Three 3-ounce raw foie gras slices, trimmed and soaked (see page 13)

Sauce

Reserved apple trimmings from burgers, above
½ cup apple cider vinegar
3 tablespoons apple cider
½ cup veal demi-glace (see page 22)

Garnish

1 cup frisée (or the center leaves of curly endive)
1 teaspoon minced fresh chives
1 teaspoon minced fresh parsley
2 teaspoons olive oil
1 teaspoon vinegar
Salt and freshly ground pepper to taste

To prepare the burgers: Preheat the oven to 400°F. Cut two ½-inch-thick slices from the stem end of each apple. Trim the apple slices to perfect circles, removing any seeds and tough core material. Reserve the rest of the apples and the trimmings and season the apple slices with salt and pepper.

Place a 10-inch sauté pan or skillet over medium-high heat and add the duck fat or olive oil. Sauté the apple slices in the fat until glazed and tender, about 2 to 3 minutes on each side. Sprinkle the slices with the sugar and cook an additional 30 seconds on each side. Remove from the pan with a slotted spatula and keep warm.

In the same pan, sauté the porcini mushrooms for 2 to 3 minutes, or until tender. Season with salt and pepper and set aside.

Season the foie gras slices well on both sides with salt and pepper. Place a dry cast-iron skillet over medium-high heat and heat until the pan is very hot. Place 2 slices of foie gras in the pan and sear the slices on one side for 30 seconds, or until the foie gras is a crisp, caramelized brown. Turn and cook for 10 to 15 seconds, then remove the foie gras from the heat and blot on paper towels. Chop the remaining slice of foie gras into ½-inch cubes and cook in the same way. Set the cubes of foie gras aside on paper towels to drain.

Fresh Burgers of Duck Foie Gras with Apples; Christian Delouvrier, Les Célébrités, New York

To make the sauce: Add the reserved apple pieces and trimmings to the foie gras and sauté over medium heat until tender, about 2 to 3 minutes. Add the apple cider vinegar and cider, then increase the heat to high, stirring to scrape up the browned bits from the bottom of the pan. Add the demi-glace and heat for 1 minute more, stirring frequently. Strain the sauce through a fine-meshed sieve; set aside and keep warm.

To make the garnish: In a small bowl, combine the frisée with the chopped chives and parsley and dress lightly with the olive oil, vinegar, salt, and pepper. Toss well to combine, then divide between 2 plates.

To assemble: Cover the bottom apple slice with a slice of foie gras, then top with the mushroom and the other apple slice. Place the burgers in an ovenproof dish with the cubes of foie gras and set aside.

To serve: Heat the burgers in the preheated oven for 3 minutes. Place 1 burger on each plate, garnish with the foie gras cubes, and drizzle the sauce around the plate.

CHRISTIAN DELOUVRIER
Les Célébrités, New York, New York

Les Célébrités, Christian Delouvrier's restaurant in New York's Essex House, the North American flagship hotel for the Japanese Nikko chain, features not only fine cuisine, but a series of rotating art exhibits. In keeping with its name, Les Célébrités exhibits paintings by celebrities for whom art is a personal passion.

Yet it is Delouvrier's dishes, called "spectacular creations" by *Zagat's 1993 New York Restaurant Guide,* that have earned the restaurant three stars from the *New York Times* and four stars from *Newsday.* Before joining the Essex House in 1989, Delouvrier was with the Hotel Parker Méridien in New York, where he opened the award-winning Maurice restaurant in 1981 and garnered a four-star rating from *Forbes* magazine for four years in a row. Delouvrier came to the Hotel Parker Méridien from L'Archestrate in Paris. Prior to that, he was executive chef for Air France Concorde in the United States.

The lavishly framed art works at Les Célébrités, by actors and entertainers including James Dean and Phyllis Diller, are rotated after being auctioned or sold, and the proceeds have raised hundreds of thousands of dollars for charity, since all of the featured artists are affiliated with the Permanent Charities Committee of the Entertainment Industries.

The luxurious decor of Les Célébrités, with its lavish table settings of Bernardaud china and Christofle silver, complements but never outshines Delouvrier's signature dishes such as Fresh Burgers of Duck Foie Gras with Apples.

JEAN-LOUIS PALLADIN
Jean-Louis at the Watergate/Palladin, Washington, D.C.

Jean-Louis Palladin might well be one of the busiest men in Washington. Not content to rest on the laurels from his namesake restaurant, Jean-Louis at the Watergate in the Watergate Hotel, Palladin has transformed the city's formerly sleepy food scene into his personal domain.

In the past two years, the man *GQ's* Alan Richman called "America's finest interpreter of classic French cuisine" has expanded into a variety of new ventures that showcase his bottomless energy and talent: He opened Palladin, a brasserie-style restaurant in the space directly over Jean-Louis; with partner Roberto Donna he founded Pesce, a combination seafood market and trattoria; and, with former sous-chef and friend Jimmy Sneed, he has played a major role in launching The Frog and the Redneck restaurant in Richmond, Virginia.

Palladin calls his combination of classical training and constant experimentation "instinctive cuisine." That same instinct propelled him into a restaurant kitchen in his native Gascony at age twelve. After receiving more training at a hotel school in Toulouse, Palladin was hired as saucier at the Hôtel de Paris in Monte Carlo. After a stint at the famous Plaza Athénée in Paris, Palladin returned to his home town of Condom and renovated a fourteenth-century monastery into his own restaurant, La Table des Cordeliers. When he was awarded two Michelin stars at age twenty-eight, he was the youngest chef ever to receive such an accolade.

Since coming to the United States in 1979, Palladin has focused on locating and encouraging sources for the finest possible ingredients in the world. As a result, his menus for Jean-Louis at the Watergate are handwritten every day depending on ingredient availability.

Upstairs at Palladin, diners will find such innovative brasserie food as Pot au Feu with Bone Marrow; Cod Chowder with Leeks, Potatoes, and Garlic; Celery Root Soup with Shad Roe; and rich Bread Pudding for dessert. There is another menu at Palladin, called "For the Adventurous Gourmet Customer," and featuring dishes that must be ordered forty-eight hours in advance, such as Nage of Stone Crab with Lemongrass.

Both Jean-Louis and Palladin draw on the same phenomenal wine cellar that has been awarded the *Wine Spectator's* Grand Award for the past ten years.

Celery Root Soup with Shad Roe

*Jean-Louis Palladin, Jean-Louis
at the Watergate
Washington, D.C.*

Serves 4

A member of the herring family, the shad is particularly prized for its delicately flavored roe, which is available only for a short season in the early spring. To enjoy this soup at other times of the year, substitute shrimp for the roe.

Soup
1 celery root (about 8 ounces)
2 tablespoons fresh lemon juice
1 boiling potato (about 6 ounces)
6 tablespoons olive oil
1 small onion, finely diced
1 shallot, minced
2 fresh thyme sprigs
2 cups heavy (whipping) cream or
   half-and-half
1 cup milk
3 cups veal consommé, veal stock
   (see page 21), or chicken stock
   (see page 20)
Salt and freshly ground white pepper
   to taste
1 Bartlett pear
2 pieces shad roe, or 1 pound raw
   medium shrimp, peeled and deveined

Garnish
2 tablespoons fresh lobster roe, sieved to
   obtain individual eggs (optional)
2 tablespoons minced fresh chives

Peel the celery root with a sharp paring knife, cut the root into 1-inch cubes, and immediately rub the pieces with some of the lemon juice to prevent discoloration. Peel the potato, cut it into 1-inch cubes, and place the cubes in a bowl of cold water. Set aside.

Heat 2 tablespoons of the olive oil in a large saucepan over medium-high heat. Add the onion and shallot, and sauté, stirring constantly, for 3 to 4 minutes, or until the onion is translucent. Add the celery root, drained potato, thyme, cream or half-and-half, milk, and consommé or stock. Bring to a boil, partially cover, and simmer over medium heat for 30 minutes, or until the vegetables are tender.

Remove the vegetables from the pan with a slotted spoon and place them in a blender or food processor with 1 cup of the liquid. Puree until smooth and strain the soup through a fine-meshed sieve. Season with salt and pepper. Set aside and keep warm.

Peel and core the pear and rub it with the remaining lemon juice to prevent discoloration. Cut the pear into ¼-inch cubes. Heat 2 tablespoons of the olive oil in a small sauté pan or skillet over medium heat and sauté the pear for 3 to 4 minutes, or until golden brown. Season with salt and pepper to taste. Set aside and keep warm.

Rinse the shad roe in cold water and blot dry on paper towels. If the fishmonger has not done so, cut into the thick membrane covering each lobe with a small sharp knife and remove it carefully, but do not cut the thin inner membrane. Place the 2 connected lobes into ice water for 5 minutes, then drain and gently pat dry with paper towels. The 2 lobes should be separated before cooking.

Heat the remaining 2 tablespoons olive oil in a small sauté pan or skillet over low heat. Add the shad roe and cook it for 5 minutes on a side, seasoning it with salt and pepper to taste. (If using shrimp, sauté them for 2 to 3 minutes in the olive oil, or until they have turned bright pink.)

To serve: Place some of the sautéed pear in the bottom of each soup plate. Slice the shad roe and place several slices on top of the pear. Carefully pour celery soup around the roe without covering it. Garnish with a sprinkling of the lobster roe and the minced chives.

Celery Root Soup with Shad Roe; Jean-Louis Palladin, Jean-Louis at the Watergate, Washington D.C.

Cod Cakes with Bacon and Wilted Greens

*Jasper White, Jasper's
Boston, Massachusetts*

Serves 6 to 8

Cod cakes are as much a part of New England as baked beans or lobster. Traditionally, they are rather heavy and blandly seasoned, but these are light and fluffy, and the potato coating adds a crisp texture to the dish. The sautéed greens and bacon create a perfect balance of color and flavor.

Cod Cakes

1 pound boneless salt cod
2 pounds boiling potatoes, peeled and halved
4 tablespoons unsalted butter
¼ cup finely chopped onion
1 tablespoon Colman's dry mustard
Few dashes of Worcestershire sauce (optional)
½ cup minced fresh parsley
4 eggs, lightly beaten
½ cup white bread crumbs or dried cracker crumbs
Freshly ground black pepper to taste
Salt to taste (optional)
1 Idaho (baking) potato
Peanut oil for frying

Greens

8 ounces bacon, cut into ⅜-inch strips
1 pound frisée, Belgian endive, escarole or radicchio
2 tablespoons cider vinegar
Salt and freshly ground pepper to taste

To make cod cakes: As least 1 day before serving, place the salt cod in an 8-cup bowl of cold water, cover and refrigerate for 24 hours or more, changing the water at least 4 times.

Remove the fish from its soaking liquid, place it in a 12-inch skillet, and cover the cod with fresh cold water. Bring the liquid to a boil over medium heat, reduce heat to low and simmer the cod for 5 minutes, or until the fish is barely cooked through and has lost translucency. Remove the cod from heat and drain well. Flake the fish with a fork, remove any skin or bones, and set aside.

Cover the potatoes with cold salted water in a large saucepan and bring to a boil over high heat. Reduce heat to a slow boil and cook the potatoes for approximately 30 minutes, or until tender. Drain the potatoes thoroughly in a colander, shaking it to remove excess moisture. Push the potatoes through a food mill or ricer, or mash them with a potato masher.

Melt the butter in an 8-inch sauté pan or skillet over medium heat. Add the onion and sauté for 3 minutes, or until the onion is translucent. Combine the onion, potatoes, flaked fish, dry mustard, Worcestershire sauce (if used), and minced parsley in large bowl. Add the beaten eggs and bread crumbs and mix very thoroughly with a fork or your hands. Season with black pepper. Check the mixture for seasoning before adding salt (it is rarely necessary). At this stage, this cod-potato mixture will seem fairly wet.

Cod Cakes with Bacon and Wilted Greens; Jasper White, Jasper's, Boston

Divide the mixture into 12 to 16 balls (2 per serving) and place them on a waxed paper–lined baking sheet. With a pancake turner, flatten the balls into ovals and chill the cakes until firm, at least 20 minutes.

Peel the Idaho potato and grate it into a bowl of ice water through the large holes of a box grater. Drain the grated potato on paper towels and place it on a plate. Remove the cod cakes from the refrigerator and coat them on all sides with a thin layer of grated potato. Pour peanut oil into a 12-inch sauté pan or skillet to depth of ½ inch. Heat the oil over medium heat to a temperature of 375°F, or hot enough so that a ring of bubbles appears when a bread cube is added to the pan. Add the fish cakes, being careful not to crowd the pan, and fry them until they are golden brown and crisp, about 3 to 4 minutes per side. Remove the cakes from the pan with a slotted spatula and drain them well on paper towels. Keep the cakes warm in a low oven while cooking the greens.

To make the greens: Place the bacon in a cold 12-inch sauté pan or skillet. Cook over medium heat until the bacon is crisp. Remove the pan from heat and remove the bacon pieces with a slotted spoon. Drain the bacon on paper towels and set aside.

Pour off all but 2 tablespoons of the bacon fat and place the pan over low heat. Add the greens to the pan with the cider vinegar, salt, and pepper. Cook and stir the greens for several minutes until they are heated through but not limp.

To serve: Divide the greens evenly on the plates. Lean 2 cod cakes on each plate, one on either side of the pile of greens, and garnish with the pieces of reserved bacon.

Note: The cod cakes may be made up to 1 day in advance, covered, and refrigerated. Fry them just before serving.

JASPER WHITE
Jasper's, Boston, Massachusetts

In 1983, when Jasper White took over an old molasses warehouse on Boston's waterfront and transformed it into his elegant restaurant Jasper's, he wanted to create a place that was "lively, but still calm enough for people to enjoy conversation with their friends." Now, more than a decade since Jasper's opened, it remains the only restaurant to earn 4½ stars from Robert Levey of the *Boston Globe*.

While growing up on a farm near the South Jersey shore, White was an avid hunter and fisherman, and these activities gave him an early respect for what he calls "food in its most unadulterated state." Though not a New England native, White relocated to Boston in 1978 to work in the Copley Plaza Hotel restaurant. When he left to open the Biltmore Hotel in Providence, Rhode Island, he began a lasting friendship and collaboration with Lydia Shire. The two both left the Biltmore after only six weeks and moved back to Boston to the Parker House Hotel.

White soon became a self-appointed spokesperson for the often misunderstood and misinterpreted cooking of New England. He aided his cause, though White calls himself "not the type to look for causes," by writing *Jasper White's Cooking from New England* (Harper & Row, 1989), which won him the Tastemaker Award for the Best Regional Cookbook for that year.

White brings what he calls "casual elegance" to his restaurant, striving to approach cooking not as an art, but rather as a craft, in order to "avoid cooking that becomes forced." Jasper's now serves an almost entirely seafood menu. His dishes are extraordinary, as one critic noted, because of the "level of honesty and flavor" with which the dishes are served.

The significance of Jasper's location on the edge of Boston's historic North End is not lost on the half-Italian, half-Irish chef. His Portuguese Mussels, and Portuguese Pork Rib-Eye with Clams and Garlic Sauce, he explains, illustrate "the wide view I take of northeastern cooking." White's Cod Cakes with Bacon and Wilted Greens, a reworking of the Yankee classic, "pays homage to New England and tastes great."

A graduate of the Culinary Institute of America and named Best Chef in the Northeast by the James Beard Foundation in 1991, White continues to run Jasper's with Nancy, his wife of fourteen years and business partner, and to help raise their children Jasper Paul, Mariel, and Hayley.

GORDON HAMERSLEY
Hamersley's Bistro, Boston, Massachusetts

Find the folks wearing baseball caps in Paris, and you've found the American tourists. Find the chef wearing a baseball cap in his French bistro, and you've found Gordon Hamersley, a Boston Red Sox fan and chef-owner of Hamersley's Bistro in Boston, Massachusetts.

Hamersley began working in restaurant kitchens as a dishwasher. When he realized that washing dishes and playing in a rock and roll band couldn't keep the food he wanted on the table, Hamersley switched to cooking. Though he has no regrets, Hamersley says, "I became a chef almost by default."

Hamersley trained under European chefs and spent three years in the kitchen of Ma Maison in Los Angeles working under Wolfgang Puck, who made famous the baseball-cap-in-lieu-of-the-toque look. Hamersley says Puck "opened up a potential for food I had never considered." After working as the day chef at Ma Maison, Hamersley went to France and, he says, "spent 1983… eating and drinking." When he returned to the States, he continued working as a chef and began searching for a location for his own bistro.

In 1988, Hamersley and his wife Fiona opened Hamersley's Bistro, introducing to Boston the kind of food that the Bostonians had never imagined.

"Life is nothing without garlic," is the Hamersley motto, and he is constantly "working on ways to cook garlic," he says. These unique creations include Garlic Custard with Broken Pasta Sauce, and Roasted Garlic Custards with Mushrooms and Green Onions.

Awards accumulated early for Hamersley's Bistro. In 1988, it was voted Best New Restaurant by *Boston* magazine and one of America's Best New Restaurants by *Esquire* magazine, Hamersley himself was voted one of America's Best New Chefs by *Food & Wine* magazine.

The list of awards and rave reviews continues to grow. To date, the Bistro has received more than fifty great reviews. As one Red Sox fan put it, "If the chef could bat like he cooks, we might actually get and stay on a winning streak."

A great Boston evening is a meal at Hamersley's Bistro and a game at Fenway Park. A perfect Boston evening is a meal at Hamersley's Bistro, and a game at Fenway Park that the Red Sox win.

Roasted-Garlic Custards with Mushrooms and Green Onions

Gordon Hamersley, Hamersley's Bistro
Boston, Massachusetts

Serves 4

Savory custards flavored with nutty roasted garlic are topped with an unusual sauce of sliced garlic, mushrooms, green onions, and pasta. This is a stunning appetizer, and can become the star of a meal if the entree is simple.

Mushroom Stock
1 Portobello mushroom
2 cups chicken stock (see page 20) or vegetable stock (see page 21)

Custards
1 cup heavy (whipping) cream
1 garlic clove, crushed
2 eggs
1 egg yolk
5 to 8 roasted garlic bulbs (½ cup puree; see page 14)
Salt and freshly ground white pepper to taste

Sauce
2 tablespoons unsalted butter
2 tablespoons olive oil
Salt and freshly ground black pepper to taste
2 garlic cloves, thinly sliced
4 green onions, cut into 2-inch pieces
¾ cup dry sherry
1½ cups Mushroom Stock, above
¼ cup broken dried fettuccine pasta
½ teaspoon minced fresh thyme

To make the mushroom stock: Twist the stem off the mushroom, wipe it with a damp paper towel, and chop it coarsely. Slice off the dark gills from the underside of the cap and reserve the cap. Combine the stem pieces, gills, and stock in a medium saucepan, and bring to a boil over high heat. Reduce the heat and simmer the stock uncovered for 30 minutes, or until reduced to 1½ cups. Set aside.

To make the custards: Preheat the oven to 325°F. Place the cream in a saucepan over medium heat with the garlic clove and bring to a boil. Remove the garlic and keep the cream hot. In a large bowl, whisk the eggs and the egg yolk together. Add the cream in a thin stream, whisking constantly. Whisk in the roasted garlic puree until the mixture is smooth and season with salt and pepper.

Butter four 6-ounce ramekins. Fill the ramekins with the custard mixture and place them in a shallow roasting pan. Place the pan in the oven and fill the pan with enough boiling water to come halfway up the sides of the ramekins. Cover the pan with aluminum foil and bake for 50 minutes to 1 hour, or until the custards are set and a knife inserted in the middle of each comes out clean. Remove the ramekins from the water bath. Let the custards sit for 5 minutes, then run a knife around the inside of each ramekin. To unmold the custards, place a dinner plate over each ramekin and turn it over quickly.

While the custard is baking, prepare the sauce: Slice the reserved Portobello mushroom cap and heat the butter and olive oil in a medium sauté pan or skillet over medium-high heat. When the butter foam begins to subside, add the sliced mushroom and sauté until tender, about 3 minutes. Sprinkle the mushroom with salt and pepper. Add the sliced garlic and green onions to the pan. Sauté over medium heat until the garlic is translucent, about 3 minutes. Add the sherry and boil over high heat until the liquid is reduced by three fourths, about 2 minutes. Add the mushroom stock to the pan along with the broken pasta and thyme. Lower heat and boil gently for 6 to 8 minutes, or until the pasta is al dente.

Arrange some mushrooms, garlic, and onions around each custard, then ladle the sauce around the custard and serve.

Note: The mushroom stock, custard mixture, and sauce—up to addition of the pasta—may be prepared 1 day in advance and refrigerated separately. Add 8 to 10 minutes to the baking time for the custards.

Roasted Garlic Custards with Mushrooms and Green Onions; Gordon Hamersley, Hamersley's Bistro, Boston

Foie Gras with Cactus Pears; Alain Borel,
L'Auberge Provençal, White Post, Virginia

Foie Gras with Cactus Pears

Alain Borel, L'Auberge Provençal
White Post, Virginia

Serves 6

This dish is a study in surprising contrasts: Crisp fried slices of bright orange sweet potato and a vivid red cactus pear sauce flecked with pomegranate seed matched with buttery foie gras.

Sweet-Potato Chips
1 sweet potato, peeled
4 cups vegetable oil

Cactus Pear Puree
2 cactus pears, peeled and sliced
   ¼ inch thick
¾ cup ruby port, divided

Foie Gras
Six ¼-inch-thick slices duck foie gras,
   trimmed and soaked (see page 13)
Salt and freshly ground black pepper
   to taste

2 tablespoons veal demi-glace
   (see page 22)
4 tablespoons unsalted butter
1 pomegranate, seeded (6 tablespoons
   pomegranate seeds)
Fresh sage leaves for garnish

To make the sweet-potato chips: Cut the sweet potato into ¹⁄₁₆-inch-thick slices. Heat the vegetable oil in a heavy pot or deep-fryer to 375°F, or until almost smoking. Cook the sweet potato slices until golden and crisp, about 2 minutes. Using a slotted spoon, remove the slices, and drain on paper towels. Keep warm in a very low oven.

To make the cactus pear puree: Cook the pears with ½ cup of the port in a very low oven in a medium saucepan over medium heat for 5 minutes. Mash the cooked pears with a fork to incorporate them into the liquid. Remove the pears from the heat and puree in a blender or food processor for 15 to 20 seconds. Strain the puree through a fine-meshed sieve. Set aside and keep warm.

To prepare the foie gras: Preheat a dry skillet over high heat. Season the foie gras with salt and pepper on both sides. Cook the foie gras for about 15 seconds on each side, or until lightly browned. Remove the foie gras immediately from the skillet and set aside. In the same pan, add the remaining ¼ cup of the port and boil until reduced by half. Add the cactus pear puree and the veal demi-glace. Add the butter, whisking gently until smooth. Check the seasoning and adjust with salt and pepper if necessary. Add the pomegranate seeds and remove from heat.

To assemble the dish: Divide the sauce among 6 warmed plates. Add the sweet potato chips in a circle around the sauce. Put a slice of foie gras in the middle of the sauce. Decorate each plate with fresh sage leaves and serve immediately.

Note: The sweet potato chips and sauce base may be prepared up to 6 hours in advance and kept at room temperature. The foie gras should be fried and the sauce completed just prior to serving.

Mignon Salmon Roulade; Alden "Binet" Lanier, Blackie's House of Beef, Washington, D.C.

Mignon Salmon Roulade

*Alden "Binet" Lanier, Blackie's House
of Beef
Washington, D.C.*

Serves 6

This updated version of "surf and turf"
combines salmon and beef tenderloin in
a roulade that is spiced with Cajun
seasoning, seared, and served with a
roasted-corn relish.

Corn and Black Bean Relish
4 tablespoons unsalted butter
3 cups cooked fresh or thawed frozen
    corn kernels
1 cup cooked black (turtle) beans
3 tablespoons balsamic vinegar
1 teaspoon sugar
3 tablespoons olive oil
Salt and freshly ground black pepper
    to taste

Roulade
1 pound beef tenderloin, trimmed and
    cut into 6 even slices
1 pound fresh salmon fillet, skinned
1 large bunch fresh sage
1 large bunch fresh basil
1 large Portobello mushroom, thinly sliced
1¼ cups Cajun spice blend
½ teaspoon ground cumin
½ cup olive oil

To make the corn relish: Place the butter
in a large sauté pan or skillet over
medium-high heat. Add the corn and
beans, and cook until the corn is heated
through. Remove the pan from the heat
and add the remaining ingredients to the
relish, mixing with a slotted spoon. Set
aside at room temperature.

To make the roulade: Place a large sheet
of plastic wrap on a work surface and
place the tenderloin slices on top of it.
Cover the beef with another sheet of
plastic wrap and pound the meat with
the smooth side of a meat mallet or the
bottom of a heavy saucepan until the
meat is about ¼ inch thick.

Slice the salmon fillet into equally
thin slices. Place the salmon slices over
the tenderloin, then layer the salmon

ALDEN "BINET" LANIER
Blackie's House of Beef, Washington, D.C.

Growing up in the Louisiana lowlands, Alden "Binet" Lanier earned
small fees guiding tourists through the swamps in search of largemouth
bass and bluegill breams. Now he has made the leap to executive chef at
Blackie's House of Beef, a Washington, D.C., restaurant since 1949.

The Cajun-born chef moved to South America at the age of nineteen
to work as the cook for an oil and gold mining company. Being responsible for feeding fifty men in the jungle taught Binet adaptability. "That
was a true test of my abilities, to use what was on hand and make it tasty
and hearty," he says.

Binet had a partnership in a small steak restaurant, 102 North Market
in Charleston, South Carolina, but the establishment was destroyed by
Hurricane Hugo in 1989. Fortunately, it was at this time that Gregory
Auger and Gary Namm asked Binet to help design the menu for LuLu's
New Orleans Cafe, in Washington. After serving authentic Creole food
for four months, Binet became executive chef for Blackie's, owned by
Auger's parents. Now he serves up signature dishes like Blackie's Prime
Rib, and, as a sign of the ever-changing culinary times, his dishes also
include lighter fare like Binet's Mignon Salmon Roulade

Binet brought with him age-old techniques of curing country ham, as
well as aging and preparing beef. "Cooking is easy," Binet says. "To be
good at it you must like it; to be very good, you must love it."

with the sprigs of sage and basil. Layer
the mushroom slices over the herbs.
Starting at one edge, roll the tenderloin
into a tight cylinder and secure the edges
with toothpicks.

Sprinkle the spice blend and cumin
onto a plate and dredge the rolls in the
mixture, covering the outside in an even
layer. Place a large sauté pan or skillet
over high heat. When the pan begins to
smoke, dip the roulade briefly in the
olive oil and place it in the pan. Sear for

a total of 5 minutes on both sides, turning frequently.

Transfer the roulade to a cutting
board and cut into ½-inch-thick slices.
Divide the roulade among the plates,
garnish with the corn relish, and serve.

Note: *The rolls may be prepared for seasoning and searing up to 4 hours in advance
and refrigerated, tightly covered with
plastic wrap. The relish may also be made
at that time.*

Poblanos Rellenos

Zarela Martinez, Zarela
New York, New York

Serves 6

The dried fruits in the chicken filling balance the savory spicing and salty olives, making this a very special version of a classic Mexican dish. Serve this with a tossed salad and some sautéed corn or zucchini.

6 large poblano chilies
Vegetable oil for frying

Stuffing
½ cup (1 stick) unsalted butter
1 onion, chopped
2 garlic cloves, minced
½ cup pimento-stuffed green olives, drained and sliced
½ cup coarsely diced pitted prunes
½ cup coarsely diced dried apricots
½ cup coarsely diced dried peaches
1½ teaspoons ground cumin
1½ teaspoons ground cinnamon
¼ teaspoon ground cloves
2 cups shredded cooked chicken
Salt and freshly ground black pepper
   to taste

Roasted-Tomato Sauce
1½ cups heavy (whipping) cream
8 large garlic cloves, unpeeled
1 onion, unpeeled and halved crosswise
4 large ripe tomatoes
Salt and freshly ground black pepper
   to taste

   Preheat the oven to 500°F. Make a 1- to 1½-inch-long lengthwise slit in each poblano chili. In a large, heavy skillet, pour oil to a depth of ½ inch and heat over high heat until almost smoking. Fry the chilies, 2 at a time, turning once or twice with tongs, until the skin blisters and turns olive-beige in color. Remove the chilies from the pan and submerge them in a bowl of ice water. Repeat with the remaining chilies. Once the chilies have cooled, peel off the blistered skin. Using a teaspoon, gently scrape the seeds out of the chilies through the slit, being careful not to tear the flesh. Set aside.

ZARELA MARTINEZ
Zarela, New York, New York

   Zarela Martinez began cooking out of necessity. Married to a widower with three children, and pregnant with twins, she supplemented her income as a social worker in Mexico by selling Christmas cookies and catering her sister's parties. Cooking quickly became a vocation for Martinez, who in 1987 opened Zarela, now a New York landmark for lovers of authentic regional Mexican food.

   Martinez began by gathering friends' recipes from her home state of Chihuahua, Mexico. She credits her success to her willingness to travel and learn. "I had little formal culinary training, but early in my catering career I took cooking lessons around the country. I traveled incessantly throughout Mexico, tasting and learning—and soon developed a style based on layers of flavors, combining elements from the different culinary regions." Signature dishes include her *Poblanos Rellenos,* as well as *Salpicon de Huachinango* (Red Snapper Hash), which was adapted from a dish she sampled at a bar in Tampico, Mexico.

   Traveling and taking lessons in America, Martinez captured the attention of Paul Prudhomme, who served as her mentor and placed her in the national spotlight. In 1983, she was asked to design a menu to be served at Ronald Reagan's ranch in California for Queen Elizabeth II. That same year, she was one of the chefs selected by Craig Claiborne for the Economic Summit in Williamsburg.

   In 1987, four years after relocating to New York City to design the menu and serve as the executive chef for Café Marimba, Martinez opened Zarela, which the *New York Times* dubbed "arguably the best Mexican restaurant in New York City." And the public seems to agree, since Zarela has consistently been listed as one of the twenty-five top-grossing restaurants in the United States by *Hospitality Magazine.*

   Following the publication of her critically acclaimed *Food from My Heart* (Macmillan) in 1992, an autobiography interwoven with treasured recipes, Martinez continues to run Zarela and research her second book. "My goal is to familiarize the American public with the ingredients and flavors of my beloved native country and ancestors and with fine dining the modern Mexican way," she says.

To make the stuffing: Melt the butter in a large sauté pan or skillet over medium heat. When the bubbles begin to subside, add the onion and garlic and cook, stirring constantly, for 3 minutes, or until the onions are golden. Add the olives, prunes, apricots, and peaches, and cook, stirring frequently, for another 3 minutes. Add the cumin, cinnamon, cloves, and chicken and continue to cook, stirring to combine, for 2 minutes more. Season with salt and pepper. Carefully stuff each chili through the slit in the side. Set aside.

To make the roasted-tomato sauce: Place the cream in a saucepan and bring to a boil over medium heat; watch as it comes to a boil and stir so that it does not boil over. Cook over medium heat until reduced to about 1 cup, and set aside.

Heat a dry cast-iron griddle or skillet over high heat until a drop of water sizzles and immediately evaporates on contact. Toast the unpeeled garlic cloves and onion, turning several times, until the garlic is dark on all sides and somewhat softened and the onion is partly blackened. Set aside. Toast the tomatoes in the same way, turning several times, until blistered on all sides. Peel the onion, rubbing away any charred bits, and add to the garlic. Peel the tomatoes directly over a blender or food processor to avoid losing any juices, and add to the garlic and onion. Puree the vegetables. Combine the reduced cream and the tomato puree in a saucepan and heat for 3 to 4 minutes. Season with salt and pepper, and keep warm.

Meanwhile, preheat the oven to 500°F. Grease a baking pan with shortening or oil and place the stuffed chilies in a single layer in the prepared pan. Bake the chilies for 7 minutes, or until heated through. Spoon the warm tomato sauce onto individual plates or a large serving platter and arrange the chilies on top of the sauce.

Note: *The chilies and sauce may both be prepared up to 2 days in advance and refrigerated, tightly covered. Reheat the sauce in a small saucepan over low heat, and reheat the chilled chilies for 10 to 12 minutes at 400°F.*

Poblanos Rellenos; Zarela Martinez, Zarela, New York

Porcini Broth with Soft Polenta; Jody Adams, Michela's, Cambridge, Massachusetts

Porcini Broth with Soft Polenta
Aquacotta

*Jody Adams, Michela's
Cambridge, Massachusetts*

Serves 4

This is one of the most comforting dishes imaginable, with the creamy polenta and an aromatic serving broth as the foils to a poached egg. Add a second egg and serve with a tossed salad and some crusty bread for a casual supper.

Porcini Broth

2 tablespoons dried porcini mushrooms
3½ cups chicken stock (see page 20)
½ cup dry Marsala wine
Salt and freshly ground black pepper
  to taste

Polenta

3 cups water
½ cup polenta (coarsely ground
  cornmeal)
2 tablespoons grated Pecorino Romano
  cheese
Salt and freshly ground black pepper
  to taste

Poached Eggs

1 tablespoon vinegar
Pinch of salt
4 extra-large eggs

Topping

Four 1-ounce slices Taleggio or Teleme
  cheese
Truffle oil or extra-virgin olive oil

To make the broth: Soak the porcini mushrooms in warm water to cover for 1 hour. Strain the liquid through a fine-meshed sieve and chop the mushrooms. Combine the mushroom water, chicken stock, and Marsala in a medium saucepan. Add the mushrooms to the pan and bring the broth to a boil over medium-high heat. Reduce heat and simmer for 45 minutes. Season with salt and pepper. Set aside.

To make the polenta: Bring 1½ cups of the water to a boil in a medium saucepan. Add the polenta to the remaining 1½ cups of cold water. Slowly whisk the polenta mixture into the boiling water, lower heat, and continue to cook for 30 minutes, stirring frequently. Stir in the cheese and season with salt and pepper.

To make the poached eggs: Fill an 8-inch sauté pan or skillet with water. Bring the water to a boil over high heat, then reduce to a simmer. Add the vinegar and salt. Crack the eggs, one at a time, into a saucer and slide them into the simmering water. Poach the eggs for 3 to 4 minutes. Remove the cooked eggs gently from the pan with a slotted spoon. Transfer the eggs to a bowl of ice water and set aside until needed.

To serve: Preheat the oven to 350°F. Spoon ½ cup polenta into each of 4 shallow soup bowls. Press 1 slice of cheese into each serving of polenta. Bake in the preheated oven until the cheese begins to melt into the polenta, about 4 minutes. Meanwhile, reheat the broth.

Reheat the poached eggs in the hot broth for 30 seconds. Remove the eggs with a slotted spoon and place on top of the cheese. Divide the broth among the bowls and drizzle the truffle oil or olive oil over it.

Note: The broth may be made up to 3 days in advance and refrigerated, tightly covered. The polenta may be prepared and the eggs may be poached up to 3 hours in advance. Reheat the polenta over low heat, stirring constantly.

JODY ADAMS
Michela's, Cambridge, Massachusetts

When a young child grows up without television, great things can happen. That was certainly the case for Jody Adams, whose interest in cooking was sparked at an early age. "We were a family without a TV. I think that left a lot of room and time to do things that were creative," she remembers, "and one of them was cooking."

While studying anthropology at Brown University, Adams began working with food writer and teacher Nancy Verde Barr, and remained her apprentice all through college. She was then hired at Seasons in the Bostonian Hotel in Boston, which has played a key role in the development of many chefs. Adams was fortunate enough to work with Lydia Shire, now chef-owner of Biba, who was then the chef at Seasons. Later she joined Gordon Hamersley as sous-chef at Hamersley's Bistro.

Then Adams came to work as executive chef at Michela's, the nationally recognized regional Italian restaurant in Cambridge, Massachusetts. Her appointment to Michela's in 1990 was a fortuitous one, since it was the only available job in Boston that attracted her. Adams brings her own New England orientation to traditionally inspired rustic Italian cooking, reflected in such signature dishes as Porcini Broth with Soft Polenta.

"People say that the choices on the Michela's menu range from really rich to downright heart-healthy. My first concern is taste and, happily, Italian cuisine offers people the best of both worlds," says Adams.

Adams recently formed a partnership with restaurateur Michela Larson and restaurant general manager Christopher Myers and opened Rialto in the Charles Hotel in Harvard Square. The menu will feature regional cuisine from the southern European countries that Adams fell in love with during her travels in France, Italy, and Spain. She is known for her careful research of regional cooking and plans to be "true to particularly regional culinary traditions of the Latin Crescent of Europe." Adams' signature pizza and pasta dishes will be an integral part of Rialto's fare, as will local seasonal ingredients with particular attention paid to fresh fish and vegetables.

Her love of Mediterranean cuisine earned Adams the 1991 Best Chef de Cuisine award from *Boston* magazine. Of her chosen profession Adams raves, "It's physical; it's creative; it's immediate; it makes people happy."

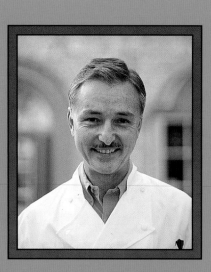

MARCEL DESAULNIERS
The Trellis Restaurant, Williamsburg, Virginia

Dispensing punishment was one of the tasks of the House of Burgesses in Williamsburg, the colonial capital of Virginia, but it's doubtful that anyone was sentenced to death by chocolate. But that is what diners in today's restored Williamsburg line up to receive as the ending to a meal at Marcel Desaulniers' The Trellis Restaurant.

Each Death by Chocolate serving weighs more than one pound and includes chocolate brownies, chocolate ganache, cocoa meringue, mocha mousse, and more. Desaulniers also offers diners Chocolate Devastation, Double-Mocha Madness, Chocolate-Lover's Cake, and Chocolate Phantasmagoria. His most recent cookbook, *Death by Chocolate: The Last Word on a Consuming Passion* (New York, Rizzoli, 1992), which received the 1993 James Beard Award for the best baking and dessert cookbook, makes Desaulniers' creations available to those not visiting Virginia's historic Tidewater area.

Perched in Merchant's Square between Colonial Williamsburg and the College of William and Mary, The Trellis Restaurant has become a destination point for travelers and locals. The menu changes both daily and seasonally, and the food is based on locality, simplicity, and freshness and is prepared with imagination and care. Dishes such as the everchanging Cheesecake (a fluffy take on quiche) and the Potato, Leek, and Watercress Soup with Grilled Smoked Duck are among the reasons that Desaulniers received the 1993 James Beard Award as Best Chef in the Mid-Atlantic States.

A 1965 graduate of the Culinary Institute of America, Desaulniers is no stranger to awards. Nationally, he has been named to *Food & Wine* magazine's Honor Roll of American Chefs and recognized by *Cook's Magazine* in their "Who's Who of Cooking in America." In addition, The Trellis has received the prestigious Ivy Award from *Restaurants & Institutions* magazine.

If you are not a chocophile but want to experience the Desaulniers' other creations, there are plenty of opportunities. His first cookbook, *The Trellis Cookbook* (Simon & Schuster) is now available in paperback. He is also the author of *The Burger Meisters* (Simon & Schuster), a compilation of forty-five burger recipes from fellow CIA graduates, and he is now writing *Desserts to Die For* (Simon & Schuster), to be published in 1995.

Potato, Leek, and Watercress Soup with Grilled Smoked Duck

Marcel Desaulniers, The Trellis Restaurant Williamsburg, Virginia

Serves 6

The addition of the peppery watercress and succulent smoked duck creates a far more interesting dish than the classic vichyssoise on which this soup is based. The time-consuming aspect of the recipe is the smoked duck, which also may be purchased at specialty foods stores or by mail; see Mail-Order Sources, page 243.

2 tablespoons unsalted butter
1 tablespoon water
6 leeks, white part only, chopped
2 celery stalks, sliced
1 onion, chopped
1 garlic clove, crushed
Salt and freshly ground pepper to taste
6 cups chicken stock (see page 20)
1½ pounds boiling potatoes, peeled and quartered
¼ cup half-and-half
1 large bunch watercress, stemmed
8 ounces thinly sliced Smoked Duck Breast (recipe follows)

Heat the butter and water in a 5-quart saucepan over medium heat. Add the chopped leeks, celery, onion, and garlic. Season with the salt and pepper, and sauté, stirring frequently, for 5 minutes, or until the onion is translucent. Add the chicken stock and potatoes to the pan. Bring the mixture to a boil over medium heat, lower the heat, and simmer slowly for 45 minutes, or until the potatoes are tender.

Remove the soup from the heat and puree it with a hand-held blender or in a blender or food processor; if using a blender or food processor this may have to be done in batches. Place the soup over low heat and bring to a simmer. Add the half-and-half and adjust the seasoning with salt and pepper.

Arrange equal portions of watercress in a ring along the outside edges of each of 6 warm soup plates. Pour the soup into each soup plate and arrange equal amounts of the grilled smoked duck over each. Serve immediately.

Note: *The soup may be made up to 2 days in advance; reheat over low heat, stirring frequently. Some milk or half-and-half may have to be added if the soup has thickened from the starch in the potatoes.*

Smoked Duck Breast
(Makes 12 ounces to 1 pound)

1 fresh duck (4½ to 5 pounds) or
  Muscovy duck breast (1 to 1¼ pounds)
2 cups warm water
½ cup kosher salt
2 tablespoons sugar

2 cups hickory, apple, or other aromatic wood chips, soaked in water for 30 minutes

If using a whole duck, remove the whole breast from the duck, reserving the legs and carcass for another use. Scrape the skin back from the duck to remove the fat, but leave the skin attached to the breast.

Prepare a brine by combining the water, salt, and sugar in a large non-aluminum bowl. Submerge the breast in the brine for 5 minutes, weighting it with a glass jar of food. Remove the duck from the brine and pat it dry with paper towels.

Lightly coat the bottom rack of a smoker with vegetable oil. Drain the wood chips and place them in the smoking chamber. Place the duck breast on the rack and smoke it for 2½ hours, or until cooked through.

Remove the breast from the smoker and grill it over a low charcoal or wood fire for 2½ to 3 minutes on each side, or until the juices run clear. Or, roast the duck in a preheated 350°F oven for 5 minutes. Let the breast cool to room temperature, then refrigerate it, uncovered, until thoroughly cool, about 1 hour.

Note: *To store, wrap the whole breast tightly in plastic wrap and refrigerate up to 5 days. Do not slice the breast until just before serving.*

Potato, Leek, and Watercress Soup with Grilled Smoked Duck; Marcel Desaulniers, The Trellis Restaurant, Williamsburg, Virginia

Pumpkin Soup with Fig Quenelles

Peter Platt, Wheatleigh
Lenox, Massachusetts

Serves 4

This is the perfect fall dish, and an elegant appetizer for Thanksgiving dinner. The soup is flavored with ginger and herbs, and the fig and whipped cream quenelles add a sweet accent to the hot soup. Butternut squash may be substituted for the pumpkins.

Pumpkin Soup

4 small pie pumpkins, about 8 inches in diameter
½ teaspoon kosher salt
1½ teaspoons ground nutmeg
4 fresh parsley sprigs
4 fresh thyme sprigs
4 small bay leaves
12 black peppercorns
4 tablespoons unsalted butter
3 onions, thinly sliced
4 cups chicken stock (see page 20)
1 cup heavy (whipping) cream
1 teaspoon ground ginger
½ teaspoon cayenne pepper
2 teaspoons salt

Fig Quenelles

6 dried figs
1 tablespoon dark rum
½ cup heavy (whipping) cream

Garnish

2 thin slices prosciutto ham, cut into
    ¹⁄₁₆-inch julienne
2 tablespoons minced fresh chives

To make the soup: Preheat the oven to 375°F and line a baking sheet with aluminum foil or parchment paper. Cut the tops from the pumpkins and scrape out the seeds and strings. Sprinkle the cavities with the salt and a little of the

Pumpkin Soup with Fig Quenelles; Peter Platt, Wheatleigh, Lenox, Massachusetts

nutmeg. Place 1 parsley sprig, 1 thyme sprig, 1 bay leaf, and 3 peppercorns in each pumpkin. Bake the pumpkins on the prepared pan for 1 hour, or until the flesh is tender.

While the pumpkins are baking, melt the butter over medium heat in a large saucepan, add the onions, cover, and cook for 3 to 4 minutes. Add the stock and cook uncovered for 20 minutes.

Remove the pumpkins from the oven. Scoop the cooked flesh from the inside, leaving the shells intact to use as bowls. Puree the cooked pumpkin and the onions and stock in a blender or food processor until smooth; this may have to be done in batches. If the soup is too thick, add more stock to thin as needed. Return the soup to the saucepan and add the cream, ginger, cayenne, salt, and the remaining nutmeg. Stir to combine the seasonings and bring to a boil over medium heat, stirring occasionally. Simmer for 3 minutes, then remove the pan from heat and set aside.

To prepare the quenelles: Place the dried figs in a small saucepan and add enough water to cover. Bring to a boil over medium heat, then reduce heat and simmer for 30 minutes. Drain the figs and let them cool. Puree the figs and rum in a blender or food processor. In a deep bowl, whip the cream until it holds stiff peaks. Fold the pureed figs into the whipped cream. Form the fig mixture into oval-shaped quenelles with 2 teaspoons.

To serve: Reheat the pumpkin shells in a 300°F oven for 10 to 15 minutes, or until warm. Fill the pumpkin shells with the hot soup up to 1 inch from the top; alternatively, divide the soup among four flat soup bowls. Place the quenelles on top of the soup. Garnish the soup with the prosciutto and minced chives.

Note: *The soup may be prepared up to 2 days in advance; refrigerate it, tightly covered, if prepared more than 6 hours in advance. Loosely cover the pumpkin shells with plastic wrap and store at room temperature.*

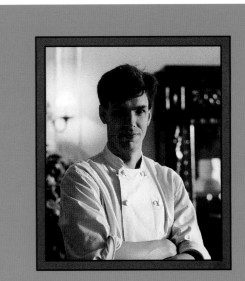

PETER PLATT
Wheatleigh, Lenox, Massachusetts

A Chicago native, Peter Platt learned to love the Berkshire Mountains of Massachusetts while attending Williams College in the western part of the range. In 1985 he opened the Wheatleigh, an inn offering what he calls "a contemporary interpretation of classical French" food, and the restaurant has garnered rave reviews; *Elle* magazine's Katherine Pancal admits, for example, "It's useless to hide it: it's my favorite."

Platt studied at Cordon Bleu in London and later worked with Lydia Shire and Jasper White at the Parker House Hotel in Boston. Over the past ten years at the Wheatleigh, he says, his cuisine has "become lighter, simpler, and hopefully more elegant. We are constantly trying to improve by finding fresher and higher-quality ingredients." In this quest, Platt has spent considerable time and energy developing a large network of local purveyors and farmers, particularly organic farmers, who meet his standards.

Signature dishes like Pumpkin Soup with Fig Quenelles and Halibut Enrobed in a Crisp Potato Crust reflect his commitment to the freshest ingredients available. The *New York Times* called the Wheatleigh dining experience "a table fit for a prince," and, in fact, the inn, which Platt describes as "a country-house hotel with a European-style flavor," is a replicated sixteenth-century Florentine palazzo built in the Berkshires by an American industrialist as a wedding gift for his daughter.

Platt elaborates on his goals as a career chef: "I want to create a place where one can come to celebrate, romance, conduct business, or focus on a sophisticated culinary experience."

Sea Scallops with Wild Mushrooms; Yves Labbé, Le Cheval d'Or, Jeffersonville, Vermont

Sea Scallops with Wild Mushrooms
Noix de Coquilles Saint-Jacques aux Champignons des Bois

Yves Labbé, Le Cheval d'Or
Jeffersonville, Vermont

Serves 4

Tender, sweet sea scallops need little augmentation, and the wild mushrooms in this quick and easy sauté dish are the perfect complement. Serve on a piece of toast with a tossed salad for a wonderful dinner.

1 pound sea scallops
2 cups mixed wild mushrooms (shiitakes, cèpes, oysters, chanterelles)
6 tablespoons unsalted butter, divided
1 shallot, thinly sliced
1 tablespoon minced garlic
Salt and freshly ground black pepper to taste
Flour for dredging
3 tablespoons olive oil
2 tablespoons minced fresh parsley
1 teaspoon fresh lemon juice

Rinse the sea scallops and remove any hingelike muscle on the side of each one. Set aside. Cut the mushrooms into ¼-inch-thick slices and set aside.

In a 12-inch sauté pan or skillet, melt 2 tablespoons of the butter over medium-high heat. Add the sliced mushrooms and cook until they are limp, about 3 to 5 minutes. Add the shallot and 1 teaspoon of the garlic, and sauté for 1 minute. Add salt and pepper and set aside.

Dredge the scallops lightly in enough flour to coat them evenly, shaking off any excess. Place a large cast-iron skillet over very high heat, add the olive oil, and heat until almost smoking. Add the scallops and sear on one side for 1 minute, or until golden brown; this may have to be done in batches so as not to crowd the pan. Add the remaining 4 tablespoons butter, the remaining garlic, and the parsley, and turn the scallops. Add the mushroom mixture and cook, stirring the mushroom mixture occasionally, for 1 minute, or until the scallops begin to give off their juices. Remove from heat and add the lemon juice. Adjust the seasoning, and serve.

Note: *The center of each scallop should be translucent and just warmed through. The mushrooms may be sautéed up to 1 hour in advance and kept warm in a very low oven.*

Risotto with Wild Mushrooms
Risotto con Funghi Misti

Lidia Bastianich, Felidia
New York, New York

Serves 4 as an entree, 6 as an appetizer

There is really no mystery to perfect risotto; it results from lovingly stirring the rice as it absorbs the liquid and becomes a creamy consistency from the starch that is released into the stock. This dish is flavored with earthy wild mushrooms, and the flavor is amplified by the dried porcini.

1 tablespoon dried porcini mushrooms
½ cup hot water
5 tablespoons olive oil
12 ounces mixed fresh wild mushrooms (such as stemmed shiitakes, chanterelles, porcini, oyster mushrooms), sliced

Risotto with Wild Mushrooms; Lidia Bastianich, Felidia, New York

Salt and freshly ground pepper to taste
1 cup minced onions
2 tablespoons minced shallots
2 cups Arborio rice
½ cup dry white wine
6½ cups chicken stock (see page 20),
    heated
½ teaspoon salt, or to taste
2 tablespoons unsalted butter,
    cut into bits
½ cup (2 ounces) freshly grated Parmesan
    cheese

Soak the dried mushrooms in ½ cup hot water for 20 minutes. Drain and chop the soaked dried mushrooms, reserving the mushroom water as well as the soaked mushrooms.

In a medium sauté pan or skillet, heat 2 tablespoons of the olive oil over medium-high heat. Add the fresh mushrooms and sauté them for 4 to 5 minutes, stirring frequently, or until they are brown and tender. Sprinkle with salt and pepper and set aside.

In a medium saucepan, heat the remaining 3 tablespoons of olive oil over medium heat. Add the onions and shallots and sauté, stirring frequently, for 3 to 4 minutes, or until golden. Add the rice to the pan and stir to coat. Cook for 2 minutes, stirring constantly.

Add the wine, ½ cup of the hot stock, and the ½ teaspoon salt. Cook, stirring constantly, until all the liquid is absorbed. Add the sautéed fresh mushrooms, chopped soaked mushrooms, and reserved mushroom water, and stir until it is almost absorbed. Continue to add the hot stock by ½-cup amounts, and cook until each successive batch has been absorbed before adding the next, stirring almost constantly.

When all the stock has been added the rice should be al dente and the dish should be creamy. Remove the risotto from the heat. Stir in the butter and cheese, season with salt and pepper, and serve at once.

LIDIA BASTIANICH
Felidia, New York, New York

Lidia Bastianich, wrote Jay Jacobs in *Gourmet* magazine, "is wedded nunlike to her calling. As she talks of food and its preparation, it soon becomes obvious that for her the service of a meal is an act of love."

Perhaps that is because the meals that Bastianich prepares are reminiscent of those cooked by her grandmother, who was her first cooking teacher. Or because Bastianich's food pays tribute to her first home in Istria, a peninsula in the Adriatic Sea. Once part of Italy, today Istria is part of Croatia. Recipes inspired by her grandmother and Istria are included in Bastianich's *La Cucina di Lidia,* an autobiographical cookbook.

Felidia, which Bastianich owns with her husband, Felice (hence the name Felidia), is part of an enclave of excellent Italian restaurants in New York City. The appetizer offerings include Wild Mushroom Soup, Blood Orange Salad, Grilled Portobello with Truffles, and Mussels Triestina, among others. The main courses are divided into Pasta and Rice, and Fish and Meat, with earthy dishes like Risotto with Wild Mushrooms, Orecchiette with Broccoli Rabe, and Calves' Liver with Balsamic Vinegar. Felidia has received honors for its food and its wine, including the Best Award for Excellence from the *Wine Spectator.*

Bastianich is more than a creator of wonderful meals. She is an educator, an editor, and an ambassador of Italian-Istrian cuisine. She has taught food anthropology as well as numerous cooking classes. Along with writing her own cookbook and contributing to others, Bastianich has edited "A Celebration of Life," an annual insert on Italian food, wines and lifestyle for the *New York Times Magazine,* and was featured in Time-Life's *60 Minute Cookbook.*

Her leadership and achievements have been honored by many. In 1990 she was the chair of Bon Appetit Taste of the Nation, a national benefit fund-raiser for Share Our Strength at Lincoln Center. She has been named Woman of the Year by NYU's Center for Food and Hotel Management. She is currently the vice-president of the New York chapter of Ordine Ristoratori Professionisti Italiana. She is one of the founding board members of the International Association of Women Chefs and Restaurateurs, and is a member of the prestigious *Who's Who of Cooking in America.*

EVERETT REID

American Seasons, Nantucket, Massachusetts

A visit to Nantucket Island wouldn't be complete without a pancake breakfast. Those who live where the screen doors bang know where to find the fluffiest ones with the most blueberries.

But those who truly know Nantucket's food offerings know that the best pancakes on the island aren't served for breakfast. The Smoked Lobster and Wild Mushroom Pancakes with Crème Fraîche and a Trio of American Caviars are available at dinner at the American Seasons restaurant and are the creation of chef-owner Everett Reid.

American Seasons, which Reid and his wife Linda opened in 1987, features diverse American dishes and regional ingredients. The interior of American Seasons is as full of color and nuance as the menu. The tables are all hand-painted to resemble game boards such as Chinese checkers and dominos, and the silver is casually tied in the napkins.

The Wild West portion of the menu includes Spicy Duck Taco with Ranchero Sauce and Orange-Jícama Salad. Representing the Pacific Coast are such dishes as Fresh Napa Valley Snails with a Brioche Tart. New England specialties include a nontraditional surf and turf of Charred Smoked Beef and Fried Oysters, and Pan-fried Skate Wings with Yellow Pepper Coulis. In the Down South menu component, you'll find Smoky Oyster and Wild Boar Gumbo with Andouille Sausage and Red Rice.

The inventor of these entrees credits his parents with his fearless attitude toward food. "My parents were always adventurous in introducing us to new foods—be it sweetbreads, kidneys—things other children in the neighborhood were not eating," says Reid. Besides his studies at the family dinner table, Reid studied at the Culinary Institute of America and at Cordon Bleu in London.

Continuing the tradition of family's "great interest in food and wine," Reid gives careful attention to the pairing of food and wines in his restaurant, and American Seasons has received a *Wine Spectator* award for its excellent wine list.

Smoked Lobster and Wild Mushroom Pancakes with Crème Fraîche and a Trio of American Caviars

Everett Reid, American Seasons
Nantucket, Massachusetts

Serves 6

Succulent lobster, aromatic from wood smoke, and woodsy wild mushrooms flavor pancakes topped with red, gold, and black caviar. This is a fabulous dish for a brunch or an elegant supper.

Pancakes

1 cup hickory chips or mixed hickory, apple wood, and pecan chips
1 live lobster, 1½ to 2 pounds
3 tablespoons unsalted butter
6 tablespoons olive oil, divided
3 cups mixed wild mushrooms such as chanterelles, oyster mushrooms, porcini, and stemmed shiitakes, cut into 1-inch pieces
Salt and freshly ground black pepper to taste
2¼ cups all-purpose flour
1 tablespoon baking powder
½ teaspoon salt
2 eggs, lightly beaten
1¾ cups milk
6 green onions, white part and 2 inches of green tops, thinly sliced
Freshly ground black pepper to taste

Garnish

6 to 9 tablespoons crème fraîche (see page 20)
3 tablespoons red salmon caviar
3 tablespoons golden whitefish caviar
3 tablespoons black American sturgeon caviar
3 tablespoons minced fresh parsley
12 fresh chives

To make the pancakes: Light a fire in a charcoal grill and place the wood chips in water to cover. Kill the lobster by inserting a knife at the base of the body and cutting through the tail. Cut the tail off the body and split it down the middle lengthwise. Cut the claws off and crack the shells with a knife. Reserve the body for making fish stock.

When the coals are glowing red, drain the soaked wood chips and sprinkle them over the coals. Place the lobster on the cooking rack and cover the grill. Grill the lobster for 5 minutes, then turn the claws and cook an additional 3 minutes. Remove the lobster from the grill and, when cool enough to handle, remove the meat from the shell and cut it into ½-inch dice.

Heat the butter and 2 tablespoons of the olive oil in a large sauté pan or skillet over medium-high heat. Add the mushrooms and sauté, stirring often, for 3 to 5 minutes, or until they are browned and tender. Season with salt and pepper, set aside, and let cool.

Combine the flour, baking powder, and salt in a large bowl. Combine the eggs and milk in a large measuring cup and add to the dry ingredients. Stir to combine, then add the green onions and pepper.

Heat a small skillet over medium-high heat. Add 2 teaspoons of the remaining olive oil and swirl to coat the pan. When the oil is very hot, add ½ cup of the pancake batter, swirling to distribute it evenly. Place one sixth of the lobster and mushrooms on top of the batter. Fry the pancake until browned on the bottom and beginning to dry on the surface. Turn the pancake with a spatula and cook the other side. Keep the pancake warm in a very low oven and repeat with the remaining batter until 6 pancakes are fried.

To serve: Place one pancake on each of 6 small plates and divide the crème fraîche and caviars on top of each. Sprinkle with the parsley and place 2 chives on each.

Note: The lobster and mushrooms may be prepared 1 day in advance, covered, and refrigerated. Do not make the batter or fry the pancakes until just prior to serving.

Smoked Lobster and Wild Mushroom Pancakes with Crème Fraîche and a Trio of American Caviars; Everett Reid, American Seasons, Nantucket, Massachusetts

Steamed Mussels
Mouclade de Moules

Georges Perrier, Le Bec-Fin
Philadelphia, Pennsylvania

Serves 4

Steamed mussels in an aromatic and flavorful sauce are a classic French dish; in this version, a hint of curry adds an interesting note to the creamy sauce.

3 tablespoons unsalted butter
2 shallots, minced
1 teaspoon curry powder
½ cup dry white wine
4 pounds mussels, scrubbed and debearded (see page 16)
1½ cups heavy (whipping) cream
1 pound spinach, stemmed
¼ cup minced fresh chives

Place a stockpot large enough to hold the mussels over medium heat and add 1 tablespoon of the butter. Add the shallots and curry powder and cook for 2 minutes over low heat, stirring constantly. Stir in the white wine and cook another 3 to 4 minutes. Add the mussels to the pot, cover the pan, and raise heat to medium-high. Cook until the mussels open, about 4 to 5 minutes, shaking the pan a few times to rearrange the mussels. Remove the pan from heat and strain the liquid into a medium saucepan, reserving the mussels. Discard any mussels that have not opened.

Return the liquid to heat and boil until the liquid is reduced by half. Add the heavy cream to the reduced sauce, stirring well to combine, and cook to and reduce by half again. Place a 10-inch sauté pan or skillet over high heat and add the remaining 2 tablespoons butter and the spinach. Cook, turning constantly, until the spinach is just wilted, about 1 to 2 minutes.

To serve: Remove the top shell from each of the mussels and arrange the mussels on 4 plates. Divide the wilted spinach into 4 portions and place in the middle of each plate. Ladle the sauce over the mussels and sprinkle with the chives.

Note: While the dish is served hot at the restaurant, it also may be served at room temperature.

Ravioli with Bay Scallops

Jimmy Sneed, The Frog and the Redneck
Richmond, Virginia

Serves 4

No portion of this dish is difficult to make; however, be warned that there are a great number of steps that must be accomplished just prior to serving. This would be a good dish to make when there are several people sharing the cooking duties.

Seaweed Salad
1 cup edible seaweed*
1 tablespoon toasted sesame oil*
2 tablespoons rice wine vinegar*
1 tablespoon sesame seeds

Pasta Dough
½ cup semolina flour
½ cup all-purpose flour
1 egg
½ teaspoon saffron threads, crushed into a fine powder in a mortar

Filling
4 to 6 sea scallops (½ cup), muscle removed
Salt and freshly ground black pepper to taste
½ cup heavy (whipping) cream
4 bay scallops
1 egg, lightly beaten
4 cups chicken stock (see page 20)

Sauce and Garnish
½ cup Champagne
2 shallots, minced
1 tablespoon olive oil
8 sea scallops, muscle removed, sliced crosswise into halves
8 bay scallops, preferably in the shell
¼ teaspoon salt
2 tablespoons cold unsalted butter
1 tablespoon minced fresh parsley

To make the salad: Combine the seaweed with the sesame oil, vinegar, and sesame seeds. Toss to combine well, cover, and refrigerate for at least 30 minutes.

To make the pasta: Combine the flours, egg, and saffron in a food processor and pulse to combine. Form the dough into a ball, cover it with plastic wrap, and let sit for at least 30 minutes.

Roll the pasta dough through the widest setting of a pasta machine, and continue to roll it, moving the rollers 1 setting closer together each time to make the pasta as thin as possible. Set the dough aside.

To make the filling: Season the sea scallops with salt and pepper on both sides. Place the sea scallops in a blender or food processor and pulse until finely pureed. Add the cream and pulse again just to combine. (Avoid over-processing, or the cream will turn to butter.) Transfer the mousse to a chilled bowl and keep cool until ready to use.

Spoon approximately 1 tablespoon of the mousse at 2-inch intervals onto one

Steamed Mussels; Georges Perrier, Le Bec-Fin, Philadelphia

half of the pasta dough. Press a bay scallop into the center of each mound, then top the bay scallop with another dollop of mousse. Brush the other half of the pasta with the beaten egg, then drape that half over the mounds of filling. Cut around the ravioli with a scalloped cookie cutter. Crimp the outside to seal the ravioli, making sure to expel any air pockets. Cover the ravioli with a damp cloth and set aside. Place the chicken stock in a stockpot and bring to a low boil.

To make the sauce and garnish: Combine the Champagne and shallots in a medium saucepan and place over medium-high heat. Simultaneously, barely coat the bottom of a heavy cast-iron skillet with the olive oil and place over high heat. Add the ravioli to the pot of boiling stock and cook for 3 minutes. While the ravioli are cooking, sear the sea scallops in the cast-iron skillet until they are golden brown on one side, about 2 minutes. When the Champagne has been boiling for approximately 4 minutes, add the bay scallops and steam until just open. (If you are using shucked bay scallops, add them to the Champagne and poach for no more than 1 minute.) Turn the sea scallops and cool on the other side for 45 seconds. Remove the bay scallops from the Champagne and set aside, keeping warm. Add the salt, then lower the heat and swirl in the cold butter, whisking to combine. Swirl in the parsley and set aside.

To serve: Drain the ravioli and blot quickly on paper towels. Arrange a mound of seaweed salad in the center of each plate. Place 4 disks of seared sea scallop on one side of the salad, then place 2 bay scallops (preferably in a scallop shell if available) beside them. Divide the ravioli among the plates. Drizzle the champagne sauce over each of the 3 scallop preparations and serve.

*Available in some supermarkets and in Asian markets.

Note: *The unrolled ravioli dough may be prepared 1 day in advance and refrigerated, wrapped in plastic wrap. The remainder of the dish must be prepared just prior to serving.*

GEORGES PERRIER
Le Bec-Fin, Philadelphia, Pennsylvania

Few restaurants are so highly regarded that they are featured in an eighteen-page magazine article, but Le Bec-Fin, whose name is a French idiom meaning "the good taste," is such a spot. Opened in 1970, Le Bec-Fin is no flavor-of-the-month place—it is a food mecca, and food critic Jim Quinn was willing to sit on milk crates in its kitchen for a year and a half researching an article for *Philadelphia* magazine that explains why.

The why is the chef: Georges Perrier. This formerly married chef, his brother says, "cannot really be divorced. He will always be married—to the restaurant."

Originally from Lyon, Perrier began his career as an apprentice at age fourteen. Before his training started, he thought that being a chef would mean not having to work as hard as his jeweler father and doctor mother. He says, "I will be a chef. A chef! What I didn't know is, I work more days, more hours than my father and my mother together." Perrier trained for more than nine years in France, and then moved to Philadelphia in 1967. Three years later he opened Le Bec-Fin.

While many might consider Philadelphia to be a little outside the East Coast culinary mainstream, its location has not hindered the restaurant's popularity or its chef's fame. Since the first year, Perrier and Le Bec-Fin have received some of the highest awards in the hospitality industry.

The restaurant has enjoyed five-star status with *Mobil Travel Guide* since 1985 and five-diamond status with the American Automobile Association since 1989. In all of the United States and Canada, only two other restaurants received both awards for 1992.

In 1976, Perrier was inducted in the Maîtres Cuisiniers de France, the premier international society of French chefs. Its two hundred members include the finest French chefs in the world. In 1989, the members voted Perrier Chef of the Year and awarded him the Silver Toque, the most coveted trophy in the world of French haute cuisine.

Perrier's style is modern French classical cooking, and his food is as close to perfect as the style gets. As he says, "Everybody makes mistakes…me, the chefs, the waiters, everybody. No one can be perfect in this world. I understand that. I believe that. But I cannot accept it!" Diners, including the most seasoned restaurant critics, appreciate his ongoing quest for culinary perfection.

Cold Appetizers and Salads

a few decades ago even the finest restaurants represented in this book defined a salad as a plate of tossed greens with a vinaigrette dressing. Today those greens may also be the pale ivory-green of endive or the vivid red of radicchio or red oak leaf lettuce, and whole leaves of fresh herbs are often used to add a more vibrant flavor.

Salads that include a variety of other ingredients, such as meat, fish, or fruit, raw or blanched vegetables, have become mainstays for the first course on today's menus. In this chapter you will find a range of salads, many of which could be enlarged to become a light lunch or supper.

The Sweetbread Salad with Mango, for example, is a triumph of satiny sweetbreads topping greens flecked with grilled red onion and bright orange mango, while the Squab Salad and Couscous with Curried Vinaigrette and Chutney has all the elements of a complete meal right on the plate.

In addition to salads, this chapter contains some easy and elegant cold appetizers. The Carpaccio of Sirloin is merely thinly pounded meat, but the genius of the dish lies in the three variations on garlic mayonnaise surrounding it.

Due to the influence of French cooking in the eastern states, this chapter includes several terrines, the forcemeat loaves of classic French cuisine. But these dishes are far from the traditional pork and/or veal loaves. Rabbit Terrine is a colorful blend of vegetables and rabbit bound by a savory custard, and Leek and Foie Gras Terrine with Raspberry Vinaigrette combines these foods in a stunning pattern.

Lasagne of Two Salmons and Savoy Cabbage; Michel LeBorgne, Inn at Essex/New England Culinary Institute, Montpelier, Vermont

Debra Ponzek, Montrachet
New York, New York

Serves 4

This is a delicious dish full of bright colors and vivid flavors that can be served as an appetizer or in a larger portion as an elegant summer lunch or dinner. It cannot be impromptu, however, since the curry oil must be made at least 2 days ahead and the sweetbreads must be prepared several hours to 1 day ahead before their final quick sauté.

Curry Oil
One 4-ounce can red curry paste (available at Asian markets)
1 cup olive oil

Sweetbreads
1 pair veal sweetbreads (about 1 to 1¼ pounds)
4 cups cold water
1 tablespoon fresh lemon juice or white wine vinegar
Salt and freshly ground black pepper to taste

1 red onion, thinly sliced
2 teaspoons plus 2 tablespoons olive oil
Salt and freshly ground pepper to taste
Flour for coating
2 cups mixed baby greens
Sherry Vinaigrette (recipe follows)
1 ripe mango, peeled and cut into a ¹⁄₁₆-inch julienne

   To make the curry oil: In a small saucepan combine the red curry paste and olive oil, and whisk until smooth. Bring to a simmer over low heat and simmer for 5 minutes, stirring occasionally. Remove the curry oil from the heat, cover, and refrigerate for 2 to 3 days. Spoon the red oil from the top of the paste (use the paste to season other dishes). Place the oil in an airtight glass jar and refrigerate indefinitely.

   To prepare the sweetbreads: Rinse the sweetbreads in cold water. Place the sweetbreads in a glass or ceramic bowl, add water to cover, and soak in the refrigerator for 1 to 2 hours, changing

DEBRA PONZEK
Montrachet, New York, New York

   Debra Ponzek was studying engineering at Boston University when she decided to trade her slide rule for a sauté pan. It was the right move, and her star has been ascending ever since.

   Ponzek transferred to the Culinary Institute of America, where she pursued her true vocation and graduated in 1984. Following graduation, she became the sous-chef at the Tarragon Tree in Chatham, New Jersey, then the chef at Toto, a steakhouse in Summit, New Jersey. Influenced first by nouvelle cuisine, Ponzek has broadened her style over the years. Her gastronomic exploration in France has contributed to her development.

   Her move in 1986 to Drew Nieporent's Montrachet, in New York's TriBeCa neighborhood, allowed her creativity to blossom. Attracted by the restaurant's combination of elegant atmosphere with straightforward food presentation, she was appointed chef not long after her arrival.

   Recognition and honors were not far behind. Soon after Ponzek took over the kitchen, Montrachet was awarded three-star status by the *New York Times* and *Newsday,* and in 1989 at the young age of twenty-eight, Ponzek was selected by *Food & Wine* magazine as one of the Ten Best New American Chefs. She left Montrachet in 1994, and is writing a book.

   In 1990, Ponzek was named Chef of the Year by the Chefs of America Association. The James Beard Foundation bestowed her with the Rising Chef of the Year award and in 1994 she became the first American ever to receive the Moreau Award.

   She describes her approach as "French—more modern than classical and more Provençal and Mediterranean—with lighter sauces, broths, and vinaigrettes." She uses lots of fresh herbs and infusions, and aspires to simplicity in her approach, as exemplified by her Sweetbread Salad with Mango. While Ponzek generally stays away from cream in her sauces, one of her signature dishes, Pasta with Wild Mushrooms, includes a bit of cream with mushroom stock. "A moderate amount of cream or butter is not the worst thing!" she says.

the water several times. Drain the sweet-breads, put them in a medium saucepan, and add the 4 cups water, lemon juice or vinegar, salt, and pepper. Bring to a boil over medium heat and simmer covered for 10 minutes. Drain the sweetbreads and rinse in cold water. Carefully remove the duct connecting the lobes and the membrane covering each lobe.

Place the sweetbreads on a plate or tray and cover with a plate. Weight the plate with a 5-pound pan or bag of sugar. Refrigerate for at least 2 hours or overnight until the sweetbreads are firm.

Light a fire in a charcoal grill. When the coals are lightly covered with a gray ash, brush the onion slices with the 2 teaspoons olive oil and grill for 3 to 4 minutes, or until tender. Set aside.

Just before serving, cut the sweet-breads into diagonal slices, about ⅜ to ½ inch thick. Season the sweetbreads with salt and pepper and lightly coat with flour. In a medium sauté pan or skillet, heat the 2 tablespoons olive oil over medium heat and sauté the sweet-breads for about 3 to 4 minutes, or until golden brown on both sides. Drain the sweetbreads on paper towels; set aside and keep warm.

Toss the baby greens in enough sherry vinaigrette to lightly dress them. Add the julienned mango and grilled red onion slices and toss to combine. Divide the salad among 4 salad plates. Arrange sweetbread slices around each salad and drizzle 1 teaspoon of the red curry oil over the sweetbreads. Serve at once.

Sherry Vinaigrette
(Makes ⅔ cup)

1 large shallot, minced
1 teaspoon minced fresh thyme
2 tablespoons sherry vinegar
½ cup olive oil
Salt and freshly ground black pepper
    to taste

In a small bowl, combine the shallots, thyme, and vinegar. Slowly whisk in the oil until the vinaigrette is emulsified. Season with salt and pepper.

Sweetbread Salad with Mango; Debra Ponzek, Montrachet, New York

Squab Salad and Couscous with Curried Vinaigrette and Chutney

Alfred Portale, Gotham Bar and Grill /
One Fifth Avenue
New York, New York

Serves 4

Couscous is actually not a grain, but a finely milled pasta made from semolina; it now comes in a quick-cooking form that does not require the traditional steaming. All the elements of this Asian-inspired salad, which is perfect for a summer dinner, are united by the flavor of curry.

Couscous
¾ cup chicken stock (see page 20)
1 tablespoon unsalted butter
¼ cup dried currants
½ cup quick-cooking couscous
3 tablepoons Curry Vinaigrette (recipe follows)
2 green onions, finely chopped
1 tablespoon harissa (see Note)
Salt and freshly ground black pepper to taste

Salad
1 small head red oakleaf lettuce
1 small head frisée (curly endive)
1 small head Bibb lettuce
Two 14- to 16-ounce squabs
Salt and freshly ground white pepper to taste
½ teaspoon Chinese five-spice powder
2 tablespoons olive oil
2 tablespoons unsalted butter
¼ cup raisins
⅓ cup Curry Vinaigrette (recipe follows)
¼ cup chutney

To make the couscous: Bring the stock and butter to a boil in a 2-quart saucepan. Remove the pan from heat, add the currants and couscous, stir well, and cover the pan. Let sit until the liquid has been absorbed, about 5 to 8 minutes. Fluff the couscous with a fork and moisten it with the curry vinaigrette. Add the green onions and harissa, then season with salt and pepper. Set aside.

To make the salad: Core the lettuces; rinse, dry, and refrigerate the leaves in plastic bags. Remove the breast halves from the squabs, including the first wing joint. Cut off the thigh-and-leg quarters. Season with salt, pepper and five-spice powder.

Heat the olive oil in a 10-inch sauté pan or skillet over medium-high heat. When the oil is hot, add the squab leg quarters, skin-side down, and fry for 2 minutes. Add the breasts and fry for 2 minutes. Turn the squab pieces and

Squab Salad and Couscous with Curried Vinaigrette and Chutney; Alfred Portale, Gotham Bar and Grill/One Fifth Avenue, New York

spoon the olive oil out of the pan. Add the butter and cook the breasts for an additional 2 minutes and the leg quarters for an additional 3 minutes, spooning the butter over the pieces as they cook. Remove the pan from heat and let the squab sit for 10 minutes.

To serve: Divide the couscous among 4 plates, sprinkling the raisins on top. Break the lettuce leaves into small pieces, toss with the vinaigrette, and divide among the plates. Place 1 leg quarter on each plate, carve 1 breast on a slight diagonal, and fan the slices along the bottom of the plate. Garnish each plate with some fruit chutney.

Note: *Harissa is sold in tubes at Middle Eastern groceries and many specialty foods stores. It is a paste made from hot chilies flavored with coriander, caraway, garlic, and salt.*

Curry Vinaigrette
(Makes 1¼ cups)

⅓ to ½ cup fresh lemon juice
1 teaspoon curry powder
¾ teaspoon salt
½ teaspoon dry English mustard
¼ teaspoon freshly ground white pepper
¼ teaspoon ground ginger
3 tablespoons minced fresh cilantro
½ teaspoon minced garlic
⅔ cup peanut oil

Place ⅓ cup lemon juice in a medium bowl and whisk in all the ingredients except the peanut oil. Add the peanut oil in a slow stream, whisking constantly. Beat for an additional 30 seconds, taste the dressing, and add more lemon juice if desired.

Note: *The couscous and dressing may be prepared up to 2 days in advance, covered, and refrigerated. Bring the couscous to room temperature and shake the dressing well to recombine before using.*

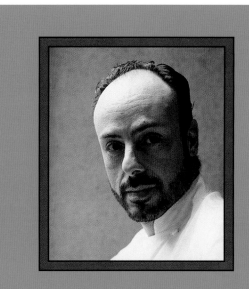

ALFRED PORTALE
Gotham Bar and Grill/One Fifth Avenue, New York, New York

In a city known for its skyscrapers, Alfred Portale's food at the famed Gotham Bar and Grill mirrors New York's architecture: His towering plates are as legendary for their complex presentations as for their complex flavors.

Portale's interest in food was piqued by reading Julia Child's *Mastering the Art of French Cooking;* his subsequent career change from jewelry designer to world-class chef began with an education at the Culinary Institute of America, where he graduated first in his class in 1981. For three years Portale worked with some of France's most renowned chefs—Michel Guerard, the brothers Troisgros, and Jacques Maximin—during which time he continued to refine and master classical French technique. As he gained experience, a personal style evolved, and Portale became one of the founders of new American cuisine.

Eager to share his wealth of knowledge and creativity back in New York, Portale became chef of the Gotham Bar and Grill, which was awarded three stars by the *New York Times* in 1986 and again in 1989.

Influenced by his mother, who learned Italian cooking from her mother and then adapted it to American ingredients, Portale borrows from several cultures to infuse his dishes with a wide range of flavors. In his Squab Salad and Couscous with Curried Vinaigrette and Chutney, for example, Portale combines the tastes and textures of the Mediterranean and India.

In 1992, Portale opened a seafood restaurant to fill the city's gap between high-end and "cheap eats" seafood offerings. Today, One Fifth Avenue has become New York's fish restaurant of choice, supplied daily by a salmon farm and by a fisherman in Maine. In these dishes, Portale combines the gutsy flavors of the Mediterranean, the abundance of the Atlantic coast, and the technical flourishes of France.

Whether he is with his family in Buffalo, New York, where he was born, or at home with his wife Helen and his two daughters, Portale is never far away from the kitchen. He is actively involved in charities dedicated to providing food for the needy, such as Share Our Strength and Citymeals-on-Wheels, and has participated in the American Chefs' and Winemakers' Tribute to James Beard, and Wolfgang Puck's Annual American Food and Wine Festival. In 1990 he was awarded the Ivy Award by the respected trade magazine *Restaurants & Institutions.*

ANTOINE BOUTERIN
Le Périgord, New York, New York

Growing up in sunny St-Rémy de Provence, Antoine Bouterin, chef at New York's Le Périgord, always knew he was destined to become a chef. "I come from a family where the men were farmers, but I knew," he says. It was "the wonderful colors, smells, and tastes of the powerful Provence" that forever made an impression on him.

Unlike many chefs, Bouterin is as adept with pastries as he is with main courses, and his cooking never fails to inspire superlatives among food critics, who are quickly transformed into fans. As John Mariani, food writer for *Esquire* magazine, notes, "I've had some of the best meals of my life at Le Périgord." When the *New York Times Magazine* ran a feature called "Stargazing," which asked noted professionals in New York to spotlight the rising stars in their respective fields, André Soltner of Lutèce chose Antoine Bouterin.

Bouterin's star status is shared by Le Périgord, which has been called "a fixed star by which to measure the wanderings of assorted New York restaurants" (Peter Gianotti of *Newsday*). For thirty years, Le Périgord has been the establishment of choice for diners seeking the finest in French cuisine, and for over a decade, Bouterin has been at the helm of the kitchen.

Bouterin apprenticed in two-star restaurants in his native France, including La Riboto de Taven, not far from his family's farm, and L'Escale, on the coast of the Mediterranean near Marseilles. This influenced his culinary flair. As he writes in his book *Cooking with Antoine at Le Périgord* (G.P. Putnam's Sons), "I have always let my own inspiration influence my style of cooking. I love to create, but it is important to me that I respect the integrity of the food."

He quotes seventeenth-century moralist Jean de La Bruyère to further illustrate his food philosophy: "Sometimes art spoils nature in seeking to perfect her." He achieves his goal of simplicity by preparing fare that he calls "mainly light with a lot of fresh herbs," and sees his cooking as "moving in the direction of my roots, which is Provence." His signature dishes include Red Snapper with Shallots and Crabmeat Crust, and Smoked Salmon Tarts.

The culinary life continues to excite and inspire Bouterin. "I live to cook and create new dishes. My kitchen is my world," he says.

Smoked Salmon Tarts

Antoine Bouterin, Le Périgord
New York, New York

Makes 4 tarts; serves 4

Buttery smoked salmon contrasts with crisp puff pastry in tarts that are easy to make with purchased fresh or thawed frozen puff pastry dough. Serve them as elegant appetizers for a special dinner, or surround with some dressed greens for a lunch dish.

1 tablespoon unsalted butter at room temperature
8 ounces puff pastry dough
2 tablespoons peanut or corn oil
4 large leeks, cleaned and thinly sliced, white part only, (see page 16)
Salt and freshly ground black pepper to taste
1 teaspoon sugar
1 tablespoon minced fresh thyme
1 garlic clove, minced
1 tablespoon minced shallot
8 very thin slices smoked salmon
1 teaspoon minced fresh basil
1 teaspoon olive oil

Preheat the oven to 400°F. Grease a heavy baking sheet (or stack 2 baking sheets) with the butter. On a lightly floured surface, roll the pastry to a thickness of ⅛ inch. Cut four 4- to 5-inch-diameter circles from the pastry. Place the puff pastry circles on the prepared baking sheet and bake them for 15 to 20 minutes, or until puffed and brown. Let cool, then cut each circle in half horizontally into 2 very thin circles. Return these pastry circles to the oven and bake another 5 to 7 minutes, or until very crisp.

Heat the oil in a medium sauté pan or skillet over medium-high heat. Add the leeks, season lightly with salt and pepper, and sauté for 5 minutes, stirring frequently. Add the sugar, thyme, garlic, and shallot. Reduce heat to low and sauté for 10 minutes, or until the leeks are golden brown and wilted, stirring frequently.

To assemble the tarts: Preheat the broiler. Heap caramelized leeks generously on the bottom half of a pastry circle and arrange 2 slices of smoked salmon lightly over the leeks, ruffling the salmon decoratively. Sprinkle generously with pepper and top each tart with ¼ teaspoon chopped basil and 2 to 3 drops of olive oil. Place under the broiler for 20 to 30 seconds, or just until the salmon is warmed but not cooked. To serve, place a tart in the middle of a small plate and place the top half of the pastry circle at an angle leaning on the tart.

Note: *The pastry may be baked and the leek mixture made up to 6 hours in advance and kept at room temperature. The tarts should be assembled just before serving.*

Smoked Salmon Tarts; Antoine Bouterin, Le Périgord, New York

Tossed Seasonal and Bitter Greens with Raspberry-Walnut Vinaigrette; Scott Williams, Americus at the Sheraton Washington, Washington, D.C.

Tossed Seasonal and Bitter Greens with Raspberry-Walnut Vinaigrette

*R. Scott Williams, Americus at the
   Sheraton Washington
Washington, D.C.*

Serves 6

The raspberry puree and walnut oil in the dressing are a delicious combination. Also try this dressing with a pasta or chicken salad.

Salad
1 bunch arugula, stemmed
1 small head Bibb lettuce, cored
1 small head radicchio, cored
1 small head red leaf lettuce, cored
1 small bunch watercress, stemmed
3 red onion slices, halved and separated
   into rings
½ to ¾ cup Raspberry-Walnut
   Vinaigrette (recipe follows)
2 tablespoons chopped walnuts, toasted
   (see page 16)
2 tablespoons crumbled feta cheese
1 cup fresh raspberries

Rinse, dry, and refrigerate the greens in plastic bags. Add the onion rings to the raspberry-walnut vinaigrette and marinate for 10 minutes. Remove from the vinaigrette with a slotted spoon and set aside.

To serve: Toss the greens with dressing to taste. Arrange the greens on 6 plates, then sprinkle each salad with the marinated onion rings, walnuts, feta cheese, and raspberries.

Raspberry-Walnut Vinaigrette
(Makes 1¾ cups)

¼ cup minced shallots
2 tablespoons honey
½ cup raspberry vinegar
1 cup walnut oil
⅓ cup fresh raspberries, pureed
Salt and freshly ground black pepper
   to taste

Combine the shallots, honey, and raspberry vinegar in a small bowl. Slowly whisk in the walnut oil until emulsified. Add the raspberry puree and season with salt and pepper.

Note: The dressing may be made up to 3 days in advance and refrigerated tightly covered. Whisk well to recombine before serving.

Scallop Salad with Grainy Mustard Vinaigrette

*Eric Ripert, Le Bernardin
New York, New York*

Serves 4

This salad is easy to make and elegant to serve. The earthy taste of the walnut oil in the dressing and the sesame seeds in the salad contrast with the sweetness of the scallops.

Grainy Mustard Vinaigrette
1 tablespoon whole-grain mustard
2 tablespoons red wine vinegar
3 tablespoons peanut oil
3 tablespoons walnut oil
Salt and freshly ground black pepper
   to taste

Scallop Salad with Grainy Mustard Vinaigrette; Eric Ripert, Le Bernardin, New York

Salad

2 Belgian endives, cored, leaves cut into
  $\frac{1}{16}$-inch julienne
2 tablespoons finely diced tomato
2 teaspoons minced fresh chives
1 teaspoon minced fresh cilantro
1 teaspoon sesame seed, toasted (see
  page 16)
2 tablespoons olive oil
Juice of 1 lemon
Salt and freshly ground black pepper
  to taste
4 large sea scallops
Fresh seaweed (see Note)

To make the dressing: Whisk the
mustard and vinegar together in a small
bowl. Slowly whisk in the peanut oil and
walnut oil. Season the dressing with salt
and pepper, and set aside.

To make the salad: In a medium bowl,
toss the julienned endives with the
tomato, chives, cilantro, sesame seed,
olive oil, and lemon juice. Season with
salt and pepper. Heat a medium nonstick
sauté pan or skillet over high heat.
Season the scallops with salt and pepper,
and sear the scallops for 1 to 2 minutes
on each side.

To serve: Place a bed of seaweed on
each of 4 serving plates and place a scallop shell (available in cookware shops) in
the center. Divide the mustard vinaigrette
among the shells and top with a seared
scallop. Divide the endive mixture over
the scallop and serve immediately.

Note: *Most seafood stores have seaweed
since lobsters are shipped packed in it.*

ERIC RIPERT
Le Bernardin, New York, New York

His formal schooling was in France, but Eric Ripert, chef at the New
York offshoot of the late Gilbert Le Coze's popular Parisian restaurant, Le
Bernardin, received his true culinary training from some of the brightest
stars in the French constellation.

Growing up in the tiny republic of Andorra in the eastern Pyrenees
between France and Spain, and in Barcelona on the Spanish Mediterranean coast, Ripert says he ate lots of seafood and wonderful desserts as
a child. So it's not surprising that he chose to be educated at the nearby
French Culinary School in Perpignan.

Besides a stint as executive chef in the French military service, Ripert
apprenticed in Paris at Tour d'Argent, and at Robuchon with Joel
Robuchon, whom he considers his mentor. In his position as *chef-
poissonnier* at Robuchon, Ripert was responsible for the kitchen's fish
station, where he directed a small team and concocted sauces.

In 1988, Ripert came to the United States to assume the position
of sous-chef for Jean-Louis Palladin at his Jean-Louis at the Watergate,
a four-star restaurant located in the Watergate Hotel in Washington,
D.C. Since 1991, Ripert has worked as executive chef at New York's Le
Bernardin, the restaurant credited with setting the standard for American
seafood preparation and presentation.

Light and *elegant* characterize Ripert's signature dishes developed for
the all-fish menu of Le Bernardin, such as Seared Tuna with Truffled
Herb Salad; Chinese-spiced Red Snapper with Port Sauce and Crepes;
and Scallop Salad with Grainy Mustard Vinaigrette. The restaurant's
atmosphere reflects these same adjectives; admirers have observed that
the interior is reminiscent of one of Monet's water lily paintings, with
its rich blue carpet and its chairs upholstered with a tapestry fabric in
soothing sea tones.

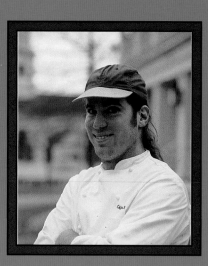

CHRISTOPHER CAPSTICK
The Old Inn on the Green, New Marlborough, Massachusetts

Born and raised in Greenwich Village, Christopher Capstick was exposed from an early age to the energy and excitement of Manhattan's ethnic diversity and began to cook in restaurants while still in high school. A growing passion for cooking combined with a genuine interest in foods and traditions inspired Capstick to travel and sample the regional cuisines of the United States. At the same time, he developed and maintained an affinity for French country cooking.

Between winters in such culinary capitals as Paris, New York, and New Orleans, Capstick worked in the ranks of the kitchen at the Old Inn on the Green in New Marlborough, Massachusetts, and eventually grew into his current position as executive chef.

A Greek Revival building with only six guest rooms, the Old Inn on the Green was built in western Massachusetts around 1760 on what was then a stagecoach road. Dinners, featuring such Capstick signature dishes as Terrine of Quahog, Shiitakes, and Local Mustard Greens; Rabbit Terrine; and Herb-infused Pheasant au Jus, are served solely by candlelight, invoking the Inn's colonial heritage.

Rabbit Terrine

Christopher Capstick, The Old Inn on the Green
New Marlborough, Massachusetts

Serves 6 to 8

This colorful terrine of red peppers, mushrooms, and rabbit is wrapped in bright red leaves of kale and bound with a smooth custard flavored with roasted garlic.

Terrine Layers
½ head red cabbage, cut into fine shreds
1 cup dry white wine
Salt and freshly ground black pepper
  to taste
8 red bell peppers, roasted, peeled,
  and seeded (see page 11)
20 shiitake mushrooms, stemmed
4 tablespoons olive oil
¼ teaspoon white pepper
1 tablespoon minced fresh thyme
4 rabbit legs, boned
½ head red kale, stemmed

Custard
4 eggs
2½ cups heavy (whipping) cream
1 salsify, cut into ½-inch pieces
8 roasted garlic cloves, pureed
  (see page 14)
Salt and freshly ground black pepper
  to taste

Sauce and Garnish
2 cups rich chicken stock (see page 20)
2 tablespoons cold unsalted butter
1 cup unpeeled pearl onions

Preheat the oven to 375°F. In a 12-inch sauté pan or skillet, cook the cabbage over medium heat with the white wine, salt, and pepper until the cabbage is tender and almost translucent, about 25 to 30 minutes. Set aside to cool.

Cut the roasted peppers into ½-inch dice and place in a strainer to drain. In a medium sauté pan or skillet, sauté the mushrooms with 2 tablespoons of the olive oil and the salt, white pepper, and thyme until tender, about 3 to 5 minutes. Transfer the mushrooms to a small bowl and set aside to cool.

To the same pan used to cook the mushrooms, add the remaining 2 tablespoons of olive oil and place over medium-high heat. Add the rabbit legs and sauté them until they are lightly browned but still rare, about 6 to 8 minutes. Remove the rabbit from heat and let cool. Chop the meat into ½-inch pieces and let cool.

To assemble the terrine: Oil the inside of the terrine. Line the terrine with the largest red kale leaves, making sure to overlap the pieces and to leave the excess hanging over the top edge of the mold. Layer the red cabbage evenly in the bottom of the terrine so that it reaches 1 inch up the side.

To make the custard: Combine the eggs, cream, salsify, and roasted garlic puree and whisk until well blended. Add the salt and pepper. Pour enough custard over the cabbage to cover, pressing it down to distribute the custard evenly. Top the custard with half of the chopped

Rabbit Terrine; Christopher Capstick, The Old Inn on the Green, New Marlborough, Massachusetts

rabbit pieces. Cover with another custard layer and press to release any air bubbles and to distribute evenly. Layer the red peppers over the custard, then top with more custard and the remaining rabbit. Top with the shiitakes, alternating the direction of the caps. Cover the mushrooms with the custard and fold the kale leaves over the terrine.

Cover the mold with aluminum foil. Place the terrine mold into a larger roasting pan and place it in the oven. Pour enough boiling water into the pan to come halfway up the sides of the terrine. Bake for 1½ to 2 hours, removing the lid after 30 minutes, or until a knife inserted in the center comes out clean. Remove the terrine from the oven, allow it to cool, and transfer it to the refrigerator overnight before serving.

To make the sauce: Heat the stock to a boil, then lower the heat and whisk in the butter. Set aside and keep warm. Bring a small pot of lightly salted water to a boil. Add the pearl onions and cook until tender, about 4 to 6 minutes. Remove from heat and peel.

To serve: Slice the terrine and spoon the warm sauce around each portion. Garnish with the pearl onions.

Note: 4 small boneless, skinless chicken breasts may be used in place of the rabbit. The terrine may be made up to 2 days in advance and refrigerated.

Potato and Bacon Pie; André Soltner, Lutèce, New York

Potato and Bacon Pie
Tarte aux Pommes de Terre

André Soltner, Lutèce
New York, New York

Serves 6

Potatoes and bacon are a classic combination from chef Soltner's native Alsace. While he serves this tart of potatoes, eggs, and bacon moistened with tangy crème fraîche as an appetizer, it makes a perfect brunch or supper dish when served with a green salad.

Crust
1¾ cups all-purpose flour
¾ teaspoon salt
9 tablespoons cold unsalted butter, cut up
1 egg yolk
Ice water as needed

Filling
5 ounces sliced bacon (about 12 slices), cut into ⅛-inch pieces
1¼ pounds boiling potatoes, peeled, cut into ⅛-inch-thick slices, and placed in cold water
Salt and freshly ground pepper to taste
¼ cup minced fresh parsley
5 hard-cooked eggs, thinly sliced
½ cup crème fraîche (see page 20)
1 egg
2 teaspoons cold water

To make the crust: Mix the flour and salt in a large bowl. Cut in the butter using a pastry blender or your fingertips until the mixture resembles a coarse meal. Place the egg yolk in a measuring cup and beat it lightly with a fork. Add enough ice water to the cup to fill it to the ¼-cup mark. Make a well in the center of the dough and add the yolk mixture. Stir it with a fork or your fingertips until the flour is evenly moistened and the dough holds together when pinched between the fingers. (This can also be done in a food processor using an on-and-off pulsing action to incorporate the butter as well as the liquid. Take care that the dough does not form a ball, or it will be tough.)

Form the dough into a ball, wrap it tightly in plastic wrap, and refrigerate it for at least 5 hours, or overnight. Divide the dough in half, and roll each half into a 12-inch circle. Fit one circle into a 9- or 10-inch false-bottomed tart pan, pressing it in well. Chill the shell for 10 minutes.

To make the filling: Place the bacon in a cold 10-inch sauté pan or skillet and cook over medium heat until browned. Remove the bacon from the pan with a slotted spoon and drain it well on paper towels.

Preheat the oven to 400°F. Remove the potato slices from the water and pat them dry on paper towels. Sprinkle the slices with salt and pepper, and place a layer of overlapping slices in the bottom of the tart pan. Sprinkle them with the cooked bacon and minced parsley, and top with a layer of overlapping egg slices. Spread the crème fraîche over the eggs and top with another layer of potatoes.

Moisten the edges of the pastry and place the second sheet of pastry on top of the pie. Trim to 1 inch larger than the dish and crimp the edges of the pastry. Beat the egg with the water and brush the top of the pie with the mixture. Cut steam vents in the top of the pie.

Bake the pie in the center of the preheated oven for 20 minutes, then reduce the heat to 350°F and bake 1 hour longer. Reduce the heat again to 300°F and bake for 10 minutes, or until the top is brown and a knife inserted into the pie goes in easily. If the pie begins to over-brown, cover the edges or the entire pie loosely with a sheet of aluminum foil.

Remove the pie from the oven and let sit for at least 10 minutes before cutting into wedges. The pie may be served hot or at room temperature.

Note: *The pie may be baked up to 4 hours in advance and kept at room temperature; it does not reheat well.*

Oysters with Champagne Sauce

Paul Milne, 208 Talbot
St. Michaels, Maryland

Serves 4

The Champagne butter sauce is a perfect foil for the briny flavor of the oysters, and the sprinkling of salty prosciutto and crunchy pistachios adds textural contrasts to the silky texture of the mollusk.

20 oysters, shucked (see page 17)
Champagne Sauce (recipe follows)
¼ cup thinly sliced imported prosciutto, cut into ¹⁄₁₆-inch julienne
¼ cup chopped pistachio nuts
4 fresh parsley sprigs

Preheat the oven to 450°F. Place the oysters on a baking sheet and bake them for 3 to 4 minutes, or until the edges of the oysters begin to curl.

Spoon the Champagne sauce over the oysters and top the oysters with the prosciutto and pistachios. Return the oysters to the oven for 45 seconds to warm the sauce.

To serve: Place a bed of rock salt on each of the dishes and arrange 5 oysters on each. Garnish each plate with a sprig of fresh parsley.

Champagne Sauce
(Makes 1¼ cups)

1 tablespoon minced shallot
½ cup dry Champagne
2 tablespoons Champagne vinegar
½ cup heavy (whipping) cream
4 tablespoons unsalted butter, cut into small pieces
Salt and freshly ground white pepper to taste

Place the shallot, Champagne, and vinegar in a small saucepan over medium heat. Bring to a boil and cook to reduce by one third. Add the cream to the pan, and cook to reduce again by one third.

Remove the pan from heat but keep the burner on low. Whisk in the butter one piece at a time. Return the pot to the burner for a few seconds if the sauce cools too much to melt the butter. Season the sauce with salt and pepper, adding a minimum of salt since the prosciutto is salty. Strain the sauce through a fine-meshed sieve and keep it warm over hot water.

Note: The sauce may be made up to 2 hours in advance and poured into a warm thermos.

Oysters with Champagne Sauce; Paul Milne, 208 Talbot, St. Michaels, Maryland

Marinated Salmon

Phillipe Roussel, La Metairie
New York, New York

Serves 2

Cured salmon dishes are popular today, from variations on gravlax to sashimi. This is a very subtle dish, since the paper-thin slices are marinated only briefly on the plate.

Salmon

6 black trumpet mushrooms or
   golden chanterelles
4 tablespoons olive oil
Salt and freshly ground black pepper
   to taste
6 ounces fresh salmon fillet
Juice of 1 lemon
1 teaspoon dried pink peppercorns
1 heaping tablespoon minced fresh dill
1 heaping tablespoon minced fresh chives
4 fresh chervil sprigs

Garnish

2 cups mixed baby greens
2 teaspoons olive oil
½ teaspoon fresh lemon juice
Salt and freshly ground black pepper
   to taste
6 to 8 whole fresh chives

Marinated Salmon; Phillippe Roussel, La Metairie, New York

To prepare the salmon: Clean the mushrooms by wiping them with a damp paper towel, then cut them into quarters. Heat 2 tablespoons of the olive oil in a small sauté pan or skillet over medium-high heat. Add the mushrooms and sauté for 3 minutes, or until they are tender. Season with salt and pepper and let cool.

Cut the salmon into lengthwise paper-thin slices no more than ⅛ inch thick. Fan the slices around the bottom of each plate so that the flat surface is almost completely covered. Sprinkle with salt and drizzle the plate with the lemon juice and the remaining 2 tablespoons olive oil. Sprinkle the salmon with the peppercorns, dill, mushrooms, and chives. Garnish with the chervil sprigs.

To prepare the garnish: Toss the baby greens with the olive oil, lemon juice, salt, and pepper in a medium bowl. Place the greens in a mound to the side of the plate, allowing the salmon to show through. Stand whole chives in the greens and serve.

Note: Do not make this dish prior to serving, or the fish will "cook" from the lemon juice and discolor. Thin slices of tuna may be used in place of the salmon.

PHILLIPPE ROUSSEL
La Metairie, New York, New York

Having worked in such grand kitchens as those of the three-star Restaurant Michel Guerard in France and the Hotel Plaza Athénée in New York, Philippe Roussel must find the kitchen at La Metairie in the arty Greenwich Village section of New York almost Lilliputian.

Former *New York Times* restaurant critic Bryan Miller described La Metairie as a "warm and welcoming French bistro," adding that it "is such a pint-sized place it gives the resident of a Manhattan studio apartment the impression of returning home to Gracie Mansion after dinner."

Miller has called the dishes here "solid bistro food that is as honest as a country prior," and dishes such as Roussel's Marinated Salmon certainly fit that definition.

Roussel trained at the Ecole Hôtelière in Rennes, then apprenticed at the Michelin two-star Le Lion d'Or in Liffre. He then worked in France and on St. Martin in the Caribbean before moving to New York in 1988. His first job was as sous-chef at Espace, and he quickly moved to the top of the World Trade Center as sous-chef at Windows on the World.

All of these large restaurant kitchens seemed small by comparison, however, since one of Roussel's first jobs was as a chef for the officers of the French Army.

But all of that has now changed, and he is commanding a mini-brigade at one of New York's smallest—but finest—restaurants.

VINCENT VANHECKE
Inn at Perry Cabin, St. Michaels, Maryland

As one critic noted, "Vincent Vanhecke has had enough Michelin-starred experiences to start his own constellation." Named one of the Ten Best Young Chefs in America by *Esquire* and one of the Great Country Inn Chefs by the James Beard Foundation in 1992, Vanhecke has made great strides since what he calls his "late start" in formal training at age seventeen.

Vanhecke's fascination with food began early, however, and from cake experiments at age ten he rapidly progressed to making pancakes to accompany his afternoon tea at age fourteen. Three years later, as an apprentice in nouvelle cuisine at the one-star La Terrasse outside of Lyons, Vanhecke came to the conclusion that he didn't like the small food portions.

His is an untrendy and heartfelt food philosophy: "My favorite food is food where calories, fats, and sodium are not taken into consideration. Like every chef, I am cooking lighter, more health-conscious dishes," but, he says, he can't stop his nagging belief that "I don't think that you can enjoy them as much."

Belgian-born and London-raised, Vanhecke remembers hunting mushrooms and small game as a child. The day he found morel mushrooms and shot two wood pigeons, which his family ate for dinner that evening, Vanhecke recalls, "I thought I was in heaven."

After going to work at the famous Boodles Club in St. James, Vanhecke was discovered by Sir Bernard Ashley of Laura Ashley fame and the owner of the Inn at Perry Cabin in St. Michaels, Maryland. Vanhecke went to work as the Inn's executive chef and, inspired by the Laura Ashley decor and the Inn's tranquil location on the Miles River off Maryland's Eastern Shore, he created such signature dishes as Leek and Foie Gras Terrine with Raspberry Vinaigrette.

Vanhecke now works as executive chef of the El Encanto Hotel and Garden Villas in Santa Barbara, where he counts "spending as much time as possible with my wife" as his favorite recreation, and points out that he would have "plenty of ambition for other hobbies if I had the time."

Leek and Foie Gras Terrine with Raspberry Vinaigrette

Vincent Vanhecke, Inn at Perry Cabin
St. Michael's, Maryland

Serves 8 to 10

Although this terrine is not difficult to make, it is a show-stopper for an elegant dinner. The richness of the foie gras is beautifully complemented by the savory leeks and the sweet-tart dressing.

Leek and Foie Gras Terrine
3 pounds baby leeks or halved larger
   leeks, cleaned
1 fresh foie gras (1 to 1½ pounds),
   trimmed and soaked (see page 13)
Salt and freshly ground black pepper
   to taste
½ ounce fresh black truffle, grated
   (optional)

Garnish

4 cups mixed baby greens, rinsed
   and dried
¼ to ⅓ cup Raspberry Vinaigrette
   (recipe follows)
Fresh chervil and parsley sprigs
½ cup fresh raspberries

Preheat the oven to 375°F. Bring a
large pot of lightly salted water to a boil
and trim the leeks to the length of
the terrine.

Cook the baby leeks in the boiling
water for 3 to 4 minutes, or until they
are bright green but still firm; larger leeks
will need up to 6 minutes. Drain the
leeks in a colander, pressing out the
excess liquid with the back of a large
spoon, and drain on paper towels.

Cut the soaked foie gras into long
slices at least ¼ inch thick and place the
slices on a baking sheet. Season both
sides with salt and pepper, and bake in
the preheated oven for 3 minutes. Pour
off and reserve the fat, and set the foie
gras aside.

Line a 9-by-5-inch terrine or loaf pan
with plastic wrap, allowing the excess
plastic wrap to hang well over the sides
of the pan. Roll the leeks in the reserved
foie gras fat and line the bottom of the
loaf pan, alternating the direction of the
white base of the leeks. Top the leeks
with slices of foie gras and sprinkle the
slices with grated truffle, if used. Repeat
the layering until the terrine is full and
all the ingredients have been used.

Fold the overhanging plastic wrap
lengthwise over the terrine, but do not
fold over the sides, so that the excess foie
gras fat can escape. Place a second terrine
or loaf pan bottom-side down on top of
the terrine and weight it with 4 to
5 pounds of canned food, bricks, or
weights. Place the terrine on a platter or
pan to catch the fat drippings and refrigerate for at least 12 hours.

To serve: Unmold the terrine and slice
with a sharp serrated knife. Toss the
greens with dressing to taste in a large
bowl. Garnish each plate with the dressed
greens and herb sprigs. Drizzle some

additional vinaigrette on each plate, dot
with fresh berries, and serve.

*Note: The terrine may be prepared up to
2 days in advance and refrigerated.*

Raspberry Vinaigrette

(Makes 1½ cups)

¼ cup raspberry vinegar
¼ cup strained raspberry puree
½ cup olive oil
½ cup walnut oil
Salt and freshly ground black pepper
   to taste

Combine the raspberry vinegar and
raspberry puree in a small bowl. Add
the olive oil in a thin stream, whisking
constantly, then add the walnut oil in
the same fashion. Season with salt and
pepper and set aside.

*Note: The dressing may be made up to
3 days in advance and refrigerated, tightly
covered. Shake or whisk well to recombine.*

Inn at Perry Cabin, St. Michael's, Maryland

Lasagne of Two Salmons and Savoy Cabbage

*Michel LeBorgne, Inn at Essex /
New England Culinary Institute
Montpelier, Vermont*

Serves 2

In this elegant appetizer, the "lasagne" is made of layers of fresh and smoked salmon, separated by crinkly Savoy cabbage and topped with a sauce of roasted red pepper and cream.

Red Pepper Sauce

1 tablespoon unsalted butter
2 shallots, sliced
4 mushrooms, sliced
2 fresh parsley sprigs
1 teaspoon crushed black pepper
1 fresh thyme sprig
½ cup sherry vinegar
1 cup heavy (whipping) cream
1 red bell pepper, roasted, peeled, seeded, and cut into ½-inch dice (see page 11)
Salt and freshly ground white pepper to taste

Fried Potatoes

2 all-purpose potatoes, peeled
4 cups vegetable oil for frying

Lasagne

8 to 10 leaves Savoy cabbage
1 tablespoon butter
Salt and freshly ground black pepper to taste
8 ounces salmon fillet, cut into ⅛-inch-thick slices
2 ounces smoked salmon, cut into ⅛-inch-thick slices
1 tablespoon fresh chives for garnish

To make the sauce: Heat the butter in a medium saucepan over medium heat. Add the shallots, mushrooms, parsley, pepper, and thyme, and sauté, stirring frequently, until the shallots are translucent, about 3 minutes. Add the sherry

Lasagne of Two Salmons sand Savoy Cabbage; Michel LeBorgne, Inn at Essex/New England Culinary Institute, Montpelier, Vermont

vinegar and cook to reduce by three fourths. Add the heavy cream and cook to reduce by half, or until thickened.

Remove the pan from heat and strain the mixture through a fine-meshed sieve. Pour the mixture into a blender or food processor, add the roasted pepper, and puree until smooth. Add the salt and pepper. Set aside and keep the sauce warm.

To make the potatoes: Cut the potatoes into ½-inch dice. Heat the oil to 375°F, or until a bread cube turns brown in 10 seconds. Add the potatoes and fry until brown and crisp. Remove them from the pan with a slotted spoon and drain on paper towels. Keep warm in a low oven.

To make the lasagne: Remove the leaves from the cabbage. Bring a large saucepan of salted water to a boil and blanch the cabbage leaves in the water for 2 to 3 minutes, or until the leaves are pliable. Remove the leaves from the boiling water with tongs and immerse them in a bowl of ice water. Dry the leaves with a towel. Cut each leaf into a 4-by-3-inch rectangle.

Melt the butter in a sauté pan or skillet placed over low heat and heat the cabbage leaves. Season with salt and pepper and keep warm.

Heat a nonstick sauté pan or skillet over medium-high heat. Add the salmon slices and cook for 30 seconds on each side. Place a cabbage leaf on each plate and top with 2 salmon slices and a slice of smoked salmon. Repeat, then cover with a layer of cabbage. Drizzle warm red pepper sauce on top. Sprinkle with chopped chives, garnish with fried potato cubes, and serve.

Note: *The sauce may be prepared up to 2 days in advance and refrigerated, tightly covered. Reheat in a small saucepan over low heat, stirring often. The cabbage leaves may be blanched and cut up to 1 day in advance.*

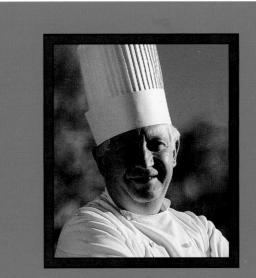

MICHEL LEBORGNE
Inn at Essex/New England Culinary Institute, Montpelier, Vermont

In 1968, Michel LeBorgne, now the vice-president of culinary affairs at the New England Culinary Institute in Vermont, became the executive chef at Yale University. Perhaps that is why Yale is not known for student protests in the late 1960s: The students may have been politically discontented, but they were well fed.

As the son of two great cooks, LeBorgne always wanted to become a chef. He began his apprenticeship at age fourteen and worked in renowned European kitchens in Paris and in Lausanne, Switzerland. He came to the United States in 1964 and worked in New York City and then as the chef at La Rôtisserie Normande in New Haven before joining the Ivy League. When asked to describe his style of cooking, LeBorgne uses one word: *simple.* "Simplicity leaves no room for errors," he says. As a corollary, he adds, "There is a fine line between success and disaster." LeBorgne encourages his students to refine their techniques and to pursue the simplicity that has become his trademark.

The Institute's Inn at Essex restaurant is "informal and cozy," LeBorgne says, and it is there that customers enjoy his signature Lobster Hash made only with New England products. They also can sample such dishes as Warm Goat Cheese and Potato Salad with Chive Dressing, and Lasagne of Two Salmons and Savoy Cabbage. "Cabbage is underrated," says LeBorgne. "Here, its crispy texture works perfectly with the soft salmon."

When he's not creating in the kitchen, LeBorgne likes to cross-country ski and photograph the countryside of rural Vermont. No doubt, the folks in not-so-rural New Haven miss him still.

ANNE ROSENZWEIG
Arcadia, New York, New York

In Sir Philip Sidney's sixteenth-century prose romance *Arcadia*, shepherds gather to recite poetry to one another. Anne Rosenzweig's Arcadia, an intimate restaurant located on New York's East Side, captures the spirit of that long-ago place as it marries earthy foods with sophisticated preparation. Chef-owner Rosenzweig says that what she serves is "hearty food with rural roots and urban polish."

"In our kitchen," says Rosenzweig, "we take classics and give them unexpected twists. Quail, for example, is paired with earthy kasha, a dish people find at once unusual and reassuringly familiar."

A meal at Arcadia is more than wonderful food. With her partner Ken Aretsky, Rosenzweig has created a place to remind the visitor of "unspoiled hills, flowing streams, and rolling farmland," she says.

In keeping with the rustic atmosphere, the menu at Arcadia changes with the seasons. Says Rosenzweig, "There's great enjoyment in rediscovering food we haven't tasted in awhile, so that every meal is a celebration of seasonal abundance."

The dishes are both seasonal and original. When *Food & Wine* asked top chefs to create a cold soup for a hot day, Rosenzweig offered Pea Soup with Coconut. Rosenzweig's Lamb Ravioli is yet another example of her simple, hearty style.

Her fearlessness with food is, perhaps, the result of her first, albeit short-lived, career. After graduating from Columbia University with a degree in anthropology, Rosenzweig spent several years doing field work in Africa and Nepal. During this time she became interested in food and its preparation.

Rosenzweig began her formal food training as an unpaid apprentice in several New York restaurants. In the early 1980s she became, in turn, the brunch, pastry, and head chef at Vanessa in Greenwich Village. It was there that food critic Mimi Sheraton first singled Rosenzweig out for her originality and creativity.

Before opening Arcadia in 1985, Rosenzweig served as a consultant for restaurants and became part of the team that was assembled to rejuvenate the '21' Club in the late 1980s. Her talents are often sought, and she was one of the chefs approached by the Clintons to become White House chef. But she declined, and her heart and her food remain in Arcadia.

Lamb Ravioli

Anne Rosenzweig, Arcadia
New York, New York

Serves 4

These "ravioli" are made with slices of grilled medium-rare lamb layered with ratatouille. At Arcadia this is served as an appetizer, but it also could be an elegant summer entree if accompanied with a larger portion of greens and a potato or pasta salad.

Marinated Lamb Loin
2 tablespoons juniper berries
2 tablespoons black peppercorns
2 garlic cloves
¼ cup olive oil
½ teaspoon kosher salt
Two 8-ounce boneless lamb loins

Ratatouille
3 tablespoons olive oil
2 shallots, minced
1 onion, chopped
2 garlic cloves, minced
1 eggplant, peeled and cut into
    ¼-inch dice
1 red bell pepper, seeded, deribbed,
    and chopped
1 zucchini, cut into ¼-inch dice
Salt and freshly ground black pepper
    to taste
½ cup tomato puree

Garnish
Mixed baby greens

To prepare the lamb: Place the juniper berries, peppercorns, and garlic in a blender or small food processor and chop coarsely. Add the olive oil and salt and blend until the mixture becomes a coarse paste. Spread the paste evenly over the lamb loins. Marinate the lamb for 2 hours at room temperature, or cover and refrigerate for up to 2 days.

To make the ratatouille: Heat the olive oil in a large sauté pan or skillet over medium heat. Add the shallots, onion, and garlic and sauté for 2 minutes. Add the eggplant, red pepper, and zucchini. Sprinkle with salt and pepper, and cook the vegetables over low heat for 5 to 6 minutes, or until tender. Add the tomato puree and cook for an additional 5 to 6 minutes, or until the mixture has thickened slightly. Scrape into a bowl and cool, then cover and refrigerate.

Remove the lamb from the refrigerator and light a fire in a charcoal grill. When the coals are glowing red, place the lamb loins on the center of the cooking rack. Drizzle the reserved marinade through the cooking rack onto the coals to create a flame around the lamb. Sear the lamb for 1½ to 2 minutes on each side for rare, or 2½ to 3 minutes for medium rare. Transfer the lamb to a plate, cover, and chill for at least 2 hours.

To serve: Slice the lamb into ¼-inch-thick slices. Place 3 medallions on each plate, top with a mound of ratatouille, then arrange another slice of lamb on top. Garnish with baby greens and serve at once.

Note: The ratatouille may be made up to 2 days in advance, and the lamb may be grilled and chilled up to 6 hours in advance.

Lamb Ravioli; Anne Rosenzweig, Arcadia, New York

Warm Goat Cheese and Potato Salad with Chive Dressing

*Robert Barral, Inn at Essex / New England Culinary Institute
Montpelier, Vermont*

Serves 4

In the past decade, small U.S. cheese-makers have begun rivaling France in the quality of their goat cheese. In this salad, thinly sliced potatoes are sautéed, then layered with herbed goat cheese to make a roulade, which is sliced and served warm over the greens. The contrast of the creamy cheese with the rich potatoes makes a delicious and stunning salad.

Goat Cheese Roulade

2 boiling potatoes
1 cup duck fat or clarified butter
   (see page 19)
4½ ounces fresh mild white goat cheese,
   preferably from Vermont, at room
   temperature
¼ cup minced fresh parsley
¼ cup minced fresh chives
Salt and freshly ground black pepper
   to taste

Chive Dressing

1 bunch fresh chives
Salt and freshly ground black pepper
   to taste
2 tablespoons sherry vinegar
¼ cup olive oil

Salad

½ head baby oakleaf lettuce
⅛ head romaine lettuce (center
   leaves only)
⅛ head red leaf lettuce
½ head Belgian endive

2 tablespoons vegetable oil
2 tablespoons unsalted butter
Flour for dredging

To make the roulade: Peel the potatoes and cut them into ⅛-inch-thick slices. Fill a deep, heavy pot with water and bring the water to a boil. Boil the potato slices for 2 minutes, drain them, and pat them dry on paper towels. Heat the duck fat or clarified butter in an 8-inch sauté pan or skillet over medium-high heat until the fat begins to smoke. Lower the heat slightly and cook the potato slices in small batches for 2 to 3 minutes each, or until tender. Remove the slices from the pan with a slotted spoon and pat dry with paper towels. Repeat with the remaining potato slices.

Combine the cheese with the parsley, chives, salt, and pepper. Mix well with a fork and set aside at room temperature.

Place a sheet of plastic wrap on the counter or a baking sheet. Arrange the potatoes in a rectangle, overlapping them in a fish-scale pattern. The finished rectangle should be approximately 6 by 8 inches. Spread the goat cheese mixture evenly on top of the potato rectangle. Using the plastic wrap as a guide, roll the potato rectangle into a tight cylinder. Twist the ends to tighten, and place the roll in the freezer for at least 15 minutes or in the refrigerator for at least 30 minutes, or until firm.

To make the dressing: Set aside 8 of the chives for garnish. Bring a small saucepan of lightly salted water to a boil and immerse the remaining chives for 20 seconds. Remove the chives from the water with a slotted spoon and immediately plunge them into a bowl of ice water to stop the cooking. When they are cool, drain them well on paper towels and chop them. Place the chopped chives in a small blender or food processor and add the salt, pepper, and sherry vinegar. Puree the mixture for 2 to 3 minutes, or until smooth. With the motor running,

Inn at Essex / New England Culinary Institute

add the olive oil in a thin stream. Strain the dressing through a fine-meshed sieve and set aside.

To make the salad: Arrange the lettuce leaves on a plate. To serve, heat the vegetable oil and butter in a medium sauté pan or skillet over medium heat. Place the flour in a shallow dish. Remove the goat cheese–potato roulade from the refrigerator or freezer and cut it into ½-inch-thick slices. Dredge the slices lightly in the flour. When the butter foam begins to subside, gently place the slices in the pan and cook for 2 minutes on each side, turning the slices carefully with a pancake turner.

While the roulade slices are cooking, dress the salad with the chive dressing and garnish each plate with the reserved chives. Remove the roulade slices from the pan and divide among the salad plates. Serve immediately.

Note: The roulade and dressing may be made up to 2 days in advance, covered, and refrigerated. Whisk the dressing well to recombine it.

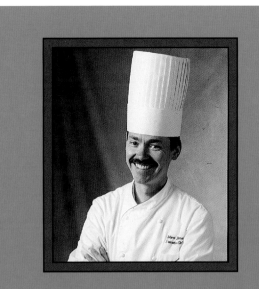

ROBERT BARRAL
Inn at Essex/New England Culinary Institute, Montpelier, Vermont

Robert Barral grew up in Montpelier, France, where he attended culinary school. Today he teaches at a culinary school in Montpelier, Vermont. Barral remembers fondly the aromas of the food in his mother's kitchen, some of which he confesses he is still unable to duplicate, and he raves about her rabbit stew made with olives and thyme gathered from their backyard.

After additional training at the Lycée Hôtelier de Grenoble in France, Barral apprenticed in both France and Switzerland, then moved to Canada where he worked for Four Seasons hotels in both Montreal and Edmonton. He next moved to the United States and became executive sous-chef at the Ritz Carlton Hotel in Chicago for five years, then worked as executive chef at the Four Seasons Hotel in Boston.

In 1987, Barral decided to become a teacher. He moved to the New England Culinary Institute in Montpelier, Vermont, as a banquet chef and is now corporate executive chef. He also is responsible for running the Inn at Essex, with its two restaurants staffed by the New England Culinary Institute.

Although his training was "extremely classical," he says, Barral sees his frequent career changes as helping him to acquire a variety of fundamental kitchen skills. In fact, he believes that his experience, coupled with a childhood diet that included little meat, culminated in his "light and healthy" approach to cooking.

At the New England Culinary Institute, which has more than four hundred students, two campuses, and several restaurants, Barral has developed such signature dishes as Sautéed Shrimp with Basil, and Warm Goat Cheese and Potato Salad with Chive Dressing.

Barral holds his students to a high standard, matched, he says, by the high expectations of the guests dining at the school's restaurants. Refinement and simplicity are the hallmarks of Barral's tenure at NECI and, we can assume, of a whole generation of chefs to come.

SETH RAYNOR
The Boarding House, Nantucket, Massachusetts

His childhood was spent eating local wild game and fish from Long Island's Great South Bay, so it is not surprising that after travels, college, and professional training, Seth Raynor returned to the sea; he now calls Nantucket Island home. Raynor is executive chef and owner, along with his wife Angela, of the Boarding House, located in the center of historic Nantucket village. Under his direction, the restaurant has garnered rave reviews.

During college in Virginia, Raynor enrolled in the outdoor education program to pursue his interests in boating, fishing, and camping. At the same time, he took a job as the day-kitchen manager in a small restaurant and quickly realized that the kitchen called to him as strongly as the outdoors.

He then transferred to the New England Culinary Institute in Montpelier, Vermont. This formal training enabled him to intern with Jean-Charles Berruet, chef at Chanticleer on Nantucket, where he was able to see classical French techniques put into practice. Raynor credits Berruet with teaching him the importance of food coordination.

Other than a stint at the Joshua Wilton House in Harrisonburg, Virginia, Raynor honed his skills on Nantucket, working at Chanticleer, 21 Federal, and American Seasons. While his style is consistent with new American cuisine, Raynor uses French techniques and specializes in Asian and Italian ingredients, resulting in such dishes as Carpaccio of Sirloin, and Sautéed Flounder with Shrimp Wontons. His aim is to produce vibrantly flavored food with consistency and simplicity. One of his signature dishes was developed after spending time in San Francisco's Chinatown restaurants: Rare Grilled Tuna with Wasabi Aïoli with Thai Pesto Noodles.

Raynor prides himself on the amount of repeat local clientele who dine at the Boarding House, which was given the Best Outdoor Dining award by *Cape Cod Life* in June 1993.

Carpaccio of Sirloin

Seth Raynor, The Boarding House
Nantucket, Massachusetts

Serves 4

Unlike the classic Italian Carpaccio that is merely drizzled with oil, this American version adds three flavors of aïoli, roasted-pepper bruschetta, and spicy onion rings. This dish is easy to create, and it looks as good as it tastes.

Four 2-ounce, ¼-inch-thick beef
  sirloin slices

Aïoli
1 egg
1 egg yolk
1 tablespoon water
6 garlic cloves
1½ cups olive oil
Juice of ½ lemon
1 teaspoon achiote paste
1 teaspoon water
1 tablespoon Dijon mustard
3 fresh basil leaves, cut into fine shreds

Bruschetta Spread
3 red bell peppers, roasted, peeled,
  and seeded (see page 11)
½ cup Kalamata olives, pitted
  and chopped
1 tablespoon olive oil

Spicy Onion Rings
1 cup all-purpose flour
1 tablespoon cayenne pepper
2 teaspoons chili powder
1 teaspoon ground cumin
1 teaspoon freshly ground black pepper
Salt to taste
1 large yellow onion, thinly sliced
2 cups canola or any other mild
  vegetable oil

Twelve ½-inch-thick slices Italian
  bread, toasted
Salt and freshly ground pepper to taste

Place the sirloin slices between 2 sheets of plastic wrap. Using the dull side of a meat pounder or the bottom of a heavy pan, pound the meat until it is paper thin. Remove the plastic wrap and check the meat for and remove any fat or gristle. Separate the meat slices with plastic wrap and refrigerate.

To make the aïoli: Place the whole egg and the egg yolk in a blender or food processor and combine. Add the water and garlic and puree for 30 seconds. With the motor running, add the olive oil a few drops at a time at the beginning, then gradually in a thin stream. Add the lemon juice and pulse to combine. The mixture should now be a light, garlicky mayonnaise.

Divide the aïoli among 3 bowls. Combine the achiote paste with the water. Add this mixture to one bowl and stir to combine. Add the Dijon mustard to the second bowl of aïoli, and stir until well blended. Stir in the basil shreds into the third bowl and set all 3 bowls aside.

To make the spread: Combine all ingredients in a small bowl, and let sit for at least 15 minutes to blend the flavors.

To make the onion rings: Combine the flour, cayenne, chili powder, cumin, black pepper, and salt. Dredge the onion slices in the seasoned flour, shaking off any excess. In a heavy pot or deep-fryer, heat the oil to 375°F, or until a bread cube dropped in the oil browns in 10 seconds. Cook the onions in the hot oil until golden brown, about 3 to 4 minutes. Remove them from the pan with a slotted spoon, drain on paper towels, and keep warm in a low oven.

To assemble: Place a slice of sirloin in the center of each plate. Spoon 1 tablespoon of each aïoli around the outside of the Carpaccio. Spread each bread slice with the red pepper and olive mixture, then place 3 toasts on each plate. Sprinkle the sirloin with salt and pepper and top the sirloin with a mound of fried onions.

Note: *The meat and sauces may be prepared 6 hours in advance and refrigerated, tightly covered. The toasts may be prepared at the same time and kept at room temperature.*

Carpaccio of Sirloin; Seth Raynor, The Boarding House; Nantucket, Massachusetts

Warm Salad of Asparagus and Artichokes

~~

Daniel Boulud, Restaurant Daniel
New York, New York

Serves 4

A most unusual salad, aromatic with fresh herbs and tart with lemon, this could become an entire meal with an addition of poached fish or roasted poultry.

4 large globe artichokes
3 tablespoons olive oil divided
16 asparagus spears, blanched for 2 minutes, drained, and cut into 2-inch pieces
1 *each* red and yellow bell pepper, roasted, peeled, seeded, and cut into ¼-inch-thick slices (see page 11)
2 lemons
4 cups mixed fresh herbs such as tarragon, green and purple basil, dill, cilantro, chervil, chives, chicory, parsley and celery leaves
Salt and freshly ground black pepper to taste
1 cup cherry tomatoes, halved
2 tablespoons basil oil (see page 19)

Bring a large saucepan of salted water to a boil. With a large knife, cut off the top third of each artichoke. Pull off all of the leaves and cut off the stems. Add the artichoke bottoms to the boiling water and simmer, covered, for 15 to 20 minutes, or until tender. Drain the artichokes upside down. When cool enough to handle, scoop out the hairy chokes and slice the hearts into ½-inch-thick slices.

Warm Salad of Asparagus and Artichokes; Daniel Boulud, Restaurant Daniel, New York

Heat 2 tablespoons of the oil in a medium sauté pan or skillet over medium heat. Add the artichoke slices, asparagus, and bell pepper. Cook for 2 minutes over medium heat, then set aside.

Scrape the zest from 1 lemon with a zester and squeeze the juice from the lemon. In a large bowl, toss the fresh herbs with the lemon juice, zest, and remaining 1 tablespoon of olive oil. Season the salad with salt and pepper. Add the cherry tomatoes and toss. Squeeze the juice from the remaining lemon and pull the pulp out of the rind with your fingers. Discarding the seeds, place the pulp and juice in a blender or food processor, puree, and set aside.

To serve: Arrange the warm artichokes, asparagus, and peppers on 4 serving plates. Top the vegetables with the salad. Sprinkle the lemon pulp and juice over the salad. Drizzle the basil oil around the vegetables.

DANIEL BOULUD
Restaurant Daniel, New York, New York

Daniel Boulud's career as chef follows a family tradition. His grandfather started a small cafe in southeastern France nearly a century ago, and Boulud grew up on a nearby farm. At the age of fourteen, Boulud began his career in food with an apprenticeship at Nandro, a Michelin two-star restaurant in Lyons. He then worked with a constellation of Michelin-starred chefs, including Georges Blanc, Roger Verge, and Michel Guerard, and in Copenhagen at Denmark's highest-rated restaurant, Les Etoiles.

In the 1980s, Boulud moved to New York, first to become chef at the Westbury Hotel and then at the Plaza Athénée Hotel, where he opened and brought prominence to its restaurant, Le Régence.

In 1986, Boulud became executive chef at the legendary Le Cirque, which has been chosen regularly by the international press as one of this country's best restaurants. Under Boulud's command, Le Cirque was awarded four stars by the *New York Times* in 1987 and again in 1992.

The next step in a career of superlatives was to open his own restaurant. Restaurant Daniel, on East 76th Street, is in the space formerly occupied by Les Pléiades, one of the chic New York French restaurants in the 1970s. Following a ten-month renovation during which the interior was transformed to a lively, young setting with European accents and artwork on loan from neighboring galleries, Daniel opened in 1993.

Contemporary French cuisine is Boulud's strong suit. He uses the freshest and highest-quality ingredients for a menu based on seasonal dishes, such as summer's Warm Salad of Asparagus and Artichokes.

More than two hundred of his recipes and his artful food styling are featured in a cookbook published in late 1993, *Cooking with Daniel* (Random House).

Poultry and Meat Dishes

*U*ntil a few years ago many of the delicious recipes in this chapter would have been frustrating for the home cook, since only commercial suppliers carried game birds and meats. Today, however, all the purveyors needed to create this bevy of stunning entrees may be found in Mail-Order Sources, page 243.

Many of these recipes were conceived by the chefs as appetizers or first courses. They were moved here because the amount of effort required to make them and the size of the portions were deemed more appropriate for main dishes; the same is true for some of the dishes placed in the following chapter of fish and shellfish recipes.

The late M. F. K. Fisher wrote about the glory of the perfect roast chicken, but very few restaurant chefs feature simple chicken dishes on their menus, as most diners eat chicken more than twice a week at home. Instead, chefs create culinary delights with more flavorful game birds. Quail is perhaps the most popular restaurant bird, since one or two make a serving, depending on whether or not they are stuffed. They also take well to a number of quick cooking methods. Susanna Foo's Eight-Treasure Quail with Chinese Sausage and Lotus Seed, stuffed with sticky rice, sautéed Portobello mushroom, and sausage, are fit for a Mandarin emperor; another memorable combination is the sweet crabmeat and local Surry sausage in Jimmy Sneed's Boneless Quail Stuffed with Crabmeat.

Regardless of the trend toward lighter eating, many diners still order red meat in restaurants. More popular with chefs than beef today are lamb and game, and this chapter includes such vividly flavored dishes as Rack of Lamb with Persimmon Chutney and Peanut Crust, and Loin of Venison, which is marinated in red wine and is bursting with hearty flavor.

Stuffed Quail and Peppered Beef Tenderloin; Hans Schadler, Williamsburg Inn, Williamsburg, Virginia

Venison Loin Chop

Andrew Wilkinson, The Rainbow Room
New York, New York

Serves 6

Venison chops, one of the leanest cuts of red meat as well as one of the most tender and flavorful, are complemented here by a sauce of reserved marinade, demi-glace, and red currant jelly. Serve this dish with Rosemary Spaetzle (page 159) and Baked Spaghetti Squash (page 158).

6 center-cut venison loin chops,
  about 12 ounces each
Salt and freshly ground black pepper
  to taste

Marinade
3 cups dry red wine
¼ cup red wine vinegar
2 bay leaves
1 tablespoon black peppercorns, crushed
6 fresh thyme sprigs
1 tablespoon juniper berries, crushed
6 fresh rosemary sprigs

3 tablespoons clarified butter
  (see page 19)

Sauce
¾ cup reserved venison marinade, above
¾ cup veal demi-glace (see page 22)
¼ cup red currant jelly
4 tablespoons unsalted butter

ANDREW WILKINSON
The Rainbow Room, New York, New York

In 1987, the colored lights were turned on again, and the completely refurbished Rainbow Room reentered New York night life. With its domed ceiling, revolving dance floor, and extensive art collection, this Art Deco supper club on the sixty-fifth floor of Rockefeller Center is as glorious as when it first opened in 1934.

Diners flock to the Rainbow Room because of its romantic history and its fabled interior, but they return because of its food. The team of chefs at the Rainbow Room was joined by Andrew Wilkinson in 1991.

Ironically, the chef for this glamorous night spot began his career in a fairly unglamorous setting, working long mornings on the lobster docks and restaurants of the Maine shore. From Maine, Wilkinson went south to the Culinary Institute of America. After graduation he spent time in the Black Forest of Germany at the two-star Kur Hotel Traube and at the Hotel Clio Court in Hakata, Japan. Wilkinson's skills were eagerly sought by legendary restaurateur Joe Baum, the developer of the new Rainbow Room.

The dishes offered at the Rainbow Room reinforce the theatrical feel of its decor and its panoramic views of the city; one of the appetizers, for example, is a Coast to Coast Shellfish Extravaganza. While there are contemporary options, Wilkinson aims for old-fashioned luxury in the Dishes with Tradition section of the menu, which includes such historic fare as Lobster Thermidor, Tournedos Rossini with Truffle Sauce and Pommes Soufflés, and Herb-roasted Rack of Lamb—all dating from the 1930s.

While Wilkinson, who has now moved to Boston, added many of his own unique dishes, such as Venison Loin Chop served with spaghetti squash and spaetzle, to the Rainbow Room menu, he stayed true to the traditions of the room. His goal was always "to inject new elements of fine dining to join the music and dancing—to add to the romance of the Rainbow Room by building new memories." The Rainbow Room continues to glow.

The day before you wish to serve the dish, season the venison with the salt and pepper.

To make the marinade: Combine the red wine, vinegar, bay leaves, peppercorns, thyme, juniper berries, and rosemary in a large non-aluminum baking pan. Add the venison, cover, and refrigerate for 24 hours, turning the chops occasionally.

Preheat the oven to 400°F. Drain the venison, reserving the marinade for the sauce. Place a large ovenproof sauté pan or skillet over high heat and add the clarified butter. When the butter is almost smoking, add the venison chops and sear for 2 minutes, then turn the chops with tongs and cook 2 minutes on the other side. Transfer the chops to the preheated oven and roast for 4 to 6 minutes for rare, or until cooked to the desired doneness. Remove the chops to a heated serving platter and let sit for 10 minutes.

To make the sauce: While the meat is resting, return the pan to high heat and add the reserved marinade, stirring to scrape up the brown bits from the bottom of the pan. Add the demi-glace and the red currant jelly, stirring well to incorporate. Whisk in the butter, 1 tablespoon at a time. Adjust the seasoning if necessary. Pool the sauce on 6 plates, top with the venison chops, and serve.

Note: The same marinade may be used for any venison steaks or roasts; however, the cooking times will vary depending on the cuts.

Venison Loin Chop, Andrew Wilkinson, The Rainbow Room, New York

Loin of Venison

*Patrick Grangien, Cafe Shelburne
Shelburne, Vermont*

Serves 4

Deer are plentiful in the woods of New England, and this is a classic way to prepare lean and flavorful venison. The sauce is a reduction of the red wine and herb marinade. Serve this dish with Potato Roses (page 162) and Celery Root Charlotte (page 161).

2½ pounds venison loin on the bone

Marinade
2 cups dry red wine
2 carrots, peeled and thinly sliced
1 small onion, thinly sliced
4 fresh parsley sprigs
1 celery stalk, sliced
1 bay leaf
4 fresh thyme sprigs
1 garlic clove, minced
½ teaspoon black peppercorns
1 large tomato, seeded and diced

Stock
¼ cup vegetable oil
1 tablespoon unsalted butter
Reserved trimmings and bone from venison loin, above
Reserved marinade, above
4 cups water

Salt and freshly ground black pepper to taste
3 tablespoons unsalted butter
2 shallots, minced
¼ cup dry red wine

Two days before you wish to serve the venison, trim the meat of most visible fat, cut the meat off the bone, and slice the meat into 2 steaks. Cut the bone into small pieces. Cover and refrigerate the trimmings.

To make the marinade: In a non-aluminum baking pan, combine the red wine with the carrots, onion, parsley, celery, bay leaf, thyme, garlic, peppercorns, and tomato. Add the venison, cover, and refrigerate for 24 hours, turning the venison occasionally.

The next day, remove the meat from the marinade, cover it with plastic wrap, and return it to the refrigerator; reserve the marinade.

To make the stock: In a Dutch oven, heat the vegetable oil and butter over medium-high heat. Add the reserved venison trimmings and bone and brown for 20 to 30 minutes, stirring frequently

Loin of Venison; Patrick Grangien, Cafe Shelburne, Shelburne, Vermont

and making sure the fat does not burn. Discard the grease from the pan and add the reserved marinade. Raise heat to high and stir the liquid, scraping the bottom of the pan to dislodge the brown bits. Add the water and cook the liquid over high heat until reduced by three fourths to an almost syrupy consistency. When ¾ to 1 cup liquid remains, remove the stock from heat, strain it through a fine-meshed sieve, cover, and refrigerate.

The next day, season the marinated venison with salt and pepper. Melt 2 tablespoons of the butter in a medium sauté pan or skillet over high heat. Sear the venison steaks on each side for 1 minute. Reduce heat to medium-high and cook the steaks for 2 to 3 minutes on each side for rare, or longer if you prefer. Remove the venison from heat and place on a warmed serving platter.

To finish the sauce: Place the pan in which the venison was cooked back on the stove over medium heat. Add the shallots and sauté, stirring constantly, for 3 minutes, or until the shallots are browned. Add the red wine to the pan, stirring to scrape up the brown bits on the bottom of the pan, and cook to reduce until the wine has almost evaporated. Add the reduced stock and cook to reduce to ½ cup, or until the sauce coats a spoon. Add the remaining 1 tablespoon butter, stirring to incorporate, and strain the sauce through a fine-meshed sieve. Adjust the seasoning with salt and pepper, if necessary.

To serve: Slice the venison steaks and fan the meat out on serving plates. Nap the meat with the red wine sauce and sprinkle with herbs for garnish.

Note: *While the chef begins this dish 2 days in advance, 1 day will work almost as well. Make the stock early in the day to allow it to chill before making the sauce.*

PATRICK GRANGIEN
Cafe Shelburne, Shelburne, Vermont

Although he claims he started cooking by "pure accident," Patrick Grangien's cuisine has evolved into world-class fare. Raised on the west coast of France, Grangien recalls going to market with his mother, who bought fish only if they were still "flapping on the table." Little wonder that Grangien went on to win the National Seafood Challenge in 1988.

Since 1985, Grangien has brought the same standards of freshness and quality to his Cafe Shelburne, in Shelburne, Vermont. Grangien trained with some of the finest chefs in France: He was *chef saucier* for Paul Bocuse in Lyons, sous-chef for Jacques Maximin at the Hotel Negresco in Nice, and accompanied Michel Guerard on his first job in New York.

Although he won the Taste of Vermont award in 1986 and 1987, Grangien is modest when discussing signature dishes. "You get ideas from everybody," he notes, naming his Rabbit Salad and his Raspberry Gratin, as well as the entree that won him the National Seafood Challenge in Charleston, South Carolina, Monkfish on a Bed of Spinach with Tomatoes and Mushrooms. "I like simple food, well presented," he says. Other examples are Loin of Venison, and Maple Syrup Gratin.

He has seen food evolve in the last fifteen years. "Everything is much lighter," he observes. "We're not trying to disguise fresh products with some French-flavored thing."

Cafe Shelburne, which Grangien runs with his wife Christine, is intimate. It has only forty-five seats, and strives to maintain a casual atmosphere. "We know most everyone who comes in our restaurant," he says, noting that they try to avoid the coldness sometimes associated with fine French restaurants. "We want people to feel good. Sometimes you feel like the restaurant's doing you a favor by letting you come in. We're the opposite."

PATRICK CLARK
Hay Adams Hotel, Washington, D.C.

When the Clintons were looking for a new chef for the White House, they set their sights on Patrick Clark, chef at the historic Hay Adams Hotel across Lafayette Square. Clark declined the White House job, explaining, among other reasons, that a government salary was inadequate to take care of his large family: a wife and five children.

The Chief's first choice for top chef was not the only recent honor conferred on Clark. In May 1994, he was named the Best Chef of the Mid-Atlantic Region by the James Beard Foundation.

Born in Brooklyn, New York, Clark entered the kitchen at an early age. His father was a chef with Restaurant Associates in New York when the company operated the Four Seasons and La Fonda del Sol, so Clark learned early to play with ingredients. He experimented for five years until, at the age of seventeen, he perfected a recipe for cheesecake. He also credits the influence of his mother's cooking, with its highly charged flavors and seasonings.

Like his father, Clark trained at New York City Technical College, but the real turning point in his career came when he was offered the opportunity to train with Michel Guerard in France. "My first meals in France were mind-blowing because I didn't realize then what wonders could be created with fine food and fine, fresh ingredients," Clark recalls.

Clark returned to New York and soon built a national reputation for his role in elevating the status of Odéon, Café Luxembourg, and his own Metro to two stars from *The New York Times Guide to Restaurants*. Later, he moved to Los Angeles to become executive chef at Ristorante Bice.

Clark's aim at the Lafayette, the Hay Adams' dining room, is to blend the influences of Asia and Europe into light but boldly flavored dishes. "I like combining luxurious foods with wonderful staples," he says of his Roasted Lobster with Polenta, and his Veal Chops with Oven-dried Tomatoes and Wild Mushrooms.

Disdainful of being called a rising young African-American chef, Clark wants to be known simply as a chef, but he regrets the paucity of African-Americans in his profession. As a result, he is active in the community, teaching children about cooking and giving motivational speeches at high schools.

Veal Chops with Oven-dried Tomatoes and Wild Mushrooms

Patrick Clark, Hay Adams Hotel
Washington, D.C.

Serves 4

Drying tomatoes in the oven gives them the intense flavor of sun-dried tomatoes but a softer texture. The combination of delicate veal with woodsy mushrooms, licorice-scented crunchy fennel, and tomatoes is superb. Serve this dish for an elegant dinner party.

Oven-dried Tomatoes
12 ripe Roma (plum) tomatoes
2 teaspoons sugar
1 teaspoon salt
1 tablespoon minced fresh thyme

Mushrooms
6 tablespoons unsalted butter, divided
1 cup sliced stemmed shiitake
  mushrooms
⅓ cup water
¼ cup heavy (whipping) cream
2 tablespoons minced fresh chives
2 teaspoons fresh lemon juice
Salt and freshly ground black pepper
  to taste

Veal
2 tablespoons unsalted butter
Four 12- to 14-ounce veal chops
2 tablespoons water

Braised Fennel (see page 158)
Fresh chervil sprigs for garnish

To prepare the tomatoes: Preheat the oven to 200°F. Cut out the stem end of each tomato, cut the tomato in half lengthwise, and carefully scrape out seeds. Place the tomato halves, cut-side up, on a wire rack placed in a baking pan. Season the tomatoes with the sugar, salt, and thyme, and bake them in the preheated oven for about 4 to 5 hours, or until they look dry and shriveled but are still slightly moist. Let cool on the rack.

To make the mushrooms: Melt 2 tablespoons of the butter in a medium sauté pan or skillet over medium-high heat. Add the mushrooms and water, and sauté the mushrooms for 3 to 4 minutes, or until the liquid is evaporated. Add the cream to the pan and bring to a boil. Add 4 tablespoons butter and cook for 1 to 2 minutes. Stir in the chives and lemon juice, and season with salt and pepper. Set aside and keep warm.

To cook the veal: Melt the butter in a large sauté pan or skillet over medium-high heat. Sauté the veal for about 8 minutes on each side, or until an instant-read thermometer registers 150°F (for medium). Remove the veal from the pan and keep warm. Add the water to the pan and cook over medium heat, stirring to scrape up the brown bits on the bottom of the pan. Pour the veal juice over the chops.

To serve: Place one fourth of the fennel on the center of each plate and place a chop on top. Surround the chop with alternate tomatoes and dabs of the mushrooms, and garnish with sprigs of chervil.

Note: *The tomatoes may be made up to 1 day in advance and kept loosely covered at room temperature, and the mushrooms may be made up to 4 hours in advance and reheated over low heat before serving.*

Veal Chops with Oven-dried Tomatoes and Wild Mushrooms; Patrick Clark, Hay Adams Hotel, Washington, D.C.

Roasted Squab with Bacon and Sage; Sylvain Portay, Le Cirque, New York

Roasted Squab with Bacon and Sage

Sylvain Portay, Le Cirque
New York, New York

Serves 4

In this wonderful dish for a brisk, cold night, the hearty flavor of squab is augmented with smoky bacon and aromatic sage. The buttery Yukon Gold potatoes are infused with another dimension of flavor by being cooked with herbs.

Squab

4 large squab, about 16 to
   20 ounces each
4 very thin slices bacon
4 large sage leaves

Potatoes

2 pounds small Yukon Gold potatoes,
   about 1½ inches in diameter
1 fresh sage sprig
1 fresh rosemary sprig
1 bay leaf
1 garlic clove, crushed
Salt to taste

Stock

2 tablespoons unsalted butter
1 tablespoon olive oil
1 garlic clove, crushed
Reserved squab legs and backbones
1 cup rich chicken stock (see page 20)

2 tablespoons unsalted butter
1 fresh Italian parsley sprig,
   coarsely chopped
¾ cup minced fresh chives
Freshly ground black pepper to taste

1 tablespoon olive oil
Four 3-ounce pieces fresh foie gras,
   trimmed and soaked (see page 13)
Salt to taste
5 leaves fresh basil, cut into shreds
1 small bunch fresh chervil, stemmed
   and coarsely chopped
1 tablespoon sherry vinegar

To prepare the squab: Remove the legs and the backbone from each bird, and reserve. Gently loosen the skin from the double breast with your finger. Slide 1 slice of bacon and 1 sage leaf under the skin of each double breast, then return the skin so that it covers the breast. Cover, and refrigerate the breasts until ready to cook.

To make the potatoes: Scrub the potatoes and place them in a large saucepan with the sage, rosemary, bay leaf, and garlic clove. Fill the pan with cold water and salt the water lightly. Bring the potatoes to a boil over high heat, reduce heat to medium-high, and boil until the potatoes are tender, about 12 to 15 minutes. Allow the potatoes to cool in their cooking liquid, then slice them into ¼-inch slices, cover, and set aside.

To make the stock: Place a 7-inch sauté pan or skillet over medium-high heat and add the butter, olive oil, and garlic. When the butter is very hot, add the reserved squab legs and backbones. Sear the legs and bones for about 10 minutes, or until golden brown. Add the chicken stock and boil for 5 minutes, stirring to scrape up the browned bits from the bottom of the pan. Strain and set the liquid aside.

Melt the butter in a small sauté pan or skillet over medium heat and add the potatoes. Add the parsley, minced chives, and black pepper and sauté the potatoes in the hot butter until they are warmed through. Remove the potatoes from heat, set aside, and keep warm.

Add the olive oil to a medium sauté pan or skillet and place over medium heat. Add the squabs, skin-side down, and cook for approximately 10 to 12 minutes, turning to brown evenly.

To serve: Divide the potatoes among 4 serving plates. Remove the squabs from heat and place on top of the potatoes. Return the pan to heat and sear the foie gras for about 30 seconds on each side, then sprinkle with salt and arrange on each of the plates. Pour off and discard the foie gras fat and add the reserved stock to the pan, stirring to scrape up any browned bits from the bottom of the pan. Add the basil, chervil, and vinegar. Adjust the seasoning if necessary and pour the sauce over the squabs.

Note: The squabs, potatoes, and stock may be prepared up to the point of sautéing the potatoes 6 hours in advance. Keep the squabs and foie gras refrigerated, tightly covered with plastic wrap.

SYLVAIN PORTAY
Le Cirque, New York, New York

At thirty-one, Sylvain Portay attained "instant star status," according to *Newsday,* when he became executive chef at Le Cirque in New York City. Some might have thought it was hubris for so young a chef to take over the country's most consistently highest-rated restaurant. But Portay's "star status" was not as instant as many New Yorkers might have thought.

At fifteen, Portay began his apprenticeship with Jean-Louis Palladin at La Table de Cordeliers in Condom, France, before Palladin moved to Washington, D.C., to open Jean-Louis at the Watergate. Portay trained throughout France with some of the finest, including Jacques Maximin at the Hotel Negresco in Nice, and Alain Ducasse at Le Louis XV in Monaco, a restaurant that was elevated to Michelin three-star status during Portay's tenure.

So when Portay took over the kitchen at Le Cirque in 1992 in the midst of the December food madness that grips the city each year, the elegance of his Warm Lobster Salad; Pasta with Black Truffles and Foie Gras; and Roasted Squab with Bacon and Sage, followed by miniature pistachio ice cream Christmas trees, may have surprised many who were unaware of the chef's extensive career.

According to the *New York Times Magazine,* Portay's menu at Le Cirque symbolizes "a new classicism in food." His "gratins enriched with marrow bones and chickens stuffed with an old-fashioned marriage of liver and truffle… signaled yet another merge of peasant fare and haute cuisine," writes food critic Molly O'Neill.

Michael Batterberry of *Food Arts* explains the love Americans have for this style of cooking. "We've moved beyond Minimalism," he writes, "and we're dipping deeply into traditional haute technique and tastes to soften the edges of Post-Modern cooking."

The menu of Le Cirque also offers variations on Italian cuisine, which Portay learned during his stay in Florence. As he brings his fresh talent and new insight into a legendary establishment like Le Cirque, Portay will, no doubt, continue to surprise.

JOHANNE KILLEEN & GEORGE GERMON
Al Forno Restaurant, Providence, Rhode Island

Johanne Killeen and George Germon of Al Forno Restaurant share more than a marriage license and ownership of their restaurant. They co-authored *Cucina Simpatica: Robust Trattoria Cooking* (HarperCollins) together, based on the country French and rustic Italian dishes served at their restaurant. Like the restaurant, the book received rave reviews. Long before they were great chefs, however, they were both artists, and this artistic spirit has translated to their culinary careers.

Killeen's physician-mother was widowed when Killeen was young, and Killeen's earliest impressions of food come from the holidays, when her mother and her extended family had the time to plan and prepare wonderful, celebratory feasts, highlighted by her Aunt Sophie's legendary butter cookies and Polish pierogis.

It wasn't until Killeen traveled to Italy after graduating from college to study photography that she discovered her true love of food. Eating in the *trattorias* of Florence and the surrounding towns made a deep impression on her, and on her return to Providence and the darkroom she began cooking for friends. In order to pay some photography bills, she took a job in a small restaurant and soon was asked to develop the dessert menu.

A talented sculptor and potter with an architectural bent, George Germon taught at the Rhode Island School of Design program in Italy, where he, too, spent much of his time in the *trattorias*. Back in Providence, Germon slowly made the transition from art to food. He met Killeen when they both worked in a restaurant that he had designed, and they fell in love over a hot stove.

The couple's combined sense of design, proportion, and color shows in the restaurant's interior. Just as fine art is destined to please or stimulate the viewer, Killeen and Germon approach the experience of a meal at Al Forno—which means "from the oven"—as something that should linger and create memories.

Inspired by the raised-hearth fireplaces in Italian *trattorias,* Germon designed Al Forno around its open-flame grill. The oven is fueled with a variety of woods, including apple wood, grapevines, and lilac branches, which are integral to such creations as Roasted Sausages and Grapes. Al Forno's nationally acclaimed signature dish is grilled pizza, with its smoky, very crisp crust studded with such toppings as fresh pumpkin, home-grown tomatoes, sweet corn, herbs, and goat cheese.

Killeen's passion shapes the list of desserts, mostly rustic individual tarts, such as Cranberry-Walnut Crostata, prepared to order. Some are elaborate and others are light and simple, such as the Lemon Meringue Tart, which was presented the Golden Dish Award as one of the ten best dishes of 1993 by *GQ* magazine.

In 1991, the couple won the James Beard Award for Best Chefs of the Northeast, and the restaurant received the Hall of Fame award from *Nation's Restaurant News* in 1992. Patricia Wells, in the *International Herald Tribune,* recently rated Al Forno as the No. 1 restaurant in the United States for casual dining.

Roasted Sausages and Grapes

George German, Al Forno
Providence, Rhode Island

Serves 6 to 8

Just as salty prosciutto and succulent figs are a natural flavor combination, so are sausages and grapes. Use more sweet sausages and fewer hot ones for a milder dish, but do use Italian sausages, as their fennel and garlic flavors are essential to this dish.

1½ pounds hot Italian sausage,
    cut into 3-inch lengths
1½ pounds sweet Italian sausage,
    cut into 3-inch lengths
3 tablespoons unsalted butter
2½ pounds red or green seedless grapes,
    stemmed (6 to 7 cups)
¼ cup balsamic vinegar
Mashed Potatoes (recipe follows)

Preheat the oven to 500°F. Bring a large pot of water to a boil over high heat. Prick the sausages with the tip of a knife or a metal skewer and add them to the boiling water. Boil the sausages gently for 8 minutes, then drain them and set aside.

Melt the butter in a large roasting pan over low heat. Add the grapes to the pan and toss to coat them with the butter. With tongs, transfer the parboiled sausages to the pan and push them down into the grapes so that the sausages will not brown too quickly.

Roast the sausages and grapes in the preheated oven, turning the sausages once, until the grapes are soft and the sausages have browned, 20 to 25 minutes. With a slotted spoon, transfer the sausages and grapes to a heated serving platter.

Place the roasting pan on top of the stove over a medium-high flame and add the balsamic vinegar. Stir to scrape up the browned bits on the bottom of the pan and cook the vinegar and juices until they are thick and syrupy.

Pour the sauce over the sausages and grapes and serve immediately, accompanied with mashed potatoes.

Mashed Potatoes
(Serves 6 to 8)

2 pounds small red potatoes, peeled
½ cup heavy (whipping) cream
½ cup (1 stick) unsalted butter
    at room temperature
1 teaspoon kosher salt, or to taste

Quarter the potatoes and place them in a large pot. Add lightly salted water to cover by 1 inch. Bring the water to a boil over high heat, lower heat to a simmer, and cook the potatoes uncovered for 15 minutes, or until tender.

Drain the potatoes in a colander and return them to the saucepan. Place the pan over very low heat and coarsely mash the potatoes with a potato masher or 2 large meat forks or force them through a ricer into a bowl; do not use a whisk or an electric mixer or the potatoes will become gummy. Slowly add the cream and butter to the potatoes and stir in the salt. Serve immediately.

Roasted Sausages and Grapes; George Germon, Al Forno Restaurant, Providence, Rhode Island

Roasted Red Pepper Ravioli with Braised Duck

Lynne Aronson and Toni D' Onofrio, Lola
New York, New York

Serves 6

Hot stuff! describes this delicious dish, not one to serve to the meek of palate. Each element is loaded with flavor, from the red pepper pasta to the duck and wild mushroom topping and the chili broth.

Pasta

½ red bell pepper, roasted, peeled, and seeded (see page 11)
2 cups all-purpose flour
¼ cup minced fresh chervil
¼ minced fresh cilantro
2 large eggs
1 teaspoon coarse salt

Braised Duck

5 duck legs, skin on
Salt and freshly ground black pepper to taste
¼ cup olive oil
5 celery stalks, coarsely chopped
3 carrots, peeled and coarsely chopped
1 onion, coarsely chopped
4 garlic cloves, crushed
4 fresh thyme sprigs
4 cups chicken stock (see page 20)
2 cups dry red wine

Chili Broth

1 large red bell pepper, seeded and deribbed
4 chipotle or ancho chilies
2 poblano chilies, seeded and deribbed (see page 11)
2 celery stalks, cut into 1-inch pieces
2 red onions, cut into 1-inch dice
2 carrots, peeled and cut into 1-inch dice
1 fennel bulb, stalk removed, cut into 1-inch slices
1 cup (8 ounces) 1-inch slices peeled fresh ginger
Bottom 3 inches of 2 lemongrass stalks
4 Kaffir lime leaves (optional)
1 cup tomato paste
8 cups chicken stock (see page 20)
½ cup fresh lime juice
Salt to taste

Wild Mushrooms

2 Portobello mushrooms, 4 to 6 inches in diameter, stemmed
Olive oil for coating, plus 2 tablespoons
8 ounces black trumpet mushrooms or golden chanterelles

Ricotta Filling

½ cup ricotta cheese
¼ cup minced fresh chives

To make the pasta: Puree the roasted pepper in a blender or food processor. Place the flour on a flat work surface in a mound and form a well in the center. In the well, place the pureed red pepper, chervil, cilantro, eggs, and salt. With a table fork or your hands, move the flour from the outside of the well into the mixture and incorporate thoroughly. If the dough is too sticky, gradually add just enough floor to make it supple. Form the dough into a ball. Place in a lightly oiled bowl, cover, and chill for 1 hour.

To roll out the pasta: Divide the dough into 6 equal pieces. Working with 1 piece at a time, crank the dough through the largest setting of a pasta machine. Continue to press the dough through the machine, adjusting the setting until the sheets are as thin as possible. Cut each sheet into two 4-by-4-inch squares to make 12 squares. Place the squares between lightly floured waxed paper or parchment. Set aside.

To prepare the braised duck: Preheat the oven to 350°F. Season the duck legs with salt and pepper. Place a heavy skillet over medium heat and add the duck legs, skin-side down. Cook the legs, turning occasionally, until they are lightly browned and the skin is crisp, about 20 to 30 minutes. Pour the duck fat out of the pan, add the olive oil, and return the pan to heat. Add the chopped celery, carrots, and onion. Cook, stirring occasionally, until vegetables are browned, about 8 to 10 minutes.

Place the duck legs and vegetables in a large roasting pan. Add the garlic, thyme, chicken stock, and red wine. Cover the roasting pan with aluminum foil and place in the preheated oven for 1 to 1½ hours, or until the duck meat is falling off the bones. Remove the duck meat from the bones, discarding the skin and bones. Shred the meat and set aside.

To make the chili broth: Combine the red bell pepper, chilies, celery, onions, carrots, fennel, and ginger in a blender or food processor and pulse to chop coarsely. (This may have to be done in 2 batches.) Cut the lemongrass into shreds by hand. (Lemongrass is too fibrous to shred in a machine.)

In a stockpot or large saucepan, combine the chopped vegetable mixture, lemongrass, Kaffir lime leaves (if used), and tomato paste. Add the chicken stock and bring to a boil over medium heat. Reduce heat to low and simmer uncov-

Roasted Red Pepper Ravioli with Braised Duck; Lynne Aronson and Toni D'Onofrio, Lola, New York

ered for 45 minutes. Strain and discard the vegetables. Add the lime juice and salt. Set aside and keep warm.

To prepare the wild mushrooms: Light a fire in a charcoal grill or preheat the broiler. Gently clean the mushrooms with a damp cloth. Lightly coat the Portobello mushroom caps with oil. Place them on a grill over hot coals or under the broiler and cook for 2 to 3 minutes on each side, or until well browned. Let cool and cut into ½-inch-thick strips. Place a medium sauté pan or skillet over medium heat and add the 2 tablespoons olive oil. When the oil is hot, add the trumpet mushrooms or chanterelles and sauté until they have released their liquid, about 4 to 6 minutes. Keep cooking until the liquid evaporates and remove the pan from heat. Combine the trumpet mushrooms with the Portobello strips and set aside.

To make the filling: Combine the ricotta cheese and chopped chives in a small bowl and set aside.

To assemble the ravioli: Warm the duck meat and mushrooms together in a saucepan, using just enough chili broth to moisten them. Pour some olive oil into a shallow bowl or deep plate. Fill a large stockpot with lightly salted water and bring to a boil. Add the pasta squares and cook for about 45 seconds to 1 minute. Quickly remove the pasta squares from the pan with a slotted spoon, running it through the olive oil to keep the squares from sticking together.

To serve: Heat the chili broth. Take a pasta square, shake to remove any excess oil, and place the pasta on the bottom of each of 6 shallow soup bowls. Portion the duck meat evenly on top of the pasta in each bowl. Spoon 1 heaping tablespoon of the ricotta filling over the duck meat and place a second pasta square on top of the cheese. Ladle hot chili broth gently into each bowl to fill it halfway. Serve immediately.

Note: *All components up to the cooking of the pasta may be made 1 day in advance and refrigerated, tightly covered. Reheat the duck mixture and chili broth over medium heat.*

LYNNE ARONSON
Lola, New York, New York

Although Lynne Aronson's career change from painting and the graphic arts appears to be worlds away from the kitchen, she has simply transferred her creativity from the visual arts to the culinary arts. Part-owner and executive chef at Lola since 1990, Aronson was named one of the ten best young American chefs by *Esquire* magazine in 1992 and has ushered her Caribbean restaurant into the New York limelight.

After graduating from the New York Restaurant School, Aronson started on the lunch line at the Union Square Cafe, where she thrived on the frenzy. She then became the sous-chef and the only woman in the kitchen at The Frog, a seafood restaurant in Philadelphia. Returning to New York, she refined and enlarged on her skills as executive chef at John Clancy's.

At Lola, Aronson uses accents from Southeast Asia and the American Southwest in such specialties as Fried Louisiana Shrimp with Asian Barbecue Sauce and Peanut Sauce; and Szechuan Peppercorn–seared Monkfish with Ancho Chili Sauce. Called a "master of frying" by John Mariani of *Esquire,* she continues to offer one of the house signature dishes, Lola's 100-Spice Caribbean Fried Chicken.

Not only are the flavors bursting at Lola, but so is the activity. Sunday brunch with live gospel music is a favorite, and patrons have been known to dance on their chairs. The restaurant is festive yet elegant, with softly colored salmon walls. Jazz suppers and "splash festivals" feature music, as well as the fruits and flavors of the Caribbean in tingling drink concoctions and tropical desserts. What is unexpected, however, is the finesse of such offerings as the chef's Scallion Corn Cakes; Grilled Rack of Lamb with Cardamom Sauce; and Roasted Red Pepper Ravioli with Braised Duck.

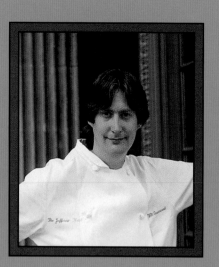

WILL GREENWOOD
Jefferson Hotel, Washington, D.C.

Just as the writings of Thomas Jefferson have influenced the course of American history, so has the culinary philosophy of the nation's foremost gourmand guided the culinary innovations of Will Greenwood, the former executive chef of the Jefferson Hotel in Washington, D.C.

It was after studying Jefferson's culinary writing that Greenwood, now thirty-five, began to create his version of Virginia cuisine. Using foods native to the Chesapeake Bay and the Shenandoah Mountains, he imbues traditional dishes with a contemporary spirit.

"Maybe this is just another example of how everything old is new again," he says. "As I learn more about Jefferson, I realize that it was he who really started new American cuisine and lightening traditional dishes."

Greenwood's cuisine has been hailed by the press and by his peers alike. He has been the subject of profiles in *Bon Appetit, Food Arts,* and *USA Today,* among others, and he has appeared on *Good Morning America.* And for the past two years the Jefferson Restaurant has been listed in the city's top fifty by the *Washington Post.*

Such dishes as Plantation Corn Cake with Smoked Salmon and Chive Cream; Crab and Lobster Cake with Pommery Mustard Sauce; and Rib-Eye Steak with Venison Chili and Twice-baked Potatoes are examples of how Greenwood combines traditional Virginia dishes with the popular foods of today.

The Oklahoma native graduated from the prestigious Culinary Institute of America. His secondary training was with the legendary Madeleine Kamman at the Beringer Vineyards New School for American Chefs in St. Helena, California.

Chef Greenwood came to the Jefferson Hotel in 1989, after launching Gaspard's in Winchester, Virginia. "Openings are a true test of management skills, organization, patience and self-control, and one's passion for one's work. We created a fine dining restaurant on the culinary frontier," he says.

Prior to that position, he had served as executive chef for the Maryland Inn in Annapolis as well as in other hotel restaurants such as the highly acclaimed La Brasserie in the Peabody Court Hotel in Baltimore.

Rib-Eye Steak with Venison Chili and Twice-baked Potatoes

Will Greenwood, Jefferson Hotel
Washington, D.C.

Serves 6

A delicious and hearty dish for a cold fall or winter night: garlic-flavored steaks; pumpkin, bean, and venison chili; and baked potatoes stuffed with goat cheese.

Steaks
3 tablespoons minced garlic
1½ cups olive oil
Salt and freshly ground black pepper
   to taste
6 rib-eye steaks (also called Delmonico),
   10 to 12 ounces each

Venison Chili
1 cup dried Christmas beans or
   dried lima beans
1½ pounds venison, cut into ½-inch
   chunks
4 cups rich beef stock (see page 21)
2 tablespoons tomato paste
Salt and freshly ground black pepper
   to taste
1 cup ½-inch-diced fresh pumpkin, acorn
   squash, or butternut squash
2 tablespoons chili powder
½ teaspoon ground turmeric
½ teaspoon ground cumin

Twice-baked Potatoes
6 medium baking potatoes
8 ounces mild fresh white goat cheese
   at room temperature
½ cup (1 stick) unsalted butter, cut into
   tablespoon-sized pieces
½ cup heavy (whipping) cream
Salt and freshly ground black pepper
   to taste
5 tablespoons minced fresh chives

2 tablespoons olive oil

Combine the garlic, olive oil, salt, and pepper in a shallow non-aluminum container. Add the steaks, cover, and refrigerate overnight.

To make the chili: Soak the beans in a large bowl of water overnight. Or, place the beans in a large pot, add water to cover, bring to a boil, and boil for 1 minute. Remove from heat, cover the pot, and let sit for 1 hour. Drain the beans and cook them as soon as possible.

In a large saucepan, combine the venison with the stock, tomato paste, salt, and pepper. Simmer for 45 minutes, then add the beans, pumpkin, chili powder, turmeric, and cumin. Simmer for 35 minutes, or until the venison and pumpkin are tender.

While the chili is simmering, make the potatoes. Preheat the oven to 400°F. Prick the potatoes with the tip of a paring knife and bake them for 1 hour, or until tender. Remove the potatoes from the oven and cut them in half lengthwise. Scoop out the potato flesh, reserving 6 half shells. Force the potatoes through a ricer or sieve into a bowl. Add the cheese and butter, and mix to combine. Add the cream and check the mixture for seasoning. Adjust with salt and pepper if necessary, then transfer the potato mixture to a pastry bag fitted with a large fluted star tip. Pipe the filling into the reserved potato halves and sprinkle with the chives.

Increase the oven temperature to 425°F and bake the stuffed potatoes for 30 minutes or until heated through. While the potatoes are baking, place the olive oil in a 12-inch sauté pan or skillet over high heat. Sear the marinated steaks for 4 to 6 minutes on each side for medium rare, or longer if you prefer. Spoon some chili over one end of each steak and garnish with a potato half.

Note: The chili and potato mixture may be prepared 1 day in advance, covered, and refrigerated. Reheat the chili slowly over low heat. Fill the potato shells and bake them again just prior to serving.

Rib-Eye Steak with Venison Chili and Twice-baked Potatoes; Will Greenwood, Jefferson Hotel, Washington, D.C.

Pan-roasted Quail with Port Sauce; Michael Lomonaco, The '21' Club, New York

Pan-roasted Quail with Port Sauce

*Michael Lomonaco, The "21" Club
New York, New York*

Serves 4

Game birds, especially quail, take well to
a bit of sweetness in their preparation,
and this easy-to-make dish is a stellar
example. The quail derive flavor from the
port and maple in the marinade, and the
heady port is the dominant flavor in the
stock-reduction sauce. Serve this dish
with Vegetable Couscous with Foie Gras
(page 156).

8 fresh boned quail

Marinade
½ cup dry red wine
¼ cup good-quality port, preferably
　not too sweet
¼ cup olive oil
2 tablespoons balsamic vinegar
2 tablespoons maple syrup
2 tablespoons low-salt soy sauce
2 bay leaves
1 teaspoon freshly ground black pepper
2 garlic cloves, crushed
4 fresh thyme sprigs
½ teaspoon juniper berries, crushed, or
　2 tablespoons gin

Port Sauce
2 pounds quail, chicken, or duck bones,
　necks, and wing tips
2 carrots, peeled and coarsely chopped
1 onion, diced
3 celery stalks, chopped
1 bay leaf
½ teaspoon dried thyme
1 garlic clove, minced
3 quarts water
½ cup rich veal or beef stock
　(see page 21)
1 cup port

¼ cup olive oil
2 tablespoons unsalted butter
2 tablespoons port

Rinse the quail under cold running water. Combine all of the marinade ingredients in a large nonaluminum bowl and whisk well. Add the quail and make sure some of the marinade enters the cavities. Marinate the quail for 2 hours at room temperature, or cover and refrigerate overnight.

To make the port sauce: Preheat the oven to 375°F. Combine the bones, necks, and wing tips with the carrots, onion, celery, bay leaf, thyme, and garlic and seasonings in a roasting pan and roast for 45 minutes to 1 hour, or until the meat and vegetables are well browned. Transfer the bones and vegetables to a stockpot and cover with the cold water. Bring the water to a boil, add the stock and port, reduce heat to a simmer again, and cook until the liquid is reduced to 1½ cups. Strain the sauce through a fine-meshed sieve. Set aside and keep warm.

Place the olive oil in a cast-iron skillet and place over high heat. Drain the quail of excess marinade and pat them dry with paper towels. Add the birds to the hot pan and cook until they are a deep mahogany in color, about 6 to 8 minutes, turning with tongs to brown them evenly on all sides. Remove the quail from the skillet, place them in a roasting pan, and bake in the preheated oven for 6 to 8 minutes.

Immediately before serving, add the butter and port to the sauce and cook until the sauce is glossy. Serve the quail immediately, surrounded by the port sauce.

Note: The quail may be marinated 1 day in advance. The sauce may be cooked 1 day in advance, up to adding the butter and 2 tablespoons port.

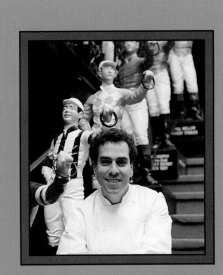

MICHAEL LOMONACO
The '21' Club, New York, New York

Once, when asked if he missed the theater, actor-turned-chef James Beard replied, "No. Why should I? We're not out of it. This is just another branch of it." Michael Lomonaco, a former member of the touring companies of *Jesus Christ Superstar* and *Hair* and currently the chef of the '21' Club in New York City, agrees.

"The fact is," says Lomonaco, "that the communication aspect of cooking is growing daily, especially with television and cable, and now TVFN," an all-food network in New York. "I have more opportunities to perform on television as a chef than I have ever had as an actor."

While television may provide a larger audience for chef Lomonaco, his most devoted audience appears daily at the '21' Club. The former speakeasy is itself a stage, filled with decades of collectibles including everything from a ten-thousand-dollar silver saddle to model trains. It's a stage on which Lomonaco appeared only after careful study of his part.

After beginning as an actor, Lomonaco studied at the New York City Technical College's Department of Hotel Management, then eventually went to work at Le Cirque with Alain Sailhac and Daniel Boulud. For his work at the '21' Club, Lomonaco has been named one of New York's Great Chefs, an honor bestowed, without former-actor favoritism, by the James Beard Foundation.

Before he began introducing his own version of the American cuisine on which the '21' Club had staked its reputation for decades, Lomonaco took the trouble to learn all the variations of the kitchen's venerable standbys, such as Cold Whole Maine Lobster Salad, and Chicken Hash.

The menu now reflects the variety and inventiveness found in the best of today's American cuisine. Soups like Yellow Pepper Gazpacho and Spicy Cuban Black Bean, and signature entrees like Pan-roasted Quail with Port Sauce, and Warm Venison Salad with Maple-baked Peaches and Chili Pepper Jam show both the '21' Club's continuing growth as a place for fine dining and Michael Lomonaco's continuing growth as a chef.

Lomonaco credits his mother Mary with his love of food. "She was a wonderful cook," he says. "I learned a love of honest, hearty flavors in that kitchen."

SUSANNA FOO
Susanna Foo Chinese Cuisine, Philadelphia, Pennsylvania

Food has been a life-long love for Susanna Foo. As a child in northern China and Taiwan, she accompanied the family cook to the market and learned how to select produce. At home, her brothers encouraged her baking experiments.

Even after earning her B.A. in history from the University of Taiwan and a master's degree in library science from the University of Pittsburgh, the kitchen still intrigued her. At the urging of their families, Foo and her husband, E-Hsin, opened Hu-Nan of Philadelphia in 1979.

Jack Rosenthal, a founder of the Culinary Institute of America, stopped in for lunch one day and took an interest in Foo's culinary development. It was under his tutelage that Foo was introduced to French cooking techniques, and she trained for eight weeks at the CIA.

Foo integrates French and Chinese cooking methods. She prepares sauces from reduced stocks—a departure from traditional Chinese cuisine—but adds Asian spices, soy, or wine. In such dishes as Eight-Treasure Quail with Chinese Sausage and Lotus Seed, she retains the lightness of classic Chinese cuisine, but enhances the flavors and textures through her adaptation of French techniques.

However, Foo does not restrict her ingredients to those used in French and Chinese cooking. Her dishes also utilize everything from lemongrass and Thai basil to sun-dried tomatoes and ancho chilies. She loves salads, which also are not traditionally Chinese, and her Fresh Water-Chestnut Salad with Balsamic Vinegar is a Philadelphia favorite.

In 1987, Foo and her husband opened Susanna Foo Chinese Cuisine in downtown Philadelphia, and in 1989 Susanna was named one of America's ten best new chefs by *Food & Wine* magazine. *Eating Well* magazine named Foo the Best Chinese Cook in the Country in 1992, and Zagat's Restaurant Survey has repeatedly designated Susanna Foo Chinese Cuisine as one of Philadelphia's most popular restaurants.

Eight-Treasure Quail with Chinese Sausage and Lotus Seed

Susanna Foo, Susanna Foo Chinese Cuisine
Philadelphia, Pennsylvania

Serves 4

This dish is based on the Chinese tradition of sweet and sour foods, but those flavors are augmented with the five-spice accent of Chinese sausage and the flavors of the Portobello mushroom and liqueurs.

Quail
¼ cup soybean oil
3 garlic cloves, crushed
2 tablespoons minced fresh ginger
1 lemongrass stalk, bottom 3 inches only, crushed and sliced
2 tablespoons soy sauce
3 tablespoons brandy
8 boned quail

Stuffing
8 ounces lean Chinese sausages*
1 pound asparagus, trimmed, or Chinese cabbage
½ Portobello mushroom, or 4 stemmed, shiitake mushrooms
2 tablespoons soybean oil
4 shallots, minced
2 tablespoons dried shrimp,* minced in a blender or food processor
1 cup Chinese sweet rice,* soaked 2 hours to overnight in 2 cups cold water
1 teaspoon kosher salt
Freshly ground black pepper to taste

Glaze
¼ cup sugar
2 cups water
½ cup dried lotus seed, soaked in 1 cup water for 1 hour
1 tablespoon unsalted butter
6 fresh kumquats, thinly sliced and seeded
3 tablespoons Grand Marnier or other orange-flavored liqueur

To make the quail: Mix the soybean oil, garlic, ginger, lemongrass, soy sauce and brandy in a large nonaluminum bowl. Gently turn the quail inside out and marinate at room temperature for 30 minutes.

Eight-Treasure Quail with Chinese Sausage and Lotus Seed; Susanna Foo, Susanna Foo Chinese Cuisine, Philadelphia

To make the stuffing: Cut two thirds of the sausages into ¼-inch-thick diagonal slices. Cut the remaining sausages into ⅛-inch dice. Cut the asparagus into ½-inch-thick diagonal slices and set aside (if using cabbage, cut it into 1-inch pieces). Cut the gills from the bottom of the Portobello mushroom and cut the stem and cap into thin matchsticks; if using shiitakes, cut the caps into matchsticks.

Heat the oil in a large sauté pan or skillet over medium-high heat. Add the shallots and sauté for 4 or 5 minutes, or until lightly browned. Add the sausage cubes, sliced mushrooms, and dried shrimp. Cook over low heat until the mushroom(s) is tender. (Although mixture may seem a little dry, you should add only as much oil as needed to make a loose stir-fry.)

Turn off heat and add the soaked rice, salt, and pepper. Mix thoroughly and transfer to a shallow dish. Place a large bamboo steamer over a 10-inch skillet filled with 1 inch of boiling water. Lay the sausage slices and the asparagus on top of the stuffing mixture, then place the pan of rice in the bamboo steamer for 10 minutes, or until the asparagus is tender. (The fat from the sausage will season the stuffing mixture.) Remove the sausage slices and asparagus from the stuffing, and keep warm.

Turn the quail right-side out and stuff each with 3 tablespoons of the stuffing mixture. Arrange the quail breast-side down, cross the legs to seal, and place on a heatproof dish.

To make the glaze: Heat the sugar with 1 cup of the water in a small saucepan. Add the drained soaked lotus seeds and cook for about 20 minutes, or until the seeds are slightly translucent and tender; strain (discard the sugar water). When the lotus seeds are cool enough to handle, break them in half with your fingers and discard the black core, if one is present. Return the lotus seeds to the saucepan. Add the butter, sliced

kumquats, and Grand Marnier or other liqueur. Bring to a boil over medium heat, stirring occasionally, and turn off heat. Set aside and keep warm.

To finish the dish: Preheat the broiler and broil the quail about 6 inches from heat for 4 minutes; turn the quail gently, using tongs, and broil for an additional 3 minutes, or until they are golden brown.

To serve: Spoon asparagus onto each plate and top with 1 quail. Arrange the sausage slices around the quail and spoon the lotus seed sauce over the quail.

*Available at Asian food stores.

Note: *The stuffing may be prepared up to 1 day in advance and refrigerated, tightly covered. Bring it to room temperature before stuffing the quail. If making the stuffing in advance, the asparagus should be steamed separately while the quail are broiling.*

Boneless Quail Stuffed with Crabmeat; Jimmy Sneed, The Frog and the Redneck, Richmond, Virginia

Boneless Quail Stuffed with Crabmeat

Jimmy Sneed, The Frog and the Redneck
Richmond, Virginia

Serves 6

The combination of sausage with crab is traditional in Virginia cooking, and this flavorful stuffing for the quail makes this a sensational dish.

Quail

6 boned quail

Stuffing

12 ounces Surry sausages
  (see Mail-Order Sources, page 243)
¼ cup water
¼ cup olive oil

1 pound shiitake mushrooms,
  stemmed and sliced
Salt and freshly ground black pepper
  to taste
2 large shallots, minced
2 garlic cloves, minced
4 ounces boneless, skinless chicken
  breast meat
⅔ cup heavy (whipping) cream
8 ounces crabmeat
1 bunch fresh chives, minced
4 ounces caul fat (optional)

Sauce

2 cups unsalted veal stock (see page 21)
  or chicken stock (see page 20),
  cooked to reduce to ¾ cup
3 shallots, sliced
1 tablespoon grainy mustard
Salt and freshly ground black pepper
  to taste
2 tablespoons unsalted butter

Preheat the oven to 450°F. Rinse the quail, pat dry with paper towels, and set aside. Prick the sausages with a fork and place the sausages in a medium sauté pan or skillet with the water. Cover the pan, place it over high heat, and cook the sausages for 5 to 7 minutes, turning once, to cook them through. Drain any remaining water from the pan, place the pan uncovered over medium heat, and brown the sausages on all sides, turning them with tongs. Remove the sausages from the pan and dice them into small chunks. Set aside.

Add the olive oil to the pan and heat it over medium-high heat. Add the sliced mushrooms and sauté for 3 to 4 minutes, or until they are brown and limp, stirring constantly. Sprinkle the mushrooms with salt and pepper, and add the shallots and garlic to the pan. Reduce heat to low and sauté an additional 3 minutes, or until the shallots are translucent. Set aside.

Place the chicken meat in a blender or food processor and puree until smooth. Scrape down the sides of the container, add the cream along with some salt and pepper, and puree until smooth, scraping down the sides of the container as necessary.

Scrape the chicken mousse into a mixing bowl with a rubber spatula and stir in the sausage, mushroom mixture, crabmeat, and chives. Stuff the quail cavities as full as possible with the mixture. If using the caul fat, wrap each quail in a double layer; otherwise, skewer the neck and body cavitiy closed with toothpicks.

Place the quail in a shallow roasting pan. Roast them in the preheated oven for 25 to 30 minutes, or until they are brown and a meat thermometer inserted into the center of the stuffing registers 175°F. Remove the quail from the oven and let sit for 10 minutes before serving.

To make the sauce: While the quail are roasting, or in advance, combine the reduced stock and shallots in a small saucepan. Bring to a boil over medium heat, reduce heat to low, and simmer for 5 to 7 minutes, or until the shallots are tender. Strain the shallots from the sauce, reserving the reduced liquid. Puree the shallots in a blender or food processor and return them to the liquid. Stir in the mustard, salt, and pepper. Place the pan over medium heat and swirl in the butter until melted.

To serve: Place a bed of the sauce on a plate and top with the roasted quail.

Note: *The stuffing and sauce may be prepared 1 day in advance and refrigerated, tightly covered. Allow the stuffing to reach room temperature before stuffing the quail, and reheat the sauce in a small saucepan over low heat; do not swirl in the butter until just before serving.*

JIMMY SNEED
The Frog and the Redneck, Richmond, Virginia

Judging by the name alone, The Frog and the Redneck would not seem like a location for fine dining. But Jimmy Sneed's endeavor in Richmond, Virginia, named one of the Best New Restaurants in America by *Esquire* magazine, has been the talk of food circles and the destination for countless road trips since its opening in 1993.

The story of The Frog and the Redneck's birth is one that Sneed—who wouldn't allow people to call him a chef until his Windows on Urbanna Creek restaurant started receiving national attention—loves to tell.

"I spent a year in France in 1973, learning the language and culture, taking some courses at the Sorbonne and selling newspapers cafe to cafe. It was a great experience, but I was getting hungrier by the day. I decided to get a job where I could also get fed, and headed over to the Cordon Bleu." There he became a French translator for American and Japanese culinary students.

Once back in Washington, D.C., Sneed worked for some mediocre restaurants, then decided that he "needed to find a master to work with, or else change professions." For the young Sneed, *master* meant French, so he drove over to the French embassy and asked to speak to the chef. The embassy chef referred Sneed to his friend Jean-Louis Palladin, chef at the famed Jean-Louis at the Watergate. The interview consisted of one question—"You speak French?"—followed by the affirmative *"oui"* of Sneed, and Sneed soon ascended to the rank of Palladin's sous-chef. He left to start Windows on Urbanna Creek, near Williamsburg, Virginia, in 1987, because he wanted his children to be raised in a tranquil country setting. His decision to open The Frog and the Redneck is premised on Sneed's belief that there is little, if any, difference between modern French and modern American food.

"So there you have it," writes Sneed in his newsletter. "The Frog in question is a tribute to what the French, generally, and Jean-Louis, specifically, have given me." The Redneck in the title refers to Sneed himself.

As the creator of such signature dishes as Boneless Quail Stuffed with Crabmeat, and Ravioli with Bay Scallops, Sneed believes that "food can no longer be categorized as being either French or American cuisine. Indeed, one of the most difficult questions to answer is, 'What type of food do you serve?' "

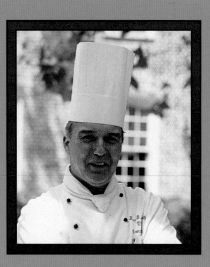

HANS SCHADLER
Williamsburg Inn, Williamsburg, Virginia

When Hans Schadler was offered the position of executive chef for the White House in 1987, he turned it down to stay in Williamsburg, Virginia. He has remained at the Williamsburg Inn, a *Mobil Travel Guide* five-star establishment, for twelve years, serving as the executive chef and food director.

Born outside Frankfurt, Germany, Schadler had an early fascination with the autobahn and dreamed of being a mechanic. However, the influence of life on a large farm prevailed, he says, recalling his fondest food memory: crisp potato cakes with warm applesauce and beef rouladen. Today, he describes his cuisine as "simple but good food," including such signature dishes as Virginia Ham with Crisp Sweet-Potato Cake; Stuffed Quail and Peppered Beef Tenderloin; and Apple Complicity.

After working as the caterer for the Norwegian royal family in Oslo, Schadler joined the Norwegian American Cruise Line and soon rose to the rank of executive chef. Aboard ship he met his wife Liv, a fellow employee, and they moved to the Caribbean. His time away from the "mainland" instilled in him an appreciation for the local produce of the Northeast, since, he says, "the import of all foods created certain restrictions" in the Caribbean.

Shadler also missed being in touch with fellow chefs and, on moving to America, he founded the Central Vermont Chefs' Association and the Rockresort Apprenticeship Program. He recently served as president of the Virginia Chefs' Association.

Now Schadler brings his classical French training and German upbringing to the Williamsburg Inn and Lodge, balancing European entrees with fresh regional specialties. "I like our guests to feel relaxed, pampered, and to have an unsurpassed quality experience; one which they will remember and tell their friends about."

Stuffed Quail and Peppered Beef Tenderloin

Hans Schadler, Williamsburg Inn
Williamsburg, Virginia

Serves 4

Roast quail and pepper-coated beef are a great combination. The quail are stuffed with a chicken mousse dotted with ham, herbs, and pine nuts, and red wine sauce unites the two portions of the entree. Serve this dish with Lentil Ragout (page 155) or Wild Rice and Barley Pilaf (page 156), and Root Vegetable Puree (page 157).

Stuffing
8 ounces skinless, boneless
  chicken breasts
½ teaspoon salt
½ teaspoon freshly ground white pepper
½ cup heavy (whipping) cream
¼ cup ice water
¼ cup finely diced ham
2 tablespoons pine nuts, toasted
  (see page 16)
2 tablespoons minced mixed fresh herbs
  (rosemary, parsley, thyme)

Quail
4 boned quails
Salt and freshly ground white pepper
  to taste
Stuffing, above
4 lean bacon slices
4 tablespoons unsalted butter, melted

Peppered Tenderloin
Four 2-ounce beef tenderloin steaks
  (preferably tail pieces)
¼ cup olive oil mixed with
¼ cup Dijon mustard
¼ cup mixed peppercorns (green, black,
  white, and pink), crushed with a
  rolling pin or coarsely cracked in
  a grinder

Red Wine Sauce

1 tablespoon olive oil

1 shallot, minced

2 garlic cloves, minced

½ cup dry red wine

1 cup rich veal stock or chicken stock
    (see page 21)

Salt, freshly ground black pepper, and
    cayenne pepper to taste

¼ cup dried cranberries

To make the stuffing: Cut the chicken into 1-inch pieces and place them in a blender or food processor. Add the salt, pepper, and cream, and puree the chicken until smooth. Add the ice water and process until the chicken reaches a gummy consistency. Transfer the chicken puree to a chilled nonaluminum bowl. Fold in the ham, pine nuts, and herbs. Adjust the seasoning and set aside.

To prepare the quail: Rinse the quail under cold running water, pat them dry with paper towels, and season with salt and pepper. Fit a large pastry bag with a large plain tip and fill the bag with the stuffing mixture. Stuff the quail, wrap each one with a slice of bacon to close the cavity, and secure the bacon with a toothpick. Brush the quail with the butter and set aside.

To prepare the tenderloin: Brush the beef with the olive oil and mustard, then roll each piece in the cracked peppercorns. Set aside.

To make the red wine sauce: Heat the olive oil in an 8-inch sauté pan or skillet over medium heat. Add the shallot and garlic, and sauté, stirring frequently, until the shallot is translucent, about 3 minutes. Add the red wine, bring to a boil, and cook to reduce the liquid by half. Add the stock, then cook to reduce by half again, or until the sauce is thick enough to coat the back of a spoon. Adjust the seasoning with salt, pepper and cayenne. Add the cranberries, remove from heat, and set aside.

Preheat the oven to 375°F. Roast the quail for 15 to 20 minutes, or until the birds are golden, the juices run clear, and an instant-read thermometer inserted into the center of the stuffing reads 175°F.

While the quail are roasting, sear the tenderloins in a 12-inch nonstick sauté pan or skillet over high heat for about 2 minutes on each side. Transfer the tenderloins to a roasting pan. Roast the beef in the preheated oven for 10 to 12 minutes for medium rare, or longer if you prefer. Remove the quail and the beef from the oven and let sit for 5 minutes before serving. Place 1 quail and 1 beef medallion on each plate to serve.

Note: The stuffing and sauce may be prepared 1 day in advance, and the beef may be coated at the same time. Refrigerate all, tightly covered. Do not stuff the quail until just prior to cooking.

Stuffed Quail and Peppered Beef Tenderloin; Hans Schadler, Williamsburg Inn, Williamsburg, Virginia

Oven-roasted Pork and Rabbit
Arista e Coniglio Arrosto al Forno

Francesco Ricchi, Ristorante i Ricchi
Washington, D.C.

Serves 8

Pork and rabbit are an excellent combination when infused with garlic and rosemary; however, this dish could also be made with pork alone.

2½ pounds boneless pork loin
Leaves from 4 fresh rosemary sprigs
4 garlic cloves, thinly sliced
Salt and freshly ground black pepper
   to taste
½ cup (1 stick) unsalted butter
1 rabbit (about 3 pounds)
¼ cup olive oil
2 cups dry red wine

   Preheat the oven to 400°F. Trim the pork loin of excess fat, slice it almost in half lengthwise, and set aside. Mince the rosemary and garlic together and sprinkle with salt and pepper. With a sharp knife, make 5 evenly spaced 1½- to 2-inch-deep incisions all around the pork loin. Place ½ teaspoon of the garlic-rosemary mixture in each pocket, then add ½ teaspoon butter to each pocket. Sprinkle the inside of the loin with salt, pepper, and half of the rosemary mixture and dot with 2½ tablespoons butter. Roll up the loin with the rosemary mixture on the inside, then tie the roast closed with kitchen twine at 1-inch intervals.

   Trim the rabbit of any excess fat and place the carcass on its back. Pull each leg away from the body, then use a sharp knife to cut through the meat and the joint to separate the leg from the loin.

Oven-roasted Pork and Rabbit; Francesco Ricchi, Ristorante i Ricchi, Washington, D.C.

Locate the breastbone and use a heavy knife to split and remove it. Run your finger down the rabbit's ribcage to locate the backbone. Use the tip of the knife to scrape each rib bone away from the meat along one side, stopping when you reach the thin skin at the base of the backbone. Repeat with the other side of the rabbit and remove the breastbone.

Season the inside of the rabbit with salt, pepper, and the remaining rosemary mixture. Top with 1½ tablespoons butter and fold the rabbit's skin like a package. Tie the rabbit using the same method as the pork loin. Make 2 incisions in each of the reserved legs at 1-inch intervals and stuff each one with the remaining herb mixture and 1 teaspoon butter.

Place the pork and the rabbit in a large roasting pan. Drizzle the meats with the olive oil and roast in the preheated oven for 40 to 50 minutes, turning the meat regularly to ensure even browning. At this point the pork should register 155°F on an instant-read meat thermometer.

Remove the pan from the oven and place it on the stove over medium-high heat. Add the wine to the pan, stirring to dislodge the browned bits on the bottom of the pan. Continue to turn the roasts occasionally while cooking the wine to reduce it by two thirds to a syrupy consistency. Transfer the meat to a serving platter, slice, and serve with the roasting juices and wine reduction.

Note: *The meats may be prepared for roasting up to 1 day in advance and refrigerated, tightly covered. Let the meats sit at room temperature for 30 minutes before roasting.*

FRANCESCO RICCHI
Ristorante i Ricchi, Washington, D.C.

In a very small Italian town called Cercina, just beyond the hills north of Florence, lived a family that for generations served *cucina rustica* to hungry travelers and townspeople alike. The family's son, raised in the kitchen that was "full of aroma" and "something magic," took his grandmother as a role model and became a great chef in a big city across the ocean.

This is the true story of Francesco Ricchi, who, with his wife Christianne, opened Ristorante i Ricchi in Washington, D.C., in 1988. George Bush added to the restaurant's fame when he visited it immediately following his presidential inauguration in January 1989. Since coming to the United States, Ricchi believes his style of cooking has become "more complex," but his goal remains "to prepare and serve traditional Tuscan cuisine and defend [its] authenticity."

Ricchi achieves this goal. *Washington Post* restaurant critic Phyllis Richman says, "Nowhere else in this country have I had such authentic Tuscan food. In fact, only in a handful of Florence's restaurants is such tradition available." Traditional dishes such as *Arista e Coniglio Arrosto al Forno* (Oven-roasted Pork and Rabbit), *Ribollita, Pappa al Pomodoro, Fettunta con Fagioli, Penne Strasciate, Tortelloni di Ricotta,* and others have found their way to American hearts.

Honors have followed effort. In 1989, the restaurant was *Esquire* magazine's Best New Restaurant in the United States. *Washingtonian* named it Best Italian Restaurant three years in a row. Most recently, i Ricchi received the Distinguished Restaurant of North America Award for 1992–93 and was selected by *Food & Wine* magazine as one of the Twenty-Five Best Restaurants in North America.

The boy from the small town shares his success in the big city. Ricchi donates his time to Share Our Strength, Food for Friends, and the Neediest Kids, among many others. Both Ricchi's story and his career are filled with good taste.

ALAIN BOREL
L'Auberge Provençale, White Post, Virginia

Only a chef with a pilot's license could spot the site for a French country inn from a small plane flying above the rolling hills of Virginia. Since L'Auberge Provençale opened in July 1981, this full-service inn has been a haven for Washingtonians who make the short trip to the Shenandoah Valley.

A fourth-generation chef, Borel began his training "the old-fashioned way," he says, starting at age seven by peeling potatoes for Hôtel du Louvre, his grandfather's two-star Michelin restaurant in Avignon, France.

After his family relocated to Key West, Florida, Borel eventually bought his father's restaurant, Chez Emile, and later opened a small cafe called the Deck. "When I had my restaurants in Key West I began to use more tropical ingredients, which opened up my creativity," he says.

His cuisine remains firmly rooted in his native Provence, however, drawing heavily on such ingredients from the Mediterranean kitchen as fresh herbs, tomatoes, and olives for signature dishes like Apple Wood–smoked Rabbit served with Fresh Basil Pasta; Pheasant with Rosemary and Vanilla; and Fois Gras with Cactus Pears.

The atmosphere of L'Auberge Provençale is also decidedly French, with the three dining rooms decorated in French fabrics and French country antiques that range from a Louis XIV lavabo to a duck press to hand-painted plates. The extensive collection of original art, from Picasso to Dufy, completes the Inn that Chef Borel calls "not pretentious" but "a respite from the otherwise hectic world."

Borel divides his time between running L'Auberge Provençale with his wife Celeste and coaching soccer for his son Christian. He is also the gardener for his inn, drawing the freshest ingredients from his orchards and crops. "For the future I see my cuisine evolving, yet I do not believe in nouveau ideas or trends. Being in the country allows me to pace my progress to maintain the highest standards of quality," says Borel.

Pheasant with Rosemary and Vanilla

Alain Borel, L'Auberge Provençal
White Post, Virginia

Serves 6

Waffles belong at other meals besides breakfast, as this dish demonstrates. Here, savory cornmeal and onion waffles form the base for slices of pheasant and are served with an unusual but delicious sauce flavored with rosemary and vanilla.

Pheasants
Three 2½-pound pheasants
Salt and freshly ground black pepper
  to taste
1 tablespoon unsalted butter
1½ cups mushrooms with stems, diced
3 garlic cloves, minced
2 shallots, minced
1½ cups diced carrots
1½ cups diced celery
1½ cups diced onions
1½ fresh rosemary sprigs
¼ cup vegetable oil

Rosemary and Vanilla Sauce
½ cup sun-dried cherries
¼ cup port
4 tablespoons (½ stick) unsalted butter
2 shallots, minced
½ vanilla bean, split lengthwise
1 fresh rosemary sprig
½ cup bourbon
1½ cups veal demi-glace (see page 22)
Salt and freshly ground black pepper
  to taste

Cornmeal Waffles
½ cup cornmeal
1¼ cups all-purpose flour
¼ cup sugar
1 tablespoon baking powder
1 teaspoon salt
¼ cup vegetable oil
1 cup milk
1 egg, slightly beaten
1 cup finely diced onion

To prepare the pheasants: Preheat the oven to 350°F. Season the pheasants with salt and pepper. Melt the butter in a 12-inch sauté pan or skillet over medium heat. Add the mushrooms, garlic, and shallots and sauté for 3 minutes. Add the carrots, celery, and onions, and cook, stirring occasionally, for 6 to 8 minutes, or until the vegetables are tender. Remove the pan from heat, let the mixture cool slightly, and use it to stuff the pheasants. Put ½ sprig rosemary in each pheasant. Thread a trussing needle with kitchen twine and tie the wings of each pheasant to the body by pushing a needle through the ends of the drumsticks and the tip of the breastbone in the middle. Wrap the string around the back of each bird, pull it taut, and tie it.

Pour the vegetable oil into a 12-inch sauté pan or skillet and place over high heat. Brown the pheasants one at a time on all sides, then transfer to a roasting pan. Roast the pheasants in the preheated oven for 25 to 30 minutes, or until an inner thigh registers 170°F on a meat thermometer.

To prepare the sauce: While the birds are cooking, in a small bowl, combine the cherries and port and set aside to soak. Melt the butter in a small saucepan over medium-high heat. Add the shallots and sauté for 1 minute, stirring constantly. Add the vanilla bean and rosemary, stirring gently. Add the bourbon and boil until the total volume is reduced by half. Add the demi-glace and simmer for 5 minutes, or until the mixture is thick enough to coat the back of a spoon. Add salt and pepper. Set aside and keep warm.

To prepare the waffles: Combine the cornmeal, flour, sugar, baking powder, and salt in a medium bowl. Stir in the vegetable oil a little at a time. In a small bowl, mix the milk and egg together and add to the dry ingredients with a few swift strokes. Add the onion and stir a few strokes just to mix. Set aside until

needed. To cook, ladle the batter into a preheated waffle iron sprayed with vegetable oil. Cook until golden, according to the manufacturer's directions, about 3 minutes. Set aside and keep warm.

To serve: Cut the waffles into triangles. Cut the pheasant breasts into diagonal slices. (Use the thighs for another dish.) Spoon the sauce onto heated plates.

Arrange the pheasant slices in a fan. Add 2 waffle triangles to each plate and dot with the port-soaked cherries.

Note: The sauce may be prepared up to 2 days in advance and refrigerated, tightly covered. The waffles may be made a few hours in advance and reheated in the oven for 5 minutes, or until crisp.

Pheasant with Rosemary and Vanilla; Alain Borel, L'Auberge Provençale, White Post, Virginia

Pheasant and Polenta

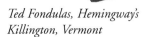

*Ted Fondulas, Hemingway's
Killington, Vermont*

Serves 8

A medley of wild mushrooms, cooked separately to keep their own character, is a woodsy garnish for the tender pheasant; creamy polenta flecked with Cheddar cheese completes the presentation.

4 pheasants, about 2 pounds each

Pheasant Stock
1 onion, quartered
1 carrot, peeled and cut into
    1-inch chunks
1 celery stalk, cut into ½-inch chunks
8 white peppercorns
6 fresh parsley stems
Reserved carcasses and wings
    from pheasants, above

Polenta
3 cups milk
2 tablespoons unsalted butter
1 cup cornmeal
¾ cup grated Cheddar cheese
Salt and freshly ground black pepper
    to taste
½ teaspoon ground nutmeg

Sauce
4 shallots, finely diced
1½ cups dry white vermouth
1 star anise
¼ teaspoon grated orange zest
Stems from shiitake and
    oyster mushrooms, below
4 cups Pheasant Stock, above
¼ teaspoon cornstarch mixed with
    1 teaspoon cold water

Wild Mushrooms
2 tablespoons olive oil
8 ounces shiitake mushrooms, stemmed
    (reserve stems)
2 tablespoons duck fat or vegetable oil
8 ounces (2½ cups) morel mushrooms or
    sliced Portobello mushrooms
2 tablespoons clarified butter
    (see page 19)
8 ounces oyster mushrooms, stemmed
    (reserve stems)
Salt and freshly ground black pepper
    to taste

4 tablespoons olive oil
Salt and freshly ground pepper to taste
¼ cup peas
1 small ripe tomato, peeled, seeded, and
    chopped (see page 18)

To prepare the pheasants: Remove the heads at the base of the neck, if attached. Remove the feet at the first joint with a cleaver, then remove the wings from the body with a sharp knife. Cut off the breasts and thighs, cover, and refrigerate. Set the carcass and wings aside.

To make the pheasant stock: Combine the onion, carrot, and celery in a heavy pot with the peppercorns and parsley stems. Add the pheasant carcasses and wings, then add water to cover, about 3 to 4 quarts. Bring to a boil over medium-high heat, skimming the scum from the surface as the mixture comes to a boil. Reduce heat to low and simmer for 3 to 4 hours; there should be 4 cups stock remaining. Strain through a fine-meshed sieve, discard the solids, and set aside.

To make the polenta: Place the milk and butter in a medium saucepan and bring to a boil over medium-high heat. Gradually add the cornmeal to the milk, whisking vigorously. Stir for 5 minutes over low heat. Remove the pan from the heat and add the Cheddar cheese, stirring until incorporated. Add the salt, pepper, and nutmeg.

While the mixture is still warm, spoon it into eight 4-ounce ramekins. Refrigerate for about 2 hours, or until the polenta sets.

To make the sauce: Place the shallots, vermouth, star anise, zest, and mushroom stems in a medium saucepan. Bring the mixture to a boil over high heat and cook to reduce by half. Add the pheasant stock and reduce by half again. Whisk in the cornstarch and water mixture, stirring constantly to prevent lumps. Set the sauce aside and keep it warm.

To cook the mushrooms: Place the olive oil in a large sauté pan or skillet over medium-high heat. Add the shiitake mushrooms and sauté for about 3 minutes, or until they are tender and brown. Remove the mushrooms from the pan and place in a pie pan. Wipe the oil out of the pan with paper towels and add the duck fat or oil. Return the pan to heat and sauté the morels or Portobellos

Pheasant and Polenta; Ted Fondulas, Hemingway's, Killington, Vermont

in the duck fat for 2 to 3 minutes. Remove the mushrooms from the pan and place in a separate pie pan. Wipe the pan out again, add the clarified butter, and sauté the oyster mushrooms very briefly over high heat, about 30 seconds. Remove the oyster mushrooms from the pan and place in a separate pie pan. Season all the mushrooms with salt and pepper to taste, and set aside.

Preheat the oven to 350°F. Unmold the polenta ramekins, place in a large ovenproof pan, brush the polenta with 2 tablespoons of the olive oil, and set aside.

Season the pheasant breasts and thighs with salt and pepper. Heat the remaining 2 tablespoons olive oil in a 12-inch sauté pan or skillet over medium-high heat. Add the pheasant pieces, skin-side down, and sear for 3 to 5 minutes. Turn the pheasant pieces with tongs and cook another 3 minutes, or until rare to medium-rare. Transfer the pheasant to a roasting pan and place in the oven for another 4 to 6 minutes. At the same time, place the polenta in the oven and bake for 10 minutes, or until heated through. Remove the pheasant from the oven and let sit in a warm place to rest for 5 minutes before carving. Reheat the sauce over medium heat, if necessary, and place the mushrooms in the oven to heat. Meanwhile, cook the peas in a small saucepan in lightly salted water for 3 minutes. Drain and set aside.

To serve: Slice the pheasant breasts on a slight diagonal and arrange in a fan shape on each plate. Spoon the warm sauce around the breast, place 1 thigh on each plate, and add the mushrooms and polenta. Distribute the peas and tomato evenly among the plates.

Note: The stock may be prepared up to 3 days in advance and refrigerated, tightly covered. The sauce, polenta, and mushrooms may all be made 1 day in advance and refrigerated.

TED FONDULAS
Hemingway's Restaurant, Killington, Vermont

A culinary epiphany in Europe led Ted Fondulas and his wife Linda to open Hemingway's Restaurant, an elegant eatery in Killington, Vermont. "Throughout the French countryside we found two- and three-star restaurants," says Fondulas. "We discovered that the fine restaurants weren't just in the cities, and we wondered if the same could hold true in America. So we decided to find out by establishing a sophisticated restaurant where we live in rural Vermont."

Both husband and wife had degrees in literature, and they named their restaurant for their literary hero Ernest Hemingway. Since its opening in 1982, Hemingway's has garnered four stars from the *Mobil Travel Guide* and four diamonds from the AAA; it was listed by *Food & Wine* magazine as one of the top twenty-five restaurants in America in 1992. Built in the 1860s, the structure was originally a stagecoach stop that offered room and board for seventy-five cents a night.

Now Fondulas strives to create dishes that are regional classics in a setting that combines what he considers to be the important dining elements. "The guest must be enveloped by your idea and feel a part of it," he believes. "There must be a complete balance of all of the elements: food, wine, service, and ambiance."

Still a part-time fiction writer, Fondulas finds that his culinary style and his literary style have a great deal in common. Both are "an amalgam of everything you've done, your mood, who you are that day," he says. In such signature dishes as Halibut and Lobster with Vanilla and Sweet Corn, and Pheasant and Polenta, Fondulas notes that "classical elements underpin a movement to combine what is in front of you: your culture and the products that surround you." Balance is paramount to Fondulas, and he considers it "the single unifying element in my style: balance of ingredients, space, flavor, culture, ideologies."

This fusion of a number of different elements is evident in Fondulas's life philosophy as well: "I believe it is impossible to be a restaurateur unless it permeates, for better or worse, your life. It is a way of life—that is the point, the attraction."

Herb-infused Pheasants au Jus

Christopher Capstick, Old Inn on the Green
Marlborough, Massachusetts

Serves 6

This recipe enhances the subtle flavor of pheasant with herbs and a creamy mousse, and the simple sauce of reduced stock reinforces the flavor.

Pheasants and stock

3 pheasants, 2½ to 3 pounds each
2 tablespoons olive oil
1 onion, cut into ½-inch dice
1 carrot, peeled and cut into ½-inch dice
1 celery stalk, cut into ½-inch dice
2 bay leaves
Salt to taste
½ teaspoon black peppercorns
Fresh parsley stems
1 fresh thyme sprig

Stuffing

6 garlic cloves, minced
Leaves from 6 fresh thyme sprigs, minced
Leaves from 3 fresh rosemary sprigs, minced
1 tablespoon grated orange zest
1 tablespoon grated lemon zest

Mousse

6 pheasant breast tenderloins from pheasants, above
½ cup heavy (whipping) cream
2 egg whites
Salt and freshly ground black pepper to taste
1 teaspoon minced fresh thyme

2 tablespoons olive oil

To make the pheasants: Rinse the pheasants, pat them dry with paper towels, and remove any excess fat. With a sharp knife, cut along the breastbone to remove the breasts. Pull the tenderloins away from the breasts and reserve for the mousse. Pull each leg away from the body of each pheasant, slice through the skin to expose the socket, then press down on the leg to cut around the socket and remove the leg with the thigh meat intact; the leg meat should remain with the thigh and only the bone be removed. Cover and refrigerate.

Preheat the oven to 400°F. Place the pheasant carcasses in a roasting pan and roast in the preheated oven for 15 to 20 minutes, or until brown. Heat the olive oil in a large Dutch oven or heavy pot and sauté the onions, carrots, and celery for 8 to 10 minutes, or until

lightly browned. Remove the pheasant bones from the oven and add them to the pot with the vegetables. Add water to cover, along with the bay leaves, salt, peppercorns, parsley stems, and thyme. Bring to a boil over high heat, then reduce heat and simmer for 2 hours, skimming the foam from the top of the pot regularly.

To make the stuffing: Mince the garlic and the herbs and combine them with the zests. Insert your fingers underneath the skin of each pheasant breast to loosen it while keeping the sides intact. Stuff 1 tablespoon of the herb mixture between the skin and the breast. Pat the skin back down, distributing the herb mixture evenly, and set the breasts aside.

To make the mousse: Place the pheasant tenderloins in a blender or food processor, and puree for about 20 seconds, or until smooth. Add the cream and egg whites, then pulse several times until incorporated. Do not over-process or the cream will separate. Scrape the mixture into a medium bowl.

Season the mousse with salt and pepper and add the minced thyme. Spoon the mixture into the deboned thighs and secure with toothpicks to close. Season the breasts and thighs with salt and pepper on both sides.

To serve: Heat the 2 tablespoons olive oil in a medium sauté pan or skillet. Add the breasts and thighs and sauté for 5 to 7 minutes, or until the skin is crisp and brown. Remove the pheasant pieces to a roasting pan, turn them once, and roast for 10 to 15 minutes, or until just slightly rare. Slice the breasts and thighs and arrange on plates. Nap with the reduced stock and serve.

***Note:** The stock may be made up to 2 days in advance and refrigerated, tightly covered.*

Herb-infused Pheasants au Jus; Christopher Capstick, The Old Inn on the Green, New Marlborough, Massachusetts

Blackie's Prime Rib; Alden "Binet" Lanier, Blackie's House of Beef, Washington, D.C.

Blackie's Prime Rib

Alden "Binet" Lanier, Blackie's
House of Beef
Washington, D.C.

Serves 6 to 8

Blackie's has been part of the Washington restaurant scene for decades, and prime rib is one of the popular options at this steakhouse. The pickling spice adds the subtle flavor of a variety of herbs and spices to the meat.

One 12-pound standing rib roast,
   with the fat cap left on
2 quarts beef stock (see page 21)
1 cup pickling spice
1 tablespoon cracked black pepper
1 tablespoon garlic powder
1 tablespoon salt
2 yellow onions, thinly sliced

Preheat the oven to 450°F. Pull back the fat cap from the roast and brush the meat all over with some of the stock. Coat the meat all over with half of the pickling spice and rub it in. Combine the black pepper and garlic powder with the salt, then divide this mixture in half and sprinkle half of it over the meat. Leave the onions in whole rings and layer them over the meat. Return the fat cap to its original place. Tie the roast back together with kitchen twine at 2-inch intervals.

Place the meat in a large, deep roasting pan. Pour the remaining stock into the pan. Season the outside of the meat with the remaining pickling spice and remaining spice-salt mixture, then roast for 30 minutes. Reduce the oven temperature to 350°F and cook an additional 2½ hours for rare, or longer if you prefer. Remove the meat from the oven and let sit in a warm place for 20 minutes before slicing. Slice the roast, discarding the fat cap, and serve.

Karsky Shashlik Supreme

Paul Ingenito, The Russian Tea Room
New York, New York

Serves 4

This marinated and grilled lamb is the centerpiece for an elaborate presentation at the Russian Tea Room, but it is just as delicious with a simple tossed salad and a crusty loaf of bread. All of the accom-

paniments are found in the Little Touches chapter because they may be used with a variety of other main dishes.

1 boneless loin of lamb or boned leg,
   about 2 pounds

Marinade
1 cup peanut oil
1 cup finely chopped onion
2 tablespoons fresh lemon juice
1 tablespoon minced garlic
2 tablespoons minced fresh parsley
1 teaspoon salt
1 teaspoon freshly ground black pepper

Optional Accompaniments
Basmati Rice and Lentil Pilaf (page 155)
Braised Red Cabbage (page 157)
Cucumber and Red Onion Salad
   with Mint Chutney (page 159)
Red Pepper Chutney (page 160)

Trim the lamb of all fat and cut the meat into 4 even pieces. Combine all the ingredients for the marinade in a non-aluminum bowl and mix thoroughly. Place the 4 pieces of lamb loin in the marinade and turn to coat evenly. Cover and refrigerate for 8 hours or overnight, turning occasionally.

Light a fire in a charcoal grill. Drain the lamb, reserving the marinade. Let sit at room temperature while the coals are heating. When the coals are lightly covered with gray ash, grill the lamb uncovered for about 4 to 5 minutes per side for rare, 5 to 7 minutes for medium, and 8 to 10 minutes for well done, basting the lamb with the reserved marinade as it grills. Transfer the lamb to a warm platter and let sit for 10 minutes before carving.

To serve: Slice each section of lamb into 3 pieces and place in a triangular pattern on the plate, surrounding the slices with the desired accompaniments.

Note: *The lamb may marinate for up to 24 hours before grilling, and once grilled it may be served at room temperature as well as warm.*

Lamb Stew with Spring Vegetables
Navarin d'Agneau Printanier

*Alain Sailhac, The French
   Culinary Institute
New York, New York*

Serves 6

A classic of French cooking, simple lamb stew is a meal in itself with a tossed green salad and some crusty bread. This version is flavorful with herbs and garlic, and sautéing the vegetables separately rather than cooking them with the meat keeps them brightly colored.

Stew

½ cup olive oil
2½ pounds boneless lamb shanks or lamb stew meat, trimmed of fat and cut into 1-inch chunks
1 large onion, peeled and diced
2 carrots, peeled and diced
Cloves from 1 whole garlic head, minced
4 celery stalks, trimmed and cut into ¼-inch dice
Salt and freshly ground black pepper
3 tablespoons tomato paste
4 fresh parsley sprigs
1 fresh thyme sprig
1 bay leaf
1 bottle dry white wine
4 large tomatoes, peeled, seeded and cut into ½-inch chunks (see page 18)
2 cups lamb stock, or veal stock (see page 21), or water

Vegetables

3 carrots, tournéed (see page 18) or peeled and cut into ½-inch chunks
3 turnips, tournéed or peeled and cut into ½-inch chunks
1 pound unpeeled pearl onions (frozen onions may be substituted)
½ cup (1 stick) unsalted butter
1 pound whole mushrooms
4 small red potatoes, tournéed or peeled and cut into quarters
8 ounces fresh peas, or one 10½-ounce package thawed frozen baby peas
4 ounces haricots verts or baby green beans, or green beans cut in half lengthwise
2 tablespoons minced fresh parsley

To make the stew: Heat the olive oil in a large Dutch oven over high heat. Add the lamb chunks, being careful not to crowd the pan; this may have to be done in batches. Brown the lamb on all sides, remove it from the pan with a slotted spoon, and set aside.

Drain the fat from the pan. Lower heat to medium and add the onion. Cook for 3 minutes, or until golden, stirring frequently. Add the carrots, garlic, celery, salt, and pepper. Cook over low heat, stirring frequently, for 5 minutes. Add the tomato paste, parsley, thyme, and bay leaf, and stir for 1 minute. Remove the vegetables from the pan with a slotted spoon and set aside along with the lamb.

Increase the heat to high and pour the white wine into the pan a little at a time while stirring to scrape the brown bits from the bottom of the pan. Cook until the liquid has reduced to about 3 cups. Return the meat and the vegetables to the pan and add the fresh tomato chunks and stock or water. Cover the pan and

Lamb Stew with Spring Vegetables; Alain Sailhac, French Culinary Institute, New York

bring to a boil over medium heat. Reduce heat to low and cook for 1½ hours, or until the lamb is tender.

To prepare the vegetables: Bring lightly salted water to a boil in a large saucepan. Add the carrots and turnips, and boil for 4 minutes. Remove the vegetables with a slotted spoon and immediately place them in a bowl of ice water to stop the cooking. Add the pearl onions to the pan and boil for 2 minutes (1 minute for thawed frozen onions). Remove them from the pan with a slotted spoon and place them in another bowl of ice water. Trim the root end and pop the pearl onions out of their skins. Set aside.

In a small saucepan, cover the potatoes with lightly salted cold water and bring to a boil over high heat. Boil the potatoes until tender, about 20 minutes, then drain them and set aside. In another small saucepan, bring lightly salted water to a boil and boil the peas for 2 minutes, or just until they turn bright green. Remove the peas from the pan with a slotted spoon and add them to the ice water. Boil the green beans for 3 minutes and cool at once in the same manner. Set aside.

Remove the lamb from the pan to a bowl and keep it warm. Skim as much fat as possible from the top of the liquid with a spoon, then cook the liquid over high heat for 15 minutes. Strain the reduced liquid through a fine-meshed sieve, pressing the vegetables with the back of a spoon against the sides to extract as much liquid as possible. Melt the butter in a 12-inch sauté pan or skillet over medium heat. Add the carrots, turnips, and onions. Sauté the vegetables for 3 minutes, or until tender, then add the mushrooms and cook for another 5 minutes.

Add the lamb to the pan liquid, then mix in the sautéed vegetables. To serve, spoon the lamb stew on plates, then top with the blanched peas, green beans, diced tomatoes, and parsley.

Note: The stew part of the recipe may be completed up to 2 days in advance.

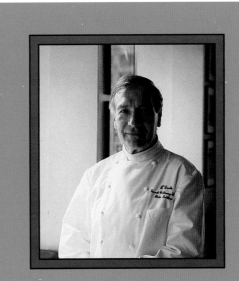

ALAIN SAILHAC
French Culinary Institute, New York, New York

Julia Child once noted that "Anyone who aspires to be a serious cook, in my opinion, needs a thorough training in modern French classical techniques." Serious cooks in training flock to New York's French Culinary Institute. Alain Sailhac, more patriarch than dean, oversees each stage of their studies.

"I have a very special relationship with each student," says Sailhac. "Like a father I shape them from beginning to end, rigorously interviewing each applicant, teaching them, and upon graduation, placing them in jobs. It is that which makes me proud."

Sailhac demands as much as he gives. "You must be willing to give more than 100 percent to succeed in this program," he tells his students. "You have to put your whole physical and mental spirit into your work." His charges must be listening, for some of them are found in today's most highly esteemed kitchens both nationwide and abroad.

Sailhac began his culinary studies at age fifteen when, six days a week, he would bicycle at dawn to a restaurant in his hometown of Millau to clean the kitchen floor and shovel the coal for the oven fires. He would then work in the kitchen until 11 P.M.

The journey from stoking the kitchen fire to stoking the creative fires of tomorrow's chefs has been a forty-year international journey. From his hometown in Millau, France, Sailhac went to Paris, where but for two years of military service and a brief sojourn at the Normandy Hotel, he spent the better part of twenty years.

Sailhac then went to work on the Greek islands of Corfu and Rhodes, and on Guadeloupe in the Caribbean. His travels as a chef took him to New York where, in 1965, he became the sous-chef at the Plaza Hotel.

His fame comes primarily from his work in New York. He was *chef de cuisine* at Le Cygne in the mid-1970s, and executive chef at Le Cirque as it gained international fame from 1978 until 1987. Under Sailhac's direction at the French Culinary Institute, one may sample modern French classical favorites such as Onion Soup, Apple Charlotte, and Lamb Stew with Spring Vegetables.

Sailhac's career has spanned four decades, the larger part of the Western world, and some of the most important restaurants of the twentieth century. Still, his greatest contribution may be yet to come, when his students themselves become teachers.

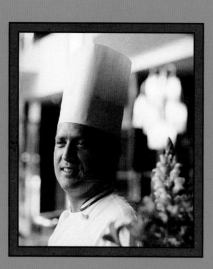

R. Scott Williams
Americus at the Sheraton Washington, Washington, D.C.

In Washington, D.C., even a chef can find himself involved in complex negotiations affecting many people. In 1992, Scott Williams found himself serving a grilled main-course lunch salad to fifteen hundred visiting chefs, perhaps one of the largest juries of one's peers ever assembled and fed. Such is the fate of the restaurant chef at Americus Restaurant in the Sheraton Washington, one of the capital city's largest convention hotels.

Fortunately, Williams is accustomed to large numbers. His inspiration to pursue a culinary career came from helping his mother prepare meals for their family of ten. During those years, Williams says, he learned "to eat fast." One of his favorite foods to inhale was chipped beef with mushrooms and peas on toast or a biscuit.

Today Williams' list of favorite foods has grown, and he believes in the importance of color, texture, and presentation as well as taste. He explains his goal is "infusing flavors together without masking the foundation" and serving them in "creative, modern plate presentations."

An example of his innovative cuisine is a side dish simply called Mixed Grains. It includes barley, green and white basami guineo—a prehistoric grain used mainly in South America—and white and wild rice tossed with dried cherries and fresh thyme. This dish illustrates why Williams calls his style "distinctive original cuisine."

A complete meal at Americus might include Mixed Grains with Pennsylvania-raised Rack of Lamb with Persimmon Chutney; Grilled Portobello Mushrooms with Glazed Chèvre and Mascarpone Cheese; and Tossed Seasonal and Bitter Greens with Raspberry-Walnut Vinaigrette.

Born and raised in Columbus, Ohio, Williams studied in New Hampshire and Maine. He has won many awards, including the 1990–91 award from Chefs in America as well as numerous first-place awards at the annual Culinary Salon.

When Williams goes home to Ohio, he doesn't prepare any elaborate salads. His mother cooks his old favorite, chipped beef, and since his siblings are grown and there is no party of fifteen hundred waiting to be fed, he can eat slowly and savor the past.

Rack of Lamb with Persimmon Chutney and Peanut Crust

R. Scott Williams, Americus at the Sheraton Washington Washington D.C.

Serves 4

Rack of lamb is perfect for an elegant dinner party. This version adds an Indonesian accent with a coating of chutney and peanut, sweet and spicy flavors that pair well with rich, rosy lamb.

2 racks of lamb, Frenched (see page 16)
Salt and freshly ground pepper to taste

Lamb Stock
4 pounds lamb bones and trimmings
3 quarts cold water
1 onion, chopped
1 carrot, peeled and chopped
1 celery stalk, chopped
5 tablespoons tomato paste
¼ cup red Burgundy wine
½ garlic clove, minced
½ bay leaf
¼ teaspoon dried thyme
¼ teaspoon whole black peppercorns
3 whole cloves
2 fresh parsley stems

Lamb Sauce
¼ cup olive oil
1 pound lamb scraps,
  trimmed of excess fat
½ cup coarsely chopped peeled carrot
¼ cup coarsely chopped onion
¼ cup coarsely chopped celery
½ cup red Burgundy wine
4 cups lamb stock, above
Leaves from ½ bunch fresh thyme,
  minced
1 fresh rosemary sprig
Salt and freshly ground white pepper
  to taste

Persimmon Chutney
2 ripe Hachiya persimmons
1⅓ cups Major Grey's chutney, pureed
¾ cup fresh peach puree
½ cup coarsely stone-ground mustard

Peanut Crust

2 tablespoons roasted peanuts,
  finely chopped
2 tablespoons minced fresh parsley
6 tablespoons fresh bread crumbs
Salt and freshly ground pepper to taste

Marinade

½ cup vegetable oil
2 garlic cloves, minced
1 shallot, minced
2 teaspoons minced fresh rosemary
2 teaspoons freshly ground black pepper

The day before serving the dish, season the lamb racks with salt and pepper, cover, and refrigerate until needed, then make the stock.

To make the stock: Preheat the oven to 375°F. Place the lamb bones and trimmings in a large shallow roasting pan and bake in the preheated oven, turning them occasionally, for 30 minutes, or until evenly browned. Transfer the bones and trimmings to a large stockpot, reserving the roasting pan. Add the water to the stockpot and bring to a boil over high heat. Reduce heat to a simmer and skim the scum that rises to the surface for the first 10 to 15 minutes. Simmer for 3 hours, uncovered.

While the bones are simmering, place the roasting pan over medium-high heat and add the onion, carrot, celery, and tomato paste. Cook the vegetables, stirring occasionally, until they are golden and caramelized, about 8 to 10 minutes. When the vegetables are browned, add the wine to the pan and cook, stirring to scrape up the browned bits from the bottom of the pan; set aside. When the bones have simmered for 3 hours, add the browned vegetables and the remaining stock ingredients to the stockpot. Pour the water into the stockpot and continue to simmer for an additional 3 hours. Remove the stock from heat and strain through a fine-meshed sieve. Chill well, then discard the layer of fat that has congealed on the top.

To make the lamb sauce: Heat the olive oil in a deep, heavy pot and sauté the lamb scraps until brown, about 7 to 9 minutes. Add the carrot, onion, and celery, and cook until golden, about 5 to 7 minutes. When the vegetables are cooked, add the Burgundy and stir to scrape up the browned bits from the bottom of the pan. Add the lamb stock, thyme, and rosemary. Simmer uncovered until reduced by half, about 1½ to 2 hours. Add salt and pepper, strain, cover, and refrigerate.

The next day, make the persimmon chutney: Puree all the chutney ingredients in blender or food processor until smooth, about 30 seconds. Strain through a fine-meshed sieve and set aside.

To make the peanut crust: Combine all the ingredients and set aside.

Preheat the oven to 400°F. Combine all the ingredients for the marinade in a shallow pan and mix well. Add the lamb racks, coating them well with the marinade, and marinate at room temperature for 10 to 15 minutes. Remove the racks of lamb from the marinade and sear them on a grill over hot coals, or in a heavy sauté pan or skillet, for 2 minutes on the first side, then 1 minute on the other side. Take the lamb from the grill or pan and coat both racks with the persimmon chutney mixture. Dust the chutney coating with the peanut crust and transfer to a shallow roasting pan.

Roast the lamb in the preheated oven for 18 minutes for rare, 22 minutes for medium rare, and 28 to 30 minutes for medium. While the lamb is cooking, reheat the sauce in a small saucepan and adjust the seasoning. To serve, slice the lamb racks into four 4-bone portions and serve on a pool of the lamb sauce.

Note: The stock and sauce may be made up to 3 days in advance and refrigerated, or they may be frozen for up to 3 months.

Rack of Lamb with Persimmon Chutney and Peanut Crust; R. Scott Williams, Americus at the Sheraton Washington, Washington, D.C.

Smoked Roasted Capon Breasts with Sweet-Potato Fries

Jeff Buben, Vidalia
Washington, D.C.

Serves 6 to 8

The smoky flavor of hickory or apple wood enhances the marinated capon, and the roasted tomato sauce and vegetable garnishes add color and textural interest to the plate. Breasts from roasting chickens, which are far easier to locate than capon breasts, work equally well in this dish.

Capon

4 capon breasts, about 12 ounces each
⅔ cup red wine vinegar
⅓ cup olive oil
2 fresh thyme sprigs
Cracked black pepper to taste
Salt to taste

Sauce

6 tomatoes, peeled, seeded, and diced (see page 18)
3 garlic cloves, minced
½ tablespoon minced fresh sage
1 shallot, minced
2 tablespoons olive oil
6 tablespoons veal stock (see page 21) or chicken stock (see page 20)
Salt and freshly ground black pepper to taste

1 cup hickory or apple wood chips
4 ounces (about 8 thin slices) bacon, cut into ⅛-inch-wide strips
1 shallot, minced
1 pound Swiss chard, coarsely chopped
2 tablespoons veal stock (see page 21) or chicken stock (see page 20)
Salt and freshly ground pepper to taste

1 pound sweet potatoes
2 tablespoons unsalted butter
8 ounces shiitake mushrooms, stemmed
1 teaspoon minced fresh thyme
1 tablespoon olive oil
Vegetable oil for frying
½ tablespoon minced fresh sage

Place the first 6 ingredients in a shallow non-aluminum bowl and marinate at room temperature for 1 hour.

To make the sauce: Preheat the oven to 375°F. Combine the tomatoes, garlic, sage, shallot, and the oil in a heavy roasting pan and roast in the preheated oven for 20 minutes, or until lightly charred. Puree in a blender or food processor with the stock. Season with salt and pepper, and keep warm.

Light a fire in a charcoal grill and place the wood chips in water to cover. Drain the wood chips and sprinkle them over the hot coals. When the coals are lightly covered with gray ash, bank the coals to one side of the grill. Remove the capon breasts from the marinade and place them on the opposite side of the cooking rack from the coals. Partially close the vents in the lid of the grill, cover the grill, and smoke the capon for 20 minutes.

When the capon is almost done, place the bacon in a medium sauté pan or skillet and cook over medium-high heat until the bacon is crisp. Add the remaining shallots and the chopped Swiss chard, and sauté for 1 minute. Add the veal stock, salt, and pepper, and cook until wilted. Set aside.

Smoked Roasted Capon Breasts with Sweet-Potato Fries; Jeffrey Buben, Vidalia, Washington, D.C.

While the capon is smoking, cut the sweet potatoes in half, square off the sides, and cut into ¼-inch-thick slices. Cut again lengthwise into fries. Transfer the potatoes to a saucepan, cover with cold water, and bring to a boil. Boil for 7 minutes, or until tender. Drain and set aside.

In a small sauté pan or skillet, melt the butter over high heat and quickly sauté the shiitake mushrooms. Sprinkle with the thyme, olive oil, and salt and pepper. Set the mushrooms aside and keep them warm.

Transfer the capon breasts from the grill to a shallow roasting pan and place in the preheated oven to cook for 8 to 10 minutes, or until the juices run clear. Let sit for 10 minutes before carving.

Place the oil in a medium saucepan to a depth of 2 inches and heat to 375°F, or when a cube of bread browns in 10 seconds. Fry the sweet potato fries until golden brown, about 1 to 2 minutes. Drain the fries on paper towels, season them with salt and pepper to taste, and keep warm.

To assemble the dish: Add the remaining sage to the sauce and reheat, if necessary. Spoon the warm tomato sauce on the plate. Slice the capon breasts at an angle, and fan the slices out on the tomato sauce. Arrange the wilted Swiss chard, sweet-potato fries, and shiitake mushrooms around the capon.

Note: The sauce may be prepared up to 2 days in advance and refrigerated, tightly closed. All remaining components of this dish should not be done more than 4 hours in advance.

JEFFREY BUBEN
Vidalia, Washington, D.C.

With its country-manor motif and its dishes that draw on foods from the nearby Chesapeake Bay and surrounding Virginia farmlands, Vidalia has been an oasis for Washington, D.C., natives and an instant success for Jeffrey Buben since it opened in 1993.

Named for the sweet onion that is native to Georgia, Vidalia is "purely American," says Buben. American regional folk art adorns the ledges, antique sideboards, and cupboards of the restaurant, and local artists are invited to showcase their talents on Vidalia's walls.

Buben has worked in several formidable restaurants in the Washington area, including Aux Beau Champs in the Four Seasons Hotel. As *chef de cuisine,* he also developed the award-winning concept for Nicholas, a restaurant in the historic Mayflower Hotel. For six years prior to the opening of Vidalia, Buben worked as executive chef for the Occidental Restaurant and Grill in Washington.

Buben runs Vidalia with his wife and restaurant manager Sallie, who previously worked at Mark Miller's Red Sage. He continues to perfect such signature dishes as Baked Vidalia Onion, and Shrimp with Creamed Grits and Thyme Sauce. A graduate of the Culinary Institute of America, Buben was attracted to the culinary profession because "it didn't seem like a job at all, so it fit well," he says.

Deemed "a wondrous homage to Southern food and comfort" by the *Washington Times,* Vidalia's charm derives both from its decor, which includes classic bric-a-brac and collectibles, and from such culinary surprises as Smoked Roasted Capon Breasts with Sweet-Potato Fries.

With his farm-raised turkey from Virginia, Vidalia onions from Georgia, and oysters, crabs, and rockfish from the Chesapeake Bay, Buben has created a classic dining experience for his patrons. "It is a warm and comfortable place that evolves with the seasons," he says.

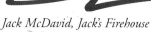

Capon with Rosemary

Jack McDavid, Jack's Firehouse
Philadelphia, Pennsylvania

Serves 2 to 4

Aromatic rosemary and rich foie gras are a secret surprise awaiting guests as they cut into the brown and tender capon breasts. This is an easy dish to prepare, and roasting-chicken breasts may be substituted for the capon breasts.

Two 12-ounce capon breast halves,
   boned but unskinned
Salt and freshly ground black pepper
   to taste
2 fresh rosemary sprigs
Two 3-ounce slices fresh foie gras,
   trimmed and soaked (see page 13)
3 tablespoons olive oil
1 pound fresh asparagus, trimmed
1 red bell pepper, seeded, deribbed, and
   cut into ½-inch strips
1 cup capon or chicken stock
   (see page 20)

Preheat the oven to 500°F. Make a slit almost all the way through each capon breast to form a deep pocket, then turn the top half of the meat over without detaching it from the bottom layer. Sprinkle each breast lightly with salt and pepper.

Pull the leaves off both rosemary sprigs, discard the stems, and divide the leaves between the inside of each capon breast. Slice the foie gras into ½-inch-thick slices and lay the slices down the middle of the capon breast. Reshape the breasts by folding them over the foie gras and press the edges together to seal.

Heat 2 tablespoons of the olive oil in a large ovenproof sauté pan or skillet over high heat. When the oil is beginning to smoke, place the capon breasts in the pan, skin-side down, and sear for 2 to 3 minutes, or until the capon is golden brown. Turn the breasts over and place in the preheated oven for 20 minutes, or until both sides are golden and the breasts are opaque throughout.

JACK McDAVID
Jack's Firehouse, Philadelphia, Pennsylvania

The name's Jack. Not John, not Jacques, not anything fancy—chef Jack McDavid is a guy who looks like a Jack in his overalls and a baseball cap. Chef-owner of Jack's Firehouse in Philadelphia, McDavid is a butcher, a baker, a farmer, and a cook.

He is what one would call, of course, a Jack of all trades. McDavid hails from Virginia, and it was there he learned the tenets of raccoon stew and "pork pull," a sandwich piled high with spicy shredded pork, and how to use "the whole deer from toes to tail."

He may not have converted everyone in Philadelphia into toes-to-tail eaters, but he has convinced them that down-home haute is the way to eat.

McDavid is committed to local farms: "We've invested in greenhouses. We've invested in farms. I've signed contracts guaranteeing to buy a farmer's crop for the next five years… People say, 'How can you afford to do it?' I say, 'How can I afford not to?'"

The chef's investment in ingredients convinces farmers to raise produce and cattle organically. When you're at Jack's Firehouse you can be sure that the meat and vegetables in such dishes as Lancaster Mixed Greens, or Roasted Eggplant and Peppers with Cheese and Smoked Ham, have been raised without artificial hormones or pesticides. Signature dishes include his Capon with Rosemary, and his Black Bear with Coca-Cola–Lime Sauce. The bear for this dish is raised on a South Dakota game farm.

It's not just organic ingredients that matter to this chef, it's also the environment. At Jack's Firehouse, everything is recycled, and the uneaten food is sent to pig farmers in Lancaster County.

But there isn't much food left uneaten. McDavid was named one of the Top Ten Chefs in 1991 by *Food & Wine* magazine. Jack's Firehouse was named one of the best new restaurants in the country by *Esquire.*

McDavid's entrees may seem outrageous, but his goal is to stir things up in the culinary world, and to educate the American palate, convincing his customers to take some risks and try something new. Among his many specialities are such foods as squirrel, possum, spearing, bear, hog jowls, chinquapins, spelt, and rattlesnake. That's "down-home haute," and that's Jack.

While the capon is cooking, arrange the asparagus in a flat layer on a baking sheet. Place the red peppers in a parallel layer over the asparagus. Season the vegetables with salt and pepper, and drizzle with the remaining 1 tablespoon oil. Roast in the oven for 5 minutes, or until lightly toasted.

Remove the capon breasts from the oven and transfer to heated serving plates. Arrange asparagus and peppers around each breast. Return the pan used to cook the capon to high heat. When the oil begins to sizzle, add the stock and cook to reduce until it is syrupy, stirring to scrape up the browned bits from the bottom of the pan. Pour this sauce over the meat and serve.

Note: *The capon breasts may be prepared for cooking up to 6 hours in advance and refrigerated, tightly covered.*

Black Bear with Coca-Cola–Lime Sauce

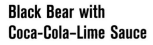

*Jack McDavid, Jack's Firehouse
Philadelphia, Pennsylvania*

Serves 6

In all honesty, this was one of the last recipes tested because of its title. The intensely flavored sweet and sour sauce

Capon with Rosemary; Jack McDavid, Jack's Firehouse, Philadelphia

turned out to be the perfect complement to the rich taste of the meat. The sauce is also excellent with sautéed beef steak.

4 large parsnips (about 8 ounces), peeled and cut into ¼-inch julienne
Freshly ground black pepper to taste
8 tablespoons olive oil, divided
2 cups beef stock (see page 21)
1 top round of black bear, about 2½ to 3 pounds, silver skin removed (see page 17)
All-purpose flour for dredging
Juice and julienned zest of 2 limes
One 12-ounce can Coca-Cola
6 cups stemmed fresh spinach
Salt to taste

Preheat the oven to 500°F. Lay the parsnips on a baking sheet in a single layer and sprinkle with pepper. Drizzle

with 2 tablespoons of the olive oil and bake in the preheated oven for 12 to 14 minutes, or until golden brown.

While the parsnips are roasting, boil the stock in a small saucepan over high heat until it is reduced by half; set aside. Slice the top round into six 1-inch-thick steaks. Dredge the meat lightly in flour and set aside.

Place a large cast-iron skillet over very high heat and add 3 tablespoons of the olive oil. When the oil is hot, sear the steaks for 4 to 6 minutes on each side. Remove the steaks to warmed serving plates. Add the lime juice, lime zest, and the Coca-Cola to the pan and boil for 3 minutes, stirring to scrape up the browned bits from the bottom of the pan. Add the reduced stock, stirring to combine. Turn up the heat as high as possible and cook to reduce the liquid to ½ cup. Set aside and keep warm.

Place a medium sauté pan over high heat and add the remaining 3 table-spoons olive oil. Add the spinach and cook, stirring constantly, until it is wilted, about 1 minute. Season with salt and pepper.

To serve: Place 1 steak on each plate. Mound some of the spinach at the base of each steak and arrange toasted parsnips across the center of each plate in a band. Pour the warm sauce over the meat and serve.

Note: *Carrots may be substituted for parsnips.*

Black Bear with Coca-Cola-Lime Sauce; Jack McDavid, Jack's Firehouse, Philadelphia

Baby Rack of Lamb with French-fried Shepherd's Pies

David Burke, Park Avenue Cafe
New York, New York

Serves 4

In this delicious pairing of lamb dishes, a simple rack is complemented by shepherd's pies baked inside a ring of French-fried potatoes. The pies are not easy to make, however, and the method given below comes after much experimentation, since few home cooks have the commercial fryer used by the chef.

4 small lamb racks, Frenched
  (see page 16)
Salt and freshly ground black pepper
  to taste

Shepherd's Pie
12 ounces ground lamb
6 slices (4 ounces) bacon,
  cut into ½-inch dice
2 teaspoons minced fresh rosemary
1 teaspoon salt
½ teaspoon freshly ground pepper
½ teaspoon ground cumin
4 cups vegetable oil for frying
6 large Idaho potatoes, peeled and
  cut into 3-inch-long,
  ¼-inch-thick square fries

Whipped Potatoes
2 large boiling potatoes, peeled and
  cut into 1-inch cubes
½ cup milk, heated to boiling
4 tablespoons unsalted butter
Salt and freshly ground black pepper
  to taste

Garnish
1 carrot, peeled and cut into ¼-inch dice
2 celery stalks, cut into ¼-inch dice
8 pearl onions (thawed frozen onions
  may be used)
½ cup fresh or thawed frozen peas
2 tablespoons unsalted butter
Salt and freshly ground black pepper
  to taste

Season the lamb racks with salt and pepper and set aside.

To make the shepherd's pies: Combine the ground lamb with the bacon, rosemary, salt, pepper, and cumin in a medium bowl and set aside.

Place the oil in a deep, heavy pot or deep-fryer and heat over medium heat until the oil reaches 325°F. Cook the French fries in batches for 60 to 90 seconds, or until lightly colored. Remove the potatoes from the oil with a slotted spoon and drain them on paper towels.

Spray the inside of four 3-inch-diameter, 2½-inch-deep ring molds with vegetable oil spray or rub them with butter. Line the French fries vertically along the inside of the ring mold until they are firmly packed along the inside perimeter. The tops of the French fries should rise about 1 inch above the top of the ring mold, and the fries should fit too snugly to move. Divide the reserved ground lamb mixture among the 4 molds. Firmly pack the meat into the bottom of each mold. Cut any leftover French fries into cubes and pack them into the underside of the mold to protect the meat from overcooking on the bottom. If you don't have ring molds, tie the potatoes with 2 rounds of twine, one near the top of the potatoes and one at the bottom.

Baby Rack of Lamb with French-fried Shepherd's Pie; David Burke, Park Avenue Cafe, New York

Preheat the oven to 425°F. Place the 4 rings and the racks of lamb in a foil-lined roasting pan in the preheated oven and bake for 30 to 40 minutes for medium rare.

While the lamb is cooking, make the whipped potatoes: Pour 6 inches of cold water into a medium saucepan, lightly salt the water, and add the potatoes. Bring the pan to a boil, uncovered, and cook the potatoes until tender, about 20 to 30 minutes. Drain the potatoes. While the potatoes are still hot, push them through a ricer or a food mill. Add the hot milk and the butter to the potatoes and beat until combined. Season with salt and pepper. Set aside and keep warm.

To make the garnish: While the potatoes are cooking, bring another pot of lightly salted water to a boil. Add the diced carrots and cook for 3 to 4 minutes, or until tender. Remove the carrots from the water with a slotted spoon and add the celery. Cook the celery for 2 to 3 minutes, or until tender, then drain in the same way. Add the pearl onions and cook for 3 to 4 minutes, adding the peas 2 minutes into the cooking time. Drain all the vegetables well. Slip the peels from the onions. Melt the butter in a small sauté pan or skillet over medium heat. Add all the blanched vegetables and cook for 2 minutes to glaze them with the butter. Season with salt and pepper.

Remove the lamb and molds from the oven and let sit for 10 minutes before carving the lamb. Unmold or untie the pies. Transfer the whipped potatoes to a pastry bag fitted with a large round tip. Pipe the whipped potatoes over the top of the lamb layer of the pies, top with the vegetable garnish, and serve.

Note: *The ground lamb mixture may be prepared 1 day in advance and refrigerated, tightly covered. The remainder of the dish must be done just before serving.*

DAVID BURKE
Park Avenue Cafe, New York, New York

Ingenious is the word for David Burke, executive chef of New York's Park Avenue Cafe. One day, Burke noticed that the collarbone of the whole trout looked like a miniature veal chop. After some research, he discovered that on each side of a swordfish the same cut was as large as a veal chop. And thus the Swordfish Chop became a trademark dish of the Park Avenue Cafe.

Burke was also one of the first chefs to use flavored oils such as basil oil, curry oil, and lemongrass oil. Spice mixes also intrigue him, and he predicts that Americans will gradually use more and more diverse spices, such as cumin and cardamom.

Burke worked in restaurants during his teenage years and graduated from the Culinary Institute of America. He furthered his experience in restaurants in Burgundy and southwest France, and as the personal chef to a shipping tycoon in Norway, and he served under such well-known chefs as Marc Meaneau and Georges Blanc. He also studied pastry arts at the prestigious Ecole Lenôtre.

Later, Burke served for a time as sous-chef, then returned to become executive chef of Brooklyn's River Cafe, also the launching spot for Larry Forgione.

In 1992, Burke developed a menu of hearty American food for the Park Avenue Cafe, where he manages the kitchen. So confident and relaxed is he that the restaurant has a glassed-in table (No. 88) in the middle of the kitchen, from which diners can watch the preparation of such dishes as Baby Rack of Lamb with French-fried Shepherd's Pie.

In 1991, Burke was named Chef of the Year by his peers in Chefs in America. He lectures regularly, gives cooking demonstrations nationwide, and is currently writing a cookbook to be published by Alfred A. Knopf.

Bobby Flay, Mesa Grill
New York, New York

Serves 2

Ancho chilies give color as well as flavor to this dish. The combination of pan-frying and baking leaves the hens moist and tender, while the crust is crisp. Bobby Flay serves this dish with Cranberry-Apricot Relish (page 161) and Sweet Potato Gratin (page 160), or on a bed of sautéed leeks, shiitake mushrooms, corn kernels, and wilted spinach.

BOBBY FLAY
Mesa Grill, New York, New York

"My favorite, favorite [restaurant] is Mesa Grill," says *New York* magazine's restaurant critic Gael Greene. "I wake up in the morning longing for a Tuna Tostada and Sweet Potato Gratin." Since restaurant critics are loath to play favorites, this is a ringing endorsement of Mesa Grill and its chef, Bobby Flay.

A Manhattan native who trained at the French Culinary Institute of New York, Flay is now spicing up the city with the flavors of the Southwest. Greene describes the scene at Mesa Grill: "Through the soaring kitchen window, you can watch Flay and team in full frenzy, sprinkling confetti of red pepper and bright green chives, scattering matchsticks of jícama—working from a palette of tastes adventurous eaters have fallen in love with: smoked chilies; the citric edge of tomatillo and lime; the blast of pepper heat cooled by pineapple, mango, and papaya." Flay is easily identifiable by his fiery red hair, which seems to match his devilish obsession with heat and spice.

Despite his classical French training and a Manhattan upbringing, Flay opened this brilliant and original southwestern restaurant at the not-so-seasoned age of twenty-six. After graduating in 1984 from the FCI, Flay was introduced to southwestern cooking by a restaurant owner. From 1988 to 1990, Flay explored his new culinary passion at the Miracle Grill in New York, where he earned something of a cult following.

Since opening Mesa Grill, Flay has been nominated as a Rising Star Chef by the James Beard Foundation both in 1991 and 1992, and Mesa Grill is packed daily. Such entrees as Ancho-rubbed Game Hens, and Smoked and Grilled Pork Loin with Apricot-Serrano Chile Sauce, have been singled out by *Gourmet* magazine. The side dishes, like Napa cabbage, chick-pea polenta, sweet-potato gratin, horseradish potatoes, cilantro-risotto cake, and blue corn tamale, along with a sampling dessert plate, have many a critic gushing praise.

Not content simply to be written about, Flay offers his own contributions to the culinary world. His book, *Bobby Flay's Bold American Food* (Warner Books) was published in 1994. His food magazine articles and columns are extensive. *Cook's Magazine* seeks his expertise in creating homemade chili powders since, according to Flay, "store-bought chili powder is bitter and without much character."

6 dried ancho chilies (see page 11)
8 cups boiling water
2 tablespoons minced garlic
½ teaspoon salt
2 tablespoons minced cilantro
2 cups cornmeal
2 tablespoons curry powder
2 tablespoons ground cumin
Salt and freshly ground black pepper
  to taste
2 Guinea hen or Rock Cornish hen
  breasts, boned and skinned
1 cup olive oil

Preheat the oven to 400°F. Place the ancho chilies in a large bowl, cover them with the boiling water, and soak them for 30 minutes to overnight. Drain the chilies well, then remove and discard the seeds and stems. Place the chilies in a blender or food processor with the garlic, salt, and cilantro. Puree and set aside.

Combine the cornmeal, curry powder, cumin, salt, and pepper and spread in a jelly-roll pan. Spread the hen breasts generously and evenly with the chili puree, then dredge them in the seasoned cornmeal.

Place a large sauté pan or skillet over high heat, add the oil, and heat until it begins to smoke. Add the hen breasts and cook 2 to 3 minutes, or until the topping is crisp. Turn the breasts, cook the other side until crisp, then transfer the breasts to the preheated oven to cook another 5 minutes, or until opaque throughout.

Note: *The same treatment may be used for boneless chicken breasts or thighs. Bake the breasts an additional 10 minutes, and the thighs an additional 15 minutes.*

Ancho-rubbed Game Hens; Bobby Flay, Mesa Grill, New York

Fish and Shellfish Dishes

a myriad of aquatic species are native to the Atlantic Coast or imported into its urban markets, and eastern chefs have created a host of superb ways of cooking them. While home cooks are accustomed to serving fish dishes simply prepared, the recipes in this chapter will make converts of cooks when they realize the stunning results that can be accomplished with little effort.

Since New England represents half the states visited in *Great Chefs of the East,* it is not surprising we've included so many wonderful ways to cook lobster. While Todd English adds a smoky nuance to the prized crustacean's sweet flavor in his Wood-grilled Lobster with Potato Gnocchi and Toasted Walnuts, Lydia Shire creates an ethereally light lobster tempura in her Lobster Crisp in Water Chestnut Flour, which is accompanied with seared tuna and salmon.

Crabs, the first cousins of lobster, are sautéed with aromatic hazelnuts and sparked with lime and cilantro by Patrick O'Connell, while Charles Palmer nests the same delectable soft-shells on creamy polenta cakes that have been sautéed until crisp.

Thick, juicy grilled fish steaks are increasingly popular, and some wonderful recipes with assertive seasonings are included in this chapter. Chris Schlesinger's Grilled Spice-rubbed Swordfish with Indonesian Ketjap is a masterful dish that includes grilled pineapple as a garnish, and Mark Miller's Seared Spicy Tuna with Mole Amarillo may be cooked in a pan or on a grill.

Sautéed Soft-Shell Crabs with Hazelnuts; Patrick O'Connell, The Inn at Little Washington, Washington, Virginia

Sautéed Soft-Shell Crabs with Hazelnuts

*Patrick O'Connell, The Inn at
    Little Washington
Washington, Virginia*

Serves 4

Soft-shell crabs from Chesapeake Bay are a treat because they are entirely edible, shell and all. This recipe complements the sweet flavor of this prized shellfish with aromatic nuts and tart lime.

Mustard Sauce
¼ cup mayonnaise
Juice of 1 lemon
1 tablespoon Dijon mustard
1½ teaspoons dry mustard
Salt and freshly ground black pepper
    to taste

Crabs
2 tablespoons unsalted butter
1 cup all-purpose flour
1 teaspoon salt
½ teaspoon freshly ground black pepper
4 jumbo soft-shell crabs, cleaned
    (see page 13)
½ cup clarified butter (see page 19)
1 tomato, peeled, seeded, and finely
    diced (see page 18)
⅓ cup hazelnuts, peeled and chopped
    (see page 16)
1 tablespoon minced fresh cilantro
Juice of 1 lime

Garnish
1 cup green beans
2 tablespoons olive oil
2 teaspoons white wine vinegar
¼ teaspoon dry mustard
Salt and freshly ground black pepper
    to taste
Lime segments
Fresh cilantro leaves
1 tablespoon minced fresh chives

To make the mustard sauce: In a medium bowl, mix the mayonnaise, lemon juice, Dijon mustard, and dry mustard into a smooth sauce. Season with salt and pepper, cover, and refrigerate.

To prepare the crabs: Preheat the oven to 400°F. Place the butter in a small sauté pan or skillet over medium heat until the butter melts and the milk solids begin to brown and give off a nutty aroma; take care not to let the butter burn. Remove from heat and set aside.

In a pie plate, mix the flour with the salt and pepper. Dredge the dressed crabs in the seasoned flour, shaking off the excess. Heat the clarified butter in a large sauté pan or skillet over high heat. Add the crabs, top-side down, and cook for 2 to 3 minutes, or until the crabs are crusty and brown. Gently turn the crabs with a slotted spatula and cook for 1 minute. Remove the crabs with the slotted spatula and place them in an ovenproof baking dish.

Drain the liquid and remaining butter from the pan and discard. Return the pan to heat and add the browned butter, tomato, hazelnuts, and cilantro. Sauté for 1 minute, pour the mixture over the crabs, and place the crabs in the preheated oven for 3 minutes. Remove the crabs from the oven and drizzle them with the lime juice.

While the crabs are cooking, prepare the green bean garnish: Cook the green beans in boiling water for 2 minutes, drain, and set aside. Mix the oil, vinegar, mustard, salt, and pepper in a small bowl with a table fork.

To serve: Place 1 crab on each plate (reserve the sauce) and place some of the green beans alongside. Drizzle the oil-vinegar mixture over the beans. Garnish the plates with the reserved pan sauce. Drizzle the plates with the mustard sauce, garnish with the lime segments and cilantro leaves, and sprinkle with the chives.

Note: The crabs must be cooked at the last minute; however, the mustard sauce may be prepared 1 day in advance and refrigerated, tightly covered.

PATRICK O'CONNELL
Inn at Little Washington, Washington, Virginia

If Patrick O'Connell had continued on his initial career path and become an actor, it is possible that by now he would have a Tony and an Oscar on his mantel. Instead, he decided to become a chef, and his Inn at Little Washington has garnered just about every award in his field. O'Connell and his partner Reinhardt Lynch orchestrate meals at the Inn so that—as in theater—the audience is totally absorbed in the experience.

The Inn at Little Washington is located about sixty miles from "big" Washington in the foothills of the Shenandoah Mountains. Selected Restaurant of the Year by the James Beard Foundation in 1993, the Inn is one of the few American properties in the prestigious French Relais et Chateaux organization. *The Mobil Travel Guide* awarded the Inn five stars, and Zagat's guide lauded O'Connell's cuisine as the best in the region.

As a drama major at Catholic University in Washington, D.C., O'Connell worked at various eateries, both in the kitchen and as a waiter. After graduation he traveled extensively, trying to decide on a direction for his life. When he returned to Washington, he embarked on a seven-year self-styled apprenticeship in area restaurants and spent a summer at the Culinary Institute of America.

After settling in the Virginia countryside, O'Connell and Lynch began operating a catering business, and soon guests were urging them to cater to the city. Driving back and forth to Washington did not last long, however, and in 1978 they bought an old garage in the tiny hamlet of "little" Washington.

Now the same food distributors who originally were reluctant to drive so far to service the Inn clamor for their business, and local farmers raise produce especially for the restaurant. While O'Connell relies on the basics of French cooking, he is also interested in traditional Virginia dishes as well as in variations on ethnic cuisines. He uses the freshest ingredients in his kitchen, such as local hams, trout, Virginia wild duck, and herbs and garnishes from the gardens of townspeople. Dishes such as Medallions of Veal Shenandoah with Local Wild Morels; Local Asparagus Salad with Toasted Pistachios; and Sautéed Soft-Shell Crabs with Hazelnuts are examples of O'Connell's innovative style.

Desserts, too, are a favorite of O'Connell's. "I want the meal to end on a dramatic note," he says, and even the title of his White Chocolate Mousse in Bed Between Dark Silky Sheets deserves a curtain call.

CHARLES PALMER
Aureole, New York, New York

It was a home economics class in his hometown of Smyrna, New York, that introduced Charles Palmer to the joys of cooking. By the age of sixteen, he was already a pro, becoming head of the kitchen of the Colgate Inn after the Swiss chef abruptly left. Now Palmer is co-owner and chef of Aureole in New York, which has consistently been ranked one of the top twenty-five restaurants in America since its opening in 1988.

Aureole soon earned three stars from the *New York Times,* but the busy schedule following such success did not deter Palmer from fulfilling another dream: opening the Chefs Cuisiniers Club in 1990, now named Alva.

The Club is his personal culinary statement, a result, he says, of years of late nights in the kitchen with few options for his own dining late at night. Palmer and his fellow chefs keep the kitchen open until 2 A.M., and have decorated the dining room with framed menus from their favorite restaurants around the world, as well as a huge mural of famous chefs behind the bar.

Palmer trained at the Culinary Institute of America and then was chosen for a six-month fellowship in the school's classic French Escoffier Room. In 1983, he became executive chef at the River Cafe in Brooklyn, which became famous for innovative American food when Larry Forgione was the chef in the early 1980s. There, Palmer built a smoke-house, became a partner in a duck farm, and set up a network of small farmers who provided 70 percent of the produce and staples needed by the restaurant.

Palmer cites his team of cooks as critical to his restaurants' success. He looks for young chefs with three traits: a strong character, a powerful desire to cook, and an ability to maintain that interest for sixty hours a week.

His food, like Sautéed Soft-Shell Crabs with Polenta, maintains an essential balance and purity while being dramatic in presentation. Palmer is unimpressed by "tricks, gimmickry, or culinary hijinks." He holds fast to his insistence on "fine dining in a relaxed atmosphere, great service, and highly creative food."

Sautéed Soft-Shell Crabs with Polenta

Charles Palmer, Aureole
New York, New York

Serves 4

This easy-to-prepare dish is a wonderful way to enjoy the delicacy of soft-shell crabs. The creamy polenta cakes provide a textural contrast to the crabs and complement their flavor. Serve this with sautéed zucchini or summer squash.

Polenta Cakes
⅔ cup milk
2¾ cup rich chicken stock (see page 20)
Salt and freshly ground white pepper
  to taste
One 13-ounce box instant polenta
¼ cup freshly grated Parmesan cheese
⅓ cup crème fraîche (see page 20)
Flour for dusting

Crabs
8 soft-shell crabs, cleaned (see page 13)
Salt and freshly ground black pepper
  to taste
Flour for dredging
½ cup vegetable oil

½ cup clarified butter (see page 19)

Lemon-Herb Butter
3 tablespoons unsalted butter
Juice of 1 lemon
1 teaspoon minced fresh parsley
½ teaspoon minced fresh chives
½ teaspoon minced fresh tarragon

To make the polenta cakes: Combine the milk, stock, salt, and white pepper in a medium saucepan. Bring the mixture to a boil over high heat and whisk in the polenta. Reduce heat to low and cook, stirring constantly, until the mixture has thickened, about 3 to 4 minutes. Add the cheese and crème fraîche, stirring well to incorporate. Continue cooking for 1 to 2 minutes. Remove the pan from heat and spread the mixture onto a greased baking sheet, smoothing it into an even 1-inch layer with a rubber spatula.

Set aside until the polenta has cooled and hardened. Cut out 8 circles of polenta with a 3-inch round cutter. Dust the circles lightly with flour on both sides and set aside. Pat the crabs dry and season with salt and pepper. Coat the crabs with the flour and set aside.

In a large sauté pan or skillet, heat the oil over medium heat. Place the crabs top-shell down and fry for 2 minutes. While the crabs are cooking, heat the clarified butter in a 10-inch sauté pan or skillet over medium-high heat. Place the polenta cakes in the pan and sauté, turning once, until golden brown on both sides. Remove the cakes from heat and place in a very low oven to keep warm. Turn the crabs and cook for another 2 minutes. Remove the crabs and drain on paper towels.

To prepare the lemon-herb butter: Add the butter to the pan that held the crabs, increase heat to high, and cook until the butter is browned but not burned. Add the lemon juice and herbs. Adjust the seasoning if necessary.

To assemble: Arrange 2 polenta cakes on each plate and top with 2 crabs. Spoon the lemon-herb butter over each plate and serve.

Note: *The polenta may be prepared up to 2 days in advance and refrigerated, tightly covered. Dust the circles with flour and fry just prior to serving.*

Aureole, New York, New York

Mexican Hat Dance

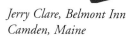

Jerry Clare, Belmont Inn
Camden, Maine

Serves 4

The dish is so named because of its lively ingredients and presentation, and also because the sea scallops dance about when they hit the hot pan. The bright flavors are not so assertive that they overwhelm the delicacy of the tender scallops.

20 fresh sea scallops (if not fresh they will stick to the pan)

Black Bean Cakes

1 cup dried black beans
3 tablespoons olive oil
1 carrot, peeled and coarsely chopped
1 small onion, chopped
2 garlic cloves, minced
1 bay leaf
2 tablespoons balsamic vinegar
3½ cups chicken stock (see page 20)
1 cup dried bread crumbs
½ red bell pepper, seeded, deribbed, and finely chopped (see page 11)

2 green onions, white part and 2 inches of green tops, finely chopped
1 tablespoon minced fresh parsley
Salt and freshly ground black pepper to taste

Chili Cream

1 small dried red chili, stemmed, seeded, and torn into pieces (see page 11)
2 cups heavy (whipping) cream

Flour for dredging
2 tablespoons vegetable oil

Garnish

Four 6- or 8-inch flour tortillas
Oil for coating tortillas
1 large tomato, peeled, seeded, and finely chopped (see page 18)
1 tablespoon minced fresh cilantro
8 chives, about 6 inches long
½ cup finely diced red onion
2 green onions, green tops sliced on the diagonal

Rinse the sea scallops and remove any hinged muscle from the side of each one. Cover and refrigerate until ready to serve.

To make the black bean cakes: Rinse the beans in a colander under cold running water, picking them over to discard any broken beans or pebbles. Place the beans in a large saucepan, cover, and bring the water to a boil over high heat. Boil for 1 minute, then remove from heat and let sit for 1 hour.

Heat the olive oil in a medium, heavy saucepan over medium heat. Add the carrot, onion, and garlic and sauté over low heat, stirring often, for 3 to 5 minutes, or until the onion is translucent. Drain the beans and add them to the pan along with the bay leaf, stirring to coat. Add the vinegar and stock and bring to a boil over medium heat. Reduce heat to low and simmer the beans uncovered until tender, about 50 minutes to 1 hour. Do not let liquid evaporate; add more stock if necessary.

Remove and discard the bay leaf. Puree ½ cup of the cooked beans in a blender or food processor and stir the puree into the beans in the pot. Let cool.

Mexican Hat Dance; Jerry Clare, Belmont Inn, Camden, Maine

Combine the beans with the bread crumbs, red pepper, green onions, and parsley; if the mixture is too loose to form patties, add more bread crumbs. Season with salt and pepper, form the beans into patties, cover, and refrigerate.

To make the chili cream: Place the chili and cream in a medium saucepan and simmer until reduced by half. Place the cream in a blender or food processor, puree until smooth, and strain through a fine-meshed sieve, pressing the solids with the back of a large spoon to extract as much liquid as possible. Cover and refrigerate the cream for at least 1 hour.

Preheat the oven to 300°F. Dredge the black bean cakes lightly in flour. Heat the oil in a medium sauté pan over medium-high heat and sauté the bean cakes until golden brown and warmed through, about 3 minutes on each side. Transfer to the preheated oven and keep warm.

Place a dry large nonstick sauté pan or skillet over high heat for 3 minutes. Pat the scallops dry with paper towels and place in the pan. Do not overcrowd the pan; cook the scallops in 2 batches if necessary. Sear the scallops on one side for about 2 minutes, then turn them with tongs and cook for 2 minutes on the other side. While the scallops are cooking, lightly coat the tortillas with oil and toast them on a grill or in a 450°F oven.

To serve: Divide the chili cream among 4 plates. Place 1 bean cake on the cream and 1 tortilla on top of the bean cake. Place 5 scallops evenly around the rim of each tortilla. Sprinkle the rim of each plate with the chopped tomato and cilantro. Garnish with 2 chives each. Divide the red onion among the plates and sprinkle each serving with green onions.

Note: The black bean cake mixture and the chili cream may be prepared up to 2 days in advance and refrigerated, tightly covered. Fry the cakes over medium heat just prior to serving.

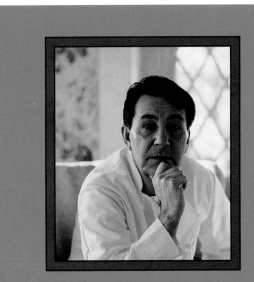

JERRY CLARE
Belmont Inn, Camden, Maine

Nantucket Island has lured many people seeking a peaceful life. Jerry Clare, now the chef-owner of the Belmont Inn in Camden, Maine, left the banking profession in Boston in 1970 and moved to the island to open a guest house. He met executive chef Michael Shannon, who still cooks on the island at the Club Car, and Shannon's food inspired Clare to become a chef.

He was hooked. By the time a 1977 vacation to Ft. Lauderdale ended, Clare owned a tiny ten-table restaurant called Victoria Park, which received praise from the *Miami Herald* and the local Ft. Lauderdale newspapers. It was a baptism by fire—Clare had never cooked professionally.

Rather than his early lessons at the Fannie Farmer Cooking School, Clare relied on a "street-sense" approach to training. "Observing what was being done around me and picking the brains of those who were doing great things with food," he says, was more valuable. Two rules have guided him: Use the freshest and best possible ingredients, and keep it simple.

Clare sold Victoria Park in 1985 and spent the next few summers working in Nantucket's notable restaurants: 21 Federal, the Boarding House, and Le Languedoc. Now he was ready for a greater challenge.

Clare was naturally drawn to the cooking style of coastal Maine, having grown up in Rhode Island eating corn chowder, clam cakes, and steamers. He and partner John Marcarella bought the Belmont Inn in Camden, Maine, in 1988. The town's oldest inn, the Belmont was transformed from a rundown boardinghouse to a gracious, flower-filled full-service Edwardian inn.

Clare's approach to dining at the Belmont Inn is to make guests feel as though they've come to his house for dinner. He uses the best that Maine's fishermen and farmers have to offer, with special twists: Lobster Pad Thai incorporates Pacific Rim flavors, and his Mexican Hat Dance dish is a scallop tortilla with black bean cake.

Clare's seasonal business gives him the opportunity to travel to such places as the beach in Thailand, where he loves the native cuisine, and to New York City to study formally, often at Peter Kump's New York Cooking School.

LYDIA SHIRE
Biba, Boston, Massachusetts

Lydia Shire's determination, drive, and talent have made her a world-class chef. Shire was making salads at Maison Robert in Boston when she realized that she needed formal culinary training if she were to continue on this career path for the rest of her life. Once she set her sights on London's Cordon Bleu, she recalls, she "kept badgering and calling them until they accepted me."

The story of a recently divorced Shire selling her diamond ring to finance her training has become something of a legend. One of the pioneers of new American cuisine in her hometown of Boston, Shire has made a permanent mark on the city's culinary community with Biba.

In its Best and Worst twentieth anniversary issue, *Boston* magazine named Biba Best Eclectic Restaurant and dubbed it "unparalleled by any restaurant in Boston." Among other recent honors, Shire has been named America's Best Chef in the Northeast by the James Beard Foundation.

Following her London stint, in 1970 Shire returned to Maison Robert as head chef of the restaurant's elegant upstairs dining room. From there she moved to the Harvest House in Cambridge, and then to hotel restaurants as executive chef at the Copley Plaza, the Parker House, and the Bostonian. In 1985 she was lured to Los Angeles to open the restaurant at the new Four Seasons Hotel as the chain's first female executive chef.

Homesickness, coupled with her dream of opening her own restaurant, brought Shire back to Boston in 1987.

Since its opening in 1989, Biba has wowed usually staid Bostonians. In fact, Shire applauds the adventurous tastes of the city's diners, citing their willingness to try anything. Her witty and often eccentric menu is divided into such categories as Legumes, Starch, Offal, Fish, Meats, and Sweets. In the Offal group, adventurous diners will find a variety of organ meats rarely found on restaurant menus. Even the bar menu is a far cry from the traditional pretzel fare, with such appetizers as Poached Marrow on Toast.

And Shire's boldness finds its pinnacle in her menu, offering an unusual combination of ingredients, both seasonal and international, in such dishes as Pork Rump, Anise, and New Garlic in a Covered Pot with Roasted Jasmine Rice Cake; and Lobster Crisp in Water Chestnut Flour.

Lobster Crisp in Water Chestnut Flour

Lydia Shire and Susan Regis, Biba
Boston, Massachusetts

Serves 4

This is a spectacular dish for a special dinner, although not one for a novice cook or one who is flustered by the prospect of last-minute work. The tempura batter gives an almost translucent look to the lobster and may be used for any tempura dish.

4 chicken lobsters (lobsters weighing from ¾ to 1 pound)

Lobster Sauce
¼ cup clarified butter (see page 19)
2 cups dry white wine
1 cup seafood or fish stock (see page 21), or bottled clam sauce
4 tablespoons unsalted butter
3 shallots, thinly sliced
2 green onions, white part and 2 inches of green tops, thinly sliced
Bottom 3 inches of 2 lemongrass stalks, crushed
1 tablespoon red curry paste*
¼ cup minced fresh cilantro
2 tablespoons grated carrot
2 tablespoons finely ground coconut (see page 12)
Liquid from 1 coconut (see page 12)
2 Kaffir lime leaves* (optional)
4 ripe cherry tomatoes
1 Thai chili,* minced
2 tablespoons fresh lime juice

Tuna and Salmon
8 ounces tuna bellies
8 ounces salmon bellies
2 tablespoons minced fresh ginger
2 garlic cloves, minced
2 tablespoons mirin*
¼ cup soy sauce
¼ cup peanut oil

Tempura
4 cups peanut oil
1 egg white
1 egg
1 cup carbonated soda water
2 cups ice
½ cup all-purpose flour

¼ cup cornstarch
2 cups water chestnut flour*
1 green onion, sliced very thin

Garnish
4 tablespoons Thai chili sauce*
Reserved fish marinade
4 green onions, trimmed, white part
 and 3 inches of green tops, cut into
 fine julienne
½ cup shaved fresh coconut
 (see page 12)
4 Thai basil* or Italian basil sprigs
4 ounces fresh green pea shoots*
¼ cup crème fraîche (see page 20)
1 teaspoon wasabi paste*

Lobster Crisp in Water Chestnut Flour; Lydia Shire and Susan Regis, Biba, Boston

Bring a large quantity of salted water to a boil in a large stockpot. Plunge the lobsters into the pot head first, and cover the pan. Once the water returns to a boil, cook the lobsters for 5 minutes. Drain them, then plunge them into a bowl of ice water. Once cool enough to handle, remove the claws from the shell. With a large, sharp knife, split the tail down the middle, leaving the shell on. Remove and discard the intestinal vein that runs down the tail. Remove and discard the sand sac between the eyes and the spongy gills along the body walls. Set aside the body sections for the lobster sauce. Thread the tail and claw meat onto 6- to 8-inch metal skewers and set aside.

To make the lobster sauce: Heat the clarified butter in a stockpot over medium-high heat. Add the reserved lobster bodies and cook for 5 minutes. Remove the lobsters from the pan and add the white wine and stock or clam juice, stirring to dislodge any brown bits from the bottom of the pan. Transfer the lobster shells and the liquid to a deep, heavy pot and place over medium heat while proceeding with the next step.

Heat 2 tablespoons of the butter in a small sauté pan or skillet over medium heat. Add the shallots, green onions, lemongrass, and curry paste, and sauté for 3 minutes, or until aromatic. Add the cilantro, carrot, coconut, coconut liquid, optional lime leaves, and cherry tomatoes to this mixture and simmer for 3 minutes. Scrape the mixture into the stockpot along with the lobster shells and bring to a boil over high heat.

Reduce heat to low and simmer the sauce for 40 minutes. Remove the shells from the pan with a slotted spoon and add the Thai chili and lime juice. Puree the mixture in a blender or food processor for 30 seconds. Strain through a fine-meshed sieve and whisk in the remaining butter, 1 teaspoon at a time. Set aside and keep warm.

To prepare the tuna and salmon: In a nonaluminum bowl, combine the tuna and salmon with the ginger, garlic, mirin, and soy sauce. Marinate for 5 minutes. Pour the peanut oil into a 12-inch sauté pan or skillet over high heat. When the oil is hot, remove the fish from the marinade (reserve the marinade) and place it in the pan, skin-side down. Without moving the fish or shaking the pan, cook the fish until deep brown and crispy on one side, about 4 minutes. Carefully turn the fish with a slotted spatula and cook the other side for 1 minute, or just enough to warm the fish through and finish the cooking. Remove from heat and keep warm.

While the fish is cooking, prepare the tempura oil and batter: Heat the peanut oil for the tempura in a deep, heavy pot or deep-fryer over high heat. Make the tempura batter by combining the egg white and the egg in a large bowl. Add the soda water and the ice, but do not mix. In a small bowl, combine the all-purpose flour and cornstarch, then add to the egg mixture and stir without

combining completely. (The batter should be lumpy, with a consistency just thick enough to coat your finger; thin with soda water as needed.) In a shallow pan, combine the water chestnut flour and the sliced green onion.

When the oil is hot but not smoking (375°F on a fat thermometer) dip the skewers of lobster into the tempura batter, dredge in the water chestnut flour, and deep-fry for 2 minutes, or until very lightly colored. Do not overcook. Drain on paper towels.

To serve: Arrange the tuna and salmon bellies on each plate and place a skewer of lobster between them. Spoon 1 tablespoon of the Thai chili sauce on each plate next to the fish and spoon 1 tablespoon of the marinade on top of the fish. On the other side of the plate, pour a larger spoonful of the lobster sauce. Sprinkle julienned green onions, shaved coconut, basil, and pea shoots on each plate. Combine the crème fraîche and the wasabi, place a dollop of the mixture on the lobster sauce, and serve immediately.

*Available at Asian markets and some supermarkets.

***Note:** The lobster may be boiled and the sauce cooked up to 1 day in advance and refrigerated, tightly covered. Heat the sauce gently over low heat and deep-fry the lobster at the last minute.*

Nitzi Rabin, Chillingsworth
Brewster, Massachusetts

Serves 2

Sweet lobster right out of Cape Cod Bay is glorified by a subtle sauce scented and lightly colored with basil. The presentation is artful without being fussy, and the dish is much easier to eat than is a whole crustacean.

2 live lobsters, 1½ pounds each
Salt and freshly ground black pepper
  to taste
3 tablespoons dry white wine
1 cup heavy (whipping) cream
3 tablespoons clarified butter
  (see page 19)
2 tablespoons Cognac
½ cup veal demi-glace (see page 21)
  or very reduced chicken stock
  (see page 20)
¼ cup minced fresh basil
16 haricots verts or baby green beans
1 tablespoon unsalted butter
1½ cups stemmed spinach
6 large basil leaves, cut into fine shreds

  Fill a stockpot with lightly salted water and bring to a boil over high heat. Add the lobsters to the pot head first, cover the pan, and cook for 5 minutes after the water returns to a boil. Remove the lobsters with tongs and place them in a bowl of ice water to cool. When the lobsters have cooled, remove the meat from the shell, discarding the sand sac just below and behind the eyes and the spongy gills along the body walls. Remove and discard the intestinal vein that runs down the tail, cut the tail portions crosswise into 4 medallions, and reserve with the claws. Extract the knuckle and leg meat and set aside separately.

  Preheat the oven to 450°F. Place the claws and the tail meat in a buttered baking dish with a sprinkling of salt and pepper and the white wine. Cover the dish with aluminum foil or parchment paper and bake for 6 to 8 minutes. Watch carefully to prevent overcooking; the meat should "steam bake" just until hot.

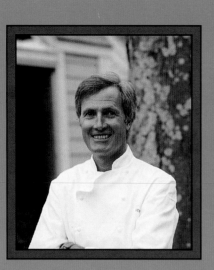

NITZI RABIN

Chillingsworth, Brewster, Massachusetts

Like many chefs, Robert "Nitzi" Rabin entered the profession through serendipity rather than by design. Trained in business, with an M.B.A. from Dartmouth College, a summer job between semesters brought Rabin and his wife Pat to Chillingsworth, and when the owner of the Brewster, Massachusetts, restaurant died, they decided to take over. That was more than twenty years ago.

Chillingsworth was established by friends of culinary great James Beard in 1956, and under the Rabins' direction the restaurant has been elevated to what one critic calls "cultural shrine" status. It has been rated the Number One restaurant by *Zagat's Boston Restaurant Survey*, and one of the Top Forty Restaurants in the Nation by the prestigious *Gault Millau* guide.

This is high praise for chef-owners who had no formal culinary training when they bought the restaurant. "I didn't have the idea to be the chef," says Nitzi. "People who want to go into this business think they're going to be managers. We weren't thinking about working full-time in the kitchen. A few disasters and there you are."

Tired of a "close enough" approach to food, the Rabins took a six-month winter course at Cordon Bleu and also trained at La Varenne in Paris. This classical French training became the foundation for Rabin's signature dishes, like Crab Cakes with Lemon-Chive Sour Cream and Golden Caviar; Plum Soufflé with Cinnamon; and Pheasant Breast, which is lightly marinated in maple syrup and molasses, grilled, and served with angel hair pasta, roasted tomatoes, and fresh basil. Pat Rabin received pastry training, became an expert, and now creates the much-loved desserts for Chillingsworth.

The Louis XV antique and reproduction furnishings, as well as the harp music floating throughout the three-hundred-year-old house, complement the French-inspired cuisine served in five elaborate dining rooms, the largest seating forty, the smallest two. Rabin's attention to detail, and his habit of never preparing a menu more than twenty minutes before the restaurant opens in order to make use of the freshest ingredients available, make it less than surprising that he is often in the kitchen from dawn until midnight. "Our intention is to do the very best possible thing. But the job gets geometrically greater as you do that," he says.

While the lobster is cooking, place the cream in a medium saucepan and bring to a boil over medium heat, stirring as it comes to a boil to keep it from boiling over. Reduce heat to low and simmer the cream until it has reduced to ¾ cup. Set aside and keep warm. Bring another pot of lightly salted water to a boil.

Place a large sauté pan or skillet over high heat. Add the clarified butter and the knuckle and leg meat. Cook for 2 to 3 minutes, then add the Cognac, stirring up any lobster meat stuck to the bottom of the pan. Cook until the liquid evaporates, then add the demi-glace or reduced stock and the reduced cream. Bring the mixture to a boil and add the minced basil. Cook an additional 1 to 2 minutes, then taste the sauce for seasoning and adjust with salt and pepper if necessary. Strain the sauce through a fine-meshed sieve. Set aside and keep warm.

Blanch the haricots verts or baby green beans in the pan of boiling water for 3 to 5 minutes, or until the beans are bright green and tender. Drain the beans, set aside, and keep warm.

While the beans are cooking, place a medium sauté pan or skillet over high heat and melt the butter. Add the spinach, season with salt and pepper, and sauté the greens until just wilted, about 1 minute.

To serve: Mound the sautéed spinach in the upper third of 2 plates to form the "body" of the lobster. Arrange the claws on either side of the spinach and place the tail meat medallions in an overlapping row to form the tail. Arrange the beans sticking out from the spinach "body" to resemble legs. Pour the lobster sauce around the dish, sprinkle with the basil, and serve immediately.

Note: *The lobster may be boiled and the sauce may be made up to 4 hours in advance, covered, and refrigerated. Finish cooking the lobster and reheat the sauce over low heat just prior to serving.*

Lobster Pad Thai; Jerry Clare, The Belmont Inn, Camden, Maine

Lobster Pad Thai

Jerry Clare, The Belmont Inn Camden, Maine

Serves 4

The sweet flavor of lobster takes well to the assertive seasoning in this version of one of the most popular Thai noodle dishes.

Four 1½-pound live lobsters
8 ounces rice stick noodles (about ¼ to ½ inch wide)*
¼ cup peanut oil
2 tablespoons minced fresh ginger
Bottom 3 inches of 2 lemongrass stalks, minced
2 tablespoons minced garlic
2 tablespoons sugar
2 tablespoons red shrimp paste*
½ teaspoon chili paste with garlic*
1 cup green onions, green tops and white parts chopped separately
2 tablespoons fresh lemon juice
2 tablespoons fresh lime juice
1 tablespoon Thai fish sauce*
1 egg

3 tablespoons water
¼ cup minced fresh cilantro
1 cup dry-roasted peanuts, ground
1½ cups fresh bean sprouts
1 lime, cut into 8 wedges
8 dried red Thai chilies*

Bring a large pot of salted water to a boil. Kill the lobsters by making a small incision with the point of a knife in the back of the shell where the chest and tail meet. Plunge the lobsters into the water head first, cover the pot, and when the water returns to a boil cook the lobsters for 5 minutes. Drain the lobsters, then place them in a large bowl of ice water to stop the cooking action. When they are cool, drain again and remove the meat from the shell, remove and discard the intestinal vein that runs down the tail, the sand sac just behind the eyes, and the spongy gills along the body walls. Cut the meat into 1-inch chunks and set aside. (Reserve the lobster bodies and shells to make seafood stock, if desired.)

In a large mixing bowl, soak the noodles in cool water for 15 minutes. Drain them well and set aside. Heat the oil in a 12-inch sauté pan or skillet over high heat. Add the lobster and sauté for 1 minute, then remove from the pan with a slotted spoon. Add the ginger, lemongrass, and garlic, tossing to coat. Add the sugar, shrimp paste, and chili paste, and toss again. Add the drained noodles, chopped green onion tops, lemon and lime juices, and fish sauce. Stir frequently. In a small bowl, beat the egg with the water and add the egg-water mixture to the lobster. Remove the pan from heat and let sit for 2 minutes.

To serve: Divide the noodles among 4 plates and sprinkle the cilantro and peanuts over the noodles. Garnish with bean sprouts, lime wedges, chilies, and the chopped white part of the green onion.

*Available in Asian markets and some supermarkets.

Note: *The dish must be made at the last minute; however, the lobsters may be blanched up to 6 hours in advance. Tightly cover and refrigerate the lobster meat.*

TODD ENGLISH
Olives, Charlestown, Massachusetts

When Todd English was growing up in Amarillo, Texas, he wanted to be a major league baseball player. But the lure of the dinner plates superseded home plate, and English is now the chef-owner of Olives, and Figs, two restaurants in Charlestown, Massachusetts, that could easily win the World Series of cooking.

Even in college in North Carolina, baseball was at the top of the list for English. But eventually the taste of fine food won his heart, and he enrolled at the Culinary Institute of America, graduating with honors. Although he apprenticed in New York at La Côte Basque, a bastion of classic French food, it was his experience in two of Italy's finest restaurants that influenced English to develop his unique style and approach to cooking. He returned to the United States and served for three years as executive chef at Michela's, an award-winning Northern Italian restaurant in Cambridge, Massachusetts.

Olives began as a fifty-seat storefront restaurant in Charlestown and gained recognition with English's interpretive European cooking. Now in a larger space, Olives was voted one of the Top Ten Restaurants by *Esquire* magazine and as the Best New Restaurant by *Boston* magazine, in 1990. His other endeavor, Figs, was named the Best Pizza Pad by *Boston* magazine in its annual Best of Boston issue.

Molly O'Neill of the *New York Times Magazine* wrote that "his cooking has all of the exuberance of youth, the sense that you better eat now, because tomorrow, who knows?" She added that his menu "is one part rustic Italian and one part American more-is-plenty." English is known for his liberal use of olive oil, huge portions of marbled meats, and food tasting of the brick hearth, wood-fired grill, and rotisserie. His signature creations, like Pizza Topped with Figs and Prosciutto and Drizzled with Olive Oil, and Wood-grilled Lobster with Potato Gnocchi and Toasted Walnuts, are typical of his restaurant, described by O'Neill as looking like "a giant fireside [hearth], something right out of the Boston of Paul Revere."

Wood-grilled Lobster with Potato Gnocchi and Toasted Walnuts

Todd English, Olives
Charlestown, Massachusetts

Serves 4

In this stunning dish, the slightly smoky flavor from the charcoal and applewood is complemented by the toasted nuts. Gnocchi are small potato dumplings. If you don't want to make them, they may be purchased frozen in many markets, or the dish is also delicious with fresh pasta.

Potato Gnocchi
2 russet potatoes, peeled and cut into
  1-inch chunks
3 egg yolks, lightly beaten
½ to ⅔ cup water
Salt and freshly ground black pepper
  to taste
1½ cups all-purpose flour

Lobster
1 cup applewood chips
4 live lobsters, 1½ pounds each
2 tablespoons olive oil
1 cup (2 sticks) unsalted butter
2 cups finely chopped walnuts

Garnish

2 tablespoons unsalted butter

1 zucchini, sliced into thin rounds

Salt and freshly ground black pepper
 to taste

Julienned zest of 1 lemon

½ bunch parsley, stemmed and minced

¼ cup freshly grated Parmesan cheese

To make the gnocchi: Place the potato cubes in a large saucepan and cover them with lightly salted water. Bring the water to a boil over high heat and cook the potatoes until tender, about 12 to 15 minutes. Drain the potatoes well in a colander. Dust a work surface with flour. Mash the potatoes through a ricer or sieve into a pile onto the work surface. Make a well in the center of the potatoes and add the egg yolks, water, salt, and pepper. With a fork or your fingers, mix in the flour a little at a time and knead gently just to incorporate.

On a floured surface, form the dough into a strip ½ inch wide and 2 to 3 feet long. Cut the strip into ½-inch pieces, then roll the pieces into balls. Using 2 forks, roll the balls the full length of the fork prong, pressing at the end to create a pocket in the middle with a fork mark at the end. Continue with the remaining dough and set the gnocchi aside.

To prepare the lobster: Light a fire in a charcoal grill and soak the applewood chips in water to cover. Kill the lobsters by making a small incision with the point of a knife in the back of the shell where the tail and chest meet. Cut off the tails and claws; reserve the bodies and knuckles for making stock (remove and discard the sand sac between the eyes and the gills along the body walls). Cut the tails in half lengthwise with a heavy knife, remove and discard the intestinal vein that runs down the tail, and set the tails aside. Bring a medium stockpot of lightly salted water to a boil and boil the claws for 3 minutes. Drain the claws and place them in a bowl of ice water to stop further cooking.

Bring a stockpot of lightly salted water to a boil. Coat the shells of the lobster tails and the lobster claws with the oil. When the coals are glowing red, drain the soaked wood chips and sprinkle them over the coals. Grill the split lobster meat-side down for 4 to 5 minutes. While the lobster is cooking, drop the gnocchi in the pot of boiling water and cook for approximately 6 to 8 minutes, or until they rise to the surface. Remove

the cooked lobster from the grill and set aside. Drain the gnocchi in a colander, set aside, and keep warm.

Melt the butter in a medium saucepan over medium heat and add the walnuts. Cook until the walnuts are toasted, about 3 to 4 minutes. Pull the lobster meat from the tail section and add, along with the claw meat still in the shell, to the butter-walnut mixture, tossing to coat well; set aside.

To make the garnish: In a small pan, melt the butter and add the sliced zucchini rounds. Cook until just tender, about 3 to 4 minutes. Season with salt and pepper and remove from heat. To serve, arrange the lobster on the plate and garnish with the sautéed zucchini. Sprinkle the lobster meat with the lemon zest and the chopped parsley. Sprinkle the finished dish with Parmesan and add the drained gnocchi. Serve at once.

Note: The gnocchi may be made 1 day in advance, tossed with cornmeal so they will not stick together, covered, and refrigerated. The lobster may be grilled up to 4 hours in advance.

Olives, Charlestown, Massachusetts

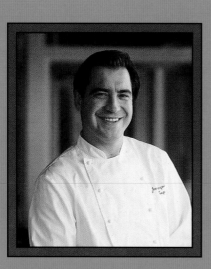

Jean-François Taquet
Restaurant Taquet, Wayne, Pennsylvania

Jean-François Taquet categorizes his restaurant, Restaurant Taquet, as a brasserie, but realizes that Americans do not readily understand the connotation. In an effort to explain, the words rush out of him. "A brasserie is fancy," he says. "It has an expensive look, an inexpensive menu, it is a place to have fun, and it must look fun." As one writer noted, Taquet has the impressive distinction of speaking English even faster than French.

This is only one of Taquet's many accomplishments. Raised in southwestern France, Taquet was inducted into the L'Académie Culinaire de France and the Maîtres Cuisiniers de France in 1993 at age thirty-five, the youngest person ever to be accorded the honor of dual membership. His signature dishes, including Fish Carpaccio with Olive Oil and Citrus; Salmon Burgers Provençale; and Raspberry Gratin with Caramel, have earned him critical acclaim for their taste as well as for their great price value, which, he notes, is "very important for the nineties."

Taquet's father is an expert small-game hunter, and Taquet learned early to share his enthusiasm for this pastime and often features game on his menu. Taquet began his formal training as an apprentice in a fine French restaurant in his native France, and went on to work as sous-chef under Jean-Louis Palladin at Jean-Louis at the Watergate in Washington. Opened in 1987 in Radnor, Pennsylvania, Restaurant Taquet moved to its current location in the Wayne Hotel in January 1992.

Describing Restaurant Taquet as "casually elegant, with exceptionally good food and attentive service," Taquet notes that "prior to 1992, the restaurant in Radnor was a formal dining establishment, which is more my background. I believe I will return to the formal style once again when the economy is better." Taquet is quick to add, "I'm having fun now, it's new!"

Salmon Burgers Provençale

Jean-François Taquet
Restaurant Taquet
Wayne, Pennsylvania

Serves 4

This dish can be described as a warm salmon tartare, or a fish version of the most flavorful hamburger you ever ate. It is easy to prepare, and it may be grilled to add another dimension of flavor.

1¼ pounds salmon fillets, skinned
1 tablespoon nonpareil capers, drained and rinsed
1½ teaspoons minced shallot
1½ teaspoons minced fresh parsley
1½ teaspoons minced fresh tarragon
2 tablespoons minced fresh basil, divided
Salt and freshly ground black pepper to taste
1¼ cups tomato sauce, preferably homemade
2 tablespoons black-olive paste or tapenade
3 tablespoons olive oil

Coarsely chop the salmon fillets by hand or in a food processor using an on-and-off pulsing action. Place the salmon in a medium bowl and add the capers, shallots, parsley, tarragon, 1 tablespoon of the basil, and the salt and pepper. Divide the mixture into 4 equal parts and shape into burgers. Set aside.

Place the tomato sauce in a small saucepan and bring to a boil over medium heat. Reduce heat to low and add the olive paste or tapenade and the remaining 1 tablespoon basil. Simmer the sauce for 2 minutes; set aside and keep warm.

Heat the olive oil in a medium sauté pan or skillet over high heat until it is almost smoking. Add the burgers and cook for 2 minutes on each side. Remove the burgers with a slotted metal spatula and drain on paper towels.

To serve: Divide the tomato sauce among 4 plates and place a warm burger on top of the sauce.

Poached Salmon in White Wine; Yves Labbé,
Le Cheval d'Or, Jeffersonville, Vermont

Poached Salmon in White Wine

Yves Labbé, Le Cheval d'Or
Jeffersonville, Vermont

Serves 4

This is an incredibly easy dish to make,
and all it needs to complete the plate
is a green vegetable such as steamed
asparagus and sautéed zucchini, and
some buttered noodles or steamed
baby potatoes.

2 tablespoons unsalted butter at
   room temperature
2 shallots, minced
2 tablespoons minced fresh parsley
Salt and freshly ground white pepper
   to taste
Four 5-ounce salmon fillets
1½ cups dry white wine
1½ cups heavy (whipping) cream
2 egg yolks, lightly beaten
2 tablespoons nonpareil capers

Preheat the oven to 500°F. Spread the
butter in the bottom of an ovenproof
sauté pan or skillet and sprinkle the shallots and parsley on top. Season with salt
and pepper, and place the salmon fillets
on top of the shallots. Gently pour the
white wine and cream over the fish and
place the pan over high heat. Cook until
the cream at the edges of the pan starts
to boil, then transfer the pan to the
preheated oven and bake for 6 to 8 minutes, or until the fish is mostly opaque
but still slightly translucent in the center;
it will continue to cook after being
removed from the oven.

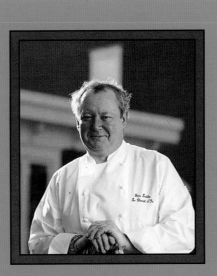

YVES LABBÉ
Le Cheval d'Or, Jeffersonville, Vermont

As a child in Montherme, a small French village near the Belgian
border, Yves Labbé often found dinner unsettling, even frightening.
In the foyer of his home, Labbé's family stored buckets of angry live eels,
secured by weighted lids. But they tasted pretty good with onion and
wine sauce, he decided. In 1962, by the age of eighteen, Labbé knew that
he wanted to enter the culinary profession, but his parents discouraged
the choice since it was not part of their family tradition.

Labbé went to art school for the next three years, but after taking a
job as a cook on a sailing yacht for the summer, he did not return to
school. Labbé's experience on ships in the Mediterranean, as well as
working in the Lesser Antilles and in the Dominican Republic, eventually led him to La Vielle Maison in Florida, where he spent the next
eleven years. During that time, the restaurant earned and kept a Mobil
five-star rating, and Labbé was invited to appear on Julia Child's television series, *Dinner with Julia.*

Labbé moved to rural Vermont in 1988 to open his own restaurant,
Le Cheval d'Or, at the Windridge Inn. He admits to being "momentarily
interested" in nouvelle cuisine, but then, he adds, "I retreated to the
more traditional domain of French country techniques and preparation."
In his cuisine, which is typified by such signature dishes as Maple Crêpes
Soufflées; Poached Salmon in White Wine; and Sea Scallops with Wild
Mushrooms, Labbé insists on simplicity, freshness, and intensity of taste.

In his scant free time, Labbé is a serious woodworker with a large,
well-equipped shop, and he also practices black and white photography.
But most of his time is spent in Cheval d'Or, where he strives to achieve
an intimate, elegant atmosphere. "We hope we give to our customers the
wonderful feeling of well-being that occurs when a fine meal has been
well served," Labbé says.

Transfer the fillets to 4 heated plates
with a slotted spatula; set aside and keep
warm. Return the pan to the stove and
whisk in the egg yolks and capers. Cook
over low heat, stirring constantly, until
the cream thickens slightly, about 2 to
3 minutes. Do not let the mixture come
to a boil or the egg yolks will curdle.
Ladle the sauce over the salmon fillets
and serve at once.

Cedar-planked Salmon with Wilted Greens and Toasted Pumpkin Seed Vinaigrette

Larry Forgione, An American Place
New York, New York

Serves 4

Cedar-planked salmon combines a Native American cooking technique with modern presentation and seasoning, and has been a signature dish at An American Place since it opened more than a decade ago. The cedar really does add to the flavor, but you also could broil the fish without it.

Toasted Pumpkin Seed Vinaigrette
½ cup apple cider
2 tablespoons pumpkin puree
4 tablespoons pumpkin seeds, toasted (see page 16)
¼ cup rice wine vinegar or apple cider vinegar
¾ cup olive oil
Salt and freshly ground pepper to taste

Salmon
1 teaspoon kosher salt
¼ teaspoon freshly ground black pepper
¼ teaspoon dry mustard
2 tablespoons unsalted butter, melted
Four 6-ounce salmon fillets, skinned and boned
2 untreated 5-by-12-inch cedar shingles or shims (available from lumber yards)

Greens
2 tablespoons olive oil
4 cups assorted greens such as dandelion, mustard, spinach, mizuna
1 small garlic clove, minced
Salt and freshly ground black pepper to taste

Garnish
2 tablespoons minced fresh chives
2 tablespoons pumpkin seeds, toasted (see page 16)

To make the vinaigrette: Combine the cider, pumpkin puree, pumpkin seeds, vinegar, and olive oil in a blender or food processor and puree until smooth. Season with salt and freshly ground black pepper, and set aside.

To prepare the salmon: Mix the salt, pepper, and mustard together in a small bowl. Brush the top of each fillet with one fourth of the melted butter and sprinkle both sides of each fillet with the mustard mixture. Preheat the broiler and soak the cedar shingles or shims in cold water for 5 to 10 minutes. Place the shingles 4 to 5 inches from the heat until browned on one side. Carefully remove the wood from the broiler.

Cedar-planked Salmon with Wilted Greens and Toasted Pumpkin Seed Vinaigrette; Larry Forgione, An American Place, New York

Immediately lay 2 fillets on the browned side of each piece of wood. Return the wood to the broiler and cook the fish for 5 to 6 minutes, until it is mostly opaque but still slightly translucent in the center.

To prepare the greens: Heat the olive oil in a 12-inch sauté pan or skillet over medium-high heat. Add the greens and cook, stirring constantly, just until wilted. Right before serving, add the garlic, salt, and pepper.

To serve: Make a bed of wilted greens in the center of each plate and top with 1 salmon fillet. Spoon the vinaigrette around the fillet and sprinkle with the chives and toasted pumpkin seeds.

Note: The vinaigrette may be made 1 day in advance and refrigerated. Let it come to room temperature and shake it well before serving.

LARRY FORGIONE
An American Place, New York, New York

When Hillary Rodham Clinton solicited the country's best chefs for guidance on how to introduce American foods to the traditionally French White House menus, she sent an unmistakable signal that the food revolution started more than a decade ago in this country's restaurant kitchens had succeeded. Larry Forgione was one of the handful of chefs selected to guide the White House, since he is acknowledged as the godfather of New American cuisine. His Manhattan restaurant, An American Place, serves only food raised and produced in the United States. Forgione's style and innovation have helped to educate the public about the inherent possibilities of American cooking.

Like many chefs, Forgione began cooking somewhat by accident. A bout with pneumonia forced him to take a semester off from college, and he went to work for a catering firm. That experience changed his career plans, and he graduated from the Culinary Institute of America in 1974. Forgione then traveled to London looking for experience and technique in the grand hotels. Forgione's sojourn in Europe reinforced his belief that the main problem facing American kitchens was an absence of high-quality ingredients. "I was there for more than two years, and each day I would see wonderful new foods that we didn't have here—the seafood from France, chanterelles and black chanterelles, tiny haricots verts," Forgione remembers. "It started to dawn on me—how come they have everything and we have nothing? Why don't we have chanterelles in the United States? We have oak trees, don't we?"

Forgione returned to New York and worked at Regine's before accepting a job as head chef of the River Cafe, a Brooklyn restaurant overlooking the Manhattan skyline. Once there, Forgione saw the opportunity for putting his untested philosophy to work. He began to encourage farmers located not only in upstate New York but throughout the country to develop and raise the ingredients he wanted: free-range chicken, native buffalo and other game, and heirloom varieties of native fruits and vegetables.

The results, such as his Terrine of America's Three Smoked Fish with Their Respective Caviars and Champagne Dressing, continue to redefine American cuisine. Another typical Forgione dish is his Cedar-planked Salmon with Wilted Greens and Toasted Pumpkin Seed Vinaigrette. His food is both vivid and modern, and sophisticated without being fussy.

TIMOTHY CARDILLO
Cranwell Resort and Hotel, Lexington, Massachusetts

Timothy Cardillo's cooking background is mirrored by the history of his family. Cardillo's grandfather immigrated to America from Naples. Settling in Stockbridge, Massachusetts, he started a dairy farm and raised eighteen children. Cardillo's father spent his younger years on the farm. He learned to hunt, garden, and butcher as part of his everyday chores, and he passed these skills on to his son.

Cardillo says, "We always had food from things around us, from the garden to foraging for mushrooms, an everyday practice when morels were sprouting deep in the woods. My father was always known for his grapes and wine, and his love of fresh greens like dandelion and cowslips."

With the foundation of his father's teaching, Cardillo went to study in various restaurant kitchens throughout New England. He credits Julia Child with influencing him greatly when she handed him a copy of *Cook's Magazine*. "It was my first hard look into the real world of cooking, who's who, and what they were doing," says Cardillo. Now he applies that early knowledge to signature dishes like his Herbed Tuna with Citrus Vinaigrette.

The boy who hunted mushrooms is now an avid golfer and the executive chef and food and beverage director at Cranwell Resort and Hotel in Lexington, Massachusetts. But if anyone should spy the chef in the woods there, he won't be looking for a chip shot gone wrong—he'll be looking for mushrooms. Really.

Herbed Tuna with Citrus Vinaigrette

Timothy Cardillo, Cranwell Resort and Hotel
Lenox, Massachusetts

Serves 4

Using vinaigrette dressings as sauces is one of the important trends in New American cuisine. This easy, colorful, and delicious one-dish meal needs only a crusty loaf of bread and some steamed rice to complete it.

Tuna
1½ pounds tuna steaks, preferably yellowfin
2 teaspoons minced fresh tarragon
2 teaspoons minced fresh cilantro
1 teaspoon freshly ground black pepper
¾ cup olive oil
¼ cup fresh lemon juice

Citrus Vinaigrette
2 teaspoons minced shallot
1 cup (3 ounces) sliced stemmed shiitake mushrooms
1 cup Chardonnay or other dry white wine
1 cup balsamic vinegar
1 cup fresh orange juice
1 *each* green, red, and yellow bell pepper, seeded, deribbed, and cut into ¹⁄₁₆-inch-thick julienne (see page 11)

Garnish

4 cups (4 ounces) mixed baby greens
2 tablespoons minced fresh cilantro
2 tablespoons minced fresh tarragon

To prepare the tuna: Preheat the oven to 350°F. Rinse the tuna and pat it dry with paper towels. Combine the tarragon, cilantro, pepper, ¼ cup of the olive oil, and the lemon juice in a shallow non-aluminum pan. Add the tuna and marinate it for a total of 10 minutes, turning it once.

Remove the tuna steaks from the marinade and pat them dry on paper towels. Heat the remaining ½ cup olive oil in a medium sauté pan or skillet over high heat. Sear the tuna steaks for 1 to 2 minutes on each side. Transfer the tuna to a baking dish and bake in the preheated oven for 3 minutes for rare and 5 minutes for medium-rare.

To make the vinaigrette: Lower heat to medium and add the shallot and mushrooms to the sauté pan or skillet. Sauté for 1 minute and add the wine. Increase the heat to high and stir the mixture to dislodge the brown bits from the bottom of the pan. Boil until the liquid is reduced by half, then add the balsamic vinegar and cook to reduce again by half. Add the orange juice and cook for 1 minute. Add the mixed peppers and cook for 1 to 2 minutes; the peppers should remain brightly colored and firm.

To serve: Arrange the mixed greens on each plate, then top with a spoonful of the vinaigrette and the pepper salad. Remove the tuna from the oven and place it on the peppers. Garnish each plate by sprinkling the fresh herbs around the fish.

Cranwell Resort and Hotel, Lenox, Massachusetts

Seared Spicy Tuna with Mole Amarillo

*Mark Miller, Red Sage
Washington, D.C.*

Serves 4

While most Americans think of *mole* as the brown sauce topping chicken in Mexican restaurants, the word *mole* means "concoction" and refers to a variety of sauces. In this dish, heady bright yellow *mole* accompanies rare tuna that has been seared with spices.

Four 6-ounce tuna steaks
4 tablespoons chili powder
1 tablespoon ground coriander
1 tablespoon coarsely ground
  black pepper
2 teaspoons crushed fennel seed
1 teaspoon dried thyme, crumbled
1 tablespoon kosher salt
Mole Amarillo (recipe follows)

Rinse the tuna steaks and pat them dry with paper towels. Combine the chili powder, coriander, pepper, fennel seed, thyme, and salt in a small bowl and mix well.

Heat a large nonstick sauté pan or skillet over high heat until it begins to smoke, at least 5 minutes. Coat both sides of the fillets in the seasoning mix. Blacken the fillets by searing them for about 2 minutes on each side; if they are thick, also sear the sides so that the seasoning mix will be cooked.

To serve: Cut each piece of tuna on the diagonal into 2 pieces. Stand 2 pieces of fillet on each of 4 plates with the cut sides upward. Spoon the Mole Amarillo around the tuna.

Seared Spicy Tuna with Mole Amarillo; Mark Miller, Red Sage, Washington, D.C.

Mole Amarillo

(Makes 2 cups)

1 tablespoon unsalted butter
1 large yellow onion, chopped
15 güero chilies, stemmed, halved,
   and seeded (see page 11)
3 yellow bell peppers, roasted, peeled,
   and seeded (see page 11)
8 fresh or drained canned tomatillos
3 roasted garlic cloves (see page 14)
½ teaspoon ground cinnamon
½ teaspoon ground allspice
1 teaspoon sugar
Pinch of ground nutmeg
Salt to taste
2 tablespoons peanut oil

Melt the butter in a large sauté pan or skillet over medium heat. Add the onion and sauté, stirring frequently, until the onion is translucent, about 3 or 4 minutes. Add the chilies and bell peppers and sauté over low heat for about 25 to 30 minutes, stirring frequently, until the chilies are tender.

Husk the fresh tomatillos, if using, and wash them with hot water. Chop the fresh or canned tomatillos and place them in a blender or food processor with the chili mixture, garlic, cinnamon, allspice, sugar, nutmeg, and salt. Puree the mixture, adding a small amount of water if necessary to make a smooth liquid.

Heat the oil in a large sauté pan or skillet over medium-high heat. Add the sauce and cook over high heat for 5 to 7 minutes, stirring continuously.

Note: *The sauce may be made up to 2 days in advance and refrigerated, tightly covered. Heat it over low heat in a small saucepan while the fish is searing.*

MARK MILLER
Red Sage, Washington, D.C.

It seems only fitting that Mark Miller should open his Red Sage restaurant in Washington, D.C., as a benefit for the National Museum of the American Indian at the Smithsonian Institution. A former student of anthropology at Berkeley and Oxford, Miller considers cooking to be a practical application of the study of culture, and he strives to re-create in food what he admires in primitive art: "intensity of forms and colors."

"Intense" has been on the lips of nearly every critic who has reviewed Red Sage, with articles marveling at the two "ring of fire" chandeliers and the "cumulus clouds" suspended from the ceilings, with strobe lights creating the effect of lightning. The food from the kitchen of this master of chilies also has created a stir, with such signature dishes as Lobster Tamales with Three Chiles; Wood Pigeon and Foie Gras Tamal; and Seared Spicy Tuna with Mole Amarillo.

Miller's decision to open Red Sage was validated when *Esquire* magazine named Red Sage Restaurant of the Year in 1992, its first year of operation. As the student of culture notes, "The world looks at America, and it thinks about the West." Speaking in the words of one excited to be a part of the historical process of food evolution, Miller notes that while the West has a glorious past, "it's still in the process of becoming. It's not about looking back. It's about bringing it forward." He has contributed to the knowledge of western cuisine through the publication of his best-selling books, all from Ten Speed Press: *Coyote Cafe* in 1989, *The Great Chile Book,* accompanied with the popular Great Chile posters, in 1991, and, most recently, *The Salsa Book.*

Miller once approached his cooking as a pragmatic endeavor, a means of relieving stress after his studies. When Alice Waters, one of the founders of New American cuisine, asked him to cook temporarily at Chez Panisse in Berkeley, California, in 1976, Miller discovered his life's calling, and stayed until 1979. He then opened the Fourth Street Grill in Berkeley, which catapulted him to culinary fame. Miller sold his interest in Fourth Street to launch his now much-imitated Coyote Cafe in Santa Fe in 1987. Critical acclaim has been heaped on the Coyote Cafe. Honors include being named by *Nation's Restaurant News* as one of the best restaurants in the country and being nominated by the James Beard Foundation as Best Southwestern Restaurant. In a special edition of *Life* magazine, Miller was named one of the most influential chefs of the decade.

Grilled Spice-rubbed Swordfish with Indonesian Ketjap

Chris Schlesinger, Blue Room/East Coast Grill/Jake & Earl's, Cambridge, Massachusetts

Serves 4

Spice rubs are easier to use than marinades since they can be added to foods at the last minute. This dish combines robustly seasoned fish with a sweet and sour sauce and succulent grilled pineapple.

Spice Rub
1 tablespoon star anise
1 tablespoon ground ginger
1 tablespoon ground turmeric
1 tablespoon ground cinnamon
1 tablespoon whole cloves
2 teaspoons dried red pepper flakes
1 tablespoon salt
1 teaspoon ground cumin seed
1 teaspoon ground cardamom seed

Four 6- to 8-ounce swordfish steaks
Four 1-inch-thick slices unpeeled
   fresh pineapple
Indonesian Ketjap (recipe follows)
Fresh cilantro sprigs for garnish
Lime wedges for garnish

To make the spice rub: Combine all of the ingredients in a 10-inch sauté pan or skillet over medium heat. Toast the spices, stirring frequently, for 5 to 7 minutes, or until they are fragrant and begin to smoke. Remove the pan from heat and grind the spices in a spice grinder, a well-washed coffee grinder, or in a mortar with a pestle.

Light a fire in a charcoal grill. Rinse the swordfish under cold running water and pat dry with paper towels. Rub the spices evenly over the swordfish steaks and set aside until the coals are covered with a light layer of gray ash and you can hold your hand at the level of the grill grid for 3 to 4 seconds.

Grill the steaks for 4 minutes on each side, or until the fish is browned but still slightly translucent in the center; it will continue to cook after it comes off the grill. Grill the pineapple for 3 minutes on

---

CHRIS SCHLESINGER
Blue Room/East Coast Grill/Jake & Earl's, Cambridge, Massachusetts

Growing up in Virginia, Chris Schlesinger became an avid devotee of barbecue, a self-described "pitmaster." It wasn't long before he was participating in barbecue competitions from San Francisco to Boston, talking to restaurant owners and cooks, and sampling other entries. Now Schlesinger and partner Cary Wheaton run an impressive group of three restaurants in Cambridge, Massachusetts. The East Coast Grill opened in 1986; Jake & Earl's, a barbecue restaurant, opened in 1989; and the Blue Room restaurant opened in 1991.

Schlesinger entered the food-service industry at the age of eighteen, fascinated by the intense energy and teamwork at the heart of any restaurant kitchen. He left college to become a dishwasher and soon graduated to line cook. He then decided to pursue a formal culinary education at the Culinary Institute of America.

Schlesinger considers barbecue a unique piece of Americana and a powerful force for bringing people together. "Eating is about having a good time," he says. "It should never be the centerpiece of a dinner; it's the background for warmth, sharing and fun." His own style of barbecue, which Schlesinger describes as "earthy simplicity, a rough style, with the emphasis on the clarity and dimension of the taste," has earned Jake & Earl's a rating as one of America's top barbecue restaurants by *People* magazine.

Schlesinger uses dry rubs—spice mixtures that include chili powder, salt, pepper, brown sugar, and cumin—to create such dishes as Grilled Spice-rubbed Swordfish with Indonesian Ketjap. "I'm basically a non-marinater," he says.

Along with John Willoughby, Schlesinger wrote *The Thrill of the Grill* (William Morrow), which was published in 1990. The two have recently collaborated on another cookbook, titled *Salsa, Sambals, Chutneys, and Chow-Chows* (William Morrow).

each side. Brush with Indonesian ketjap and grill an additional 30 seconds on each side.

To serve: Place a swordfish steak on each plate and cut the pineapple into wedges. Spoon a few tablespoons of Indonesian ketjap over the swordfish and garnish with sprigs of fresh cilantro and wedges of lime.

Note: The spice rub may be prepared up to 1 week in advance. Store in an airtight jar.

Indonesian Ketjap
(Makes 1½ cups)

1 cup pineapple juice
½ cup distilled white vinegar
¼ cup soy sauce
1 tablespoon minced fresh ginger
½ cup tomato ketchup
¼ cup firmly packed dark brown sugar
¼ cup minced fresh cilantro
¼ cup fresh lime juice

Combine the pineapple juice, vinegar, soy sauce, and ginger in a 1-quart non-aluminum saucepan. Bring to a boil over medium heat and simmer for 20 to 30 minutes, or until the liquid is reduced by half. Add the ketchup and brown sugar, stir, and simmer for 5 minutes, stirring occasionally. Remove the pan from heat and stir in the cilantro and lime juice. Let cool, cover, and store in the refrigerator for up to 1 week.

Halibut and Lobster with Vanilla and Sweet Corn

Ted Fondulas, Hemingway's Killington, Vermont

Serves 8

This dish is as colorful as it is delicious, with a medley of vegetables forming a bed for browned succulent fillets of halibut topped with New England lobster. The scent of vanilla in the beurre blanc heightens the sweet flavor of the lobster.

Halibut and Lobster with Vanilla and Sweet Corn; Ted Fondulas, Hemingway's, Killington, Vermont

Vanilla Beurre Blanc
½ cup dry white wine
2 shallots, minced
½ vanilla bean, split lengthwise
¾ cup unsalted butter (1¼ sticks),
    cut into 1-tablespoon pieces

Two 1- to 1½-pound lobsters
2 boiling potatoes, peeled and cut
    into ¼-inch dice
4 carrots, peeled and cut into ¼-inch dice
2 ears fresh corn, or one 10½-ounce
    package frozen corn, thawed
1 zucchini, cut into uniform balls with
    a ¼-inch melon baller
½ cup chicken stock (see page 20)
½ cup (1 stick) unsalted butter
¼ cup olive oil
Eight 6-ounce halibut fillets
    (1 inch thick)
Salt and freshly ground white pepper
    to taste
2 tablespoons minced fresh chives

To make the beurre blanc: In a small saucepan, boil the white wine, shallots, and vanilla bean half, until only 1 table-spoon liquid remains. Remove the pan from heat and remove the vanilla bean. Whisk in the butter 1 tablespoon at a time, making sure each piece has been incorporated before adding the next one. Keep the pan off the stove, but have a burner set on low to reheat the sauce briefly if it becomes too cool to melt the butter. The sauce should be kept hot enough that steam rises from the surface but not so hot that it boils. Set aside and keep warm over barely tepid water.

Bring a large pot of salted water to a boil over high heat. Plunge the lobsters into the water head first, and once the

water returns to a boil, cook them for 6 to 8 minutes, depending on their size. Drain the lobsters and place them in a bowl of ice water. When they have cooled, remove the meat from the shell. Remove and discard the intestinal vein that runs down the tail, the sand sac just behind the eyes, and the spongy gills along the body walls. Slice the meat into ½-inch pieces and set aside.

Bring a medium saucepan of lightly salted water to a boil. Add the potatoes and carrots and boil over medium heat until almost tender, about 4 minutes. If using fresh corn, cut the kernels off the ear with a sharp knife and discard the cobs. Drain the potatoes and carrots and return them to the saucepan along with the fresh or defrosted corn kernels, zucchini, chicken stock, and the butter. Cook over medium heat, stirring frequently, for 5 minutes, or until the corn is cooked. Set aside and keep warm.

Preheat the oven to 350°F. Heat the olive oil in a large sauté pan or skillet over high heat. Sprinkle the halibut with salt and pepper and place the fillets in the hot pan. Cook for 2 to 3 minutes on a side, or until golden brown. Place the fillets in an ovenproof baking pan and divide the lobster pieces on top of the fillets. Bake the fillets for 5 to 7 minutes, or until they are mostly opaque but still slightly translucent in the center; the fish will continue to cook after being removed from the oven.

Add the chives to the corn, potato, and carrot mixture, and simmer over low heat for 2 minutes. Spoon the vegetable mixture onto warmed serving plates and place 1 halibut fillet on each vegetable bed. Ladle beurre blanc over each fillet and serve immediately.

Note: The beurre blanc may be made up to 3 hours in advance and kept warm in a warmed Thermos bottle, and the vegetables may be made up to 3 hours in advance and reheated over low heat. The lobster may be boiled up to 1 day in advance and refrigerated, tightly wrapped.

Halibut Enrobed in a Crisp Potato Crust

Peter Platt, Wheatleigh
Lenox, Massachusetts

Serves 4

This dish joins tender New England halibut with oysters, another native crop. The halibut is topped with a crisp crust of buttery Yukon Gold potatoes that resembles fish scales. It takes some skill to turn the fillets when frying prior to baking, so this is not a dish for the novice cook.

Halibut

4 large Yukon Gold potatoes
1 cup (2 sticks) unsalted butter, melted
Salt and freshly ground black pepper
    to taste
4 halibut fillets, about 5 to 6 ounces each

Sauce

20 oysters, shucked and liquor reserved
    (see page 17)
½ cup dry white vermouth
1 teaspoon fresh lemon juice
2 tablespoons heavy (whipping) cream
½ cup (1 stick) cold unsalted butter,
    cut into 1-tablespoon pieces

2 tablespoons clarified butter
    (see page 19)

Garnish

2 tablespoons unsalted butter
1 leek, washed and cut into julienne
1 red pepper, seeded, deribbed, and cut
    into julienne (see page 11)
1 carrot, peeled and cut into julienne
Salt and freshly ground black pepper
    to taste
1 tablespoon Ossetra or Sevruga caviar

To prepare the fish: Peel the potatoes, slice them in half lengthwise and square off 3 sides of the potato half. Cut the fourth side using a round, fluted cookie or biscuit cutter to make a scalloped side. Stand the potato on end with the scalloped side facing up and slice the potatoes into ⅛-inch-thick slices. Place the slices in a bowl of ice water to prevent discoloration.

Melt the butter in a medium saucepan over medium heat. Season the butter with salt and pepper. When the butter has melted completely, drain the potato slices, pat them dry on paper towels, and add the potato slices to the butter. Cook them for 3 minutes; this should be done in batches so as not to crowd the pan.

Season the halibut fillets on both sides with salt and pepper. Taking 1 potato slice at a time, layer the potato slices over the halibut fillets to resemble scales, leaving ¼ inch between each scalloped edge. Trim the end of the potato layer to match the edge of the fish, then cover and refrigerate the fillets until ready to use.

To make the sauce: Remove the oysters from their liquor and strain the liquor through a fine-meshed sieve. In a medium saucepan, combine the vermouth and lemon juice, and bring to a boil. Cook to reduce by half, or until the liquid is almost the consistency of a glaze. Add the strained oyster liquor and cook to reduce again to the same consistency. Add the cream and reduce again until thick. Gradually whisk in the butter, 1 tablespoon at a time, making sure each piece has been incorporated into the sauce before adding the next. Set the sauce aside and keep warm over barely tepid water.

Preheat the oven to 350°F. In an ovenproof sauté pan or skillet, heat the clarified butter over medium-high heat. Carefully place the halibut fillets potato-side down in the butter. Cook until golden, about 2 minutes. Turn the fish carefully with a metal spatula and place the pan in the oven for 6 to 8 minutes, or until the fish is mostly opaque but still slightly translucent in the center.

While the fish is cooking, prepare the garnish: Melt the butter in a medium sauté pan or skillet over medium heat. Add the leek, red pepper, and carrot, and sauté, stirring frequently, for 4 to 5 minutes, or until the vegetables are crisp-tender. Season with salt and freshly ground black pepper to taste. Set aside and keep warm.

Place the vermouth sauce over medium heat, add the oysters, and cook them just until their edges begin to curl, about 2 to 3 minutes.

To serve: Arrange the vegetable mixture in 5 small mounds on each plate. Place 1 oyster on each pile of vegetables, ladle the sauce in and around the vegetable piles, and garnish the sauce with the caviar. Drain the fish briefly on paper towels, place a potato-crusted fillet in the center of each plate, and serve.

Note: *The fish may be wrapped in the potato slices and the sauce and garnish may be prepared up to 6 hours in advance. Cover and refrigerate the fish and sauce, and let the garnish sit at room temperature.*

Halibut Enrobed in a Crisp Potato Crust; Peter Platt, Wheatleigh, Lenox, Massachusetts

Sautéed Flounder with Shrimp Wontons; Seth Raynor, The Boarding House, Nantucket, Massachusetts

Sautéed Flounder with Shrimp Wontons

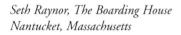

Seth Raynor, The Boarding House
Nantucket, Massachusetts

Serves 4

The use of Asian ingredients is one of the hallmarks of Seth Raynor's cooking style. These crisp wontons also make a delicious hors d'oeuvre for a cocktail party.

Sauce

1 tablespoon olive oil
2 tablespoons thinly sliced lemongrass
2 tablespoons minced fresh ginger
2 tablespoons minced garlic
4 tomatoes, peeled, seeded, and diced
   (see page 18)
¼ teaspoon salt
¼ cup dry white wine
4 cups V-8 or tomato juice
1 cup water
½ cup thinly sliced stemmed
   shiitake mushrooms

Wontons

One 8-ounce package cream cheese
   at room temperature
4 ounces smoked shrimp, finely chopped
½ cup chopped green onions (white parts
   and 2 inches of green tops)

¼ teaspoon cayenne pepper
¼ teaspoon salt
½ teaspoon fresh lemon juice
About 30 wonton skins
4 cups vegetable oil for frying

Flounder

8 yellowtail flounder fillets, 3 to
   4 ounces each
8 fresh basil leaves
Salt and freshly ground black pepper
   to taste

Garnish

8 ounces asparagus
10 ounces fresh spinach, stemmed
3 tablespoons vegetable oil
4 to 6 green onions, sliced (white part
   and 2 inches of green leaves)

To make the sauce: Heat the olive oil in a medium saucepan over medium heat. Add the lemongrass, ginger, and garlic, and cook for 2 minutes, stirring occasionally. Add the tomatoes and salt, and cook for 3 minutes. Add the wine and cook for 5 minutes. Add the V-8 or tomato juice and water, and increase the heat to high. Bring the mixture to a boil, then reduce the heat to low and simmer for 1 hour, stirring occasionally.

Strain the sauce through a fine-meshed sieve into a medium sauté pan or skillet, then add the mushrooms. Simmer the sauce over low heat for 5 minutes; set aside and keep warm.

To make the wontons: Combine the cream cheese, shrimp, green onions, cayenne, salt, and lemon juice in a medium bowl. Stir well with a wooden spoon. Brush the edges of a wonton skin with water. Place 1 teaspoon of filling at the center of the wrapper and fold it in half to form a triangle, pressing the edges together with your fingers to seal them tightly. Bring the opposing 2 corners of the triangle together, dab with water, and press to seal. Repeat until all the filling has been used; it will make about 30 wontons.

In a heavy, deep pot or deep-fryer, heat the oil over medium heat to 375°F, or until a bread cube dropped into the oil is surrounded with a ring of white bubbles and turns brown in 10 seconds.

Fry the wontons in small batches, being careful not to crowd the pan, for 1 to 2 minutes, or until golden brown. Remove the wontons from the pot with a slotted spoon, drain them on paper towels, and repeat until all the wontons have been fried. Set aside at room temperature.

To make the flounder: Preheat the oven to 450°F. Place 1 basil leaf in the center of 1 fish fillet and place another fillet on top of it at a right angle. Place another basil leaf in the center of that fillet and fold in the 4 ends to enclose the top leaf and create a woven package. Season the package with salt and pepper, and set aside.

To make the garnish: Pour ½ inch of lightly salted water into a medium sauté pan or skillet and bring to a boil. Place a stainless steel steamer in the bottom of the pan and add the asparagus. Cover the pan and steam the asparagus for 5 to 8 minutes, depending on size. Remove the asparagus from the steamer and add the spinach. Steam the spinach for 2 to 3 minutes, or until wilted. Set aside and keep warm.

To finish the dish: Heat the oil over high heat in a medium ovenproof sauté pan or skillet. Sear the flounder for 2 minutes on each side, turning it gently with a metal spatula. Transfer the pan to the bottom rack of the preheated oven for 3 minutes. Turn the fillets gently and move the pan to the center rack for an additional 2 minutes. Remove the pan from the oven.

To serve: Place a fillet in each of 4 shallow soup bowls. Arrange 3 portions of spinach around each fillet. Place the asparagus over the spinach. Pour 1 cup of sauce into each bowl and garnish with the reserved wontons and the sliced green onions.

Note: *The wontons may be prepared 1 day in advance of frying; refrigerate them lightly dusted with flour and with sheets of waxed paper separating the layers. The sauce may also be prepared a day in advance and reheated in a medium saucepan over low heat.*

Pan-fried Skate Wings with Yellow Pepper Coulis

Everett Reid, American Seasons
Nantucket, Massachusetts

Serves 2

Skate wings are a delicacy in New England, and the vivid yellow pepper sauce makes this a beautiful presentation. The sauce may also be used for any pan-fried or grilled fish fillet.

Yellow Pepper Coulis

2 tablespoons olive oil
3 shallots, minced
2 garlic cloves, minced
¼ cup chopped leek
6 yellow bell peppers, seeded, deribbed, and chopped (see page 11)
¼ cup minced fresh basil
1½ cups fish stock (see page 21) or bottled clam juice
2½ cups dry white wine
Salt and freshly ground black pepper to taste
4 tablespoons unsalted butter, or ¼ cup heavy (whipping) cream (optional)

Skate Wings

12 to 14 ounces skate wings
Salt and freshly ground black pepper to taste
¼ teaspoon cayenne pepper, or to taste
¼ cup olive oil

Garnish

¼ cup chopped yellow bell pepper
1 tablespoon minced fresh parsley

To make the coulis: Heat the olive oil in a large sauté pan or skillet over medium heat. Add the shallots, garlic, and leek and sauté, stirring frequently, until the shallots are translucent, about 2 to 3 minutes. Add the yellow peppers and basil and cook for 3 to 4 minutes, or until the peppers are tender. Pour in the fish stock or clam juice and wine, and cook over high heat, stirring frequently, for 8 to 10 minutes, or until reduced by two thirds.

Puree the peppers in a blender or food processor and strain through a fine-meshed sieve. Season the sauce with salt and pepper, and add the butter or cream, if desired. Warm the sauce over low heat and keep warm.

To prepare the skate: Season the skate wings on each side with the salt, pepper, and cayenne. Heat the olive oil in a large sauté pan or skillet over medium-high heat. Sauté the fish 2 to 3 minutes on each side, or until just barely translucent.

To serve: Pour the yellow pepper coulis onto each of 2 plates. Top the sauce with the fish. Garnish each plate with chopped yellow pepper and minced parsley before serving.

Note: *The sauce may be made up to 2 days in advance and refrigerated, tightly covered. Reheat it over low heat in a small saucepan and add the butter or cream at that time, if desired.*

Pan-fried Skate Wings with Yellow Pepper Coulis; Everett Reid, American Seasons, Nantucket, Massachusetts

Little Touches

One of the luxuries of the restaurant kitchen is the staffing to make special side dishes and garnishes for entrees and desserts. Old-fashioned side dishes were often just boiled vegetables or plain potatoes, and the garnish was the ubiquitous sprig of parsley, but contemporary chefs create intriguing little dishes to complement their main dishes.

In testing recipes for *Great Chefs of the East,* we found some of these side dishes and garnishes to be so delicious and versatile that we believed they should be included in a separate chapter.

Bobby Flay's Sweet Potato Gratin, for example, will replace candied yams on my table from this point onward, and no Moroccan couscous dish will prepare you for Michael Lomonaco's Couscous with Foie Gras, with buttery bits of liver adding their richness to the semolina nuggets.

The headnotes to the recipes indicate which recipes they were designed to accompany, and suggest other main dishes they will complement. Use your own imagination and taste in deciding when to add these "little touches" to your own menus.

Karsky Shashlik Supreme; Paul Ingenito, The Russian Tea Room, New York

Lentil Ragout

Hans Schadler, Williamsburg Inn
Williamsburg, Virginia

Serves 4

The chef serves this as one of the side dishes to Stuffed Quail and Peppered Beef Tenderloin, (page 103); however, it is a delicious side dish for any simple entree. Cooking the delicate lentils in stock or broth makes them much richer than cooking them in water.

1 tablespoon minced pancetta
2 tablespoons minced onion
1 garlic clove, minced
1 tablespoon tomato paste
½ cup (4 ounces) red lentils
2 cups chicken stock (see page 20)
Salt and freshly ground black pepper
   to taste
1 teaspoon sherry vinegar

Place a large sauté pan or skillet over medium heat and fry the pancetta until it renders most of its fat, about 3 to 4 minutes. Add the onion and garlic and sauté, stirring frequently, until the onion is translucent, about 3 minutes. Add the tomato paste and cook for another 2 minutes, stirring constantly. Add the lentils, stock, salt, pepper, and vinegar. Bring the mixture to a boil, and reduce heat to low and simmer for 20 to 25 minutes, or until the lentils are tender and the ragout has a smooth consistency. Serve immediately.

Note: *The ragout may be made up to 2 days in advance and refrigerated, tightly covered. Reheat over low heat, stirring often.*

Stuffed Quail and Peppered Beef Tenderloin;
Hans Schadler, Williamsburg Inn,
Williamsburg, Virginia

Basmati Rice and Lentil Pilaf

Paul Ingenito, The Russian Tea Room
New York, New York

Serves 4

This pilaf, one of the accompaniments to Karsky Shashlik Supreme (see page 112), contains a wonderful blend of flavors: nutty basmati rice, tangy dried apricots, smoky bacon, and a light vinaigrette dressing.

Rice

1 cup basmati rice
3 tablespoons unsalted butter
4 large shallots, minced
1½ cups water or chicken stock
   (see page 20)
1½ teaspoons salt

Lentils

4 cups water or chicken stock
   (see page 20)
1 small onion, stuck with 2 cloves
2 garlic cloves, minced
2 fresh parsley sprigs
1 carrot, peeled
1 celery stalk
1 tablespoon salt
½ cup green lentils

3 tablespoons chopped dried apricots
1 large tomato, peeled, seeded,
   and finely diced (see page 18)
4 bacon strips, finely diced

2 tablespoons minced shallots
3 tablespoons minced fresh cilantro
1 tablespoon sherry wine vinegar
3 tablespoons olive oil
Salt and freshly ground black pepper
   to taste

To make the rice: Place the rice in a bowl, cover it with water, and carefully pour off the water. Cover the rice with water again and soak it for 45 minutes, changing the water as necessary if it becomes cloudy.

Melt the butter in a medium saucepan over low heat. Add the shallots, cover, and cook for 5 minutes, stirring occasionally. Add the water or stock to the pan and bring it to a boil over high heat. Add the rice and stir as the liquid returns to a boil. Stir in the salt, reduce heat to medium-low, cover, and cook the rice for 15 minutes. Remove the pan from heat and let sit, covered, for another 10 minutes. Spread the rice onto a flat tray to cool and set aside.

To make the lentils: Bring the water or chicken stock to a boil in a medium saucepan and add the onion and garlic. Tie the parsley, carrot, and celery together with kitchen twine and add them to the pot along with the salt. Simmer the liquid for 5 minutes and add the lentils. Cook at a bare simmer for about 20 to 25 minutes, or until the lentils are just tender. Let sit off heat in the liquid for about 15 minutes.

To finish the dish, place the rice, lentils, chopped apricots, and tomato in a bowl. Place the bacon in a cold small sauté pan or skillet and fry it over medium-high heat until crisp. Remove the bacon from the pan with a slotted spoon and add the shallots to the pan. Pour the bacon fat, shallots, and bacon bits into the rice mixture. Stir in the cilantro, vinegar, and olive oil. Add salt and pepper and serve.

Note: *The pilaf may be prepared up to 2 days in advance and refrigerated, tightly covered. Let it come to room temperature before serving.*

Wild Rice and Barley Pilaf

Hans Schadler, Williamsburg Inn
Williamsburg, Virginia

Serves 4

Wild rice is the seed of an aquatic grass not related to paddy rice or barley, but its nutty flavor is similar to and its toothsome texture contrasts nicely with pearl barley. The chef serves this as an accompaniment to Stuffed Quail and Peppered Beef Tenderloin, (page 103).

½ cup wild rice
2 tablespoons olive oil
1 tablespoon diced onion
1 tablespoon diced celery
1 tablespoon diced carrot
¾ cup chicken stock (see page 20)
4 cups water
Salt to taste
½ cup pearl barley
Freshly ground black pepper to taste
1 tablespoon minced fresh parsley

Wash the rice in a bowl of cold water to dislodge any dirt or sand particles. After washing, place the rice in a bowl and add boiling water to cover. Cover the bowl and let soak for at least 1 hour. Drain and rinse the rice, then set aside.

Heat the olive oil in a medium saucepan over medium heat. Add the onion, celery, and carrot, and cook for 3 minutes, stirring frequently, or until the onion is translucent. Add the wild rice and stock and bring the liquid to a boil. Cover the pan, reduce heat, and simmer the rice for 35 to 40 minutes, or until the rice is tender and the grains are separate. Check after 25 minutes and add more stock or water if it seems the pan is dry.

In a separate saucepan, bring the 4 cups of water to a boil and salt lightly. Add the barley, cover, and cook until the grains are tender but not mushy, about 30 to 35 minutes. Drain the barley in a sieve and mix it with the cooked wild rice. Adjust the seasoning with salt and pepper, sprinkle with the minced parsley, and serve.

Note: *The dish may be prepared 1 day in advance and refrigerated, tightly covered. Reheat it in a 300°F oven or a microwave oven until warm.*

Vegetable Couscous with Foie Gras

Michael Lomonaco, The "21" Club
New York, New York

Serves 4

Unlike instant rice, which bears no resemblance in texture to steamed rice, quick-cooking couscous is an excellent product that makes the lengthy steaming and special equipment for traditional couscous unnecessary. Michael Lomonaco serves this dish with Pan-roasted Quail with Port Sauce (page 97), but it would go equally well with any poultry, meat, or game dish.

1 package quick-cooking couscous
4 tablespoons unsalted butter
1 carrot, peeled and finely diced
1 leek, white part only, finely diced
4 ounces pâté de foie gras
   (see Mail-Order Sources)
½ teaspoon ground cinnamon
¼ teaspoon ground cumin seed
½ cup minced fresh cilantro
Salt and freshly ground pepper to taste
½ cup water

Place the couscous in a bowl, cover it with water, and carefully pour off the water. Melt 2 tablespoons of the butter in a sauté pan or skillet over medium heat. Add the carrot and leek and sauté for 3 minutes, stirring often, or until the leek is tender. Set aside.

Dice the pâté into ¼-inch pieces. Combine the rinsed couscous with the vegetables, pâté, the remaining 2 tablespoons butter, the cinnamon, cumin, cilantro, salt, and pepper in a large saucepan. Add the water, cover the pan, and bring to a boil over medium heat, stirring often. Turn off the heat and let sit for 12 to 15 minutes, or until the couscous is dry. Fluff it with a fork and serve.

Note: *The vegetables may be sautéed up to 4 hours in advance, but do not steam the couscous until just prior to serving.*

Pan-roasted Quail with Port Sauce; Michael Lomonaco, The '21' Club, New York

Root Vegetable Puree

~

Hans Schadler, Williamsburg Inn
Williamsburg, Virginia

Serves 4

This simple orange-colored puree accompanies the chef's Stuffed Quail and Peppered Beef Tenderloin, (page 103), but it is perfect with almost any roasted or broiled meat or poultry.

⅓ cup diced peeled celery root
⅓ cup diced peeled turnip
⅓ cup diced peeled carrot
¾ cup diced peeled boiling potatoes
⅓ cup plus 1 tablespoon milk
4 tablespoons unsalted butter
Salt and freshly ground black pepper
    to taste
¼ teaspoon ground nutmeg

Place the celery root, turnip, carrot, and potatoes in a large saucepan of lightly salted cold water and bring the water to a boil over high heat. Cook for 6 to 8 minutes, or until tender.

While the vegetables are cooking, heat the milk in a small saucepan. Strain the vegetables and puree them through a food mill or sieve. Immediately add the hot milk and the butter, stirring well to combine. Add the seasonings and serve immediately.

Note: *The puree may be prepared up to 3 hours in advance. Cover and let sit at room temperature. Reheat in a double boiler over simmering water to serve.*

Braised Red Cabbage

~

Paul Ingenito, The Russian Tea Room
New York, New York

Serves 4

Braised red cabbage is a favorite Russian dish, so it is only natural that the chef would brighten his Karshy Shaslik Supreme (page 112) with this version. The caraway seeds add a distinctive flavor to the dish, and it pairs well with all game and pork dishes.

1 red onion, thinly sliced
½ cup red wine vinegar
3 tablespoons grenadine
1 tablespoon caraway seeds
½ head red cabbage, cored and
    thinly sliced
1½ tablespoons sugar

½ cup golden raisins
Salt and freshly ground black pepper
    to taste

In a medium nonaluminum saucepan, combine the red onion, vinegar, grenadine, and caraway seeds. Cook, stirring occasionally, over medium heat for 10 minutes, or until the onions are wilted.

Add the cabbage and cook an additional 15 minutes. Add the sugar, raisins, salt, and pepper, and cook 10 minutes longer, or until the liquid is slightly evaporated but not dry. Adjust the seasoning and serve.

Note: *The cabbage may be prepared up to 2 days in advance and refrigerated, tightly covered. Reheat it over low heat or in a microwave oven.*

Karsky Shashlik Supreme; Paul Ingenito, The Russian Tea Room, New York

Braised Fennel

Patrick Clark, Hay Adams Hotel
Washington, D.C.

Serves 4

Chinese star anise reinforces the licorice flavor of the fennel in this savory side dish. Chef Clark serves braised fennel as a bed for Veal Chops with Oven-dried Tomatoes and Wild Mushrooms (see page 87), but it is delicious with any simple meat, poultry, or fish entree.

3 tablespoons unsalted butter
¼ cup minced shallots
1 fresh rosemary sprig
1 star anise
2 fennel bulbs, trimmed and cut
    into ¹⁄₁₆-inch julienne
1 cup chicken stock (see page 20)
Salt and freshly ground black pepper
    to taste

Melt the butter in a medium sauté pan or skillet over medium heat. Add the shallots and sauté, stirring frequently, for 2 to 3 minutes, or until the shallots are translucent. Add the rosemary, star anise, and fennel to the pan. Sauté for 2 to 3 minutes, or until the rosemary is fragrant and the fennel begins to wilt. Add the stock and bring to a boil over high heat. Reduce heat to medium and cook the mixture for 4 to 5 minutes, or until the fennel is cooked but still has a slightly crunchy texture and almost all the liquid has evaporated. Discard the rosemary and star anise, season the fennel with salt and pepper, and serve immediately.

Veal Chops with Oven-dried Tomatoes and Wild Mushrooms; Patrick Clark, Hay Adams Hotel, Washington, D.C.

Baked Spaghetti Squash

Andrew Wilkinson, The Rainbow Room
New York, New York

Serves 6

Spaghetti squash has become popular only in the past decade. It is easy to cook and fun to eat, since the strands do look like spaghetti when "combed." Wilkinson serves this dish with Venison Loin Chop (page 83), and it would be equally good with almost any entree.

1 spaghetti squash
Salt and freshly ground black pepper
    to taste
4 tablespoons unsalted butter

Preheat the oven to 350°F. Cut the spaghetti squash in half and season the inside with salt and pepper. Place the squash, cut-side down, on a baking sheet. Bake in the preheated oven for 1½ hours, or until the flesh is tender. Let cool completely, then turn the halves over and scrape the flesh out in spaghettilike strings with a fork. To serve, melt the butter in a large sauté pan or skillet over medium heat. Add the squash, season with salt and pepper, and stir the squash gently to warm it through.

Note: *The squash may be baked up to 2 days in advance and refrigerated, tightly covered. Reheat it over low heat in a covered sauté pan just prior to serving.*

Rosemary Spaetzle

Andrew Wilkinson, The Rainbow Room
New York, New York

Serves 6

Spaetzle are small free-form boiled dumplings served as a starch in German and Austrian cooking. The chef serves these to accompany Venison Loin Chop, (page 83); however, they are good with any meat, poultry, or game dish.

4½ cups all-purpose flour
1 tablespoon salt
½ cup minced fresh rosemary
2 cups milk
4 eggs

Mix the flour, salt, and rosemary together in a large mixing bowl. Beat the milk and eggs together with a whisk. Make a well in the middle of the flour, add the liquid ingredients, and mix well. The spaetzle dough will be sticky but pliable. Cover and refrigerate for a minimum of 1 hour.

To cook: Fill a medium saucepan with lightly salted water and bring to a boil over high heat. Using a spaetzle-maker if available, place the dough in the top of the machine and press the dumplings through the holes into the boiling water. Alternatively, press the dough through the largest holes of a box grater or a large-holed colander directly into the boiling water. When the dumplings float to the surface of the water, they are cooked. Drain and serve immediately.

Note: *If the spaetzle are not to be served immediately, remove them from the water and plunge them into a waiting bowl of cold water and set aside until needed. Reheat the spaetzle in a saucepan with 2 tablespoons melted unsalted butter over medium heat, or in a microwave.*

Cucumber and Red Onion Salad with Mint Chutney

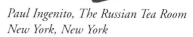

Paul Ingenito, The Russian Tea Room
New York, New York

Serves 4

This salad, served as an accent to the chef's Karshy Shashlik Supreme (page 112), is similar to Indian raita; the mint chutney adds a cooling flavor. It is excellent with any lamb or rich poultry dish.

Salad
1 European cucumber
½ small red onion, chopped
1 tablespoon cider vinegar
1 tablespoon sugar
½ cup sour cream
Salt and freshly ground black pepper
   to taste

Mint Chutney
1 cup fresh mint leaves, minced
2 green onions, white part only,
   finely chopped
1 teaspoon curry powder
1½ teaspoons sugar
¼ teaspoon cayenne pepper
Juice of 1 lemon
Salt to taste

To make the salad: Peel, seed, and quarter the cucumber lengthwise, and cut it into small horizontal slices. Combine the red onion, vinegar, sugar, and sour cream. Stir the mixture gently into the cucumber, season with salt and pepper, and set aside.

To make the mint chutney: Combine all the ingredients in a small bowl and set aside.

To serve: Place a dollop of cucumber salad on each plate and top with 1 tablespoon of the mint chutney.

Note: *The salad and chutney may be prepared 1 day in advance and refrigerated separately, tightly covered.*

Venison Loin Chop, Andrew Wilkinson, The Rainbow Room, New York

Sweet-Potato Gratin

Bobby Flay, Mesa Grill
New York, New York

Serves 4 to 5

This dish will forever replace any recipe you may have for sweet potatoes—it's a great way to enjoy their delicate flavor. Chef Flay serves this to accompany his Ancho-rubbed Game Hens (see page 123), but it would go well with any meat or poultry entree.

2 cups heavy (whipping) cream
½ canned chipolte chili
3 sweet potatoes, peeled and thinly sliced
Salt and freshly ground black pepper
    to taste

Preheat the oven to 350°F. Puree the cream and chili in a blender or food processor until smooth; be careful not to over-process or the cream will turn to butter. Arrange one fourth of the sweet potato slices in an 8-inch square baking pan. Season with salt and pepper, and cover with one fourth of the cream. Repeat the process until all the potatoes and cream are used. Bake in the preheated oven for 1 hour, or until the cream has been absorbed and the potatoes are browned. Serve warm.

Note: *The gratin may be prepared up to 1 day in advance and refrigerated, tightly covered. Reheat it in a 350°F oven for 15 minutes, or until hot.*

Ancho-rubbed Game Hens; Bobby Flay, Mesa Grill, New York

Red Pepper Chutney

Paul Ingenito, The Russian Tea Room
New York, New York

Serves 4

This is one of the many relishes that accompany the chef's elaborate lamb presentation, Karshy Shashlik Supreme (page 112). The spices add pungency to the colorful peppers and green onions, making this an excellent chutney for any grilled food.

3 red bell peppers
2 green onions
2 tablespoons olive oil
⅛ teaspoon cumin seeds
⅛ teaspoon caraway seeds
⅛ teaspoon coriander seeds
1 tablespoon minced fresh cilantro
1 tablespoon sherry wine vinegar
Salt, freshly ground black pepper, and
    cayenne pepper to taste

Coat the red peppers and green onions lightly with the olive oil and place over glowing red coals on a charcoal grill, turning frequently. The green onions should be removed as soon as they turn bright green and the outer leaves are barely blackened. The skin on the peppers should blacken thoroughly and blister.

After all sides have been charred, remove the peppers from the grill and place them in a medium mixing bowl. Cover the bowl with plastic wrap or a plate for 10 minutes, then remove the skin and seeds from the peppers. Cut the grilled green onions into 1-inch lengths and chop the peppers and onions roughly.

Place a small dry sauté pan or skillet over medium heat. Add the cumin, coriander, and caraway, and toast until the spices begin to give off a nutty aroma, about 1 to 2 minutes. Remove the pan from heat and let the spices cool. Transfer the mixture to a miniature food processor or coffee grinder and grind it into a fine powder; this also may be done by hand with a mortar and pestle. Add to the pepper-onion mixture. Stir in the cilantro, vinegar, salt, pepper, and cayenne. Check the chutney for seasoning and adjust if necessary.

Note: *The chutney may be made 1 day in advance and refrigerated, tightly covered. Allow it to reach room temperature before serving.*

Loin of Venison; Patrick Grangien, Cafe Shelburne, Shelburne, Vermont

Potato Roses

Patrick Grangien, Cafe Shelburne
Shelburne, Vermont

Serves 4

Crisp brown potato roses are a garnish for the chef's Loin of Venison, (page 85). Although these are a good deal of work and require a steady hand with a paring knife, they cause gasps of awe when served.

4 round red potatoes, peeled
1 cup clarified butter (see page 19)
Salt and freshly ground black pepper
 to taste

Using a very sharp paring knife, cut a slice off the bottom of 1 of the potatoes so that it sits flat on the counter. Holding the potato with the flat surface on the bottom, cut a continuous slice so that the potato becomes a long, curled sheet. If the potato breaks, keep slicing; the dish can be assembled later.

When you get to the center of the potato, leave a piece the size of a cork. Twirl the potato back loosely, and it will curve and form a rose shape. Place the rose gently in a bowl of ice water to prevent discoloration, and repeat with the remaining potatoes.

Preheat the oven to 350°F. Heat the clarified butter over high heat in a small saucepan. Drain 1 potato rose and blot it gently with paper towels to avoid splat-tering. Season the potato with salt and pepper, and gently lower it into the hot butter with a slotted spoon or tongs. Fry the potato for 3 to 4 minutes, or until browned. Remove it from the pan with a slotted spoon and place it in a shallow baking dish. Repeat with the remaining potato roses.

Place the potatoes in the oven and bake for 15 to 25 minutes, or until very brown. Blot gently with paper towels and serve immediately.

Note: *The potatoes may be cut, fried, and left at room temperature up to 4 hours before being baked.*

Cranberry-Apricot Relish

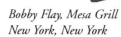

Bobby Flay, Mesa Grill
New York, New York

Makes 4 to 5 cups

Chef Flay serves this as an accompani-ment to his Ancho-rubbed Game Hens, (page 123), but it also is fabulous with turkey, chicken, or pork. The tart cran-berries and tangy dried apricots are a stellar pairing.

2 tablespoons unsalted butter
2 minced seeded jalapeño chilies
½ cup finely diced red onion
2 tablespoons minced fresh ginger
4 cups (1 pound) fresh or thawed
 frozen cranberries

2 cups fresh orange juice
2 tablespoons packed light brown sugar
½ cup honey
8 ounces dried apricots, cut into julienne
1 tablespoon curry powder
Salt and freshly ground black pepper
 to taste

Melt the butter in a medium saucepan over medium heat. Add the jalapeños, onion, ginger, and 2 cups of the cran-berries and cook for 5 minutes, or until the cranberries have popped.

Increase the heat to high, add the orange juice, brown sugar, and honey, and bring to a boil. Reduce heat to medium and simmer for 10 minutes. Add the remaining 2 cups cranberries and simmer for 5 minutes. Add the apricots, curry powder, salt, and pepper. Mix well and remove the pan from heat. Pour the relish into a shallow nonalum-inum container and let cool at room temperature. Pour the mixture into a bowl, cover, and refrigerate.

Note: *The relish will keep up to 2 weeks in the refrigerator.*

Celery Root Charlotte

Patrick Grangien, Cafe Shelburne
Shelburne, Vermont

Serves 4

The chef serves this silky custard as an accompaniment to Loin of Venison, (page 85). It is beautiful, with stripes of vegetables encasing the pale filling, and not difficult to make.

3 tablespoons unsalted butter
1 celery root, about 12 ounces to
 1 pound
1 egg, lightly beaten
Salt and freshly ground white pepper
 to taste
2 carrots, peeled and cut
 into ¹⁄₁₆-inch julienne
1 large zucchini, cut into
 ¹⁄₁₆-inch julienne
1 yellow squash, cut into
 ¹⁄₁₆-inch julienne

Use 1 tablespoon of the butter to grease the inside of four 6-ounce ramekins. Peel the celery root and slice it thinly, quickly placing the slices in a medium saucepan filled with cold water to prevent discoloration. Lightly salt the water and bring the pan to a boil over high heat. Reduce the heat to medium and boil the slices until tender, about 15 to 20 minutes. Drain, add the remaining 2 tablespoons of butter to the slices, and set aside to cool.

When the celery root has cooled, place the slices in a blender or food processor and puree until smooth. Fold in the beaten egg, season with salt and pepper, and set aside.

While the celery root is cooking, bring another pot of lightly salted water to a boil. Add the carrots and boil until tender yet still firm, about 2 to 3 minutes. Remove the carrots from the pan with a slotted spoon. Boil the zucchini for 1½ to 2 minutes and remove from the water. Cook the squash for 1½ to 2 minutes and drain. Set all the vegetables aside individually.

Preheat the oven to 350°F. When the vegetables are cool, line the inside of the ramekins with the vegetables in alternating colors (carrot, squash, zucchini). The colored side of the squash and zucchini sticks should be facing the outside of the ramekin. After each mold has been lined with the vegetable sticks, fill the molds with the celery root puree. Place the filled ramekins in a roasting pan and place it in the oven. Pour in enough hot water to come halfway up the side of the ramekins. Bake the ramekins in the water bath until the celery root mixture is set, about 15 to 20 minutes, or when a knife inserted in the center comes out clean.

Carefully remove the ramekins from the pan and let sit for 5 minutes. To serve, invert the ramekins onto small plates and move the custards to the entree plates with a large metal spatula.

Note: *The ramekins may be prepared for baking 1 day in advance and refrigerated, covered with plastic wrap. Add 10 to 15 minutes to the baking time.*

Chocolate Tuile Cookies

*Richard Leach, One Fifth Avenue
New York, New York*

Makes about 48 cookies

The chef serves these crispy wafers with his Riot in Chocolate (page 211), but they could be the stars themselves with a bowl of ice cream or as part of a cookie assortment.

½ cup (1 stick) unsalted butter at
   room temperature
¼ cup honey
½ cup all-purpose flour
1¼ cups confectioners' sugar
¼ cup unsweetened cocoa powder
¼ cup egg whites (about 2 or 3)

Preheat the oven to 375°F. Combine the butter and honey in a large bowl and beat until the mixture is smooth and pale in color, about 5 minutes. Sift the flour, confectioners' sugar, and cocoa powder together. Add to the butter and honey and mix until incorporated. Slowly add the egg whites and mix until smooth.

To bake the tuiles: Use an X-acto blade or a sharp paring knife to make a stencil from the top of a plastic deli or cottage cheese container by cutting out any shape you wish (the chef uses a leaf shape). Place the plastic top on a well-greased jellyroll pan and spread the batter in it until the batter is thin and smooth. Remove the plastic top to leave the shaped batter. Repeat until all the cookies have been made. Bake in the preheated oven for 5 to 6 minutes, or until the cookies are firm and dry. Remove from the baking sheet with a large spatula and let cool on waxed paper or parchment paper.

Note: *The cookies may also be baked into circles by pouring the batter directly onto the pan, then molded by draping them over a rolling pin, or by laying them over the upturned bottom of a cup to form a basket shape. This must be done immediately after the cookies are taken from the oven, before they cool.*

A Riot in Chocolate; Richard Leach, One Fifth Avenue, New York

Desserts

*P*astry chefs are the unsung heroes of many restaurant kitchens; they are given full credit on *Great Chefs of the East,* however, their names and biographies appear with their recipes on the following pages.

While some young American chefs create all the components of their menus, in most fine restaurants the desserts and breads are created by a specialist in a style that is harmonious with the rest of the menu.

In this chapter you will find mouth-watering sensations to serve as a sweet finale to any meal. Some of the offerings use regional foods; maple is a central ingredient flavoring an ice cream and many egg-based concoctions.

Fresh fruit is glorified in a number of ways, from Nitzi Rabin's light, vividly flavored Plum Soufflé with Cinnamon to Jacques Torres's Exotic Fruit Soup in a Sugar Cage, which combines perfectly poached fruit topped with a perforated layer of crunchy caramel. Kilian Weigand layers vibrantly colored blueberries with a caramel sauce and a creamy mousse between crisp cookies in his Mascarpone Cheesecake with Lacy Nut Wafers and Blueberry Caramel.

If wine aficionados believe that the first rule of any wine is to be red, then the dessert corollary for many people is that the first rule of any dessert is to be chocolate. Chocophiles will have a range of forms from which to choose, from Richard Leach's A Riot in Chocolate—an insurrection complete with chocolate-tea ice cream—to Dominique Leborgne's Swans with White Chocolate Mousse, an elegant offering made from crisp cream-puff dough.

Do not be intimidated by the intricacy of the desserts in some of the photographs in this chapter. In most recipes, the components of the dishes are easy, while some garnishes require advanced skills. If you like, just skip the garnishes and wow your guests with the main event.

Cool Caramel Mousse with Cinnamon-basted Fruit; Dan Rundell, Aureole, New York

Vanilla Parfait

Robert Bennett, Le Bec-Fin
Philadelphia, Pennsylvania

Makes two 9-by-5-inch loaves;
serves 12 to 16

Colorful nuts and fruits dot slices of velvety vanilla- and fig-scented mousse, a wonderful dessert for a dinner party since it may be made a few days in advance and frozen.

Parfait

1 cup (4 ounces) coarsely chopped blanched almonds, toasted (see page 16)

1 cup (4 ounces) coarsely chopped pistachio nuts, toasted (see page 16)
¾ cup candied orange peel, coarsely chopped
¾ cup brandied cherries, coarsely chopped
4 cups heavy (whipping) cream
8 egg yolks
2 vanilla beans, split lengthwise
1¼ cups sugar
⅓ cup water
1 cup Fig Jam (recipe follows)

Garnish

6 ounces bittersweet chocolate, chopped
2 bananas
2 cups caramel sauce (see page 19), chilled

To make the parfait: Line a 9-by-5-inch loaf pan with waxed paper or parchment paper and set aside.

Toss the almonds, pistachios, orange peel, and cherries together. Spread the mixture out on a baking sheet and place the pan in the freezer. Whip the heavy cream in a deep bowl until it reaches soft peaks. Set aside.

Place the egg yolks and the vanilla beans in a mixer bowl and beat with a whisk attachment at medium speed until the mixture is foamy. Combine the sugar and water in a small saucepan, swirl gently to moisten the sugar, and brush the sides of the pan with a wet pastry brush. Boil over high heat until the syrup

Vanilla Parfait, Robert Bennett, Le Bec-Fin, Philadelphia

reaches 250° to 260°F on a candy thermometer, or to the "firm ball" stage
(a droplet of the hot syrup placed in a
cup of ice water will form a ball that
feels hard when picked up and pressed
between the fingers).

Turn the mixer to high speed and
slowly stream the hot sugar syrup into
the beaten egg yolks and vanilla bean.
Continue to beat at high speed until the
mixture is thick and cool. Strain through
a fine-meshed sieve to remove the vanilla
beans. Fold the fig jam, whipped cream,
and the nuts and fruit into the egg yolk
mixture, and scrape the mixture into the
prepared loaf pan. Cover and freeze
until firm.

To make the garnish: Preheat the oven to
250°F. Place the chopped chocolate in an
ovenproof baking dish and place it in the
oven. Turn off the oven and let the chocolate remain there for 5 to 7 minutes, or
until melted. Stir the chocolate and
spread an even layer ¹⁄₁₆-inch thick onto a
piece of waxed paper or parchment
paper. Allow it to cool until almost hard.
Using a pastry scraper, scrape the chocolate into bands to form curled "ribbons."
Set aside. Peel the bananas, cut them into
¼-inch-thick slices, and stir the slices
gently into the caramel sauce.

To serve: Remove the loaf pan from the
freezer, invert it onto a platter, and
discard the waxed or parchment paper.
Place a chocolate ribbon at the top of
each plate with a slice of parfait below it.
Spoon the caramel-coated bananas at the
bottom of the plate.

Fig Jam
(Makes 1½ cups)

1 pound dried Turkish figs, quartered
Grated zest of 1 lemon
1 cup water

Combine all the ingredients in a small
saucepan and bring to a boil over medium
heat. Lower the heat and simmer the figs
until the water is absorbed and the figs
are tender. Puree in a food blender or
processor, then push through a sieve.
Cover and refrigerate to store.

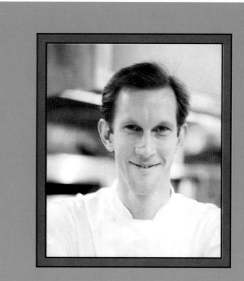

ROBERT BENNETT
Le Bec-Fin, Philadelphia, Pennsylvania

"Nothing is more a symbol of Le Bec-Fin, nothing more beloved by
its fans and addicts, than the dessert cart," says *Philadelphia* magazine's
food critic Jim Quinn. Customers can enjoy as much as they are able to
eat from the cart, which is replete with more than forty desserts a night.
Le Bec-Fin's range of confections showcases works "laced with edible
gold, slathered with the best (and most expensive) French chocolate,
packed with seasonal fruits," writes Quinn.

Classic French cuisine holds a time-honored place for dessert. But
when chef George Perrier filled the important position of pastry chef,
he chose Robert Bennett, a Virginia native, rather than one of his French
countrymen.

Bennett says that he had "plenty of time to experiment" with food
while he was growing up, because "my mother never used the kitchen." A
graduate of the New England Culinary Institute, Bennett completed his
second year of school before the end of his first year of enrollment. He
spent his remaining time working in the pastry department where,
shortly after graduation, he became the executive pastry instructor.

During his tenure, he was invited to President Reagan's second in-
augural as guest pastry chef. For the occasion, he created a gigantic cake
to serve forty-four thousand; it was a replica of Capitol Hill. Beginning
with a 6-by-8-foot base, Bennett built the cake in graduating tiers and
crowned it with a sugar replica of the U.S. Capitol.

Since joining Le Bec-Fin, Bennett has competed in the World Cup of
Pastry held in France, placing fifth. "No excuses," says the chef, "but we
only had two months to prepare. I'll do better in the next one. But it's
not so bad to be fifth in pastry—worldwide."

While the chef's fame is spreading, his desserts, including his signature Vanilla Parfait, are a highlight at Le Bec-Fin. Bennett also
contributes to the community. Among other public services, he donates
more than three thousand petits fours, chocolates, pastries, and frozen
desserts for an annual dinner to raise funds for Philadelphia's Stop Child
Abuse Now.

Charities aren't the only ones who are grateful to Bennett. Customers
of Le Bec-Fin are always thankful that they were warned to save room for
dessert.

Maple Crêpes Souffleés

Yves Labbé, Le Cheval d'Or
Jeffersonville, Vermont

Serves 8

The chef serves this maple-flavored New England dessert in the fall, garnished with vividly colored maple leaves. Many kitchen stores sell paper leaves in the same red tone.

Crêpes
½ cup all-purpose flour
1 tablespoon sugar
Pinch of salt
1 egg
1 egg yolk
¼ cup milk
¼ cup water
4 tablespoons clarified butter (see page 19), melted
1 tablespoon rum

Maple Pastry Cream
½ cup milk
1 egg yolk
2 tablespoons maple sugar
1 tablespoon flour

Soufflé Filling
1½ cups egg whites (about 12 egg whites)
½ teaspoon cream of tartar
1½ cups maple sugar
⅓ cup Maple Pastry Cream, above

Garnish
1 cup crème anglaise (see page 19), flavored with 2 tablespoons maple syrup or bourbon

To make the crepes: Mix the flour, sugar, and salt together in a blender or food processor and, with the motor running, add the egg, egg yolk, milk, water, 1½ tablespoons of the clarified butter, and the rum. Scrape the sides of the container with a rubber spatula and blend again. Cover and place in the refrigerator for at least 1 hour before using. The batter should be the consistency of light cream. If it is too thick, add enough rum or water to thin.

To cook the crepes: Brush the bottom of a 5- to 6-inch crepe or sauté pan with some of the remaining clarified butter and place the pan over medium-high heat. When the pan is almost smoking, pour ¼ cup of batter into the center of the pan. Rotate the pan quickly and evenly in a circular motion to distribute the batter over the bottom of the pan. Pour any excess back into the batter and cook the crepe until bubbles begin to form in the center and the edges begin to brown, about 30 to 45 seconds. Turn the crepe with a spatula and cook until the second side is lightly browned, about 15 to 20 seconds. Repeat to cook the remaining batter, stacking the crepes on a plate, separated by sheets of waxed paper or parchment paper.

To make the pastry cream: Bring the milk to a boil in a small nonaluminum saucepan over medium heat. While the milk is heating, mix the egg yolk and maple sugar thoroughly in a small bowl. Add the flour, stirring well, then add ¼ cup of the boiling milk to the egg mixture. Return this mixture to the milk in the pan and bring to a rolling boil over medium heat, whisking constantly. Transfer to a small nonaluminum bowl set in a larger bowl of ice, cover with a sheet of plastic wrap pressed directly into the surface, and let cool.

Preheat the oven to 550°F, or the highest the oven can be set without broiling.

To make the filling: Place the egg whites in a large bowl and beat until foamy. Add the cream of tartar and beat until soft peaks form. Slowly add the maple sugar, a few tablespoons at a time, beating until the egg whites are glossy and stiff. Place the pastry cream in a large bowl and stir in one fourth of the meringue. Gently fold in the remaining meringue.

To assemble the dessert: Fill 8 crepes with equal portions of meringue, then fold the crepes in half. Place in a shallow ovenproof pan and bake for 3 to 5 minutes, or until the crepe filling is puffed and well browned. Transfer each crepe to a dessert plate, using a metal spatula, and spoon crème anglaise around each crepe.

Note: *The crepes and maple pastry cream may be prepared up to 2 days in advance and refrigerated, tightly covered with plastic wrap.*

Maple Ice Cream in a Caramel Cage

John Foster, Hemingway's
Killington, Vermont

Makes 2 quarts; serves 8

Maple ice cream is not only elegant served in its caramel cage, but it is also the perfect topping for apple or pecan pies for Thanksgiving dinner. The creamy custard ice cream base is the perfect vehicle for the delicate taste of maple.

Maple Ice Cream
2 cups milk
6 eggs
2 cups maple syrup
2 cups heavy (whipping) cream

Caramel Cages
2 cups sugar
2 tablespoons water
1 tablespoon maple syrup
⅛ teaspoon cream of tartar

Garnish
Fresh berries
8 mint sprigs

To make the ice cream: In a heavy saucepan, heat the milk until bubbles form around the edge of the pan and a skin forms on the top; do not let it boil. Remove from heat. In a large bowl, beat the eggs and the maple syrup until well blended. Slowly whisk in the hot milk, return the mixture to the milk pan, and place over medium heat. Cook, stirring constantly, until the mixture is thick enough to coat the back of a wooden spoon so that a line drawn through it remains visible; do not let the mixture boil or the eggs will curdle. Strain the mixture through a fine-meshed sieve into a nonaluminum container; cover and let cool. Cover and refrigerate overnight.

Blend the heavy cream into the custard mixture and freeze in an ice cream maker according to the manufacturer's instructions, or see page 14 if you do not have an ice cream freezer.

Maple Syrup Gratin; Patrick Grangien, Cafe Shelburne, Shelburne, Vermont

To make caramel cages: Spray the inside and rim of a shallow soup bowl with vegetable oil spray or rub it with a lightly oiled paper towel. Wipe out any excess, then spray or oil again. Place the soup bowl on a large sheet of waxed paper and set aside.

Place a large saucepan over medium-high heat and add the sugar. Add the water and maple syrup, stirring to combine. Add the cream of tartar. Stir the mixture occasionally until the sugar has melted and begun to turn color. When the sugar is a light amber, remove the pan from heat. Working quickly, dip a fork into the hot caramel and drizzle the caramel over the inside and rim of the prepared soup bowl, turning the soup bowl to cover the surface evenly. Let the caramel cool, then tip the plate over and invert the cage. Repeat to make a total of 8 cages, reheating the caramel carefully over low heat if necessary.

To serve: Place 3 small scoops of ice cream in the center of each dessert plate and cover with an inverted caramel cage. Garnish with berries and fresh mint.

Note: The ice cream may be prepared up to 2 days in advance; let the ice cream soften for 15 minutes before serving.

Maple Syrup Gratin

Patrick Grangien, Cafe Shelburne Shelburne, Vermont

Makes six 3-inch mousses; serves 6

These creamy raspberry-filled mousses flavored with maple are a sophisticated and light dessert using Vermont's most famous culinary asset. Instead of individual servings, it also may be prepared in a large ovenproof baking dish.

Maple Base
1½ packages unflavored gelatin
3 tablespoons cold water
2 cups heavy (whipping) cream
1½ cups maple syrup
6 egg yolks
1 teaspoon cornstarch
6 egg whites
1½ cups fresh raspberries

Maple Cream Sauce
1 cup heavy (whipping) cream
¼ cup maple syrup

Garnish
Fresh raspberries
6 mint sprigs

To make the maple base: Sprinkle the gelatin over the cold water in a cup. Allow the mixture to sit for 10 minutes, or until the water is absorbed. Bring the cream to a boil in a medium saucepan over medium heat, stirring so that it does not boil over onto the stove. In a medium bowl, combine 1 cup of the maple syrup with the egg yolks and cornstarch and whisk until the mixture is light and lemon-colored. Whisk the cream into the egg yolks, return the mixture to the saucepan, and bring to a boil. Add the gelatin mixture and cook over medium heat until the gelatin is dissolved. Pour the mixture into a large bowl, cover, and chill until the mixture is cool and has begun to set.

In a small saucepan, bring the remaining ½ cup maple syrup to a boil over medium heat, then reduce the heat and cook for 2 to 3 minutes. Set aside and keep warm. In a large bowl, beat the egg whites until soft peaks form. Gradually add the heated syrup while beating to form a stiff, glossy meringue. Cover and chill the meringue for 1 hour.

Fold the meringue into the chilled egg yolk mixture. Place six 3-inch tart rings on a baking sheet. Fill the tart rings halfway with the mousse. Layer the raspberries on each mousse and fill the rings completely with the remaining mousse. Level the tops of the rings with a spatula. Chill the mousses for 2 to 3 hours, or until set.

To make the sauce: Bring the cream to a boil in a small saucepan over medium heat and simmer for 1 minute. Add the maple syrup and stir to combine; set aside and keep warm.

To serve: Place 1 mousse on each of 6 ovenproof serving plates and preheat the broiler. Run a knife around the inside rim of the tart rings and remove the rings. Place the mousses under the broiler for 20 to 30 seconds, or until lightly browned on top. Spoon the maple syrup cream sauce around each mousse and garnish with raspberries and sprigs of fresh mint.

Note: The mousses may be prepared up to 1 day in advance and refrigerated, tightly covered. Broil the mousses and make the maple sauce just before serving.

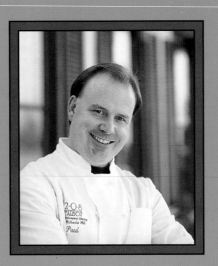

PAUL MILNE
208 Talbot, St. Michaels, Maryland

In a town known for its crab houses, finding "casual gourmet dining," as co-owners Paul Milne and Candy Chiaruttini term the fare at 208 Talbot, is a treat. One critic said that the credo at the restaurant, which opened in 1990, should be "nouvelle cuisine in ample portions." Named for its street address, the restaurant continues to attract locals and weekend visitors in the small seaside town of St. Michaels on the Chesapeake Bay.

After attending the University of Maryland Business School for three years, Milne decided that cooking was his true passion, so he enrolled in the Culinary Institute of America where he graduated first in his class. He combined his culinary and business experience as chef-partner of Kings Contrivance Restaurant, a two-hundred-seat establishment between Washington, D.C., and Baltimore. After six years of managing twenty-five cooks and serving as many as 750 dinners on holidays, Milne bought his own intimate restaurant on the eastern shore of Maryland.

The "casual gourmet" atmosphere of 208 Talbot appeals to Milne's patrons, a number of whom are boaters who dock at one of the several marinas in the historic town. "Also, a lot of the homes in St. Michaels are weekend homes for people who come from Philadelphia, New York, and Washington," says Milne. "After a week in the city, they do not want to wear a tie to dinner."

During the waterfowl season, hunters who travel to the Eastern Shore from all over the United States will often bring their ducks and geese to Milne to be prepared for the evening dinner crowds. For all diners, 208 Talbot's commitment to fresh ingredients is reflected in Milne's signature dishes, such as Oysters with Champagne Sauce. The restaurant also makes all of its ice creams, and is known for such concoctions as Coffee–Butterfinger Crunch Ice Cream.

For Milne, running a restaurant means long hours but big rewards. "Being a chef is something I have always enjoyed. It is a profession where the fruits of one's labors are experienced on a daily basis," he says.

Coffee–Butterfinger Crunch Ice Cream

Paul Milne, 208 Talbot
St. Michaels, Maryland

Makes 1½ quarts; serves 6 to 8

The ingenious part of this easy-to-make ice cream is the texture and flavor added by the candy bars. Any crunchy candy may be used in place of Butterfingers, or you may adapt the concept to your favorite flavor combinations.

2 cups half-and-half
2 cups heavy (whipping) cream
8 egg yolks
⅓ cup sugar
1 tablespoon instant coffee powder mixed with
2 tablespoons hot water
8 ounces Butterfinger candy bars, coarsely chopped

Place the half-and-half and cream in a heavy, medium saucepan. Bring the mixture to a boil over medium heat, stirring occasionally to make sure it does not boil over.

In a medium bowl, beat the egg yolks and sugar until the mixture is fluffy and pale in color. Add one fourth of the cream mixture to the eggs, then pour the egg mixture back into the saucepan. Whisk the dissolved instant coffee into the mixture in the pan.

Place the pan over low heat and stir constantly with a wooden spoon until the mixture thickens so that a line drawn on the back of the spoon does not fill in. Be careful not to let the custard boil, or the egg yolks will curdle. Strain the mixture through a fine-meshed sieve and cool in a bowl set over ice cubes.

Freeze the mixture in an ice cream machine according to the manufacturer's instructions, or use see "Making Ice Cream without a Machine" on page 14. When the mixture is almost frozen, stir in the chopped candy pieces. Continue to freeze until hard.

Note: The ice cream may be made up to 2 days in advance and kept frozen. Let sit at room temperature for 30 minutes before to serving.

Coffee-Butterfinger Crunch Ice Cream; Paul Milne, 208 Talbot, St. Michaels, Maryland

Zabaglione Sarah Venezia

Francesco Antonucci, Remi
New York, New York

Serves 6

Zabaglione, a custard flavored with Marsala wine, is a classic Italian dessert. In this version, the chef molds that zabaglione in a cookie cutter and tops it with ice cream, but you may simply mound the custard on each dessert plate.

8 egg yolks (or 10 yolks if molding
  the dessert)
⅓ cup dry Marsala wine
6 tablespoons sugar

Garnish
1 pint vanilla ice cream
2 cups fresh raspberries
1 cup fresh strawberries, hulled
6 fresh mint sprigs

Combine the egg yolks, wine, and sugar in a medium mixing bowl, and whisk well. Place the bowl over a pan of barely simmering water and continue to

Zabaglione Sarah Venezia; Francesco Antonucci, Remi, New York

whisk. Be certain that the water does not reach boiling temperature; if the water is too hot it will cook the eggs. Keep whisking the mixture over heat until the mixture has thickened enough so that whisking the yolks reveals the bottom of the bowl, then remove from heat.

If you want to mold the dessert, spoon the warm zabaglione into an upside-down cookie cutter placed on a plate (Francesco Antonucci uses a 5-inch star cookie cutter). Let the zabaglione set for 5 minutes. Alternatively, mound the zabaglione on each of 6 dessert plates.

To serve: Preheat the broiler. If using a mold, remove it at this time. Put each dessert under the broiler and cook the zabaglione until it is lightly browned, about 30 to 45 seconds. Place a scoop of vanilla ice cream in the center of each serving of zabaglione. Garnish with the fresh berries and mint sprigs and serve immediately.

Note: *The zabaglione may be made and molded or mounded up to 1 hour in advance.*

FRANCESCO ANTONUCCI
Remi, New York, New York

New York's Remi was rated the best Italian restaurant in the United States by Luigi Veronelli, Italy's premier food writer. Much of the credit goes to Remi's Venetian-born co-owner and chef Francesco Antonucci, whose Northern Italian cuisine and experimental savvy have kept customers and critics raving since its opening in 1987. One critic described Antonucci's style as more akin to alchemy than cooking, noting his talent for transforming simple ingredients into innovative dishes.

Remi has attracted young celebrities and seasoned food veterans alike to experience its Venetian food and the stunning interior design of co-owner Adam Tihany, which Antonucci describes as "our vision of traveling the Grand Canal in Venice." The restaurant's Gothic decor, with its twenty-five-foot-high ceilings, medieval arches, and room-length mural of Venice, embody Antonucci's vision of fine dining. "People eat in restaurants not just because they are hungry, but also because they are looking for something special—fun, excitement, service, energy, original cuisine, or even just an escape," he says.

The signature dishes that emerge from Antonucci's kitchen, from Ravioli Marco Polo (tuna ravioli topped with ginger) to Saffron Pappardelle with Osso Buco Sauce to Zabaglione Sarah Venezia, reflect his culinary credo: "Venetian cuisine uses only the best, most simple ingredients, yet develops into a wonderful, surprising complexity of flavors."

Antonucci trained in Milan, but says he has "always kept working in the Venetian style." In his stated quest to "discover new influences and to create new combinations," Antonucci now spends his spare time training chefs at the Remi restaurants that have opened recently in Mexico City and Tel Aviv. "I have the opportunity to learn and appreciate new flavors and tastes so that I may continue my development and keep on the cutting edge."

Indian Pudding

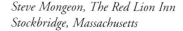

Steve Mongeon, The Red Lion Inn
Stockbridge, Massachusetts

Serves 10 to 12

Indian pudding goes back to colonial days, but a topping of vanilla ice cream or whipped cream makes this historic dish a contemporary dessert. The apple and raisins add texture to the smooth pudding.

6 cups milk
½ cup (1 stick) unsalted butter
½ cup plus 2 tablespoons cornmeal
2 eggs
2⅔ cups molasses
3 tablespoons ground cinnamon
1 tablespoon ground ginger
1 Granny Smith or other tart green
   apple, peeled, cored, and thinly sliced
½ cup raisins
Vanilla ice cream or sweetened whipped
   cream for serving

   Preheat the oven to 300°F. Butter a 2½- to 3-quart shallow ovenproof dish and set aside.

   In a medium saucepan, combine 5 cups of the milk with the butter and heat over medium heat to just below the

STEVEN MONGEON
Red Lion Inn, Stockbridge, Massachusetts

   In the Berkshire Mountains of western Massachusetts is a place of retreat known as the Red Lion Inn. Since 1773, this inn has served the needs of revolutionaries looking for a place to hide, writers searching for peace and quiet, and politicians and actors yearning for holiday privacy.

   It was here that Thorton Wilder wrote every summer for fifty years, and Norman Rockwell painted. Today it is the site where Steven Mongeon blends classic cuisine with native regional ingredients to create his eclectic but uniquely New England menu.

   At the Red Lion Inn guests can savor such dishes as Sirloin of Venison with Red Wine Sauce; Salmon with Pan-roasted Leeks and Julienned Carrots; and Indian Pudding. Not stunted by his own success in creating these signature dishes, Mongeon says, "Development of dishes is on-going, as I am constantly researching and experimenting with regional ingredients."

   Mongeon began his culinary career at age ten. He was influenced even earlier by his mother and by his grandmother, who created a roasted chicken with a unique mashed potato and bread stuffing that still lingers in the chef's memory. Mongeon says, "I have always enjoyed the wonderful feeling that comes from cooking and serving well-prepared food."

   Mongeon graduated from the Culinary Institute of America in 1973. He now teaches culinary courses at Berkshire Community College and donates much of his free time to community service programs.

   Since Mongeon has been its chef, the Inn has produced *The Red Lion Inn Cookbook* (Berkshire House), which showcases his classical New England style. He says, "My style is developing in the direction of total natural freshness and using locally raised and grown products. My goal is to serve dishes that enhance the flavors of local products rather than masking their essence in heavy sauces and marinades."

   With Mongeon cooking and creating, the spirits of a few famous New Englanders may wander the kitchen of the Red Lion Inn looking for a midnight snack.

boiling point, or until bubbles appear around the edge of the pot and steam rises. Combine the remaining 1 cup milk with the cornmeal in a medium bowl and whisk the mixture into the scalded milk. Bring the mixture to a boil over medium heat, then reduce heat to low and cook for 20 minutes over low heat, stirring frequently to keep the bottom from burning. Set aside.

In a bowl, whisk the eggs, molasses, cinnamon, and ginger together. Whisk the egg mixture into the warm cornmeal mixture until thoroughly combined. Pour the batter into the prepared casserole dish and bake in the preheated oven for 1 hour. Remove the pudding from the oven, stir in the apple and raisins, and bake for 1 additional hour, or until a toothpick inserted in the center comes out clean.

Let the pudding cool, then cover and refrigerate until chilled and thickened, at least 6 hours or preferably overnight.

To serve: Preheat the oven to 300°F. Reheat the pudding for 15 to 25 minutes, or until warm. Serve topped with vanilla ice cream or whipped cream.

Note: The pudding may be made up to 3 days in advance and refrigerated, tightly covered.

Indian Pudding; Steven Mongeon, Red Lion Inn, Stockbridge, Massachusetts

Cool Caramel Mousse with Cinnamon-basted Fruit; Dan Rundell, Aureole, New York

Cool Caramel Mousse with Cinnamon-basted Fruits

Dan Rundell, Aureole
New York, New York

Makes eight 3-inch mousses

There is a lot going on in this dessert, and all of it is delicious. The only difficult aspect of the dish is the caramel cages, so if you are intimidated by them, just make the other components without the cages.

Raisin Spice Cake
2 cups water
1¼ cups raisins
1½ cups sugar
⅓ cup unsalted butter, melted
¾ teaspoon ground cinnamon
¾ teaspoon ground nutmeg
3½ cups all-purpose flour
1 teaspoon baking soda

Caramel Mousse
8 egg yolks
2¼ cups sugar
¼ cup plus 2 tablespoons water
1 cup (2 sticks) unsalted butter, melted
2 teaspoons plain gelatin
2 cups heavy (whipping) cream

Oven-basted Fruits
2 Red Delicious apples, cored and
  thinly sliced
1 pineapple, peeled, cored, and
  thinly sliced
1½ cups sugar
1 tablespoon ground cinnamon
¼ teaspoon ground nutmeg

Caramel Cages
1 cup sugar

Garnish
Crème anglaise (see page 19)
Caramel sauce (see page 19)

To make the raisin spice cake: Preheat the oven to 300°F. Bring the water and raisins to a boil in a small saucepan over medium heat. Remove the pan from the stove and let cool. Place the raisin-water mixture in a large bowl. Stir in the sugar and melted butter. Combine the dry ingredients in a medium bowl, then stir gradually into the raisin mixture. Grease an 11-by-15 jelly-roll pan with butter. Spread the cake batter evenly on the pan and bake in the preheated oven for 18 to 22 minutes, or until golden brown, firm, and springy to the touch. Let cool to room temperature on a rack.

When the cake has cooled, take a 3-inch round cutter and cut out 8 circles of cake. Place the cake circles in the bottom of eight 3-by-2¼-inch ring molds and set aside.

To make the caramel mousse: Combine the egg yolks and ½ cup of the sugar in a medium bowl. Place the bowl over a pan of simmering water and whisk constantly until the yolks are warm. Beat until the yolks are pale yellow and form a slowly dissolving ribbon on their surface when the beater is lifted; set aside.

In a medium saucepan, combine the remaining 1¾ cups sugar with ¼ cup of the water, place over high heat, and boil rapidly until the sugar turns a light amber color. Immediately remove the sugar from heat and beat the caramel into the yolk mixture, drizzling it down the sides of the bowl to avoid cooking the eggs. Beat the caramel mixture for 1 to 2 minutes more, then gradually beat in the melted butter.

Sprinkle the gelatin over the remaining 2 tablespoons water in a small pan and let sit for 10 minutes. Dissolve the gelatin by placing the pan in the pan of simmering water. Add the gelatin to the caramel mixture and mix until well blended.

In a deep bowl, whip the cream until it holds stiff peaks. Fold the caramel-yolk base into the whipped cream until well combined. Pour the mousse into the cake-lined molds, cover with plastic wrap, and freeze for at least 2 hours or until ready to serve.

To make the oven-basted fruits: Preheat the oven to 300°F. Place the apple slices and the pineapple slices in separate bowls. Combine the sugar, cinnamon, and nutmeg in a small bowl, then divide the mixture between the pineapple and the apples. Toss the apples to coat the

DANIEL RUNDELL
Aureole, New York, New York

The development of New American cuisine has led to greater opportunities for the country's pastry chefs. Today a restaurant's signature style extends to the bread basket and the pastry cart, so calling a bakery to deliver baguettes and fruit tarts is no longer a practice of the country's top American kitchens.

This trend is reflected at Aureole in New York City, a glamorous restaurant nestled in a town house off Park Avenue. Charles Palmer commands the kitchen, but the sweet finales are produced by Daniel Rundell.

For two years, Rundell studied in the pastry program at Johnson and Wales University in Providence, Rhode Island. He then began a bakery in Utica, New York. With a move to New York City, he traded large-volume production for a position with Aureole. It took two years for him to achieve the rank of pastry chef, and since then the desserts at Aureole have gained renewed attention.

Rundell produces such classics as Crème Brûlée with Linzer Biscuits, but also offers an array of sophisticated fruit desserts such as Maple-roasted Pear Délice with Warm Pear Fritters, and Cool Caramel Mousse with Cinnamon-basted Fruit.

slices evenly. Heat a medium sauté pan or skillet over medium heat. Add the apple slices and cook, stirring frequently, until they are browned and three-fourths cooked, about 8 to 10 minutes. Toss the pineapple with the sugar and spices, then bake in a shallow pan in the preheated oven for 15 to 18 minutes, or until caramelized.

To make caramel cages: Lightly oil a small ramekin and place it upside down on a lightly oiled sheet of waxed paper. Place the sugar in a medium sauté pan or skillet over medium heat and melt, stirring constantly. Cook the sugar syrup until it turns a medium amber brown, then remove it immediately from heat. Dip a fork in the caramel and, working quickly, trail long threads of sugar back and forth across the oiled ramekin

and the waxed paper. The sugar will harden quickly. When the sugar is cool and hard, use a 5-inch round cutter to trim the circumference of the basket so that the finished product looks like a small rimmed hat. Repeat to make a total of 8 cages.

To assemble the dessert: Invert each mold and remove the mousse with a thin spatula or a sharp knife. Place on dessert plates. Invert the caramel cages, press one into the top surface of each mousse, and fill the cavity with the cinnamon-basted fruits. Garnish with caramel sauce and crème anglaise and serve.

Note: The cake, the mousses, and fruit may be prepared 1 day in advance. Refrigerate, tightly covered.

Exotic Fruit Soup in a Sugar Cage

Jacques Torres, Le Cirque
New York, New York

Serves 2

While fruit soups are uncommon in the United States, in the cuisines of Northern Europe they are served both as an appetizer and as dessert. This soup is elegant and easy to make. If you don't want to make the caramel, serve the soup with a few crisp cookies for the same textural contrast.

JACQUES TORRES
Le Cirque, New York, New York

At age twenty-six, Jacques Torres became the youngest chef ever to earn the prestigious title of *Meilleur Ouvrier de France Pâstissier,* an honor bestowed only on the top pastry chefs in France. Three years before receiving this honor, *Le Figaro,* the nationally syndicated French newspaper, reported that Mr. Torres had "extraordinary flair" and was "without a doubt the greatest pastry chef working in any restaurant in France today."

These days Torres is in New York, working at Le Cirque, which, during his tenure, has garnered the highest ratings given by of the *New York Times, New York* magazine, and *Newsday.* It has also been awarded *Gault Millau's* highest rating, 19½ out of 20 toques, and been named Best in America by international publications too numerous to mention.

To Torres, the secret of his sweet success is quite simple. "If you love to work with dough and chocolate and sugar, then you give it everything you have," he says. Add invention to effort, he recommends. "You have to come up with something new, something else, always, always," says Torres.

At Le Cirque, Torres always offers something new, but you may also find dream desserts called Swan Lake, Angel's Delight, Cupid's Coupe, or Manjari Harlequin Hearts, all of which were featured in the *New York Times Magazine,* and Exotic Fruit Soup in a Sugar Cage, featured in this book. True *pâtissier* poetry, they require the patience of Petrarch to produce.

Torres learned patience and the basics of his art in his formal training in France. He started his apprenticeship in pastry at age fifteen in the small village of Bandol, where he lived with his family. From there, he moved to the south of France to the Negresco in Nice, where he stayed for eight years.

Before moving to Le Cirque, Torres traveled extensively. In Tokyo, he received the Medal of Honor of the Confederation of Japan. In 1988, he joined the Ritz-Carlton as corporate pastry chef, for which he traveled and trained other pastry chefs throughout the United States.

Success has come early for this chef, but his talent, dedication, and determination to come up with "something new, something else, always, always," promise decades of sweet surprises.

Fruit Soup

¾ cup sugar
2 cups water
Grated zest of 1 lemon
2 bananas
1 mango
2 kiwis
1 papaya

Sugar Cage

1 cup sugar
½ cup hot water
⅛ teaspoon cream of tartar

To make the soup: Combine the sugar, water, and lemon zest in a medium saucepan. Heat the mixture over medium heat until the sugar melts, brushing any sugar crystals from the sides of the pan with a pastry brush. Set aside and let cool.

Peel the bananas and cut them into ¼-inch-thick slices. Peel the rest of the fruit and cut them into ½-inch dice. Add the sliced fruit to the syrup, cover, and refrigerate for at least 30 minutes.

To make sugar cage: Combine the sugar, hot water, and cream of tartar in a small, heavy saucepan. Insert a candy thermometer into the syrup and heat until the mixture reaches 310°F, or it just begins to turn an amber color. Turn off heat and let the sugar cool for a few minutes.

Spray a heavy baking sheet with vegetable spray, then wipe the baking sheet with a paper towel to remove any excess. Working quickly, use a fork to drizzle the caramel across the baking sheet in an 8-by-6-inch rectangle: Make

one pattern of parallel lines, then tilt the baking sheet and make cross-hatching lines on the diagonal. Let cool, then use a sharp knife to cut the cage into 2 neat rectangles.

Distribute the fruit soup into 2 shallow soup bowls and garnish with fresh mint. Lay 1 sugar cage rectangle on the side of each bowl and serve.

Note: The soup may be prepared up to 8 hours in advance and refrigerated, tightly covered. The caramel may be prepared at the same time and kept at room temperature.

Exotic Fruit Soup in a Sugar Cage; Jacques Torres, Le Cirque, New York

Crepes with Oranges

Klaus Helmin, Tivoli Restaurant
Arlington, Virginia

Makes one 6-inch torte; serves 4 to 6

Most crepe desserts are warm and require last-minute preparation. In this one, however, the crepes are stacked and filled with orange pastry cream to make a chilled torte.

Crêpes

6 eggs
¾ cup milk
2 tablespoons orange juice
1 tablespoon sugar
½ cup cake flour
2 tablespoons canola or other mild vegetable oil
¼ teaspoon salt
2 tablespoons clarified butter (see page 19)

Orange Pastry Cream

2 eggs
5 tablespoons sugar
Grated zest from 2 oranges
2 tablespoons sifted cake flour
1 cup cold milk
2 tablespoons fresh orange juice
¼ teaspoon salt

Caramel

½ cup sugar
Zest of 4 oranges, cut into julienne
4 tablespoons Curaçao or other orange-flavored liqueur

To make the crepes: Combine all the ingredients except the clarified butter in a blender or food processor. Blend for 30 seconds, or until smooth, scraping down the sides of the bowl a few times. Strain through a fine-meshed sieve, cover, and refrigerate for at least 30 minutes.

Wipe a 6-inch crepe pan with enough clarified butter to coat the surface and place over high heat. Ladle 3 to 4 tablespoons of the batter into the pan and swirl the pan so that the batter coats the bottom evenly, pouring any excess back into the batter. Cook the crepe for 30 to 45 seconds, or until the surface of the crepe looks dry. Flip with a thin metal spatula and cook another 20 to 30 seconds. Remove to a plate and repeat with the remaining batter, stacking the cooked crepes between sheets of waxed paper. You should have between 24 to 26 crepes. Chill the crepes in the refrigerator until needed.

Crepes with Oranges; Klaus Helmin, Tivoli Restaurant, Rosslyn, Virginia

To make the pastry cream: Beat the eggs and the sugar in a medium bowl until the mixture is thick and pale yellow. Add the orange zest, flour, milk, orange juice, and salt and beat well. Transfer the mixture to a medium saucepan and bring to a boil over medium heat, stirring constantly. Cook, whisking vigorously, until the pastry cream is thickened. Transfer the pastry cream to a bowl, press a sheet of plastic wrap directly into the surface to keep a skin from forming, and chill in the refrigerator.

After the crepes and pastry cream have chilled, place one crepe on a serving plate. Top the crepe with 1½ tablespoons of the pastry cream and spread. Top with another crepe and top with more pastry cream. Repeat, alternating layers, until all the crepes are used.

To make the caramel: Place a medium saucepan on the stove over medium-high heat and add the sugar. Add the orange zest and melt the sugar, stirring occasionally until the syrup has just begun to turn color. When the syrup is a light caramel brown, add the liqueur, stirring to combine, and pour over the stack of crepes. Chill for several hours.

To serve: Cut the torte into thick wedges and garnish with fresh mint sprigs.

Note: The crepes and pastry cream may be made up to 2 days in advance and refrigerated, and the torte may be assembled up to 8 hours in advance. The crepes also may be made in advance and frozen, tightly covered.

KLAUS HELMIN
Tivoli Restaurant, Rosslyn, Virginia

Klaus Helmin grew up in Berlin just after World War II, so his early childhood food memories are not what enticed him into the culinary world. "My mother prepared plain German food. Because of the war, we only had access to the bare essentials," he says. This could explain why Helmin gravitated towards Northern Italian cuisine, which he has been creating as executive chef of the critically acclaimed Tivoli Restaurant since 1983.

With its combination of stunning interior design and Helmin's cooking expertise, Tivoli has made the northern Virginia business enclave of Rosslyn, not normally noted for its after-business-hours appeal, a mecca for lunch and dinner crowds. Commenting on the restaurant's decor, one critic noted that "in Tivoli's dramatically mirrored third story dining room, the tables are set in niches, corners and at angles so that diners in the 175 seats have both a sense of privacy and of being right in the middle of the party."

The restaurant focuses on innovative Italian fare, and Helmin's signature dishes include *Terrina di Piccione e Funghi Selvatici* (Terrine of Squab Breast and Wild Mushrooms) and *Coniglio in Umido alle Olive Nere* (Braised Rabbit with Black Olives), as well as his Crepes with Oranges.

After graduating in 1957 from the Hotel and Restaurant School in Berlin, Helmin came to the United States to work in Wichita, Kansas, at the Broadview Hotel. In 1965, he opened the Washington Hilton Hotel as the executive sous-chef, and later became a partner in the Restaurant Corporation of America, which operated the Watergate Restaurant, Les Champs Restaurant, and the Watergate Pastry Shop. After selling his share of the corporation, Helmin, along with several colleagues, founded the American Restaurant Corporation, which now operates Tivoli Restaurant, two Tivoli Gourmet shops, and the Watergate Pastry Shop. Tivoli Restaurant now provides pre-theater, post-theater, lounge, full restaurant, Sunday brunch buffet, gourmet shop, and bakery services. This variety of food options does not faze Helmin. "I love to experiment with new ideas. This makes the task of creating new dishes exciting," he says.

MICHAEL KORNICK
Four Seasons Hotel, Boston, Massachusetts

"Four Seasons' clients expect their meals to be flawless; so do I," says Michael Kornick of the Four Seasons Hotel in Boston. Kornick became responsible for serving perfection on a plate when he took over New England's only Mobil five-diamond restaurant, Aujourd'hui, in 1991.

Creating flawless cuisine has been Kornick's goal since age thirteen, when he decided he wanted to become a chef. To Kornick, the creation of outstanding cuisine is often very simple. "People yearn for simple cuisine," says Kornick. "I really believe in preserving the natural integrity of the product one is working with. Chicken should taste like chicken."

When a chef preserves the integrity of food, he must begin with stellar ingredients. "I'm really into product," says Kornick. "I survey the markets all the time so I can see for myself what is fresh and what isn't. 'In season' doesn't always mean superior quality."

Kornick's culinary education has been acquired through hands-on training in restaurants and through travel. He spent time in New Mexico, New Orleans, Los Angeles, and San Francisco in an extensive effort to learn about regional American cooking. He also visited England and France, and spent several months in Asia working in a hotel restaurant and studying the indigenous cuisines.

Critics have enjoyed the range and studied simplicity of Kornick's food. Dishes such as Asparagus and Crayfish Bisque with Ossetra Caviar, Sautéed Fresh Foie Gras with Hazelnuts, and Spiced Pears with Port and Gorgonzola, have been singled out for praise. If Kornick's and the Four Seasons' standards continue to be met, these and other dishes at Aujourd'hui will continue to be flawless.

Plum Soufflé with Cinnamon

Nitzi Rabin, Chillingsworth
Brewster, Massachusetts

Makes 1 large or 6 small soufflés; serves 6

Blushingly pink, dotted with red raspberries, and light as a feather because it is made with only egg whites, this soufflé is the essence of summer. As delicious as it is pretty, it also is easy to make.

Soufflé
2 tablespoons unsalted butter, melted
1¼ cups granulated sugar
12 large ripe Black Friar plums, pitted and cut into 1-inch pieces
¼ cup water
2 tablespoons raspberry liqueur or *eau de vie*
1 tablespoon fresh lemon juice or more to taste
½ teaspoon ground cinnamon or more to taste
1 cup egg whites (about 7 or 8)
Pinch of cream of tartar
2 cups fresh raspberries
Confectioners' sugar for dusting
Crème anglaise (see page 19) for serving

To make the soufflé: Brush the inside of one 6-cup soufflé dish or six 1-cup soufflé dishes with the melted butter. Use ¼ cup of the granulated sugar to line the inside of the dish(es), rolling it around to cover all surfaces and shaking out the excess over the sink. Set the prepared dish(es) aside.

Place the cut-up plums in a large sauté pan or skillet with ¼ cup of the granulated sugar, the water, and the liqueur or *eau de vie*. Cook the plums over medium heat for 15 minutes, or until the fruit is soft enough to mash with a spoon and most of the liquid has evaporated. Add the lemon juice and cinnamon, then taste the fruit and adjust the flavor with additional sugar, lemon juice, or cinnamon as needed.

Transfer the fruit to a blender or food processor and puree until smooth. Strain the fruit through a fine-meshed sieve, cover, and refrigerate until cold, about 2 hours; this should be a very thick puree.

Preheat the oven to 400°F. In a large bowl, beat the egg whites until foamy. Add the cream of tartar, and slowly add the remaining ¾ cup granulated sugar, a few tablespoons at a time, while beating until the whites hold stiff peaks.

Place 1 cup fruit puree in a large bowl. Gently fold half of the egg whites into the puree, then fold in the remaining egg whites. Fill the prepared dish(es) halfway full with the soufflé batter, place a layer of raspberries on top of the batter, and fill with the remaining batter. Smooth the tops and form into a rounded cone.

Place the soufflés in the preheated oven and turn the heat down to 350°F for the large soufflé or 375°F for smaller soufflés. Bake 35 minutes for the large soufflé and 20 minutes for the smaller soufflés, or until puffed and golden and a skewer inserted into the middle of a soufflé comes out clean. Dust the soufflé(s) with confectioners' sugar and serve immediately with crème anglaise.

Note: *The fruit base may be prepared up to 3 days in advance and refrigerated, tightly covered.*

Spiced Pears with Port and Gorgonzola; Michael Kornick, Four Seasons Hotel, Boston

Spiced Pears with Port and Gorgonzola

Michael Kornick, Four Seasons Hotel
Boston, Massachusetts

Serves 4

Pears, Gorgonzola, and walnuts are the classic accompaniment to a fine port after dinner. Here the chef has combined the same elements to create a vividly colored dessert that is perfect for a cool evening.

Poached Pears
2 cups port wine
4 star anise
4 cinnamon sticks
4 whole cloves
¼ teaspoon ground nutmeg
½ teaspoon freshly ground black pepper
¼ cup honey
½ cup firmly packed light brown sugar
4 ripe pears
4 tablespoons unsalted butter

Garnish
Four 3-ounce slices cold Gorgonzola
  cheese
1 cup walnut halves, toasted
  (see page 16)

Bring the port to a boil in an oven-proof medium gratin dish or casserole over medium heat. Add the star anise, cinnamon sticks, cloves, nutmeg, pepper, honey, and brown sugar. Cook the mixture until the liquid is reduced by one third.

Preheat the oven to 325°F. Peel, quarter, and core the pears. Heat the butter in a medium sauté pan or skillet over medium heat and sauté the pears for 2 to 3 minutes. Add the pears and butter to the poaching liquid, and bake in the preheated oven for 20 to 25 minutes, or until tender.

To serve: Place a slice of Gorgonzola cheese on each of 4 serving plates. Spoon the pears and some of the sauce next to the cheese. Garnish with the toasted walnut halves and serve.

Note: *The pears may be poached up to 2 days in advance and refrigerated, tightly covered. Reheat them over low heat before serving.*

Plum Soufflé with Cinnamon; Nitzi Rabin, Chillingsworth, Brewster, Massachusetts

Poached Pears with Roquefort Mousse

Craig Shelton, Ryland Inn
Whitehouse, New Jersey

Serves 4

Pears and blue-veined cheeses are a traditional combination, and this elegant dessert adds the perfumes of herbs and spices. Serve this dish as a combination dessert and cheese course and, if you don't care to do the elaborate assembly, simply pipe the mousse into the pear halves.

Poached Pears

4 Bosc pears
Juice of 2 lemons
1 bottle Sauternes or other sweet white wine
¼ cup honey or more to taste
¼ cup sugar
3 whole cloves
1 cinnamon stick
1 bay leaf
½ teaspoon black peppercorns
2 quarter-size slices peeled fresh ginger
1 vanilla bean, split lengthwise

Baked Quince

1 fresh quince
1 tablespoon unsalted butter at room temperature
1 fresh rosemary sprig
1 teaspoon honey

Roquefort Mousse

1 envelope unflavored gelatin
2 tablespoons water
⅔ cup (3 ounces) crumbled Roquefort cheese, at room temperature
1 teaspoon milk
½ cup heavy (whipping) cream

Garnish

¼ cup crystallized ginger, softened in 1 cup water and finely chopped
¼ cup honey
Mint oil (see page 19)
Four 1-ounce slices cold Roquefort cheese
4 fresh mint sprigs

To make the pears: Peel the pears and place them in a bowl of cold water to which 1 tablespoon of the lemon juice has been added to prevent discoloration. Combine the wine, honey, sugar, cloves, cinnamon stick, bay leaf, peppercorns, ginger, remaining lemon juice, and vanilla bean in a large nonaluminum saucepan or Dutch oven. Bring the liquid to a boil over high heat, add the pears, and cover the pears with a clean kitchen towel to keep the pears completely submerged. When the liquid returns to a boil, reduce heat to low and simmer the pears for approximately 30 minutes, or until tender. Remove the pears from the liquid with a slotted spoon and let cool.

To prepare the quince: Preheat the oven to 350°F. Peel and seed the quince. Spread an 8-by-12-inch piece of heavy-duty aluminum foil with the butter. Place the rosemary in the center of the foil, top with the quince slices, and drizzle the fruit with the honey. Wrap the

Poached Pears with Roquefort Mousse; Craig Shelton, Ryland Inn, Whitehouse, New Jersey

foil loosely around the quince, sealing the edges tightly, and bake in the oven for 1½ to 2 hours. Set aside.

To make the Roquefort mousse: Sprinkle the gelatin over the water in a small saucepan and let soften for 10 minutes. Place the saucepan over low heat and stir until the gelatin is just dissolved and warm. Set aside.

Force the Roquefort cheese through a fine-meshed sieve into a medium bowl. Add the milk and blend to soften the cheese. Add the dissolved gelatin mixture and stir to combine. In a deep bowl, whip the cream until it holds stiff peaks. Fold the whipped cream into the cheese mixture, cover, and refrigerate for 30 minutes, or until the mousse is firm.

To assemble the dessert: Slice a pear crosswise into ¼-inch-thick slices and remove the seeds with a small spoon. Place the Roquefort mousse in a pastry bag fitted with a large fluted tip and pipe the mousse around the edge of each pear slice, stacking the slices in their original shape. Before replacing the top of the pear, pipe the mousse down through the cored center of the pear. Replace the top. Repeat to assemble all the pears.

Dice the quince and combine it with the drained crystallized ginger. Make a design on each of the 4 serving plates with the honey and the mint oil. Place 1 pear on each plate. Divide the quince mixture among the 4 plates, then garnish each with a slice of Roquefort and fresh mint sprigs.

Note: *All the components of the dish may be prepared up to 1 day in advance and refrigerated, tightly covered. Let the pears and quince sit at room temperature for 30 minutes before assembling the dessert.*

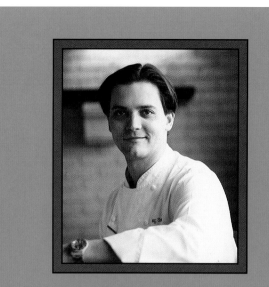

CRAIG SHELTON
Ryland Inn, Whitehouse, New Jersey

At the Ryland Inn in Whitehouse, New Jersey, Craig Shelton not only heads a brigade of eighteen cooks, but he is also master of a five-acre organic garden in which he raises 150 different types of herbs, seventy-five varieties of lettuce and eighty different vegetables. More than any purveyor could, he says, the garden gives him "a much broader palate of tastes and textures to work with than before."

"Before" was in some of the world's best kitchens, however. Shelton was sous-chef to celebrated David Bouley at Bouley in New York for three years, helping New York's top-rated restaurant achieve four-star rating from the *New York Times.*

Shelton considers Bouley his mentor, and both chefs apprenticed under famous French chef Joel Robuchon in France. In fact, Shelton is a dual citizen of both France and the United States (his mother is French), and he has vivid childhood memories of watching his grandparents, once restaurant owners in Cognac, prepare such dishes as *oeufs à la neige* and *omelette aux fines herbes.*

Prior to Bouley, Shelton held positions in other top American restaurants, such as Ma Maison in Los Angeles, and La Côte Basque, Le Bernardin, The Rainbow Room, and Le Chantilly in New York.

As chef-proprietor of the Ryland Inn, Shelton cultivates both his garden and his inclination to provide only the finest to his clientele. In his dishes, he explains, he keeps "trying to move towards fewer elements, more purity—so that nature is the star." He strives for an elegant and refined cuisine in such signature dishes as Baby Lamb; Poached Pears with Roquefort Mousse; and Bass with Three Celeries, the latter a dish designed to complement a great Chardonnay. The Ryland Inn's wine list features more than eight hundred selections and was recently voted the Best French Wine List of America by *Restaurant Hospitality* at the eighth Annual World of Wines Festival in California.

A graduate of Yale University with degrees in molecular biophysics and biochemistry, Shelton's interests are as varied as his menu. He enjoys the outdoors—sailing, gardening, and camping—but also appreciates classical music and opera. He lives in the country with his wife and five-year-old daughter.

PHILIPPE KAEMMERLÉ
French Culinary Institute / L'École, New York, New York

Alsace, located on the French and German borders, is known for dishes that draw elements from both cuisines. Philippe Kaemmerlé's career began at that intersection of culinary cultures, and he went on to create pastries for some of New York's best restaurants before starting a second career as a trainer of future pastry chefs.

Kaemmerlé began his training in the beautiful town of Strasbourg, with its narrow, winding streets, canals, and French quarter. It was an ideal setting for an aspiring pastry chef—and the passion that it instilled in Kaemmerlé served as the impetus for his work as the instructor in charge of special pastry programs at the French Culinary Institute in New York.

After his years in Strasbourg, Kaemmerlé moved to Operakallaren Restaurant to work for Werner Vogeli, the private catering chef for the king of Sweden. Upon arriving in New York, Kaemmerlé became pastry chef at the '21' Club and later at Windows on the World, the restaurant atop one of the World Trade Center towers. In 1991, after a year at Prunelle, a nouvelle French restaurant, Kaemmerlé joined the teaching staff of the French Culinary Institute as *chef-pâtissier.*

Kaemmerlé's Caramelized Pears with Chocolate Mousse in a Tulipe, garnished with a chocolate butterfly, represents years of dedication to his profession, as well as the fusing of the seasonal glory of fruit with the timeless appeal of chocolate.

Caramelized Pears with Chocolate Mousse in a Tulipe

Philippe Kaemmerlé, French Culinary Institute / L'École
New York, New York

Serves 4

This dessert has all of the flavors of spring and would make a wonderful ending to an Easter dinner. The pears are carved into the shape of eggs, poached, and coated with caramel sauce. They surround a very light chocolate mousse in a crisp cookie cup.

Poached Pears
4 large pears
3 cups water
1 cup dry white wine
1 cup granulated sugar
1 tablespoon grated orange zest
2 cloves
¼ teaspoon ground nutmeg
1 cinnamon stick, broken in half

Chocolate Mousse
2½ ounces semisweet chocolate, chopped
¾ cup heavy (whipping) cream
2 egg whites
1 tablespoon granulated sugar

Tulipe Cookies
5 tablespoons unsalted butter at
    room temperature
5 tablespoons confectioners' sugar, sifted
2 egg whites
3 tablespoons cake flour

Chocolate Butterflies (optional)
2 ounces semisweet chocolate, chopped

Garnish
1 cup caramel sauce (see page 19)
2 tablespoons Cognac
20 fresh strawberries, hulled and halved
½ cup pistachio nuts, finely chopped
4 fresh mint sprigs

To prepare the pears: Cut each pear into 5 even sections and carve each piece into an egg-shaped oval with a paring knife. Combine all the remaining ingredients in a medium saucepan and bring to a boil over medium heat. Simmer the liquid for 5 minutes, then add the pears and cook for 20 to 25 minutes, or until the pears are tender.

To make the mousse: Melt the chocolate in a large bowl set over a pan of barely simmering water, stirring until smooth. Set aside. In a deep bowl, beat the heavy cream until it holds soft peaks and set aside. In a large bowl, beat the egg whites until foamy, then add the sugar and beat until stiff, glossy peaks are formed. Fold the beaten whites into the melted chocolate, then fold in the whipped cream. Cover and chill until needed.

To make the cookies: In a medium bowl, beat the butter and the confectioners' sugar until light and fluffy. Slowly add the egg whites and the cake flour, mixing until fully incorporated.

Preheat the oven to 350°F. Lightly grease a baking sheet with butter, then dust it with flour. Drop 1 tablespoonful of dough onto the baking sheet and spread it with a thin metal spatula into a circle 4 inches in diameter. Repeat, distributing the cookies evenly across the baking sheet, leaving 3 inches between them. Bake the cookies in the preheated oven until they are golden brown, about 5 to 8 minutes. Working quickly, mold the warm cookies over a small glass or custard cup to form 2-inch-diameter cups. Return the baking sheet to the oven to warm the cookies if they are too stiff to mold. Let the cookie bowls cool, then invert and set aside.

To make the chocolate butterflies: Draw an outline of a butterfly on a piece of waxed paper or parchment paper. Fold another small piece of paper in half, then lay it over the drawing, smoothing out the fold and making sure that the folded line is in the center of the butterfly drawing. Melt the chocolate in a double boiler over barely simmering water, stirring until smooth. Let cool slightly, then transfer the chocolate to a parchment paper cone, then snip the end. Trace the outline of the butterfly drawing, then transfer the chocolate outline to the refrigerator until needed. Repeat to make 3 more butterflies. (Kaemmerle places his chocolate butterfly in special V-shaped molds to shape them.)

Transfer the chilled chocolate mousse to a pastry bag fitted with a fluted star tip. Fill the cookie bowls with the chocolate mousse and chill until firm.

To assemble the dessert: Warm the caramel sauce and add the Cognac, stirring to incorporate. Add the pears, stirring gently to coat them evenly. Place a cookie bowl in the center of each plate. Arrange 5 pear pieces in a star pattern around each cookie bowl and drizzle some caramel sauce over the pears. Place 10 strawberry halves between the pear pieces, then sprinkle the pears with the chopped pistachios. Perch a chocolate butterfly on the edge of each chocolate mousse, if you like; garnish with the mint sprigs, and serve.

Note: *All the components of this dish may be prepared 1 day in advance. Keep the cookie bowls in an airtight container, and cover and refrigerate the pears, mousse, caramel sauce, and chocolate butterflies.*

Caramelized Pears with Chocolate Mousse in a Tulipe; Philippe Kaemmerlé, French Culinary Institute/L'École, New York

Grilled Peaches with Grilled Walnut Bread; Stan Frankenthaler, Blue Room, Cambridge, Massachusetts

Grilled Peaches with Grilled Walnut Bread

Stan Frankenthaler, Blue Room
Cambridge, Massachusetts

Serves 4

The heat from the grill caramelizes the peaches and gives them a distinctive smoky flavor. This is a wonderful summer dessert, and the chutney also is excellent with any simple grilled poultry or fish.

2 cups water
2 cups sugar
½ vanilla bean, split lengthwise
1 cinnamon stick
2 whole cloves
1 whole allspice
4 ripe peaches, peeled, pitted and halved (see page 17)
Four ¼-inch-thick slices walnut bread
4 tablespoons unsalted butter at room temperature

Garnish
Peach-Walnut Chutney (recipe follows)
Balsamic vinegar
1 cup sweetened whipped cream
4 fresh mint sprigs
¼ cup fresh berries (optional)

Combine the water and sugar in a medium nonaluminum saucepan and bring to a boil over medium heat. Add the vanilla bean, cinnamon, cloves, and allspice and simmer for 15 minutes. Add the peach halves and simmer them for 3 to 10 minutes, or until they are tender; the amount of time will depend on the ripeness of the peaches. Remove the pan from heat and let the peaches cool in the syrup.

Light a fire in a charcoal grill. Rub the peaches and the slices of walnut bread with the softened butter. When the coals are lightly covered with gray ash, grill the peaches, cut-side down, for 2 minutes;

turn them gently with tongs and grill for an additional 1½ minutes. Grill the bread on the edge of the grill rack for 30 to 45 seconds on each side, or until it is toasted.

To serve: Cut each slice of walnut bread in half on the diagonal and place a peach half on each slice. Spoon 3 tablespoons peach-walnut chutney on each of 4 serving plates and surround it with 2 peach-topped bread slices. Spoon a small amount of balsamic vinegar around the chutney on each plate and garnish with whipped cream, sprigs of mint, and optional berries.

Peach-Walnut Chutney

(Makes 1¾ cups)

1 tablespoon unsalted butter
½ cup diced onion
1 tablespoon minced fresh ginger
¼ cup raisins
½ small tomato, peeled, seeded and chopped (see page 18)
1 large peach, peeled and diced
½ cup vanilla syrup reserved from poached peaches, in preceding recipe
½ cup dry red wine
¼ cup balsamic vinegar
½ teaspoon salt
¼ cup coarsely chopped walnuts, toasted (see page 16)

Melt the butter in a medium sauté pan or skillet over medium-high heat. Add the onion and ginger, and sauté for 2 to 3 minutes, stirring constantly. Add all the remaining ingredients except for the walnuts. Bring the mixture to a boil, reduce heat to low, and simmer the chutney for about 20 minutes, or until thickened; stir frequently, especially towards the end of the cooking time to ensure against scorching. Add the walnuts and simmer for 5 minutes.

Note: *The chutney may be made up to 1 week in advance without the addition of the walnuts. Refrigerate, tightly covered.*

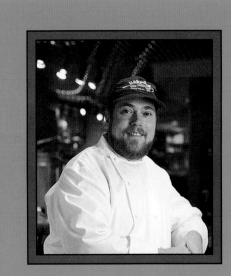

STAN FRANKENTHALER
Blue Room, Cambridge, Massachusetts

Along with the standard *batterie de cuisine,* the kitchen at Stan Frankenthaler's Blue Room in Cambridge, Massachusetts, includes a stone-lined fire pit for Chinese hot pots and fire-heated stones for baking bread.

A native of Alabama whose family "gathered around the dinner table for hours," Stan Frankenthaler remembers being "shoo'ed away from the kitchen for being too young." But he was obstinate, and at age seven began to help by shelling peas and snapping beans. In less than a decade, Frankenthaler had become the family cook.

He began cooking professionally at age seventeen, and paid his way through the University of Georgia with his restaurant earnings. It was during those years that Frankenthaler realized that cooking was his calling. He moved to Boston and spent two years at the Culinary Institute of America, where he graduated with high honors.

Honors have continued to come to Frankenthaler. During his work as sous-chef at Jasper White's restaurant, Jasper's, it received 4½ stars from the *Boston Globe* and was inducted into the *Boston* magazine's Hall of Fame. Frankenthaler's next project, a home-catering company called Choice Catering, received rave reviews: He was named Boston's Best Personal Caterer in *Boston* magazine.

In 1991, Frankenthaler teamed up with two other dedicated foodies, Chris Schlesinger and Cary Wheaton, and created the Blue Room. The menu features open-fire cooking from around the world. Frankenthaler's menu includes Cumin-rubbed Grilled Whole Snapper with Preserved Lemons; Spicy Dry-fried Shrimp and Squid; and Grilled Peaches with Grilled Walnut Bread.

When Frankenthaler isn't cooking, he is involved with public-service groups that organize food fund-raisers for local charities. He serves on the education committee for the American Institute of Wine and Food, and is actively involved in Chef's, an organization that promotes food safety.

When he goes home to Alabama on vacation, Frankenthaler may not be able to bring his fire-heated stones or fire pit with him, but he still does the cooking for family gatherings.

ERIC MEUNIER
Wheatleigh, Lenox, Massachusetts

Eric Meunier went from playing with food as a child to actually preparing it. "When I was nine years old, my mom was cooking at home and I was always behind her. She would turn from the stove for a moment and I would taste and mix and touch everything. I even used to eat the sweet dough and drink the crepes mix. I just loved to play with food," he says. Today, instead of ingesting his ingredients he creates world-class pastries for customers at the Wheatleigh in Lenox, Massachusetts.

After graduating from the Technical School of Hotel and Catering Management in Grenoble, and working in his native France, Meunier went to the Wheatleigh, where his duties ran the spectrum from making stocks to cooking meats. He became the Inn's pastry chef in 1991.

Trained in traditional French cuisine, Meunier notes, "I'm always looking to create my own interpretations of that style," as is demonstrated in his Chèvre and Raspberries in Pastry. He has fond memories of the origin of one of his signature dishes, Crepes with Caramelized Apples Flambéed with Calvados and Vanilla Ice Cream. "I came up with that for a friend of mine who loved sweets and was always hungry very late at night."

Raspberry Gratin with Caramel

Jean-François Taquet, Restaurant Taquet
Wayne, Pennsylvania

Serves 4

This dessert is the epitome of easy elegance and may be made with any fresh berries. It comes to the table slightly warm and browned, which reinforces the caramel flavor.

6 tablespoons sugar
⅔ cup heavy (whipping) cream divided
4 cups fresh raspberries
Fresh mint sprigs

In a medium saucepan over medium-high heat, cook the sugar until it turns a light golden brown, about 4 to 5 minutes. Add ⅓ cup of the cream, stirring constantly until the caramel is smooth. Transfer the caramel to a mixing bowl and chill.

Preheat the broiler. Arrange a layer of raspberries, standing upright, in concentric circles in the center of each of 4 ovenproof plates. Whip the remaining cream in a deep bowl until stiff peaks form. Fold the whipped cream into the chilled caramel. Divide the caramel mixture over the raspberries and place under the broiler just until the caramel is lightly browned, about 30 seconds; don't overcook, or the caramel mousse will collapse. Garnish with fresh mint sprigs and serve immediately.

Note: *The caramel mixture may be prepared up to 2 days in advance and refrigerated, tightly covered.*

Raspberry Gratin with Caramel; Jean-François Taquet, Restaurant Taquet, Wayne, Pennsylvania

Chèvre and Raspberries in Pastry

Eric Meunier, Wheatleigh
Lenox, Massachusetts

Serves 6

This dessert is glamorous-looking and not difficult to make. The creamy cheese mousse is a wonderful contrast to the crisp cookies and succulent fruit. This is a good dish for people who usually do not like desserts, as it is not overly sweet.

Tuile Cookies
⅔ cup confectioners' sugar, sifted
¾ cup (1½ sticks) unsalted butter at room temperature
7 egg whites, slightly beaten
1⅓ cups all-purpose flour

Chèvre Filling
¾ cup heavy (whipping) cream
¼ cup granulated sugar
8 ounces mild plain white goat cheese at room temperature
1 tablespoon framboise liqueur

Fruit Sauce
¼ cup water
¼ cup sugar
½ cup *each* fresh or thawed frozen unsweetened strawberries, raspberries, and blueberries or blackberries

Garnish
2 cups fresh raspberries
Confectioners' sugar for dusting
6 fresh mint sprigs

To make the tuile cookies: Preheat the oven to 350°F. In a large bowl, beat the sugar and butter together until light and fluffy, scraping down the sides of the bowl as necessary. Stir in the egg whites, then gradually stir in the flour until it is fully incorporated. Cut a piece of parchment paper to fit a baking sheet, then trace eighteen 3-inch-diameter circles onto the sheet of paper. Spread the batter as thinly as possibly within the area of the tracings, then bake the tuiles in the preheated oven for 3 to 5 minutes, or until golden. Set aside.

To make the filling: In a deep bowl, beat the heavy cream with the sugar until the cream holds soft peaks. In a medium bowl, beat the goat cheese and framboise together until smooth and well blended. Fold the whipped cream into the cheese mixture. Scrape the mousse into a large pastry bag fitted with a fluted star tip and set aside.

To make the fruit sauce: Simmer the water and sugar for 10 minutes in a medium saucepan. Add the berries and cook in the syrup for 5 to 6 minutes, or until barely translucent and syrupy. Remove the berries from heat and puree in a blender or food processor. Strain the sauce through a fine-meshed strainer and set aside.

To assemble: Pour a scant ¼ cup of the fruit sauce into the center of each of 6 dessert plates and swirl evenly to make a circle. Set aside. Place 6 to 7 raspberries on the outside edge of 1 cookie round. Pipe rosettes of the cheese mixture between the berries. Top with another cookie, a layer of raspberries, and a layer of cheese. Top the final cheese layer with a cookie. Dust the top of the cookie with sugar, then pipe a rosette of cheese into the center. Top the rosette with 1 raspberry and a fresh mint sprig. Using a large metal spatula, carefully move each dessert to one of the prepared dessert plates and serve.

Note: *The cookies, mousse, and sauce may all be made 1 day in advance. Keep the cookies in an airtight container, and cover and refrigerate the mousse and sauce. The desserts should be assembled just prior to serving.*

Chèvre and Raspberries in Pastry; Eric Meunier, Wheatleigh, Lenox, Massachusetts

Strawberries San Giorgio with Caramelized Walnuts

~

Zack Grumet, Blackie's House of Beef
Washington, D.C.

Serves 8

Rather than being dipped in chocolate, these strawberries are stuffed with a rich ganache, then candy-coated walnuts are added for a contrasting texture.

24 large ripe fresh strawberries

Cognac Ganache
4 ounces bittersweet chocolate, chopped
¼ cup heavy (whipping) cream
2 tablespoons unsalted butter, melted
1 tablespoon lightly beaten egg
1 tablespoon Cognac

Chocolate Sauce
4 ounces semisweet chocolate, chopped
¼ cup unsweetened cocoa powder
½ cup hot water

Caramelized Walnuts
1 cup packed brown sugar
2 tablespoons water
24 pieces unbroken walnut halves

Garnish
1½ cups crème anglaise (see page 19)
8 fresh mint sprigs

Rinse, dry, and hull the strawberries; set aside.

To make the chocolate ganache: Melt the chocolate in a double boiler set over barely simmering water, stirring until smooth. Set aside and keep warm. Place a small saucepan over medium heat and combine the cream with the butter. Bring the cream to a boil and pour, whisking constantly, into the melted chocolate. Add the egg, stirring thoroughly until the mixture is glossy. Add the Cognac, stirring to incorporate. Transfer the mixture to a clean bowl, cover, and refrigerate until it thickens but does not harden.

To make the chocolate sauce: Melt the chocolate in a double boiler over barely simmering water, stirring until smooth. Stir in the cocoa powder and hot water, mixing thoroughly. Remove the sauce from heat and set aside at room temperature.

To make the caramelized walnuts: Combine the sugar and water in a medium saucepan and bring the mixture to a boil over medium-high heat, stirring occasionally, until it is thick, syrupy, and golden brown. Using a slotted spoon, dip the walnuts in the caramel one at a time,

Strawberries San Giorgio with Caramelized Walnuts; Zack Grumet, Blackie's House of Beef, Washington, D.C.

being sure to cover each one completely. Shake the spoon carefully to remove the excess, then place the caramelized walnut halves on a sheet of waxed paper, leaving space between each one.

To stuff the berries: Transfer the ganache to a pastry bag fitted with a small star tip and pipe a rosette into the center of each strawberry. Remove the strawberries to a platter and refrigerate them until the ganache hardens slightly.

To serve: Pool some crème anglaise on each plate. Pool a little of the chocolate sauce in the center of each pool of crème anglaise. Using a toothpick or a sharp knife, pull the chocolate sauce through the crème anglaise toward the outside of the plate. Place 3 strawberries in a triangle at the center of each plate. Divide the caramelized walnuts among the plates, arranging them in a larger triangle outside the strawberries. Garnish the plates with the mint sprigs and serve.

Note: *All the components of this dish may be made up to 1 day in advance and refrigerated. Assemble the dessert just prior to serving.*

ZACK GRUMET
Blackie's House of Beef, Washington, D.C.

Zack Grumet began his culinary career as a child in Long Island, New York, where he spent every Thursday cooking with his mother. In five hours they would prepare the family's weekly supply of bread, rolls, cakes, pies, and cookies.

At age eighteen, he moved to Brookline, Massachusetts, and apprenticed at Kupel's Bake and Bagel, where he was trained in kosher-style baking by his mentor and master baker, Ralf Schwartz. Grumet fondly recalls Schwartz urging, "Make it nice or don't make it at all," as he repeatedly banged his rolling pin on the table for emphasis.

After five years, Grumet returned to New York, married, and continued to work in ethnic and specialty food shops while taking classes at the Culinary Institute of America.

He moved to Washington, D.C., to work at Sutton Place Gourmet, the region's finest gourmet store, where he applied small-shop quality to high-production gourmet operations. Grumet is now pastry chef for Blackie's House of Beef, as well as Lulu's, a New Orleans–style restaurant, and a bar and dance club called Déja Vu.

Grumet credits the credo of "practice, practice, practice" with his success. His Strawberries San Giorgio wth Carmelized Walnuts, strawberries stuffed with chocolate ganache on a bed of chocolate sauce, is a perfect example of his style. It is "simple to prepare, exquisite to look at, and tastes wonderful," he says.

DAWN ROSE
Olives, Charlestown, Massachusetts

Boston-born Dawn Rose has a versatile background in both pastry and traditional culinary pursuits. An award-winning pastry chef, she was recently featured in *Art Culinaire,* a gourmet magazine specializing in the art of food.

Rose earned her culinary degree from Newbury College in Brookline, Massachusetts, and later went to work with Todd English at Olives in nearby Charlestown. Rose shares her life and long professional hours with her chef-husband Mark Rose. The couple is in the process of opening their own restaurant in the Boston suburbs.

Dawn Rose's signature dish, Apple Tarts, is a simple rendition of the American classic.

Apple Tarts

Dawn Rose, Olives
Charlestown, Massachusetts

Makes four 8-inch tarts, serves 8 to 12

These tarts are masterful versions of the beloved apple pie. The crunchy phyllo crusts are layered with a nut filling, then filled with a layer of sweetened and spiced apple slices and topped with a caramelized dome of apple rings.

Spice Mixture

3 tablespoons ground cinnamon
1½ teaspoons ground nutmeg
⅓ teaspoon ground cloves
⅓ teaspoon ground ginger

Apple Filling

3 tablespoons unsalted butter
6 Cortland apples, peeled, cored, and
  sliced into ¼-inch crescents
½ cup firmly packed brown sugar
½ cup granulated sugar
1½ tablespoons Spice Mixture, above
Juice and grated zest of 1 lemon
¼ teaspoon salt
¼ teaspoon freshly ground black pepper

Nut Filling

½ cup pecans, toasted (see page 16)
1 cup firmly packed brown sugar
1½ tablespoons Spice Mixture, above

Crusts

1 package (1 pound) thawed frozen
  phyllo dough (see page 17)
½ cup (1 stick) unsalted butter, clarified
  (see page 19)
4 tablespoons honey

Apple Topping

4 Red Delicious apples, cored, and
  sliced into ⅛-inch-thick rings
2 tablespoons fresh lemon juice

Apple Cider Sauce

2 cups apple cider
½ cup firmly packed brown sugar
1½ cinnamon sticks
2 whole cloves
1½ teaspoons cornstarch
1 tablespoon cold water
4 tablespoons unsalted butter

Garnish

Vanilla ice cream or sweetened
  whipped cream
Caramel shards (optional)
Fresh raspberries
8 to 12 fresh mint sprigs

Preheat the oven to 350°F.

To make the apple spice: Blend all the ingredients together and set aside.

To make the apple filling: In a medium saucepan over medium heat, combine the butter, apple slices, brown sugar, granulated sugar, spice mixture, lemon juice, and zest. Add the salt and pepper, and cook over medium heat until the apples are tender and the juices are thick, about 15 to 20 minutes. Remove the apples from heat and set aside.

To make the nut filling: Combine all the ingredients in a blender or food processor and pulse until the mixture resembles a coarse meal with some nut pieces still visible. Set aside.

Line 2 baking sheets with parchment paper or brush them lightly with melted butter. Keep the phyllo covered with a damp paper towel so it will not dry out as the tarts are being assembled.

To make the crusts: Spread a phyllo sheet on a work surface and brush lightly with melted butter. Repeat with 2 more sheets, placing each layer of dough at a 45-degree angle to the preceding one to build up a large area of sheets with a thick center where the sheets overlap. Brush each sheet lightly with butter.

To add the nut filling to the crusts: Place ¼ cup of the nut filling in the center of the overlapping area of phyllo dough. Drizzle 1 tablespoon honey over the mixture. Cover the nut filling with an additional sheet of phyllo dough at a 45-degree angle to the third sheet and repeat with 2 more sheets. The nut filling should be completely covered, and the phyllo design should form a rough circle. Seal the tart by crimping the edge of the phyllo sheets and folding them over towards the center of each tart. Turn the crust, crimping the sides, until the whole crust is a neat circle with a crimped edge. Repeat to make 4 nut-filled crusts.

To make the topping: Sprinkle the apple rings with the lemon juice to prevent discoloration.

To assemble the tarts: Mound one fourth of the cooled apple filling in the center of a nut-filled phyllo circle. Lay 1 apple ring against the apple filling, then place another ring overlapping over the first so that the hole of the core is covered by the second ring. Continue with the remaining apple rings, forming a dome around the filling. Fit the last apple ring underneath the first one. Paint the tart crust and top with melted butter, then sprinkle with 1 tablespoon of the nut filling. Repeat to make 4 tarts. Transfer the tarts to the prepared baking sheets using a metal spatula, and bake in the preheated oven for 15 to 20 minutes, or until golden brown.

To make the sauce: In a medium saucepan, combine the cider with the brown sugar and spices, and bring to a boil over medium heat. Cook to reduce the cider by half, then strain through a fine-meshed sieve, discarding the spices, and return the sauce to the pan over medium heat. Combine the cornstarch with the water, making sure there are no lumps. Add the cornstarch to the simmering cider sauce and, when the sauce has thickened slightly and is clear, remove the pan from the stove. Add the butter, 1 tablespoon at a time, whisking to incorporate each piece before adding the next. Set aside and keep warm.

To serve: Remove the tarts from the oven, cut them in halves or thirds, place 1 piece on each of 8 to 12 dessert plates, and top with ice cream or whipped cream. Garnish with caramel shards, if desired, and sprinkle fresh raspberries over the tart. Tuck mint sprigs under each serving and serve.

Note: The apple filling may be prepared and the crusts made up to 6 hours in advance, and the sauce may be prepared, up to adding the butter, at the same time. Add the apple filling and apple topping just before baking.

Apple Tarts; Dawn Rose, Olives, Charlestown, Massachusetts

Warm Apple Tarts; Stephen Johnson, Hamersley's Bistro, Boston

Warm Apple Tarts

Stephen Johnson, Hamersley's Bistro
Boston, Massachusetts

Makes four 6-inch tarts; serves 4

The secret of this aromatic filling is a pinch of Chinese five-spice powder in lieu of the usual nutmeg and cinnamon. These homey tarts bake very quickly because the filling is cooked in advance.

Pastry

1½ cups all-purpose flour
½ teaspoon salt
½ cup (1 stick) cold unsalted butter, cut into small pieces
¼ cup ice water

Tarts

3 to 4 large Granny Smith or other tart green apples
1 tablespoon unsalted butter
¼ teaspoon plus 2 tablespoons sugar
¼ teaspoon Chinese five-spice powder
1 egg, lightly beaten

Caramel Sauce (see page 19)

Garnish

4 tablespoons crème fraîche (see page 19)
4 fresh mint sprigs

To make the pastry: Combine the flour and salt in a medium bowl. Cut in the butter, using a pastry blender or 2 knives, until the mixture resembles large peas. Pour in the ice water and use your fingertips to work in the water until it is completely incorporated. On a lightly floured pastry board, form the dough into a log about 8 inches long. With the heel of your hand, push down on the dough to smear it across the surface of the board. Gather up the dough, form it into a log, and repeat. Gather the dough into a ball and knead it for a minute or two. Wrap the dough in plastic wrap and let it sit in the refrigerator for at least 30 minutes.

To make the tarts: Peel and core the apples, then cut them into eighths. Melt the butter in a large saucepan over medium heat. When the butter stops foaming and begins to brown, add the apples and toss them gently to coat them with the butter. Add the ¼ teaspoon sugar and continue to cook, stirring frequently. When the apples are a dark, golden brown, add the five-spice powder and cook another 2 to 3 minutes, or until tender but not mushy. Set aside and let cool.

Preheat the oven to 350°F. On a floured board, divide the pastry into 4 balls and roll each out into a ¼-inch-thick free-form round. Divide the apples between each circle of pastry, then crimp the sides of each tart to form an edge.

Brush the tart dough with the beaten egg and sprinkle lightly with the remaining 2 tablespoons sugar. Using a metal spatula, place the tarts on a baking sheet and bake in the preheated oven for 15 to 20 minutes, or until golden.

To serve: Place each tart onto a warm plate and drizzle with the caramel sauce. Spoon 1 tablespoon of crème fraîche onto each tart and garnish with fresh mint.

Note: *The tarts may be baked up to 6 hours in advance. Reheat them in a preheated 300°F oven for 5 minutes before serving.*

STEPHEN JOHNSON
Hamersley's Bistro, Boston, Massachusetts

Inspired by his grandmother's strawberry shortcake, an interest in food as a means of transmitting cultural values, and "the desire to work with my hands, standing up," Stephen Johnson began his culinary career. With no formal training, but an intense desire to learn, he is now the sous-chef at Hamersley's Bistro in Boston, Massachusetts.

Growing up playing in the gardens, lakes, and streams of North Carolina and Virginia gave Johnson an early appreciation for "primary ingredients." His current work with programs to promote sustainable regional agriculture and his energetic promotion of urban gardening centers reflect the value he places on seasonal foods.

Johnson continues to pursue his interest in tastes, flavors, and techniques. Signature dishes like Braised Rabbit with Anchos, Cumin, and Cinnamon, and Braised Bass with Ginger, Soy, and Sesame reflect his desire to infuse traditional fare with ethnic flavor and style.

Johnson credits Gordon Hamersley with the Warm Apple Tarts recipe included in *Great Chefs of the East*. "This is Gordon's food; I simply do it—it is a great example of a beautiful, delicious, rustic, home-style pastry depending upon simple basics: deliciously prepared fruit, a well-balanced burnt-caramel sauce, and a tangy, rich *crème fraîche*," says Johnson.

Apple Complicity; Hans Schadler, Williamsburg Inn, Williamsburg, Virginia

Apple Complicity

Hans Schadler, Williamsburg Inn
Williamsburg, Virginia

Makes 2 baked apples

Baked apples were a favorite dessert in colonial Virginia. In this updated version, the apples are stuffed with a flavorful mixture of diced apples and dried fruits, and served with a light cider sauce.

Cider Sabayon
1 cup apple cider
3 egg yolks
1 egg
½ cup dry white wine
2 tablespoons maple syrup
½ teaspoon grated orange zest
½ teaspoon grated lemon zest
¼ teaspoon ground cinnamon

Stuffed Apples
¼ cup assorted dried fruits such as figs, apples, and apricots
¼ cup dark rum
2 Granny Smith or other tart green apples

1 lemon half
1 cup dry white wine
2 Red Delicious apples, peeled, cored, and cut into ½-inch dice
2 tablespoons dried currants
Grated zest of 1 orange
Grated zest of 1 lemon
¼ cup maple syrup
¼ cup small-curd cottage cheese
¼ teaspoon ground nutmeg
¼ teaspoon ground cinnamon
1 egg white, lightly beaten
¼ cup soft bread crumbs to bind the filling, if necessary
6 sheets thawed frozen phyllo dough
4 tablespoons unsalted butter, melted

Garnish
1 apple
1 lemon half
2 tablespoons unsalted butter
1 tablespoon granulated sugar
Confectioners' sugar for dusting

To make the cider sabayon: Whisk all the ingredients together in a large bowl and place the bowl over a saucepan of simmering but not boiling water. Continue whisking the mixture vigorously until the yolks are light and frothy and the mixture has begun to thicken. When whisking the mixture exposes the bottom of the bowl, the sabayon is done. Remove the bowl from the heat and allow the mixture to cool. Transfer the sabayon to a smaller bowl, cover, and chill it in the refrigerator until needed.

To make the stuffed apples: Preheat the oven to 350°F. Coarsely chop the dried fruits and place them in a small mixing bowl. Cover the fruit with the rum and set aside for 1 hour.

Cut the Granny Smith or other tart apples in half crosswise. Core both halves of the apples and scoop out two thirds of the flesh from the cavity. Rub the inside of each apple with a lemon half to prevent discoloration. Place the apples in a shallow baking dish with the white wine and bake in a preheated oven for 10 minutes. Remove the apples from the baking pan with a slotted spoon and let them cool.

In a medium saucepan, combine the diced Red Delicious apples, dried fruits, currants, orange and lemon zests, and maple syrup. Cook over medium heat until the apples are soft, about 8 to 10 minutes. Add the cottage cheese and spices. Add the lightly beaten egg white and the bread crumbs, adjusting the seasoning if necessary. Spoon the fruit mixture into each apple cavity, then return the apples to the baking dish and bake, uncovered, for an additional 10 minutes.

On a clean work surface, lay out the phyllo dough, covered with plastic wrap. Cut a sheet of pastry into 8-inch squares and brush each one with some of the melted butter. Repeat with 2 more sheets of phyllo dough, placing each square at a 45-degree angle to the preceding one. Repeat to make a second stack of phyllo.

Increase the oven temperature to 400°F. Place a baked apple in the center of each phyllo pastry stack. Gather the edges up around the apple and twist the layers of pastry at the top to resemble a package. Place the apples on a baking sheet and bake the apples for 10 to 12 minutes, or until the phyllo dough is lightly browned and crisp.

While the apples are baking, make the garnish: Core the apple and cut each section into crescent-shaped ¼-inch-thick slices. Rub the slices with the lemon half to prevent discoloration and set aside. Melt the butter in a large saucepan over high heat. Add the apple slices and cook, turning occasionally, until the apples are tender, about 3 to 5 minutes. Sprinkle the slices with the granulated sugar and cook 1 additional minute until the apples have a light brown glaze.

To assemble the dessert: Place 1 baked apple on each dessert plate and spoon a dollop of cider sabayon around the base of each apple. Garnish with the glazed apple slices, dust the top of each apple with confectioners' sugar, and serve.

Note: The apples may be prepared up to the final baking with the phyllo up to 6 hours in advance and allowed to sit at room temperature.

Cranberry-Walnut Crostata

Johanne Killeen, Al Forno
Providence, Rhode Island

Makes one 10-inch tart; serves 6 to 8

A crostata is a flat Italian fruit tart. This is an easy-to-make, not-too-sweet dessert because of the tartness of the cranberries.

Pastry
1 cup (2 sticks) cold unsalted butter,
   cut into ½-inch cubes
2 cups all-purpose flour
¼ cup superfine sugar
½ teaspoon kosher salt
¼ cup ice water

Filling
2 cups fresh or thawed frozen cranberries
½ cup chopped walnuts, toasted
   (see page 16)
2 tablespoons confectioners' sugar, sifted
2 tablespoons firmly packed
   dark brown sugar

Garnish
Confectioners' sugar for dusting
Créme anglaise (see page 19) or
   sweetened whipped cream (optional)

To make the pastry with a food processor:
Freeze the butter cubes on a baking sheet for 10 minutes. Place the flour, sugar, and salt in a food processor. Pulse a few times to combine. Add the butter cubes and toss with your fingers to coat each cube with the flour. Pulse quickly on and off 15 times, or until the butter particles are the size of small peas. Add the ice water through the feed tube and pulse on and off until the dough is moist and holds together when a small amount is pressed between your fingers. Do not let the entire amount of dough become a solid mass.

To make the pastry by hand: Cut the butter into the dry ingredients using a pastry blender or 2 knives. Add the ice water and stir with a fork until all the ingredients are moistened.

Turn the contents of the bowl onto a sheet of aluminum foil and shape into a rough ball. Wrap the dough in foil and refrigerate for at least 2 hours, or until firm.

To make the filling: Preheat the oven to 450°F. On a lightly floured surface, roll the tart dough into an 11-inch circle and transfer it to a baking sheet.

Combine the cranberries, walnuts, and sugars in a mixing bowl. Toss to combine evenly. Mound the cranberry mixture in the pastry circle, leaving a 1½-inch border around the outside edge. Fold the dough border towards the center of the tart, letting the pastry drape gently over the fruit. Press the edge of the border together. Without mashing the fruit, pinch together the soft pleats of dough that form the draping.

Bake the tart in the preheated oven for 20 to 25 minutes, or until the crust is golden and the berries are juicy. Let cool on a rack for 10 minutes, dust with confectioners' sugar, and serve warm with crème anglaise or whipped cream, if desired.

Note: *The tart dough will freeze well for up to 2 weeks. Defrost the wrapped dough on a counter for 30 to 45 minutes before rolling, or until it is still quite cold but pliable.*

Cranberry-Walnut Crostata; Johanne Killeen, Al Forno Restaurant, Providence, Rhode Island

KILIAN WEIGAND
Biba, Boston, Massachusetts

Fond memories of family dinners in his grandmother's small apartment led Kilian Weigand to become a pastry chef. "There was no room to move, so we just sat at the table for eight or nine hours. It was the focal point of the family," he says. Weigand put his expertise into practice and later became the pastry chef at Biba in Boston.

A graduate of the Culinary Institute of America, he worked at the Copley Plaza in the late 1970s, then moved to Délice Pastries. Like several other well-known Boston chefs, such as Lydia Shire and Jasper White, Weigand moved through the Parker House Hotel, the Bostonian Hotel, and the Charles Hotel before going to Biba.

Weigand also served in the U.S. Navy for six years as a mess management specialist. Surprisingly, working in military mess halls did not discourage him from becoming a chef. "The military gave me opportunity to travel, to work as a food buyer, and to have lots of exposure to different sorts of serving environments," he says.

His signature desserts, such as Hot Chocolate Cheesecake, and Mascarpone Cheesecake with Lacy Nut Wafers and Blueberry Caramel, "try to reexamine American-style desserts and take them up a notch," says Weigand. He described the atmosphere at Biba, where he worked with Lydia Shire, as "colorful, eclectic, and fun, and that's reflected in the people." Weigand is currently taking time off to collect stamps and care for his houseful of pets.

Marscarpone Cheesecake with Lacy Nut Wafers and Blueberry Caramel

Kilian Weigand, Biba
Boston, Massachusetts

Serves 6 to 8

This spectacular dessert combines layers of crisp nut wafers, a cheesecake cream made with marscarpone and cream cheese, and a violet-hued sauce. All the elements may be made in advance and assembled at the last minute. Chef Weigand uses wild Maine blueberries, but you may use any fresh blueberries.

Cheesecake Cream
8 ounces (1 package) natural cream
   cheese at room temperature
8 ounces marscarpone cheese at room
   temperature (available at specialty
   food stores, or see Mail-Order Sources,
   page 199)
1 cup granulated sugar
2 eggs
Grated zest of 1 lemon
1 tablespoon vanilla extract

Lacy Nut Wafers
¼ cup almonds or hazelnuts, toasted
   (see page 16)
1 cup granulated sugar
¼ cup water

Blueberry Caramel
2 cups granulated sugar
½ cup water
2 cups fresh or thawed frozen
   unsweetened blueberries
¼ to ½ cup water

Blueberry Compote
2 to 4 cups fresh or thawed frozen
   unsweetened blueberries
¼ cup Blueberry Caramel, above

⅛ to ¼ cup heavy (whipping) cream
4 cups vegetable oil
1 package *kataifi* dough (extruded phyllo
   dough found at Middle Eastern
   markets)
Confectioners' sugar, fresh blueberries,
   whipped cream, and 6 to 8 fresh
   mint sprigs for garnish

To make the cheesecake cream: Preheat the oven to 350°F and butter a 9-inch round cake pan. Beat the cheeses and sugar until light and fluffy, add the eggs, and beat until smooth. Scrape down the sides of the bowl and add the lemon zest and vanilla. Pour the batter into the prepared cake pan, then place the cake pan in a baking pan. Place the baking pan in the preheated oven and pour enough hot water into the pan to come halfway up the side of the cheesecake pan. Bake for 20 to 30 minutes, or until a knife inserted in the center comes out clean.

Remove the cake pan from the baking pan, let cool to room temperature, and refrigerate to chill completely.

To make the wafers: Preheat the oven to 375°F and line baking sheets with parchment paper or grease and lightly flour them. Combine the nuts and sugar in a blender or food processor and process until very finely ground. Add the water and process briefly to form a paste. Spoon 12 to 16 small mounds of 1½ to 2 teaspoons of the paste 3 to 4 inches apart onto the baking sheets. Bake until brown and bubbly, about 7 to 9 minutes. The wafers will become crisp shortly after baking; if not, return them to the oven and bake another minute or two. Let the wafers cool to room temperature on the baking sheets.

To make the blueberry caramel: Combine the sugar and water in a heavy, medium saucepan over high heat. Boil until the sugar turns an amber color, then immediately add the blueberries and stir. Cook the sauce for 2 minutes, then strain it through a fine-meshed sieve and let cool. Add water as necessary to make a pourable sauce.

To make the compote: Chop the blueberries coarsely and combine them with the caramel. Let sit at room temperature for at least 30 minutes.

To assemble the dessert: Blend the cheesecake mixture with the heavy cream to the consistency of a stiff pastry cream. Transfer the mixture to a pastry bag fitted with a No. 5 (large) star tip.

Heat the oil in a deep, heavy pot or deep-fryer to 375°F, or until almost smoking. Fry the *kataifi,* one large handful at a time, for 1½ to 2 minutes, or until light brown. Drain the fried dough on paper towels or brown paper bags and dust it heavily with confectioners' sugar while it is still hot. Repeat until all the *kataifi* is fried.

With a large spoon, drizzle the blueberry caramel onto each dessert plate in a random pattern. Place 1 wafer on each plate and pipe a border of the creamed cheesecake around the perimeter, leaving a well in the center. Fill the center with a spoonful of the blueberry compote and place another wafer on top. Fluff the *kataifi* and place a large "nest" atop each dessert, then dust the top with additional confectioners' sugar.

Garnish the plate with several fresh blueberries, a small dollop of lightly whipped cream, and a sprig of fresh mint.

Note: The cheesecake cream, blueberry caramel, compote, and wafers may all be made 1 day in advance and refrigerated, tightly covered. The kataifi may be fried a few hours in advance; however, the desserts must be assembled right before serving.

Mascarpone Cheesecake with Lacy Nut Wafers and Blueberry Caramel; Kilian Weigand, Biba, Boston

Sabayon en Hippenmasse

*Wolfgang Friedrich, Americus at the
    Sheraton Washington
Washington, D.C.*

Makes six 8-ounce custards

If making thin fences out of cookie
dough intimidates you, make just the
frozen wine-flavored custard and the red
wine sauce. The cookie fence is made
from an easy dough similar to a French
tulipe; however, the fence itself is somewhat complicated to make.

Sabayon
6 egg yolks
2 eggs
6 tablespoons granulated sugar

Juice of ½ lemon
¾ cup plus 2 tablespoons dry white wine
1 envelope unflavored gelatin
2 tablespoons rum
1 cup heavy (whipping) cream

Hippenmasse (Cookie Fences)
1 cup confectioners' sugar, sifted
4 egg whites
1 tablespoon vanilla extract
1 cup all-purpose flour
½ cup (1 stick) unsalted butter, melted
  and cooled
¼ cup unsweetened cocoa powder

Bishop Sauce
1 cup dry red wine
5 tablespoons granulated sugar
Grated zest of 1 lemon

1 cinnamon stick
1 whole clove
1½ teaspoons cornstarch
2 tablespoons cold water
1 tablespoon candied orange peel,
  finely chopped
1 tablespoon sliced almonds

Garnish
2 ounces white chocolate, chopped
1 cup Champagne grapes

To make the sabayon: Place the egg
yolks, eggs, granulated sugar, and lemon
juice in a medium bowl. Place the bowl
over a pan of barely simmering water.
Add ¾ cup of the white wine in a steady
stream, whisking the mixture until it is
very thick and pale yellow. Set aside.

Place the gelatin, rum, and the
remaining 2 tablespoons white wine in a
cup and let sit until the gelatin has softened. Place the cup holding the gelatin
in a small saucepan set over low heat to
dissolve the gelatin. Place the egg mixture
over a pan of ice water, then whisk until
cool. Stir the melted gelatin into the
sabayon.

Place the cream in a deep bowl and
whip until the cream holds soft peaks.
Fold the whipped cream into the
sabayon. Divide the mixture evenly
between six 8-ounce plastic cups or
custard cups and transfer the cups to
the freezer.

To make the Hippenmasse (Cookie Fences):
Place the confectioners' sugar and the egg
whites in a medium bowl, stirring to
combine. Add the vanilla and the flour,
mixing until fully incorporated. Add the
melted butter gradually without overmix-
ing the batter. Remove one fourth of the
batter to a separate bowl and add the
cocoa powder. Transfer the larger amount
of the batter to a parchment paper pastry
cone with a snipped tip, or a pastry bag
fitted with a small round writing tip.
Line a baking sheet with a sheet of waxed
paper or parchment paper. Pipe a row of
matchstick-sized vertical lines out of the
dough until the row is approximately
10 inches long. Transfer the chocolate
dough to another snipped parchment
paper cone or another pastry bag fitted

Sabayon en Hippenmasse; Wolfgang Friedrich; Americus at the Sheraton Washington, Washington, D.C.

with a small round writing tip. Pipe the chocolate dough in a perpendicular line across the row of dough to create a picket-fence effect. Repeat with the remaining dough to make 6 fences.

Preheat the oven to 425°F. Bake the cookies for 3 to 4 minutes, checking frequently to prevent them from burning. Working quickly, remove the cookies one at a time from the baking sheet and wrap each carefully around a rolling pin to form a round cookie fence. Set the fences aside.

To make the sauce: Combine the red wine, granulated sugar, lemon zest, cinnamon stick, and clove in a medium saucepan and bring to a boil over medium heat. Simmer for 10 minutes. Dissolve the cornstarch in the water and add, whisking constantly, to the hot wine sauce. Remove from heat and set aside. Stir the candied orange peel and almonds into the sauce just prior to serving.

To assemble the dessert: Melt the white chocolate in a double boiler over barely simmering water, stirring until smooth. Let cool slightly, then transfer the chocolate to a parchment paper cone with a snipped end. Using the mold or cookie cutter of your choice as a stencil (Wolfgang Friedrich uses a grape-leaf form), trace the outline of the mold or cutter with a thin line of white chocolate. Fill in the white chocolate outline with the red wine sauce. Remove the frozen sabayon from the freezer and dip the bottom of each cup in a hot-water bath. Invert each cup, loosening the sabayon with a thin spatula or a sharp knife. When the sabayon comes out, place each one bottom-side up in the center of a sauce outline. Fit a cookie fence over each sabayon. Garnish the top of each dessert with Champagne grapes and serve.

Note: *The sabayon cups may be made up to 3 days in advance and kept frozen, covered with aluminum foil. The cookie fences may be made 1 day in advance and kept at room temperature in an airtight container. The sauce also may be made 1 day in advance, up to adding the candied peel and almonds, and kept at room temperature.*

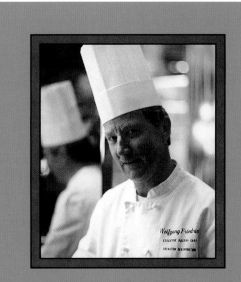

WOLFGANG FRIEDRICH
Americus at the Sheraton Washington; Washington, D.C.

Dark Chocolate and Raspberry Terrine, Fresh Coconut Custard served in a coconut, and Saybayon en Hippenmasse have sweetened many a visitor's stay in the capital city. These are the signature creations of pastry chef Wolfgang Friedrich of the Sheraton Washington hotel.

A native of Germany who grew up near the Baltic Sea and the city of Luebeck, Friedrich began his career by working in a pastry store as a teenager. After deciding he liked life in a sweet shop, he apprenticed himself to a baker and confectioner for five years. He then worked in top pastry shops in Germany and Switzerland, giving special study to cold desserts and chocolate candies.

His ambition, says Friedrich, was always "to work in hotels and to travel." Before coming to the United States in 1970, he worked in hotels in northern Europe, Greece, and Thailand. Now his pastries have found a home in Washington. His desserts are featured at Wolfgang's Pastry and Ice Cream Shop at the Sheraton, as well as at the Sheraton's Americus Restaurant.

It takes a special patience and dedication to create pastries in a 1,505-room hotel, and Friedrich has such qualities. "This is my profession," he says, "and I still like it to this day!"

A certified master chef, Friedrich has been awarded the Grand Prize in the Pastry Display Culinary Salon, a competition that judges pastry presentation held in Washington, D.C. Having outlasted several administrations, Friedrich continues to make life in the capital city more delicious for all.

ANDRÉ SOLTNER

Lutèce, New York, New York

When Lutèce opened its doors nearly thirty-five years ago, its owner made sure that the prices were high, and that people who lacked the proper social polish were turned away. He believed that there was a certain mystique in being the most expensive restaurant in New York City, and that this cachet alone would be enough to attract customers. When André Soltner became the owner in 1972, all of that changed.

Soltner's unyielding dedication to the quality of his classic French food has consistently garnered four-star ratings from the *New York Times,* five stars from the *Mobil Travel Guide,* and been rated 19 out of 20 by *Gault Millau.* The cuisine is top-notch, but the brownstone dining mecca is without affectation. Soltner's wife, Simone, whose official title is cashier, personally greets and seats each of the restaurant's customers.

This combination of a welcoming atmosphere and food prepared by a gourmet's gourmet has remained a winning recipe; Lutèce turns away one thousand customers a year. When Cornell University business students suggested that he open a second restaurant, or charge more money, Soltner refused. "Why should I have more benefit just because I'm small?" he asked.

Growing up in his native Alsace, Soltner began his apprenticeship early, and by the time he came to the United States at the age of twenty-six, he had worked at a series of restaurants in France and Switzerland. While in Switzerland, Soltner developed a love of skiing that sent him into the French alpine troops once his military service began. Since he had no particular desire to cook en masse, he told the army that he was a cabinetmaker, his father's profession.

In a profession in which twelve-hour days are the norm, Soltner has a reputation among fellow chefs of being exceedingly dedicated even by industry standards, and his love for cooking is not confined to Lutèce. The dishes that Soltner prepared for *Great Chefs of the East,* Potato and Bacon Pie, and Beignets Soufflés Crème Anglaise, are typical of Alsatian home cooking, which, he notes, "I adore to cook at home."

Beignets with Vanilla Sauce
Beignets Soufflés Crème Anglaise

André Soltner, Lutèce
New York, New York

Serves 8

Most Americans know beignets as the New Orleans version of a doughnut. Made from the same cream puff dough as éclairs, they are fried instead of baked. These are crisp and delicious, served with a creamy sauce.

1 cup water
3 tablespoons unsalted butter
¼ teaspoon salt
1 cup sugar
1 cup all-purpose flour, sifted
4 large eggs
½ teaspoon ground cinnamon
4 cups vegetable oil
1½ cups crème anglaise, heated
  (see page 19)

Combine the water, butter, salt, and ¼ teaspoon of the sugar in a deep, heavy saucepan. Bring the mixture to a boil over medium heat, stirring to dissolve the butter, then remove from heat. Immediately add the flour all at once and stir vigorously to blend. Return the mixture to medium heat and cook, stirring constantly, until the mixture pulls away from the side of the pan, forms a ball, and leaves a film on the bottom of the pan, about 3 minutes. Remove from heat and beat in 1 egg at a time with a wooden spoon. The finished paste should be very smooth. Cover and set aside.

Mix the remaining sugar with the cinnamon and place it in a deep plate or shallow soup bowl. In a deep, heavy pot or deep-fryer, heat the oil over medium-high heat to 375°F, or almost smoking. When the oil is hot, scoop up 1 heaping teaspoonful of the dough, push it off the spoon into a rounded lump with your thumb, and drop into the oil. Increasing the heat slightly, fry 10 to 12 beignets at a time, moving them around in the oil so they brown equally on all sides. Remove the cooked beignets with a slotted spoon to paper towels to drain briefly, then keep them warm in an oven on very low heat.

Repeat with the remaining dough. Roll the warm beignets in the cinnamon sugar and serve at once with the warm crème anglaise on the side.

Note: *The cream puff dough can be made up to 6 hours in advance and kept at room temperature; the puffs must be fried just prior to serving.*

Beignets with Vanilla Sauce; André Soltner, Lutèce, New York

Pecan-Rum Tart; Leslie Miller, The Old Inn on the Green, New Marlborough, Massachusetts

Pecan-Rum Tart

Leslie Miller, The Old Inn on the Green
New Marlborough, Massachusetts

Makes one 10-inch tart; serves 8 to 10

This delicious variation on pecan pie has a puff pastry crust and a crunchy rum-scented filling, which is glazed with apricot and dusted with confectioners' sugar.

½ cup (1 stick) unsalted butter at
   room temperature
1¼ cups granulated sugar
4 eggs, separated
1 tablespoon crème fraîche (see page 20)
2 tablespoons rum
1 tablespoon vanilla extract
2 cups chopped pecans, toasted
   (see page 16)
1 fully baked 10-inch puff pastry crust
   made from frozen puff pastry (a 10-
   inch pastry shell may be substituted)
1½ cups apricot jam
Confectioners' sugar for dusting

Preheat the oven to 350°F. Place the butter and granulated sugar in a medium bowl and beat until light and fluffy. Beat

in the egg yolks, crème fraîche, rum, and vanilla. Fold in the chopped pecans and set aside.

In a large bowl, beat the egg whites until stiff peaks form. Fold the egg whites gently into the nut mixture.

Pour the batter into the pastry shell and bake in the preheated oven for about 30 minutes, or until the tart is puffed and set in the middle. Let cool. Place the apricot jam in a small saucepan over low heat, stirring occasionally, until the jam is melted. Strain the melted jam through a fine-meshed sieve over a bowl and discard the solids. Let cool.

Just before serving, spread the apricot glaze over the top of the tart, dust with confectioners' sugar and serve.

Note: The tart may be made up to 8 hours in advance; do not glaze or dust with sugar until just prior to serving.

Chocolate-Lover's Cake

John Richard Twichell with
  Marcel Desaulniers; Trellis
Williamsburg, Virginia

Makes one 9-inch layer cake;
serves 10 to 12

Three chocolate textures in one dessert, with hazelnuts thrown in for good measure, make this a dream cake for chocolate aficionados. None of the three components of the recipe is difficult to make, and the cake may be assembled 1 day in advance and refrigerated, uncovered.

Chocolate Cake
2 tablespoons butter, melted, plus
   1 cup (2 sticks) unsalted butter
8 ounces semisweet chocolate, chopped
10 egg yolks
½ cup sugar
6 egg whites

Chocolate Mousse
6 ounces semisweet chocolate, chopped
1½ cups heavy (whipping) cream
3 egg whites
2 tablespoons sugar

Chocolate Ganache
1½ cups heavy (whipping) cream
20 ounces semisweet chocolate, chopped

2¼ cups hazelnuts, peeled (see page 16)

To make the cake: Lightly coat the insides of two 9-inch round cake pans with some of the melted butter. Line each pan with waxed or parchment paper, then lightly coat the paper with more melted butter and set aside. Preheat the oven to 325°F.

Chocolate-Lover's Cake; John Richard Twichell with Marcel Desaulniers; The Trellis Restaurant, Williamsburg, Virginia

Melt the 1 cup butter and the semi-sweet chocolate in a double boiler over simmering water, stirring until smooth. Set aside at room temperature.

Place the egg yolks and sugar in a medium bowl and beat until the mixture is slightly thickened and pale in color, about 4 minutes. Scrape down the sides of the bowl and beat for 2 more minutes.

Place the egg whites in a large bowl and beat until stiff peaks form. Using a rubber spatula, fold the melted chocolate mixture into the beaten egg yolk mixture. Add one fourth of the beaten egg whites and stir to incorporate, then gently fold in the remaining egg whites.

Divide the batter between the prepared pans, spreading it evenly, and bake in the preheated oven for 45 to 55 minutes, or until a toothpick inserted in the center comes out clean. Remove the cakes from the oven and let cool in the pans for 15 minutes. (During baking, the surface of the cakes will form a crust; this crust will collapse when the cakes are removed from the oven.) Invert the cakes onto cake circles or flat plates. Remove the paper and refrigerate the cakes for 1 hour.

To make the chocolate mousse: Melt the chocolate in a double boiler over barely simmering water, stirring until smooth. Remove from heat and set aside at room temperature.

Place the heavy cream in a deep bowl and beat until stiff peaks form. Set aside. Place the egg whites in a large bowl and beat until soft peaks form. Add the sugar and continue to beat until stiff, glossy peaks form. Whisk one fourth of the whipped cream into the melted chocolate. Fold the chocolate mixture, then the remaining whipped cream, into the egg whites gently but thoroughly. Cover and refrigerate.

To make the ganache: Heat the heavy cream in a medium, heavy saucepan over medium-high heat. Bring the cream to a boil, stirring so that it does not boil over onto the stove. Place the chocolate in a stainless-steel bowl. Pour the boiling cream over the chocolate, cover the

LESLIE MILLER
The Old Inn on the Green, New Marlborough, Massachusetts

Growing up in New York, pastry chef Leslie Miller remembers, "I used to pass eight bakeries every day on my way home from school—I would stop at each of them." While attending college in Boston, Miller "worked at a popular movie theater where my brownies and cookies were sold. They would disappear faster than the movie tickets."

Today, Miller's hobby has become her profession. She and her husband own and operate a tavern, The Old Inn on the Green, in New Marlborough, a town situated in the Berkshire Mountains in the western part of Massachusetts.

"The Old Inn," says Miller, "has grown and prospered beyond our wildest dreams." Several years ago, the couple acquired the turn-of-the-century Gedney Farm, just down the road from the Inn. They restored and renovated two Normandy-style barns; now one has eleven luxury guest rooms and the other is a banquet hall and meeting space.

Guests and diners at the Old Inn and Gedney Farm can enjoy a first-class inn and a restaurant that features fresh bread and pastries, such as Pecan-Rum Tart. And Leslie Miller is busy baking, hosting, and raising two children who need only stop at one bakery—hers—on their way home from school.

bowl, and let it stand for 5 minutes. Stir until smooth and set aside at room temperature.

Chop the hazelnuts to ¼-inch pieces using an on-and-off pulsing action in a food processor or chop by hand. Do not use a blender.

Combine 1½ cups of the chocolate ganache and 1 cup of the chopped hazelnuts in a medium bowl and set aside at room temperature.

To assemble and decorate the cake:
Spread the hazelnut-ganache mixture evenly over one cake layer, using a cake spatula. Reverse the other cake layer and place it right side up on top of the ganache-covered cake. Press the cake layers together. Using a very sharp serrated knife, trim the top and sides of the cake so they are even. Refrigerate the cake for 30 minutes.

Remove the cake from the refrigerator and spread ¾ cup of the chocolate mousse evenly over the sides of the cake. Chill the cake in the freezer for 30 minutes, or refrigerate for 1 hour.

Remove the cake from the freezer and pour the room-temperature chocolate ganache over the cake, spreading it evenly with a spatula to cover the top and the mousse-coated sides of the cake. Refrigerate the cake for 20 to 25 minutes to set the ganache.

Transfer the remaining chocolate mousse to a pastry bag fitted with a No. 5 (large) star tip. Remove the cake from the refrigerator and pipe mousse stars over the entire top of the cake. Press the remaining chopped hazelnuts into the ganache on the sides of the cake, coating the sides evenly. Refrigerate the cake for at least 1 hour before cutting and serving.

To serve: Cut the cake with a serrated slicer, heating the blade of the slicer under hot running water before making each slice. Allow the slices to come to room temperature for 10 to 30 minutes before serving.

Chocolate-Toffee Mountains

George Bozko, American Seasons
Nantucket, Massachusetts

Makes 8 individual tortes

Although these are not high mountains, they are certainly rich ones, with two chocolate sauces and a caramel sauce napping the individual chocolate-robed tortes. The tortes are similar to baked mousses, and are moist and delicious on their own, even without the sauces.

Chocolate Tortes

8 ounces bittersweet chocolate, chopped
1 cup (2 sticks) unsalted butter
1½ cups firmly packed dark brown sugar
¾ cup unsweetened cocoa powder
6 eggs
½ cup freshly brewed coffee
1 cup slivered almonds, toasted
  (see page 16)

Chocolate Glaze

10 ounces semisweet chocolate, chopped
1¼ cups heavy (whipping) cream
3 tablespoons corn syrup
2 teaspoons Cognac
1½ teaspoons vanilla extract

White Chocolate Sauce

1½ pounds white chocolate, chopped
1½ cups heavy (whipping) cream
2 tablespoons Triple Sec or other
  orange-flavored liqueur

Dark Chocolate Sauce

1 cup water
1 cup granulated sugar
¼ cup corn syrup
3 tablespoons unsweetened cocoa powder
4 ounces semisweet chocolate, chopped
1½ cups heavy (whipping) cream

Garnish

8 ounces Almond Roca candy
4 ounces semisweet chocolate, chilled
Caramel sauce (see page 19)

To make the chocolate tortes: Grease eight 4-ounce fluted molds with butter and preheat the oven to 300°F. Melt the chocolate and the butter in a double

GEORGE BOZKO
American Seasons, Nantucket, Massachusetts

While working as a sales representative for a wine and spirits wholesaler, George Bozko found that the most exciting part of his job was visiting restaurant kitchens. After a couple of years of just dropping by, Bozko decided to give up selling and stay in the kitchen, where his spirit and talents have blossomed ever since.

These days, Bozko's kitchen is at American Seasons restaurant on Nantucket. On this island off the coast of Cape Cod, Massachusetts, Bozko creates such signature desserts as Nantucket Daffodil Cake, California Citrus Tart, Chocolate-Peanut Butter Mud Cake, and Chocolate-Toffee Mountain.

Of Belorussian heritage, Bozko was encouraged throughout his New Jersey childhood to help create family favorites like babka (a sweet yeast bread), pirogi, and chicken soup. His formal training began at the French Culinary Institute in New York. His baking has evolved from the French classical style he learned at the Institute into what he now calls "contemporary American."

"This style," says Bozko, "involves altering but using classical cooking methods and using new flavors to develop a new taste experience that is lower in fat and sugar but full of pronounced flavors."

Freeing himself from the "ever-present wedges" of pies, cakes, and tortes, Bozko has come to favor creating individual desserts. "People seem to like something that is all their own," he says. "It also allows for more interesting presentation possibilities."

The Chocolate-Toffee Mountain is illustrative of what Bozko does best. This beautifully presented individual chocolate torte with a chocolate glaze is served with white chocolate and caramel sauces.

"Americans love gooey desserts," says Chef Bozko, "so by underbaking the cake you enhance and increase the already rich nature of the cake." This cake may not pass traditional "doneness" tests, but it passes the dessert-lover's test easily.

boiler over barely simmering water, stirring until smooth. Set aside. In a medium bowl, combine the brown sugar and cocoa powder. Add the eggs, coffee, and almonds and beat until well blended. Add the melted chocolate mixture and blend in. Divide the batter among the prepared molds. Place the filled molds in a baking pan, then fill the baking pan with enough hot water to come halfway up the side of the molds. Bake in the preheated oven for 40 to 50 minutes, until just set. The edges will be dry, but the center will not be fully cooked; do not overbake or the tortes will be dry. Allow the tortes to cool for 10 minutes. Turn out onto wire racks, let cool slightly, then refrigerate for 1 hour.

To make the chocolate glaze: Place the chocolate in a medium bowl. Combine the remaining ingredients in a small saucepan and bring to a boil. Pour the hot liquid over the chocolate and let the mixture stand for 2 minutes. Stir until melted and smooth, then strain through a fine-meshed sieve and set aside.

To make the white chocolate sauce: Place the chocolate in a large bowl. Place the heavy cream in a medium saucepan and bring to a boil. Stir in the Triple Sec or other liqueur and pour this mixture over the white chocolate. Stir until melted and smooth. Strain through a fine-meshed sieve and set aside.

To make the dark chocolate sauce: In a medium saucepan, combine the water, granulated sugar, and corn syrup over medium heat. Bring to a boil and cook for 1 minute. Stir in the cocoa powder, return to a boil, and cook for 1 additional minute. Repeat with the chopped chocolate and cream. Strain through a fine-meshed sieve and set aside.

Spoon the chocolate glaze over the chilled tortes and refrigerate them for 15 minutes. Place the candy in a heavy plastic bag and hit it with the smooth side of a meat mallet or the bottom of a heavy pot until ¼-inch shards are formed. Shave the chocolate with a vegetable peeler to make ¼ cup shavings. To serve, pool caramel sauce in middle of each plate. Place 1 torte in the center of each pool of caramel, then pour white chocolate sauce down one side of the torte and dark chocolate sauce down the other side. Garnish with the candy shards and chocolate shavings.

Note: The tortes and sauces may be made up to a day in advance, then covered and refrigerated separately. Heat the sauces over low heat until liquid and smooth before serving. The chef uses a large quantity of sauce for each dessert; the amounts may easily be cut by half.

Chocolate-Toffee Mountains; George Bozko, American Seasons, Nantucket, Massachusetts

Warm Valrhona Chocolate Cakes with Vanilla Ice Cream; Jean-Georges Vongerichten, JoJo/Vong, New York

Warm Valrhona Chocolate Cakes with Vanilla Ice Cream

Jean-Georges Vongerichten, JoJo's / Vong
New York, New York

Makes 4 individual cakes

These easy-to-make cakes are the epitome of chocolate as a comfort food because the centers remain soft, like fudge. People of all ages will adore their taste and texture.

Cakes

6 tablespoons unsalted butter
3½ ounces Valrhona bittersweet chocolate, chopped
2 whole eggs
2 egg yolks
½ cup sugar
3 tablespoons all-purpose flour

Garnish

Unsweetened cocoa powder for dusting
1 pint finest-quality vanilla ice cream, slightly softened before serving
4 fresh mint sprigs

To make the cakes: Butter and flour four 4-ounce fluted molds or custard cups and set aside. Preheat the oven to 350°F. Melt the butter and chocolate in a double broiler over barely simmering water, stirring until smooth. Set aside.

In a medium bowl, whisk together the eggs and egg yolks. Add the sugar and whisk until foamy. Add the flour and stir to combine. Pour in the chocolate mixture and stir to combine.

Pour the cake batter into the prepared molds. Bake the cakes in the preheated oven for 8 to 10 minutes, or until slightly puffed. Invert the cakes onto 4 individual dessert plates. Dust the cakes with cocoa and place a scoop of softened ice cream to one side of each cake. To serve, make a cut into the center of the cake to show the texture; the middle of the cakes should be soft and liquid. Garnish with fresh mint sprigs and serve.

Note: The cake batter may be placed in the molds up to 2 hours in advance of being baked.

JEAN-GEORGES VONGERICHTEN
JoJo/Vong, New York, New York

Like other great artists who make their work appear deceptively simple, Jean-Georges Vongerichten, chef and owner of JoJo and Vong in New York City, is constantly reminding himself and those who work for him to simplify, simplify.

The entrees listed in bold letters on the menu at JoJo read simply Codfish, Salmon, Lobster, Chicken, Lamb, and Duck. There are no titled dishes.

Such unpretentious presentation might be expected from the chef who wrote *Simple Cuisine* (Prentice Hall Press), a volume devoted to replacing the heavy sauces and pastry of French haute cuisine with vegetable juices, vinaigrettes, infused oils, broths, and phyllo dough. It becomes surprising only when you recall that this same chef made his name cooking elaborately titled traditional French food with its cream-and-butter-laden soups and sauces. And one of his signature desserts is the decidedly luxurious Warm Valrhona Chocolate Cakes with Vanilla Ice Cream.

Vongerichten was born in Alsace, France. At age fifteen he became a chef's apprentice at a Michelin three-star restaurant. His career took him to L'Oasis in the south of France, where he worked for chef Louis Outhier. Vongerichten became part of Outhier's "flying squadron of chefs," opening ten restaurants in such far-flung places as Bangkok, Singapore, Hong Kong, Portugal, London, Boston, and New York.

In New York, Vongerichten joined the Drake Hotel and led its Restaurant Lafayette to the *New York Times'* highest honor, a four-star rating. Vongerichten then opened JoJo, where he serves his very personal style of simplified cooking. Two years after opening JoJo, he combined the ingredients of Thailand and Vietnam with French techniques and opened Vong, also in New York City.

Both restaurants have received the excellent, or three-star, rating from the *New York Times*. Vongerichten's menus may modestly call entrées Lamb or Shrimp, but his dishes will never be "just" that. It's not that simple.

RICHARD LEACH
One Fifth Avenue, New York, New York

Richard Leach, pastry chef at New York's Symphony Cafe, has had his creations deemed "edible sculptures" by the *New York Times,* and *Chocolatier* magazine calls his pastries "architectural in design." For Leach, who began making pastries simply to become more knowledgeable in the kitchen, dessert has become the essential part of the meal.

As the *Times* noted, "Leach is busy reinventing the final course, moving it beyond sugar, fruit and chocolate to some new and always surprising plateau." After graduating from the Culinary Institute of America in 1987, Leach began his career as a line cook at the River Cafe in Brooklyn under chefs David Burke and Charles Palmer. Moving with Palmer to Aureole, Leach worked in the pastry department and quickly became pastry chef. After three years at Aureole, Leach became pastry chef at Lespinasse in the St. Regis Hotel, then worked at Mondrian, and One Fifth Avenue.

Leach notes that he created one of his signature dishes, A Riot in Chocolate, a bittersweet chocolate mousse with chocolate-tea ice cream, "because the bitter properties of tea and chocolate complement each other so well. People are often skeptical, but after the first bite, it gets great reviews," he says.

A Riot in Chocolate

Richard Leach, One Fifth Avenue New York, New York

Makes 6 individual mousse cakes

This dessert combines chocolate in all its most luscious forms: creamy mousse, tender cake, ice cream, and crisp cookies. The tea flavoring in the ice cream adds an unusual and delicious note to the dramatic dessert. The chef uses Valrhona chocolate, but any high-quality imported chocolate may be used.

Chocolate Mousse
8 ounces Valrhona extra-bitter chocolate, chopped
½ cup milk
2 egg yolks
1½ tablespoons sugar
½ cup (1 stick) unsalted butter, melted
2 cups heavy (whipping) cream

Chocolate Cake
1 cup (2 sticks) unsalted butter at room temperature
2¾ cups sugar
1 cup unsweetened cocoa powder
3 eggs
3½ cups cake flour
1½ teaspoons baking powder
1½ teaspoons baking soda
1 teaspoon salt
2 cups warm water

Chocolate-Tea Ice Cream
4 cups heavy (whipping) cream
2 cups milk
8 Earl Grey tea bags
1½ cups sugar
12 egg yolks
8 ounces Valrhona extra-bitter chocolate, chopped

Chocolate Wrapping
8 ounces Valrhona extra-bitter chocolate

Fresh mint sprigs
Chocolate Tuile Cookies, page 162

To make the chocolate mousse: Combine the chocolate and milk in a large bowl. Bring 1 inch of water to a simmer in a large saucepan and place the bowl on top. Stir until the chocolate is melted, then remove the bowl and keep the chocolate mixture warm.

Combine the egg yolks and sugar in another large bowl. Place the bowl over the pan of simmering water and beat until the eggs are warmed. Remove from heat and beat until the egg mixture is pale and thick, then gradually add the melted chocolate and melted butter to the eggs, mixing just until incorporated. Remove from the heat and keep warm.

In a deep bowl, whip the cream until it forms soft peaks. Fold the whipped cream gently into the chocolate mixture until fully incorporated. Place the mousse in a clean bowl, cover, and refrigerate until needed.

To make the chocolate cake: Butter an 8-inch round cake pan and set aside. Preheat the oven to 300°F. Place the butter and sugar in the bowl of an electric mixer and beat with the paddle attachment for about 5 minutes, or until the mixture is light and fluffy. Stop the machine and add the cocoa powder. Mix at low speed and slowly add the eggs, one at a time, and mix until smooth. Sift the flour, baking powder, baking soda, and salt together. Add all at once to the cocoa mixture and mix until smooth at low speed, scraping the sides of the bowl as necessary. Slowly add the warm water. Scrape the batter into the prepared cake pan and bake for 20 to 25 minutes, or until the cake is firm and springy to the touch. Cool the cake in the pan on a wire rack for 10 minutes, then remove the cake from the pan, let cool completely, cover, and refrigerate.

To make the chocolate-tea ice cream: Place the heavy cream in a large, heavy saucepan with the milk, tea bags, and 1 cup of the sugar. Bring the mixture to a boil over medium heat, then remove the pan from heat and let the tea steep for 20 minutes. Place the egg yolks and the remaining ½ cup of sugar in a medium bowl and stir to combine. Strain the tea-infused cream into a clean pot and bring to a full boil over medium heat. Quickly whisk the boiling liquid into the yolks and sugar. Immediately add the chopped

chocolate, stirring the mixture until smooth, then strain through a fine-meshed sieve into a clean mixing bowl. Place the bowl of chocolate mixture inside another bowl filled with ice. Once the custard is cold, transfer the mixture to an ice cream maker and freeze according to the manufacturer's instructions, or see page 14.

To assemble the chocolate mousse cakes: You will need six 3-by-1½-inch ring molds, a pastry bag with a No. 8 tip, and a 1-inch-diameter round cutter. Cut the cake into very thin (about ¼ inch) crosswise slices. Using the metal rings, cut out 12 disks of cake. Place a cake disk at the bottom of each ring mold. Fill the pastry bag with the chocolate mousse. Pipe chocolate mousse into the rings until it reaches ½ inch up the side of each mold. Smooth the mousse flat with a tablespoon dipped in hot water. Place a second disk of chocolate cake on top of the chocolate mousse, creating a sandwich. Press down until level and flat. Refrigerate until firm (about 1 hour). When each mousse cake is firm, remove it from the refrigerator. To garnish, dip the smaller 1-inch round cutter in hot water and cut a hole slightly off center in the chocolate sandwich disk. Remove the mousse cakes from the ring molds by rubbing each ring with your hands until the cake is released. Carefully push it out of the ring mold and refrigerate.

To make the chocolate wrapping: Preheat the oven to 300°F. Melt the chocolate in a double boiler over barely simmering water, stirring until smooth; set aside. Clean and dry the baking sheet. Place the pan in the preheated oven until it is very warm, about 30 to 45 seconds. Remove the pan from the oven and spread the melted chocolate onto the back of the sheet pan in a very thin, even layer. Place the pan in the freezer or refrigerator for 1 hour. Remove the pan and let sit at room temperature until the chocolate is warm enough to peel off the sheet pan using a paring knife, about 5 minutes. Cut 9-inch-long 1-inch-wide strips of chocolate and peel off the pan. Carefully wrap a strip of chocolate around the sides of each disk of mousse cake (so that it looks like a smooth frosting). Wrap all 6 mousse cakes and refrigerate.

To serve: Place one of the chocolate mousse cakes on each plate, add a scoop of the chocolate-tea ice cream, and garnish with fresh mint sprigs and tuile cookies.

Note: The mousse, cake, and ice cream may be made up to 1 day in advance and stored separately. The mousse cakes may be assembled up to 6 hours in advance and refrigerated.

A Riot in Chocolate; Richard Leach, One Fifth Avenue, New York

Marble Fudge Brownies

Michael Romano, Union Square Cafe
New York, New York

Makes four 4-inch round brownies;
serves 4

The best brownies are dense, rich, and loaded with chocolate. These fit the bill perfectly, and the swirl of cream cheese adds a visual and flavor contrast to the chocolate.

2 tablespoons unsweetened cocoa powder
   for dusting

Fudge Mixture
9 tablespoons unsalted butter
4 ounces good-quality semisweet
   chocolate, chopped
2 eggs
¾ cup plus 1 tablespoon granulated sugar
½ cup all-purpose flour
Pinch of salt

Cream Cheese Mixture
One 8-ounce package cream cheese
   at room temperature
¼ cup granulated sugar
½ teaspoon vanilla extract
1 egg

Chocolate sauce and ice cream
   for serving, or confectioners' sugar
   for dusting

   Preheat the oven to 350°F. Butter four 4-by-1-inch round molds and dust with the cocoa powder.

   To make the fudge mixture: Melt the butter and chocolate in a double boiler over barely simmering water, stirring to combine thoroughly; set aside to cool slightly. In a medium bowl, whisk together the eggs and sugar until well combined. Add the chocolate mixture and stir well to incorporate. Stir in the flour and salt until blended, but do not overmix.

Marble Fudge Brownies; Michael Romano, Union Square Cafe, New York

To make the cream cheese mixture: In a medium bowl, beat the cream cheese and sugar until the mixture is fluffy, scraping down the sides of the bowl from time to time. Add the vanilla and egg and continue to beat until smooth.

Fill the prepared molds three-fourths full with the chocolate mixture, then top off with cream cheese. Using a fork, swirl the layers 2 or 3 times, using a folding motion. Be careful not to overmix or to scrape the sides or bottom of the pan, or the brownies could stick.

Bake the brownies for 35 minutes in the preheated oven, or until the tops are golden and the centers are somewhat firm. Let cool on a wire rack and un-mold. Serve with chocolate sauce and your favorite ice cream, or dust with confectioners' sugar.

Note: *The brownies may be made 1 day in advance and kept at room temperature, tightly covered with plastic wrap.*

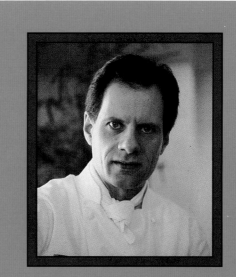

MICHAEL ROMANO
Union Square Cafe, New York, New York

Many chefs believe that a foundation in classical French technique, far from being an impediment, instead liberates creativity and stimulates improvisation. The career of Michael Romano, chef at New York's Union Square Cafe, validates this maxim.

Although Romano was born in the then-thriving Italian section of East Harlem in New York City and grew up on Neapolitan dishes, he excelled in classical French culinary training at New York City Technical College. Following graduation in 1975, he trained for several years under Michel Guerard at Regine's in both Paris and New York, and at Eugenie-les-Bains, Guerard's legendary Michelin three-star restaurant, where Romano received his training in modern sauce making. After additional apprenticeships in France and Switzerland, Romano returned to the United States in 1984 to become the first American chef in the twenty-seven-year history of New York's La Caravelle.

In the fall of 1988, Romano was lured to Union Square Cafe as executive chef by owner Danny Meyer. Meyer's instinct for adaptable talent paid off: Romano has easily traded a regimen of cooking refined French food for high-volume international food, primarily Italian with American and French accents. Each evening of the week has its own special, such as Wednesday's whole roasted pig braised with garlic and rosemary, then served with a curl of pig crackling, sautéed greens, and roasted herbed new potatoes. The meals are regularly topped off by rich desserts like Romano's Marble Fudge Brownies.

Union Square Cafe is located in the Flatiron District, at about Fifth Avenue and Eighteenth Street, an area that has experienced a rebirth in the last several years as publishers, advertising agencies, artists, and new shops have moved into the neighborhood. Romano takes advantage of the nearby Greenmarket, New York's best and largest outdoor farmer's market, where he selects fresh produce as well as meat and fish for his daily specials.

The restaurant has been awarded the coveted three-star rating by the *New York Times,* and in 1991 Romano was named by *Food & Wine* magazine as one of America's top ten chefs.

DOMINIQUE LEBORGNE
Le Palais du Chocolat, Washington D.C.

In Washington, D.C., there are many monuments but few palaces. That's why, when customers enter Dominique Leborgne's white marble Palais du Chocolat and see rows of milk chocolate pyramids, cocoa-dusted bittersweet truffles, and beautiful bonbons filled with Cointreau and Armagnac, they wonder: Are they really in Washington, D.C., or are they in Paris, or at Willy Wonka's?

Leborgne comes from Armentières, a small town in the north of France. At fifteen, he refused to work in his parent's gourmet shop, and instead apprenticed at the pastry shop across the street. Says Leborgne, "Since I was fourteen I wanted to do this, and didn't want to do anything else."

Winner of the *Grand Prix Internationale de la Chocolaterie* and a gold medalist at the World Gastronomic Exposition and the Charles Prouse competition, among many other awards, Leborgne arrived in Washington from France in 1986 to open the Willard Intercontinental Hotel as pastry chef.

Before joining the international hotel chain, Leborgne trained at the prestigious Dalloyau pastry shop in Paris. It was there he learned the ways of artistic form and dramatic presentation. Winner of the Golden Medal of St. Michel, the patron saint of pastry chefs, for a chocolate creation of a five-foot Venus rising from a bed of flowers, Leborgne makes his creations look as good as they taste. "I love the precision and artistic work," he says. This attention to taste and beauty shines through in creations like his Swans with White Chocolate Mousse.

The secret of Leborgne's chocolate creations is Guanajaa chocolate, which is 70 percent cocoa butter, unlike most American chocolate, which is usually around 40 percent. Cocoa butter reinforces the chocolate flavor, but often American chocolate makers substitute other lower-quality fats for the cocoa butter and the chocolate flavor suffers. Leborgne also uses French, Belgian, and Swiss chocolates, whichever best enhances the creations of the day.

Since all of the ingredients in his chocolates are fresh, "You cannot be sick if you eat too much of them," he says.

Swans with White Chocolate Mousse

Dominique Leborgne, Le Palais du Chocolat
Washington, D.C.

Serves 8

These decorative cream puff swans are quite simple to make, and the white chocolate mousse filling is delicious. If making the swans is intimidating, simply form the cream puff dough into round puffs or long éclairs.

Cream Puffs
½ cup water
½ cup milk
½ cup (1 stick) unsalted butter
¾ teaspoon salt
1½ teaspoons granulated sugar
½ cup plus 1 tablespoon all-purpose flour
3 eggs

White Chocolate Mousse
1½ pounds white chocolate, chopped
1 envelope unflavored gelatin
2 tablespoons Amaretto liqueur
4 eggs
4 egg yolks
3 cups heavy (whipping) cream

Garnish
6½ ounces white chocolate, chilled
1 cup fresh or thawed frozen
    unsweetened raspberries
1 tablespoon granulated sugar
1 tablespoon fresh lemon juice
Confectioners' sugar for dusting
Fresh raspberries
Mint leaves

To make the cream puffs: Preheat the oven to 325°F. Combine the water, milk, butter, salt, and sugar in a medium saucepan and bring to a boil over medium-high heat. Remove the pan from heat and add the flour all at once. Stir quickly to combine and return the pan to the heat. Cook, stirring constantly with a wooden spoon, until the mixture forms a ball and leaves a film on the bottom of the pan. Scrape the mixture into a large bowl or a food processor and beat in 1 egg at a time.

Line a baking sheet with parchment paper or butter it. Spoon some of the dough into a pastry bag fitted with a ½-inch star tip. Pipe the dough into 24 teardrop shapes 2 inches apart at one end of the prepared pan to form the bodies of the swans. Place the remaining dough in a parchment cone with a snipped tip or another pastry bag fitted with a small round tip. To make the neck and head of the swans, pipe 30 long S shapes with an oval at one end onto the other end of the pan; you will need extra neck/heads since they are very fragile and some may break in assembling the swans. Bake the puffs in a preheated oven for 20 minutes, or until light brown. Set aside and let cool.

To make the mousse: Melt the white chocolate in a bowl over a pan of barely simmering water, stirring until smooth; set aside. Sprinkle the gelatin over the Amaretto in a cup. Place the eggs and the egg yolks in a medium bowl, then place the bowl over a pan of simmering water. Beat the eggs and egg yolks until they are warmed through. Remove the eggs from

heat, add the gelatin mixture, and whisk to combine. Whisk in the melted white chocolate, and set aside.

In a deep bowl, whip the cream until stiff peaks form. Fold the whipped cream into the white chocolate mixture. Cover and chill the mousse until set.

To assemble: Cut each swan body in half crosswise and pull out any cooked dough, leaving only the crisp shell. Cut each top in half lengthwise to form the wings. Place the mousse in a pastry bag fitted with a fluted tip and pipe the mousse into the bottom part of the shell, forming the body of the swan. Use the base of mousse to anchor the head and neck piece of pastry. Add the wings, turning the browner portion to the inside. Pipe more mousse between the wings and over the base of the neck.

To make the garnish: Chop 2½ ounces of the white chocolate and melt it in a bowl over the pan of barely simmering water, stirring until smooth. Let cool slightly. Shave the remaining 4 ounces of

white chocolate with a vegetable peeler to make about ¼ cup shavings. Combine the raspberries, sugar, and lemon juice in a blender or food processor and puree. Strain the raspberry sauce through a fine-meshed sieve.

To serve: Fill the inside of each plate with the raspberry puree. Place the melted white chocolate in a parchment paper cone, snip the end, and pipe a design over the puree with the white chocolate. Place 2 or 3 swans on each plate, head to head. Top the mousse with white chocolate shavings to resemble feathers, then dust with confectioners' sugar. Arrange fresh raspberries and mint leaves around each swan and serve.

Note: The cream puffs, mousse, and raspberry sauce may be made up to 2 days in advance. Refrigerate the sauces, tightly covered. The swans must be assembled just prior to serving.

Swans with White Chocolate Mousse; Dominique Leborgne, Le Palais du Chocolat, Washington, D.C.

Menus for Entertaining

A Spring Dinner for 6

At the first sign of a reprieve from winter, serve this celebratory menu for good friends. All three dishes are reminiscent of the winter months, but fresh shad roe, tender vegetables, and berries add the rejuvenating flavors of spring. Decorate the table with tulips and daffodils in spring pastels.

Celery Root Soup with Shad Roe, page 31
Lamb Stew with Spring Vegetables, page 113
Chèvre and Raspberries in Pastry, page 189

Dinner from the Grill

Everything on this menu may be served at room temperature, which makes it perfect for warm summer evenings too beautiful to spend in the kitchen. Each dish may be assembled well in advance, then grilled at the last minute. Assertive seasoning keeps the lamb ravioli from being overpowered by the sweet and sour tang of the swordfish. Even the dessert is a study in vivid contrasting flavors: lush fruit chutney and smoky grilled bread with a comforting dollop of whipped cream. If you're dining al fresco, try lighting your dinner with festive votive candles or hurricane lamps on a table dressed with bright linens.

Lamb Ravioli, page 73
Grilled Spice-rubbed Swordfish with Indonesian Ketjap, page 147
Grilled Peaches with Grilled Walnut Bread, page 187

A Valentine's Day Dinner for Two

This classic meal is an extravagance to be lavished on a deserving romantic partner. Some low candles and good Champagne are the only necessary accompaniments. Although this menu is designed for the holiday, it also may be served whenever your guest requires some culinary pampering.

Oysters with Champagne Sauce, page 66
Lobster with Basil Cream, page 135
Warm Valrhona Chocolate Cakes with Vanilla Ice Cream, page 210

Grilled Spice-rubbed Swordfish with Indonesian Ketjap; Chris Schlesinger, The Blue Room/East Coast Grill/Jake & Earl's, Cambridge, Massachusetts

A Contemporary New England Dinner

This menu updates traditional dishes into slightly more glamorous versions. The dominant flavors are the simple and hearty staple foods of the region: smoky bacon, molasses, and cornmeal. Pewter plates on a bare wooden table would make the setting complete.

An Asian-inspired Dinner

Considerable advance preparation and adventurous, complex flavors make this menu perfect for accomplished cooks who want to deliver a show-stopping meal. Because the dinner is so elaborate, the table decoration may be as simple as branches of flowering fruit trees, preferably dramatically stark plum or cherry blossoms.

An Italian-inspired Dinner for Fall

Cooks concerned with presentation might want to add a steamed green vegetable or two to vary the palette of deep, rich browns. If the color scheme of your meal is not a priority, however, simply savor the earthy, authentic flavors of Tuscany in this dinner.

Oven-roasted Pork and Rabbit; Francesco Ricchi, Ristorante i Ricchi, Washington, D.C.

A French Bistro-inspired Dinner

In honor of the nation that perfected leisurely dining, this menu requires minimal last-minute assembly, but nonetheless possesses an unstudied chic. Serve with carafes of crisp, cool wine, and enjoy the great French tradition of lingering over your food well into the evening.

Marinated Salmon, page 67
Pan-fried Skate Wings with Yellow Pepper Coulis, page 152
Warm Salad of Asparagus and Artichokes, page 79
Warm Apple Tarts, page 196

Marinated Salmon; Phillippe Roussel, La Metairie, New York

A Bastille Day Picnic Celebration

At once rustic and luxurious, this menu adds Gallic glamour to a summer evening in the country. The tart vinaigrettes on the terrine and the salad balance the buttery foie gras and the goat cheese, while the herb-flecked salmon and the dessert fritters are pure indulgence. Since each dish may be served at room temperature, the picnic may take place in a shady outdoor setting.

Leek and Foie Gras Terrine with Raspberry Vinaigrette, page 69
Poached Salmon in White Wine, page 140
Warm Goat Cheese and Potato Salad with Chive Vinaigrette, page 75
Beignets Soufflés Crème Anglaise, page 203

A Summer Dinner Party for Six

Perfect for casual entertaining, each dish in this menu showcases bright, assertive flavors echoed by vivid colors. Soft-shell crabs are sprinkled with pungent green herbs before serving, the tuna rests on a bed of colored-pepper confetti, and the cheesecake has a dramatic violet-colored sauce.

Sautéed Soft-Shell Crabs with Hazelnuts, page 127
Herbed Tuna with Citrus Vinaigrette, page 143
Mascarpone Cheesecake with Lacy Nut Wafers and Blueberry Caramel, page 199

Pheasant with Rosemary and Vanilla; Alain Borel, L'Auberge Provençale, White Post, Virginia

Autumn Dinner

This sophisticated menu shifts gears from summer's emphasis on fish and light salads to harvesttime's savory game, here perfumed with bourbon and fruit. Welcome the cooler nights by serving this meal with a good port or dessert wine.

Pumpkin Soup with Fig Quenelles, page 45
Pheasant with Rosemary and Vanilla, page 107
Maple Crêpe Soufflées, page 167

An Elegant Summer Lunch for Two

The pale, pristine colors of this sophisticated lunch create a mood of understated elegance. Happily, each dish may be prepared in advance, then assembled in less than ten minutes, so you may concentrate on your guest without compromising the quality of the food.

Scallop Salad with Grainy Mustard Vinaigrette, page 61
Smoked Salmon Tarts, page 59
Raspberry Gratin with Caramel, page 189

New Year's Eve Dinner

In these days of increasingly casual entertaining, New Year's Eve is one of the few evenings that still calls for a formal dinner. This menu includes a traditional fish course, but the meal may also be adapted for the rest of the year by choosing either the fish or the lamb as the main course. Most of the preparation for this meal may be done well in advance, leaving you plenty of time to usher in the New Year with your guests.

Roasted Garlic Custards with Mushrooms and Green Onion, page 35
Halibut Enrobed in a Crisp Potato Crust, page 149
Rack of Lamb with Persimmon Chutney and Peanut Crust, page 116
Tossed Seasonal and Bitter Greens with Raspberry-Walnut Vinaigrette, page 61
Chocolate-Lover's Cake, page 205

Dinner Party of New American Cuisine

This ethnically eclectic menu reflects on the inventiveness of contemporary American cooking. The squab are infused with subtle Asian flavors, but paired with a fruited Moroccan-inspired couscous. The salmon dish is cooked in a uniquely American style and teamed with an unusual vinaigrette. A maple-based dessert combines American ingredients with classical French technique. Try a simple centerpiece of sunflowers or wildflowers and Queen Anne's lace.

Squab Salad and Couscous with Curried Vinaigrette and Chutney, page 57
Cedar-planked Salmon with Wilted Greens and
Toasted Pumpkin Seed Vinaigrette, page 141
Maple Ice Cream in a Caramel Cage, page 167

A Formal Winter Dinner

This glamorous dinner is perfect for chasing away the winter doldrums, as the dishes are not too far removed from traditional comfort foods. Think of it as a slightly more elegant pancake supper with a meaty veal steak, braised vegetables, and a flaky phyllo version of the traditional apple tart.

Smoked Lobster and Wild Mushroom Pancakes with Crème Fraîche
and a Trio of American Caviars, page 49
Veal Chops with Oven-dried Tomatoes and Wild Mushrooms, page 87
Braised Fennel, page 158
Apple Tarts, page 193

A Southwestern Feast

Bring out your most colorful plates, napkins, and flowers for this bold, hearty meal with layers of smoky flavors and complex spicing. Stock up on plenty of cold beer or Margaritas, then invite friends over for a casual supper. There's more flavor than heat in the four savory dishes, and the warm chocolate brownies are the perfect finale.

Poblanos Rellenos, page 39
Seared Spicy Tuna with Mole Amarillo, page 145
Ancho-rubbed Game Hens, page 123
Sweet Potato Gratin, page 160
Marble Fudge Brownies, page 213

Seared Spicy Tuna with Mole Amarillo; Mark Miller, Red Sage, Washington, D.C.

Winter Weekend Supper

This menu is the perfect antidote for frigid winter evenings when it feels too cold to prepare an overly elaborate dinner. Make the night special with a roaring fire and some low candles to fight off the chill.

Roasted Sausages and Grapes, page 92
Venison Loin Chops, page 83
Baked Spaghetti Squash, page 158
Rosemary Spaetzle, page 159
Spiced Pears with Port and Gorgonzola, page 182

A Russian-inspired Easter Dinner

A departure from the baked ham that appears on many American tables at Easter, this menu reflects a far older Russian tradition. The dinner looks elaborate enough for a czar, but the side dishes are simple to prepare and may be served on a large platter with the lamb. Cream puff swans on a ruby pool of raspberry sauce are a dramatic way to end a meal fit for royalty.

Borscht with Braised Duck, page 27
Karsky Shashlik Supreme, page 112
Braised Red Cabbage, page 157
Cucumber and Red Onion Salad with Mint Chutney, page 159
Basmati Rice and Lentil Pilaf, page 155
Red Pepper Chutney, page 160
Swans with White Chocolate Mousse, page 215

A Mediterranean Seafood Dinner

Fresh crustaceans in simple but flavorful preparations bring the flavors of the Mediterranean a little closer to home. For a truly Italian touch, toss some apple wood chips or fresh rosemary branches onto the fire before grilling the lobsters, and decorate the table with your favorite oversized dishes.

Sautéed Soft-Shell Crabs with Polenta, page 129
Wood-grilled Lobster with Potato Gnocchi and Toasted Walnuts, page 137
Cranberry-Walnut Crostata, page 198

Cranberry-Walnut Crostata; Johanne Killeen,
Al Forno Restaurant, Providence, Rhode Island

A City Supper

Find the best view of the city skyline to serve as a backdrop for this meal. For true urban sophistication, bring out your best linen napkins and oversized flatware. Set low bowls of roses and freesias on the table to complete the mood.

Carpaccio of Sirloin, page 77
Pan-roasted Quail with Port Sauce, page 97
Vegetable Couscous with Foie Gras, page 156
Cool Caramel Mousse with Cinnamon-basted Fruit, page 175

Carpaccio of Sirloin; Seth Raynor, The Boarding House; Nantucket, Massachusetts

A Grand French Dinner

While this classic French menu features traditionally rustic ingredients such as game, the results make this dinner feel like a splurge in a three-star Paris restaurant. For an over-the-top evening, decorate with your best silver and a lavish spray of flowers.

Potato, Leek, and Watercress Soup with Grilled Smoked Duck, page 43
Rabbit Terrine, page 63
Roasted Squab with Bacon and Sage, page 89
Vanilla Parfait, page 165

A Southern Country Dinner

Each dish in this year-round menu has its roots in the grand southern tradition of the opulent table. The addition of a few ingredients such as shiitake mushrooms imparts contemporary overtones while maintaining the southern nature of the menu.

Boneless Quail Stuffed with Crabmeat, page 101
Smoked Roasted Capon Breasts with Sweet-Potato Fries, page 117
Pecan-Rum Tart, page 205

Thoughts on Wine, by David L. Vaughan

*W*ine appreciation is highly subjective and idiosyncratic. If the wine pleases you, or tastes good with a particular dish, it is the right wine. Pairing food and wine is no more complex than that, and to enjoy wine you do not need to become a wine "expert." What I recommend is that you identify a few specific types of wine you particularly enjoy and focus on learning more about those. You will refine your task to a manageable one and increase your enjoyment.

How to Taste Wine

As strange as it may sound, the proper way to taste wine is from the top of the face down. First use your eyes to judge the wine's appearance, next use your nose to assess the wine's bouquet and aroma, and, finally, take the wine into your mouth and swallow it.

Appearance: To judge the wine's appearance, pour some of the wine into a large, clear glass and tilt it away from you against a white backdrop (such as a tablecloth) in good light (fluorescent light makes a red wine appear more brown). Initially, look for clarity—there should be no suspended particles in the wine. Next, look at the wine's color. Color often indicates the wine's age. A young white wine will usually have a light straw color, sometimes with a slight green tinge. As white wine ages, it gains an amber hue and gradually begins to turn brown. Red wines usually begin their life cycle with a ruby red color, sometimes with a slight purplish tint at the edge. As red wine ages, it loses clarity and gradually turns a brickish brown.

Aroma and Bouquet: Next, smell the wine. Place the glass on a flat surface and move the base of the glass in a small, circular pattern, swirling the wine around the sides of the glass. This exposes more of the wine to the air and makes it easier to smell. As you prepare to sniff the wine, be sure you concentrate on your very first sniff. The human nose quickly adjusts to any smell, and after four or five sniffs, your ability to detect aromas will be greatly reduced. With the first sniff, you can ascertain if there are any objectionable odors such as that of sulfur or vinegar. If you detect either of these smells, the wine is flawed.

Assuming you find no flaws, next decide whether the smell of the wine pleases you. Does it have an intense smell, or very little smell? Do you detect any fragrance associated with the grapes used in the wine? For instance, some wines produced from the Cabernet Sauvignon grape are said to exhibit a smell not unlike that of green bell peppers. Some wines made from the Pinot Noir grape have a scent vaguely resembling that of tar or bacon or chocolate.

Wine specialists categorize wine odor into two categories: aroma and bouquet. Aroma comprises those scents associated with the grape variety or varieties used to make the wine. Bouquet, on the other hand, arises from complex chemical processes occurring in the bottle as the wine ages. For instance, some very simple young red wines smell almost like grape juice. This is their aroma. Older red wines, particularly very good ones, on the other hand, often exhibit much more complex fragrances such as those resembling violets, truffles, etc. This is the bouquet.

Taste: Now, at last, you are ready to actually taste the wine on the palate. Most people make two mistakes here: They take too much wine in their mouths, and they swallow it too quickly. You do not need a great deal of wine in your mouth to taste it and, once the wine is in your mouth, you should roll it around inside your mouth, not unlike mouthwash, to taste it fully. Some wine tasters also inhale through the wine while it is in their mouth, making a gurgling sound. After you feel as if you have tasted all you can of the wine in your mouth, swallow the wine and pause for a brief period. Does the taste disappear immediately, or does it linger? Most high-quality wines are said to have a lingering aftertaste or, in wine speak, are "long on the palate." After swallowing a red wine, look for a drying or puckering sensation in the mouth. This is an indication of the presence of tannin, a substance naturally occurring in red wine, which indicates that the wine has further aging potential.

Other examples of tastes you might find are butter or vanilla, flavors often imparted to wine by aging in new oak barrels; grassy, or herbaceous, a flavor frequently associated with white wines made from the Sauvignon Blanc grape, such as Pouilly Fumé; spiciness, a characteristic often associated with red wines from the Rhône River in France and red wines made from the Zinfandel grape in California; and floweriness, associated with wines made from the Riesling grape.

How to Read Wine Labels

Reading wine labels can be a perplexing task. At a minimum, the label should tell you where the grapes were grown, who grew the grapes and made the wine (sometimes these are the same, sometimes they are not), and the year in which the grapes were harvested. The harvest year, sometimes called the vintage year, is important because weather conditions during the year affect the quality of the grapes that make the wine, and these conditions vary—sometimes greatly—from year to year.

Confusion often arises because wine labels sometimes state the name of the grape used to make the wine, sometimes the place where the grapes were grown, and sometimes both. Thus, if you do not know, for instance, that Merlot is a grape and Bordeaux a place, you will obviously have a problem reading those labels. To assist you, we have prepared two charts that set forth the principal grape varieties used to make red and white wines, the principal places these grapes are grown, some general characteristics of the wines, and how the wines are labeled; that is, whether by the name of the grape variety used, the name of the place, or both.

The following are generalized comments and, as with all aspects of wine, there are numerous exceptions.

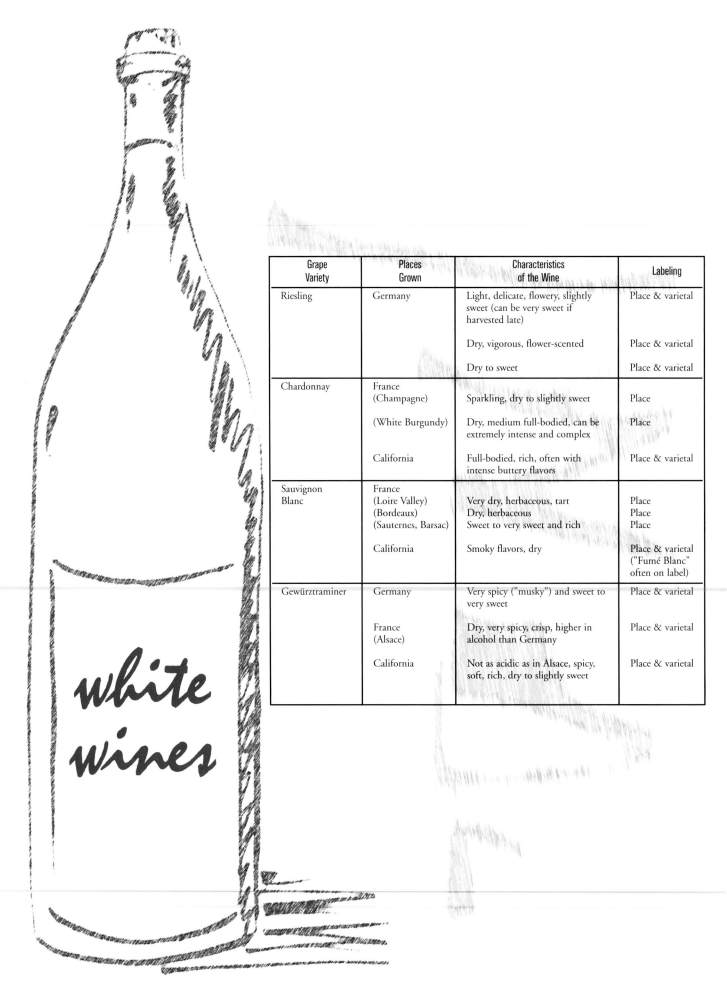

Grape Variety	Places Grown	Characteristics of the Wine	Labeling
Riesling	Germany	Light, delicate, flowery, slightly sweet (can be very sweet if harvested late)	Place & varietal
		Dry, vigorous, flower-scented	Place & varietal
		Dry to sweet	Place & varietal
Chardonnay	France (Champagne)	Sparkling, dry to slightly sweet	Place
	(White Burgundy)	Dry, medium full-bodied, can be extremely intense and complex	Place
	California	Full-bodied, rich, often with intense buttery flavors	Place & varietal
Sauvignon Blanc	France (Loire Valley) (Bordeaux) (Sauternes, Barsac)	Very dry, herbaceous, tart Dry, herbaceous Sweet to very sweet and rich	Place Place Place
	California	Smoky flavors, dry	Place & varietal ("Fumé Blanc" often on label)
Gewürztraminer	Germany	Very spicy ("musky") and sweet to very sweet	Place & varietal
	France (Alsace)	Dry, very spicy, crisp, higher in alcohol than Germany	Place & varietal
	California	Not as acidic as in Alsace, spicy, soft, rich, dry to slightly sweet	Place & varietal

Grape Variety	Places Grown	Characteristics of the Wine	Labeling
Cabernet Sauvignon	France (Bordeaux blended with other varieties)	Elegant, dry, tannic when young, aroma possibly resembling green peppers, long-lived	Place
	California	Same as above, except sometimes a minty flavor and often more intense fruit flavors with less tannin and higher alcohol	Place & varietal
Pinot Noir	France (Red Burgundy)	Velvety, round, full-bodied wine with flavors slightly resembling bacon or tar	Place
Zinfandel	California	Bramblelike, jammy, spicy, intense fruit flavors	Place & varietal
Nebbiolo	Italy (Piedmont)	Nutty, almost burnt flavors: big, complex, intense long-lived wines	Place
Merlot	France (Bordeaux, principally St-Emilion and Pomerol)	Similar to Cabernet Sauvignon, but softer and earlier maturing	Place
	California	Same as French except more intense fruit flavors, higher alcohol and lower acid	Place & varietal

How to Pair Food and Wine

Balance is the key to pairing food and wine. Neither the food nor the wine should overwhelm the other with intensity of flavor. For example, you should avoid serving a Zinfandel port with fillet of sole, since it is unlikely that you would be able to taste the sole. Similarly, a light, mildly flavored Italian white wine, such as Soave, might not be much of a complement to venison in a green peppercorn, garlic, and tomato sauce.

Choose a savory, intensely flavored wine to accompany a dish of the same description, and serve a light, mildly flavored wine with a light, mildly flavored dish.

An important exception, or footnote, to the foregoing involves deciding whether you are going to emphasize the wine or the food. If the main point of the evening is the food, you might wish to err slightly on the side of having your wine less strongly flavored and less distinctive than the food. If, on the other hand, you wish to show off your wines, you might select foods that do not compete with the wines for your guests' attention. Also, complex wines show best with simple foods.

In deciding whether your dish is strongly flavored, consider the sauce. A chicken breast prepared in a delicate Champagne sauce would require a much milder-flavored wine than it would if prepared with the green peppercorn, garlic, and tomato sauce mentioned above.

As with much of the standard learning on wine, the maxim "white wine with fish, red wine with meat" is only half true. Red wine should generally be avoided with fish as it contains tannin, which reacts with substances in the flesh of the fish to cause a bitter or metallic flavor in the mouth. If you would prefer to have red wine with your fish, either serve a light, low-tannin red such as Beaujolais, or try cooking and serving the fish in a hearty tomato and red wine sauce. The classic example of a fish dish that can stand up to a red wine is bouillabaisse with a red wine, tomato and garlic sauce.

The fact that fish almost always calls for white wine, however, doesn't mean that meat automatically calls for red wine. A "white" meat such as chicken, veal, or pork might find a better companion in a white Burgundy or a California Chardonnay. But it is rare for beef or lamb to pair with anything but a red wine.

Another principle is that extremely tart and dry wines tend to go well with salty foods—hence Champagne with caviar and Muscadet or Chablis with oysters. A good German wine at the drier end of the spectrum, such as a Kabinett, will have enough flavor to match that of ham and sufficient acidity to counterbalance the saltiness.

Another principle is never to serve a dry wine with a sweet food. The sugar in the food will accentuate the acidity in the wine, making the wine taste sour. For the same reason, desserts should always be less sweet than the accompanying wine. A delightful combination experienced recently was a lush, sweet late-harvest Riesling from California with a lemon mousse.

How To Serve Wine

Proper wine service begins with the proper glass. All good wineglasses share two attri-butes—they are large, and they are clear. They are large so that you can serve an acceptable quantity, and yet never have the glass more than one-third full, and they are clear so that you can easily assess the wine's appearance. Do not use cut glass or colored glasses. Another desirable feature in a wineglass is a rim that curves in slightly at the top to concentrate the aroma and bouquet of the wine. The classic brandy snifter is perhaps the best-known example of this attribute. White wine is often served in a tulip-shaped glass, and red wine in a spherical, or globe-shaped glass. A globe-shaped glass spreads the red wine out and makes it easier for you to assess the wine's color. How much wine to serve obviously depends upon the occasion. For a light, quick lunch, perhaps one glass is ample. For a four-hour formal dinner, perhaps five or six glasses would be more appropriate. A good rule is to be generous, but not forcing. Figure on six glasses of wine per bottle.

The order in which wines are served can significantly increase or decrease your enjoyment of them. The general rules (to which there are always exceptions) may be summarized as follows: white before red, dry before sweet, young before old, lesser before better, simple before complex, and lighter in flavor before richer in flavor. When possible, you should serve more than one wine at a meal and afford your guests the pleasurable experience of comparing wines. If you do so, serve your better wines later. A less complex, less intensely flavored wine can be a good lead-in to a complex, intensely flavored wine, but show poorly if served after the more complex, more fully flavored wine.

Wine temperature has a significant influence on its taste. Generally speaking, the colder a wine is, the harder it is to smell and taste. Accordingly, serve bad wines, if you must serve them at all, colder, and better wines warmer. Another general rule is that white wines should be served chilled, while reds should be served closer to room temperature. A lower temperature accentuates the freshness and crisp acidity of most white wines, and red wines need to be close to normal room temperature to release their aroma and bouquet and to show fully their complexity on the palate. Many lighter, less complex reds, such as lesser Beaujolais or Valpolicella, can benefit from slight chilling. Although the exact temperatures at which to serve wine are purely a matter of personal taste, here are some suggested guidelines. Serve lighter, less complex white wines from 45° to 50°F. Serve the best and most complex whites, such as great white Burgundies or California Chardonnays, between 55° and 60°F. Serve light reds between 55° and 60°F, and richer, more complex reds at around 67°F.

Glossary

a chef's larder is now as big as the world, and in American restaurant kitchens foods from different cuisines are often combined to create uniquely American dishes. Seth Raynor at the Boarding House on Nantucket, for example, uses Mexican achiote paste for the sauce to accompany an Italian-inspired Carpaccio, and Patrick Clark at Washington's Hay Adams Hotel uses Chinese star anise to reinforce the licorice flavor of his braised fennel.

This chapter contains listings for many of the foods and ingredients used in this book, as well as definitions of several cooking terms used by many chefs.

Achiote:

Dark brick-red seeds from the annatto tree that are often made into a paste; these are especially popular in the Yucatán for adding color and an earthy flavor to food.

Aïoli:

Garlic mayonnaise. Some chefs complement the garlic with roasted pureed red bell pepper, basil, or lemon zest.

Al dente:

The literal translation of this phrase, "to the tooth," applies to pasta, risotto, and vegetables that are cooked until tender but still somewhat resilient and firm.

Anaheim chilies:

Also called California, California green, *chiles verdes* or, when canned, mild green chilies. Anaheim chilies are dark green, about 7 inches long, 1½ inches wide, and mild to hot in flavor. When the chilies ripen completely in the fall, they turn red and are sweeter and milder. Their large size makes Anaheim chilies ideal for stuffing. They may be substituted for poblanos.

Ancho chilies:

Dried poblano chilies, anchos come from California (where they're sometimes incorrectly called pasilla chilies) and Mexico and range from dark red to almost black. They're about 4½ inches long and 3 inches wide and are moderately hot, with a smoky undertaste. They are wrinkled and should still be pliable if fresh. Pasilla chilies, though difficult to find, may be substituted.

Arborio rice:

A medium-grain rice imported from Italy and used primarily in making risotto, or risotto-based dishes such as fried rice balls stuffed with cheese. Adding liquid slowly to Arborio rice while stirring constantly results in a risotto that is creamy from the slow release of starch, while the grain is still firm to the bite.

Arrowroot:

A powder made from a tropical tuber and used as a thickening agent. Cornstarch may be substituted at a ratio of 2 parts cornstarch to 1 part arrowroot to achieve the same transparency in a thickened sauce. Arrowroot should be mixed with cold water before being added to hot liquid.

Arugula:

The elongated, smooth, dark green leaves of this pungent, peppery green have fairly long stems and grow in small clusters. Excellent alone or combined with sweet or bitter greens.

Balsamic vinegar:

Imported from Italy and tremendously popular due to its mild, almost sweet flavor, balsamic vinegar is made from unfermented grape juice that is aged for at least ten years. Balsamic vinegar may be used in sauces and salad dressings, and as a topping for fresh strawberries.

Basmati rice:

The word *basmati* means "queen of fragrance," and this Indian rice is the best known of the aromatic rices. Its nutlike aroma is caused by a high concentration of acetyl pyroline, a compound found naturally in all rice. A similar species is now being raised in the United States and marketed under the name Texmati.

Baton/Batonnet:

These terms, meaning "stick" and "small stick," describe vegetables that are cut into pieces about ¼ inch thick and 2 inches long.

Beets, golden:

Golden beets are related to the common red beet and have the same sweet flavor. Their advantage is that they do not bleed, so they can be added to salads and all elements will retain their natural color.

Beurre blanc:

A white butter sauce made with a reduction of white wine and shallots thickened with butter and possibly finished with fresh herbs or other seasonings.

Black Friar plums:

A large eastern plum with dark red skin and deep yellow flesh. When cooked, the puree becomes a blushing pink.

Black trumpet mushrooms:

Also called black chanterelles, these have the same shape and size as their orange cousins, and must be cooked before eating.

Blanch:

To cook food briefly in boiling water before finishing or storing it. Blanching sets the brilliant color of green vegetables and herbs, loosens the skins of tomatoes, peaches, and nuts such as almonds, rids rice and potatoes of excess starch, removes excess salt and flavor from bacon, and firms sweetbreads.

Borscht:
A beet and cabbage soup of Russian and Polish origins that may be served either hot or cold, frequently with a dollop of sour cream on top.

Bouquet garni:
A small bundle of herbs, usually bay leaf, parsley, and thyme, used to flavor stocks, braises, and other preparations.

Braise:
A cooking method in which food is seared in fat, then simmered over low heat in stock or another liquid in a covered pan until it becomes very tender.

Cactus pear:
The flavor of this light pink to red oval-shaped fruit of the nopal cactus is reminiscent of watermelon. The needles must be removed before use.

Cajun spice blend:
Sold under a number of different brand names, this seasoning contains thyme, paprika, garlic, cayenne pepper, and white pepper, and is used frequently in dishes from Louisiana.

Capers:
The pickled or preserved flower buds of a bushy plant that grows near the Mediterranean. Capers have a salty, acidic flavor and are used for garnishing, especially for meats and some sautéed fish dishes. They are available in large and small sizes. The smaller ones, called nonpareils, are more subtle in taste, and the large ones may sometimes need to be chopped before using.

Capon:
A 5- to 8-pound castrated male chicken, slaughtered at under 8 months of age. While the same size as a roasting chicken, capons are usually more tender and have more flavor. They are usually roasted, and a large roasting chicken is the best substitute.

Caul Fat:
A lacy fat from the belly of animals. It is used as a covering or binding for foods to be cooked, especially small sausages.

Caviar:
Fish roe that has been preserved by being salted.

Beluga: The eggs of the largest of the sturgeon species are large, with a delicate skin, and are light to dark gray in color. Beluga eggs are rated "O" for the darkest eggs, "OO" for eggs of medium tone, and "OOO" for the lightest eggs.

Ossetra: Dark brown to golden large eggs with a delicate skin.

Sevruga: Smaller eggs with a fine, dark gray color.

American sturgeon: Very similar to ossetra in taste, size, and color, this caviar is from sturgeon harvested in the southern states in tributaries of the Mississippi River.

Salmon roe: These large, bright red eggs from Atlantic Ocean salmon are prized for their color as well as for their flavor.

Golden whitefish: Tiny golden eggs with a delicate flavor, used primarily as a garnish.

Celery root:
A gnarled brown root with a pronounced celery flavor. Available from fall to spring, celery root (also called celeriac) discolors and must be rubbed with an acid such as lemon juice or vinegar after being peeled and cut.

Cèpes:
See Porcini.

Champagne grapes:
A variety of small round red seedless grapes used in the pressing of Champagne that are becoming popular for decoration. Any small red grape may be substituted.

Chanterelles:
Called "trumpets," due to their shape, most available chanterelles are an exotic golden color, although the colors range from a creamy white to a black. The flavor is nutty and meaty, and the flavor is aromatic and has almost peachy tones.

Cheesecloth:
A light, fine cotton gauze that has many purposes in the kitchen, including straining the impurities out of liquids and encasing foods so that they hold their shape.

Chiffonnade:
Finely shredded leafy vegetables or herbs, often used as a garnish.

Chipotle chilies:
Jalapeño chilies that have been dried, smoked, and often pickled, chipotles are usually a dark shade of brown and have a very hot smoky taste. If packed in tomato sauce, chipotles may be called *mara* and are a dark, brick red.

Chocolate:
Here is a guide to the various forms of chocolate:

Unsweetened: Also referred to as baking or bitter chocolate, this is the purest of all cooking chocolates. It is hardened chocolate liquor (which is the essence of the cocoa bean, not an alcohol) that contains no sugar and is usually packaged in a bar of eight blocks weighing 1 ounce each. Unsweetened chocolate must contain 50 to 58 percent cocoa butter.

Bittersweet: This chocolate is slightly sweetened with sugar, and the amount varies depending on the manufacturer. This chocolate must contain 35 percent chocolate liquor and is used whenever an intense chocolate taste is desired. It may be used interchangeably with semisweet chocolate in cooking and baking.

Semisweet: This chocolate is sweetened with sugar but, unlike bittersweet chocolate, it may also have flavorings such as vanilla added to it. It is available in bar form as well as in chips and pieces.

Milk: A mild-flavored chocolate used primarily for candy bars but rarely (except for milk chocolate chips) in cooking. It may have as little as 10 percent chocolate liquor, but must contain 12 percent milk solids.

Unsweetened cocoa powder: Powdered chocolate that has had a portion of the cocoa butter removed. Cocoa keeps indefinitely in a cool place.

Dutch process cocoa powder: A type of cocoa powder formulated with reduced acidity. It gives foods a more mellow flavor; however, it burns at a lower temperature than more common cocoa.

White: Actually ivory in color, white chocolate is technically not chocolate at all; it is made from cocoa butter, sugar, and flavoring. It is difficult to work with, and should be used in recipes that are specifically designed for it. Do not substitute it for other types of chocolate in a recipe.

Christmas beans:
A large red-and-white striped dried bean about the size of a large lima bean.

Cilantro:
Also called fresh coriander or Chinese parsley, and used as extensively in Asian cooking as it is in southwestern. Cilantro resembles flat-leaf Italian parsley, but is much more flavorful and aromatic. Its flavor is pungently sweet, and its scent has been compared to that of orange or lemon peel, or a combination of caraway and cumin.

Clams:
Any of a variety of bivalve mollusks that burrow in the sand in both salt- and freshwater. The word derives from Old English *clamm,* or "bond," for its clamped shell. The two main varieties of East Coast clams are softshell, or long-necked clams, and hard-shell, or littleneck clams.

Clarified butter:
Butter from which the milk solids and water have been removed, leaving pure butterfat that can be heated to a higher temperature without smoking or scorching.

Cod:
Cod, or codfish, is one of the most important food fishes in the world, both fresh and particularly salted and dried. Cod was key to the history and fortunes of America, in light of its abundance off the East Coast. See also Salt cod.

Colander:
A perforated bowl, with or without a base or legs, used to strain foods or to drain foods that have been boiled.

Coriander seeds:
The seed of fresh coriander, which is also called cilantro or Chinese parsley.

Coulis:
A thick vegetable or fruit puree used as a sauce for foods.

Couscous:
Although it resembles a grain, couscous, a staple of North African cooking, is actually a pasta made from semolina and is usually cooked by steaming. It is now also available precooked and dehydrated and is usually sold as quick-cooking couscous.

Crab:
Any of a large variety of saltwater crustaceans with a hard shell and five pairs of legs with front pincers. The blue crabs that are native from the Chesapeake Bay to New England are particularly savored in the East. Softshell crabs are blue crabs that are harvested just as they have molted their hard shell in order to grow and are in the process of growing a new shell that is initially soft.

Cranberries:
A very tart red berry grown in bogs from low, trailing vines and used in sauces, jellies, and beverages. Although there are several species in the world, the American, or large, cranberry is the only one in wide cultivation and is a major crop in Massachusetts and New Jersey.

Crème fraîche:
While its tangy, tart flavor is similar to that of sour cream, crème fraîche is less thick and is used in cooking since it will not curdle when heated as do sour cream and yogurt.

Crimini mushrooms:
These mushrooms resemble common mushrooms but are a medium brown in color and have a dense, earthy flavor that is not as strong as that of most wild mushrooms. They may be used interchangeably with common, or white, mushrooms in almost all dishes.

Cumin:
Seeds from the pods of an indigenous and plentiful southwestern plant. Cumin may be used either whole and ground and is mixed with ground chilies to make commercial chili powder and is also used in curry powder. If a recipe calls for ground red chilies and cumin, do not add additional cumin if substituting chili powder.

Deglaze:
To use a liquid, such as wine, water, or stock, to dissolve food particles and browned juices remaining in a pan after meat or poultry has been roasted or sautéed.

Degrease:
To skim the fat off the surface of a liquid, such as a stock or sauce. The

easiest way to do this is to chill the liquid and discard the fat that congeals on the surface.

Dredge:

To cover food completely with a powder, most often flour or confectioners' sugar.

Drizzle:

To randomly place droplets or a thin line of liquid on food, such as drizzling a sauce or oil over food or drizzling hot caramel to form a random pattern before it becomes hard.

Duck:

Any of a variety of web-footed birds of the family *Anatidae,* ducks may be either wild or domesticated and they inhabit open water, marshes, ponds, lakes, and rivers. The Chinese Peking duck was introduced to Long Island after the Civil War and is frequently dubbed Long Island duckling. Domestic ducks weigh between 5 and 7 pounds.

Egg wash:

A mixture of egg and milk or water that is brushed on pastry before baking to give it a glossy finish.

Emulsion:

A mixture of two or more liquids, one of which is a fat or oil and the other of which is water-based, that remained combined and homogeneous for only a short time. The most common examples are vinaigrette dressings and butter sauces.

Flatfish:

A related group of fish, all having a flat body and both eyes on one side of the head. They range in size from small sole to large halibut.

Flounder:

Any of a variety of flatfishes, sometimes mistakenly sold as sole. The main American species of flounder includes American plaice, also called the dab or sand dab, as well as Atlantic halibut.

Foie gras:

The enlarged—by four or five times—liver of a goose or duck. It has a rich, velvety, buttery texture and flavor, and is equally delicious slowly baked by itself or as part of a terrine, or quickly fried and sauced.

Free range:

Livestock that is raised unconfined, so that the musculature is better developed than that of animals raised in pens.

Frisée:

The mildest-tasting member of the chicory family, with pale green slender curly leaves and an almost yellowish-white heart. Frisée is also known as curly endive.

Ganache:

A filling or coating made from heavy cream, chocolate, and/or other flavorings. It also forms the basis for chocolate truffles.

Ginger:

A rhizome originally grown in the Asian tropics and now imported to the United States from Jamaica. Ginger is used fresh in most cooking, and it is also available crystallized and in ground form.

Glaze:

To give a food a shiny surface by brushing it with sauce, aspic, icing, or other external treatment. *Glaze* also refers to the concentrated syrupy liquid produced by reducing meat, poultry, or fish stock.

Goat cheese:

Called *chèvre* in French, goat cheese ranges in flavor from mild and tangy in its fresh form to sharp when it is aged.

Gorgonzola:

A creamy, blue-veined cheese from Italy similar in taste to a Stilton or other blue cheeses.

Güero chilies:

Also called Hungarian yellow wax chilies, these hot chilies are yellow or yellow-green in color when immature and red when ripe.

Guinea hen:

A game bird related to the pheasant. It is slaughtered at about 6 months of age and weighs ¾ to 1½ pounds. While the flavor will not be as pronounced, Cornish hen is the best substitute.

Halibut:

A term used for two large flounders, one a North Atlantic fish, the other from the North Pacific. The Atlantic halibut is quite large, reaching up to 700 pounds in weight, and may be caught from Virginia to Greenland. The fish is most commonly sold at weights between 15 and 80 pounds. The cheeks of the fish are particularly prized.

Haricots verts:

Very thin French green beans now being grown in the United States. Baby green beans or green beans sliced vertically into halves or quarters may be substituted.

Indian pudding:

A cornmeal-pudding dessert made with milk and molasses. The name comes from the fact that corn was called "Indian corn" by the early settlers, and anything containing corn or cornmeal might have the adjective "Indian." In the late seventeenth century, the dish was known as hasty pudding by colonists.

Infuse:

To steep herbs or other seasonings in liquid to extract their flavor. The liquid resulting from this process is called an infusion.

Jalapeño chilies:

A fairly small, dark green hot chili approximately 2 inches long and 1 inch wide. One of the most widely available fresh chilies. Serranos are a common substitution, although the heat from jalapeños is immediate while the serrano provides more of an afterburn. Jalapeños can vary in the level of hotness, and those with striations on the skin are older and usually hotter. It's better to start with less than the required amount, and add to suit personal taste.

Julienne:

Vegetables, potatoes, or other foods cut into thin strips about 1 to 2 inches long and ⅛ inch wide. Fine julienne is ⅟₁₆ inch wide.

Kalamata olives:

A robustly flavored brine-cured Greek black olive packed with some vinegar. Liguria or Lugano olives are the best substitutions; however, Kalamatas are widely available.

Kosher salt:

Also known as coarse salt or pickling salt, kosher salt is pure, refined rock salt that does not contain magnesium carbonate. It is milder in flavor than table salt and has larger grains. Do not substitute table salt in the same proportion in a recipe; it will make the dish far too salty. Use ½ to 1 teaspoon of table salt for each tablespoon of kosher salt specified.

Lemongrass:

Technically an herb, lemongrass is characterized by a strong citrus flavor with a spicy finish similar to that of ginger. Fresh lemongrass is used extensively in the cuisines of Thailand and Vietnam and may be found in some Asian markets.

Littleneck clams:

Small, hard-shell clams often eaten raw on the half shell or baked.

Lobster:

The American, Atlantic, or Maine lobster is a crustacean with a jointed body and two large pincer claws. The larger claw is used for crushing and the smaller one is used for catching its prey.

Maple syrup:

A sweet syrup made from the sugar-maple tree. Although it is expensive, do not substitute sugar syrup or a maple-syrup blend for pure maple syrup or the flavor will be inferior.

Marsala, dry:

An Italian wine similar in flavor and character to a medium-dry sherry, and used for such dishes as zabaglione and in a sauce for sautéed veal.

Mascarpone:

A soft, fresh Italian cheese with a high fat content used primarily in desserts and for tortas. If it is not available, combining equal parts of cream cheese and unsalted butter will produce a similar product.

Meringue:

Egg whites beaten until they are stiff but still glossy are called meringue, but the term also applies to dishes that are then sweetened and baked, such as meringue cookies and meringue toppings on pies.

Morels:

These spring mushrooms are about 1 inch long with a tall, hollow, pitted "hat." The colors range from gray to brown to black, depending on where they are found. Their flavor is rich, nutty, and meaty when cooked, and they should never be eaten raw.

Mussels:

Any of a variety of both salt- and freshwater bivalve mollusks having a blue-black shell.

Oysters:

Any of several edible mollusks found in brackish waters, marshes, inland waters, and even on the roots of submerged trees. There are many eastern varieties of oysters, including the Virginia oyster—also known as the Blue Point—Bristol, Cape Cod, Chincoteague, James River, Kent Island, and the Lynnheaven.

Oyster mushrooms:

Sometimes referred to as "shellfish of the woods," oyster mushrooms are delicate and translucent, with a silky consistency. The cap is scallop shaped, and they have a graceful appearance similar to that of a calla lily. The pale gray color may have hints of blue, yellow, and pink. Despite a slight aroma of anise, oyster mushrooms have a mild shellfish or oyster flavor.

Pancetta:

A thick Italian bacon sold in cylindrical form. Although it is salty, it does not have the heavy smoky taste of American bacon, nor is it eaten by itself. Most often, it is used as a flavoring in recipes.

Parchment paper:

A white heat-resistant paper sold in rolls at cookware stores. It is used in cooking to line baking pans and baking sheets, to cook items *en papillote,* and to loosely cover delicate foods like fish fillets during poaching.

Pasilla chilies:

Named for *pasa,* which means "raisin" in Spanish, this chili also is called *chilaca* when fresh, brown, and ripe, and *negro* when dried and black. Pasillas are mild to hot in temperature, are used in *moles,* and may be substituted for ancho or chilies.

Pastry bag:

A bag, usually made of plastic, canvas, or nylon, that may be fitted with plain or decorative tips and used to pipe out icings, thick doughs, and pureed foods.

Pheasant:

One of the leanest and most flavorful of game birds, pheasant is eaten when it is one year old or younger. To test for age, gently press the space above the breastbone; if the pheasant is young, the bone will move.

Phyllo dough:

Also called filo, these tissue-paper-thin pastry sheets made from a flour and water dough are used in layers and brushed with some sort of fat before baking. Phyllo is widely available in supermarkets.

Pilaf:

A dish of grain that has been sautéed briefly in butter or oil, then simmered in stock or water with various seasonings.

Pink peppercorns:

The slightly piquant berries of a small South American shrub, pink peppercorns are a decorative alternative to green peppercorns, or the two may be used in combination. Use sparingly; pink peppercorns can be toxic in great quantity.

Poaching:

Poaching, whether on top of the stove or in the oven, is a method of cooking food by submerging it in barely simmering liquid. The food cooks gently, leaving the flavor and texture intact. The foods most often poached are firm-fleshed fish, whole chickens or chicken pieces, and fruits.

Poblano chilies:

Large tapered chilies about 4 inches long, 2½ inches wide, and shiny dark green in color. Poblanos are mild to hot. When used in sauces, they may be interchanged with green Anaheim chilies, though the flavor will be different. If desperate, green bell peppers may be stuffed in place of poblanos, but increase the spice level of the filling.

Polenta:

Coarsely ground cornmeal, which is combined with stock or water and cooked slowly until thick. It may be served creamy, or it may be chilled, cut into shapes, and grilled.

Porcini mushrooms :

This mushroom is popular the world over, but is very important in Italian cuisine, and is used as much dried as fresh. Porcini do not have gills under the cap, but rather a mass of minuscule tubes. Their flavor is earthy, rich, and reminiscent of hazelnuts, while the texture remains delicate and the colors range from rusty brown to terra-cotta. Fresh porcini are also known as *cèpes.*

Portobello mushrooms:

Huge mushrooms with caps from 3 to 6 inches in diameter. The brown gills underneath the cap should be cut away before the mushrooms are cooked or they will give a dark brown color to a dish.

Prosciutto:

A raw ham with a slightly sweet flavor, primarily from the Parma region of Italy, prosciutto is made from pigs fed on acorns and is aged for at least nine months after being smoked.

Quahogs:

A hard-shell clam over 3 inches in diameter, which is always removed from the shell and chopped before using it since it is too tough to eat raw on the half shell. Quahogs are the basis for clam chowders and fritters, and are frequently mixed with bread crumbs and packed back into the shell for stuffed quahogs.

Quail:

Quail have pale meat, usually weigh about 4 ounces, and are subtly flavored. They are excellent for grilling, broiling, and stuffing since they are tender. Boned quail are really semi-boneless, as the body is boned but the leg bones are left in.

Quenelle:

While a traditional French quenelle is a dumpling based on ground meat or seafood and bound with egg, in contemporary American cooking they may be any sort of pureed and bound food that top a liquid; the term is used almost interchangeably with *dumpling.*

Radicchio:

Relatively new in America, radicchio is a member of the chicory family developed in Italy. The head ranges in size from that of a golf ball to that of a grapefruit. The beautifully white-veined leaves may be any shade from bright red to dark maroon, and the flavor is rather bitter. In Italy radicchio is served as a salad or is braised, grilled, or wilted, often with a splash of vinegar and oil.

Ramekin:

A ceramic ovenproof dish ranging in size from 4 to 8 ounces. They are used for baking custards and individual servings of many foods.

Reduce:

To decrease the volume of a liquid by simmering or boiling, which results in the evaporation of water and produces a thicker consistency and/or concentrated flavors.

Reduction:

The product that results when a liquid is reduced.

Render:

To produce fat by cooking meat containing a high fat content such as bacon or poultry skin or fat.

Roux:

A base of flour cooked in fat, used as a thickening agent for white sauces, gumbo, and many soufflé bases. The mixture may be cooked from pale white to dark brown depending on the usage, and the purpose of this step is to cook the flour so that the resulting dish does not have a pastelike taste.

Sabayon:

A sweetened custard made with egg yolks and liquor or wine.

Saffron:

The stigmas from a species of crocus plant, saffron is the most expensive food in the world. Modern technology has yet to invent a harvesting method to replace the delicate hand-picking, and it takes more than 250,000 crocus plants to yield one pound of spice. Saffron imparts an orange-yellow color and a slightly pungent flavor to foods. It is traditionally used in such dishes as Spanish paella, and is a great addition to sauces for simple fish preparations.

Salsa:

While salsas entered our vocabulary as vegetable sauces served with Mexican and southwestern cooking, the term has become generic and now means any chopped sauce used as a topping for food.

Salt cod:

Prior to refrigeration, salting of meat and fish was one of the only means of preservation, and salt cod was one of the major foods exported from New England. Salt cod needs to be soaked thoroughly before using in such recipes as cod cakes, a traditional New England dish.

Sauté:

A cooking method in which items are cooked quickly in a small amount of fat in a low-sided pan on top of the stove. For many dishes, aromatic vegetables such as onions and/or garlic are sautéed before other ingredients are added to the pot, so the sauté may be a preliminary step as well as a completed dish.

Savoy cabbage:

A head cabbage with bright green crinkled leaves that make a pretty garnish, but may also be shredded or stuffed.

Scallops:

A bivalve whose adductor muscle (the muscle that keeps its shell closed) and roe are eaten. The waters off New England contain both tiny bay and larger sea scallops that are harvested at different times of the year. Fresh scallops have a sweet aroma and their liquid is clear and not milky.

Sear:

To seal the surface of meat by adding it to a small amount of oil that has been heated to almost the smoking point over very high heat. Searing keeps the juices of foods from escaping during longer cooking and gives foods a rich brown tone.

Serrano chilies:

A tapered, thin, bright-green chili that is similar to but smaller than a jalapeño. Good for cooking or as a garnish, it varies in hotness as much as jalapeños and may be substituted for them.

Shallots:

A member of the onion family, their flavor is milder than that of onion and less pungent than garlic. Shallots are usually about 1 to ½ inches long, are oval in shape, and may come as one bulb or a pair. They are excellent in sauces, salad dressing, and roasted whole.

Shiitake mushrooms:

The second most widely cultivated mushroom in the world, shiitakes have a distinctive woodsy, smoky flavor, are moist and fleshy when fresh, and need to be soaked to soften when dried. They are medium to large, with an umbrella-shaped, floppy tan to dark brown cap with edges that tend to roll inward. Use only the spongy, full-bodied caps and discard the fibrous stems; they are too tough to eat.

Silver skin:

The tough, connective tissue that surrounds certain muscles.

Simmer:

To maintain the temperature of a liquid just below boiling, about 200°F. Also, a cooking method in which items are cooked in simmering liquid.

Smithfield ham:

In order to carry a Smithfield label, a ham must be salted, smoked, and aged in the town of Smithfield, Virginia, though the hogs may come from the surrounding area. The ham is sometimes called "Virginia ham," but that name is more generally applied to a specific method of roasting a smoked ham. The ham is dry, with a very salty flavor and a crumbly texture.

Soufflé:

While the word *soufflé* literally means "puffed," it refers to a hot or cold dish with a light texture that uses beaten egg whites to achieve height.

Spaghetti squash:

A bright yellow squash shaped like a football. The pale yellow flesh of the vegetable becomes stringy, like spaghetti, when cooked, and is often served like spaghetti, with cheese or a sauce.

Squab:

A domesticated pigeon that has not yet begun to fly. It is slaughtered at 3 to 4 weeks old, weighing under 1 pound. Its light, tender meat is suitable for sautéing, roasting, and grilling.

Surry sausage:

A mildly spiced Virginia pork sausage flavored with sage.

Sweat:

To cook vegetables in a covered pan in a small amount of fat until the food softens and releases moisture.

Sweetbreads:

The thymus glands of veal calves, sold in pairs, thus the plural name. They have a very delicate flavor and weigh about 1 pound per pair.

Temper:

To heat gently and gradually. May refer to the process of incorporating hot liquid into a liaison to gradually raise its temperature, or to the proper method for melting chocolate.

Tempura:

Seafood and/or vegetables that are coated with a light batter and deep-fried.

Terrine:

A loaf of forcemeat cooked in a covered mold in a water bath so that the exterior does not become crusty. Also, the mold used to cook such items, usually oval or rectangular in shape.

Timbale:

A small pail-shaped 4- to 8-ounce mold used to shape rice, custards, and other items. Also, a preparation made in such a mold.

Tomalley:

The liver of a lobster, which is located in the body cavity and green in color. It is used in lobster sauces and stocks.

Tomatillos:

Tomatillos look like tomatoes, are small and green even when ripe, and are found in markets covered with a protective brown paper-like husk. While they will not have the citric undertones, small unripe green tomatoes are the best substitute.

Truffles:

Round, irregular in shape, with a rough texture, truffles are either black or white, and most are as small as a walnut. In North America, two varieties of truffles are grown, in Texas and Oregon, and they sell for far less money than their European counterparts. Fresh truffles are in season in the fall, and black truffles are also available canned.

Truss:

To tie meat or poultry with string before cooking it in order to give it a compact, rounded shape for a better appearance or to hold in stuffing.

Vanilla beans:

The pod of a relative of the orchid, vanilla beans are green and have no flavor when picked; they are then cured by a process of sweating and drying. Once cured, the beans are either bundled whole for export or processed into extract.

Venison:

Meat from large game animals; often used to refer to deer meat.

Water bath:

A vessel of simmering water into which a cooking vessel is set in order to cook food gently. A water bath ensures that custards are velvety and not tough, and that pâtés have a uniform texture rather than being crusty on the exterior.

Yukon Gold potatoes:

These yellow-skinned boiling potatoes have sweet, moist, smooth meat and an almost buttery taste. They are excellent for mashing and whipping.

Zest:

The thin, brightly colored outer part of citrus rind. It contains volatile oils, making it ideal for use as a flavoring.

MAIL-ORDER SOURCES

If this book had been written a decade ago, many of the ingredients in the recipes would have been unavailable in supermarkets. We have advanced light years since the era twenty years ago when I had to ask my sister in New York to ship snow peas and bok choy to me in Cincinnati. Today, many supermarkets carry the basics for various kinds of ethnic cooking, along with a variety of fresh vegetables used in many cuisines.

Fresh game birds and seafood may still be difficult to find, however, in some small towns and cities. Listed below are mail-order sources for many of the fine products called for in these recipes, as well as eastern companies whose products are especially noteworthy.

Aidells Sausage Company

P.O. Box 7456
San Francisco, CA 94120-7456
800-541-2233

A wide array of traditional and innovative sausages of the highest quality and reasonably priced.

American Spoon Foods

P.O. Box 566
Petoskey, MI 49770
800-222-5886

Chef Larry Forgione and his partner, Justin Rashid, package a wonderful line of dried fruits and other ingredients for cooking, including dried cranberries and cherries, as well as many American regional specialties from other companies.

Auricchio Cheese, Inc.

5810 Highway NN
Denmark, WI 54208
414-863-2123

An excellent source of fine Italian cheeses, from fresh marscarpone to Parmesan.

Balducci's

11-02 Queens Plaza South
Long Island City, NY 11101-4908
800-225-3822

This famed New York gourmet market has created a mail-order division, with everything from fresh pastas and excellent sauces to prime meats and desserts. This is the source for such foods as pâte de foie gras, capon, quail, pheasant, squid, venison, and imported and domestic caviars.

Boyajian, Inc.

P.O. Box 26
Belmont, MA 02178
617-965-5800

Poussins, turkeys, caviar, wonderful citrus and garlic oils, imported and domestic caviars, and smoked fish.

Broken Arrow Ranch

P.O. Box 530
Ingram, TX 78025
800-962-4263

Mike Hughes was the pioneer of farm-raised game in Texas, and his venison, bear, and other products are superb.

Chesapeake Express, Ltd.

1129 Hope Road
Centreville, MD 21617
410-758-0913

This company is one of the few to ship jumbo soft-shell crabs as well as lump crabmeat and authentic Maryland crab cakes.

Clambake Celebrations

9 West Road
Orleans, MA 02653
800-423-4038

The source for an entire New England clambake in a pot to set on the stove, as well as other types of eastern seafood.

Dallas Mozzarella Company

2944 Elm Street
Dallas, TX 75226
800-798-2954

Paula Lambert's delicious array of Italian and Texas-style cheeses.

D'Artagnan

399–419 St. Paul Avenue
Jersey City, NJ 07306
800-327-8246

The only source in this country for fresh foie gras, D'Artagnan also offers fresh game birds and meats, sausages, free-range poultry, duck fat, smoked duck, heart, and pâté de foie gras.

Dodge Cove Marine Farm, Inc.

P.O. Box 211
Newcastle, ME
207-563-8168

An excellent source for farmed oysters, mussels, lobster, fresh fish, and other Maine delicacies.

Ducktrap River Fish Farm

Lincolnville, ME 04849
800-828-3825

Smoked seafood, including smoked scallops, mussels, and shrimp, made Ducktrap famous with New England food aficionados, and it remains the source for some of the best available nationally.

The Farm at Mt. Walden

P.O. Box 515
The Plains, VA 22171
800-64-TROUT

This small smokehouse in the foothills of the Shenandoahs offers wonderful smoked trout, as well as hot-smoked salmon.

Foggy Ridge Gamebird Farm

213 Highland Road
Warren, MS 04864
207-273-2357

The farm will ship a wide range of game birds, such as pheasant, grouse, Guinea hen, squab, wild duck, and wild turkey.

Gray's Grist Mill

P.O. Box 422
Adamsville, RI 02801
508-636-6075

This small mill sells white flint cornmeal for true Rhode Island johnnycakes, as well as brown-bread flour and various pancake and muffin mixes.

Gwaltney's

P.O. Box 1
Smithfield, VA 23431
800-292-2773

While many people substitute prosciutto in recipes calling for Smithfield ham, there is really no comparable product. The hams are available cooked and pre-sliced.

Harrington Ham Company

Main Street
Richmond, VT 05477
802-434-3411

A well-known source of Vermont-style cob-smoked hams, country bacon, and other smoked specialties.

Horton's Downeast Foods, Inc.

P.O. Box 430
Waterboro, ME 04087
207-247-6900

Call for their catalog of smoked seafood specialties, including plump mussels.

Jamison Farm

171 Jamison Lane
Latrobe, PA 15650-9400
800-237-5262

While every supermarket carries lamb, very few specialty butchers carry the kind of free-range organically fed lamb that can be shipped from this Pennsylvania farm.

John Dewar & Company

753 Beacon Street
Newton, MA 02159
617-442-4292

Another good source of specialty meats, venison, and game birds.

Legal Seafood

33 Everett Street
Allston, MA 02134
800-343-5804

This firm gained regional fame by offering the finest quality of seafood in its restaurants. In addition to shipping clambakes, you can count on them for many varieties of fish and shellfish as well as excellent chowder and bluefish paté.

L'Espirit de Campagne

P.O. Box 3130
Winchester, VA 22604
703-955-1014

Dried vine-ripened tomatoes in various forms: halves marinated in extra-virgin olive oil with herbs; minced, for a spreadable texture; and dried sprinkles to use like seasonings, a healthy alternative to bacon bits. The company also offers dried apples, cherries, blueberries, and cranberries, all unsulphured and with no preservatives.

Marblehead Lobster Company

Beacon and Orne streets
Marblehead, MA 01945
617-631-0787

Another fine source for lobsters of all sizes.

Montdomaine Cellars

Route 6, P.O. Box 188A
Charlottesville, VA 22902
800-829-4633

Wines from the land of Thomas Jefferson, including Chardonnay, Cabernet Sauvignon, Merlot, blush, Viognies, Marsanne, and Cabernet Franc.

Mook Seafarm, Inc.

HC 64, P.O. Box 041
Damariscotta, ME 04543
207-563-5210

Some of the best mussels, clams, and oysters in the country.

Mystique

Friendship Street
Waldoro, ME 04572
207-832-5136

One of the region's best boutique goat cheese makers, with a tart yet creamy product.

Oasis Vineyards

P.O. Box 116
Hume, VA 22639
703-635-7627

Virginia wines, including Chardonnay, Riesling, Gewürztraminer, Cabernet Sauvignon, Merlot, Cabernet Franc, Oasis Brut, Oasis Extra Dry, and Dogwood Series label.

Pines Acres Rabbitry

299 East Main Street
Norton, MA 02766
508-285-7391

It is still difficult to find good fresh rabbits in many parts of the country, and these are meaty and delicate.

The Pork Shop of Vermont

P.O. Box 99
Hinesburg, VT 05461
802-482-3617

Smoked hams, bacon, and other smoked products cured without nitrates or other preservatives.

Prince Michel Vineyards

HCR 4, P.O. Box 77
Lion, VA 22725
703-547-3707

One of the best of the Virginia wineries, producing Rapidan River Riesling, Gewürztraminer, Chardonnay, Prince Michel Vineyards Chardonnay, White Burgundy Chardonnay, Blanc de Michel, Blush de Michel, Cabernet Sauvignon, and Meritage Red.

Salumeria Italiana

151 Richmond Street
Boston, MA 02113
617-523-8743

Replicate a meal in Boston's North End, with products from one of the area's best-known purveyors.

Schartner's Mountain View Fruit and Berry Farm

Route 220, P.O. Box 82
Thorndike, ME 04986
207-568-3668

This farm ships many heirloom apple and pear varieties as well as other fruits.

Stonington Lobster Co-op

P.O. Box 89
Indian Point Road
Stonington, ME 04681
207-367-2286

This firm gathers its wares from a number of different suppliers, and offers fresh crabmeat in addition to lobster.

Summerfield Farms

10044 James Monroe Highway
Culpepper, VA 22701
702-547-9600

One of the country's best lines of game meats including venison and bear and birds, along with flavorful free-range veal, lamb, and organ meats. They also sell veal demi-glace—a real boon to cooks.

S. Wallace Edwards & Sons, Inc.

P.O. Box 25
Surry, VA 23883
800-222-4267

Hickory-smoked aged Virginia hams, bacon, Surry sausages, as well as dry-cured duck breast and Virginia seafood including crab cakes, smoked tuna, and Chesapeake Bay oysters.

Vermont Butter & Cheese Company, Inc.

Pitman Road, P.O. Box 95
Websterville, VT 05678
802-479-9371

A source for crème fraîche and European-style cheeses, including fromage blanc and mascarpone.

White Lily Flour Company

P.O. Box 871
Knoxville, TN 37901

Soft-wheat flour to use for southern biscuits or in place of cake flour for cakes.

Wolfe's Neck Farm Foundation

R.R. 1, P.O. Box 71
Freeport, ME 04032
207-865-4469

Organic Black Angus beef as good as any beef from the prairie.

York Hill Farm

York Hill Road
New Sharon, ME 04955
207-778-9741

Another small goat-cheese producer, with a line that includes a Roman-style capriano.

Credits
Great Chefs of the East©

The Book
Publisher	
Editor	
Production Services	
Book Design	
Author	
Photography	
Sales & Marketing	
Public Relations	

Great Chefs Publishing
John Shoup
Carolyn Miller
Mimi Luebbermann
Linda Anne Nix
Larry Escudier
Dwain Richard, Jr.
Ellen Brown
with Amanda Lydon
Eric Futran
Charles Flood
Brown & Whiting

Home Video
Sales & Marketing

Great Chefs Video
Thomas DeMaeyer

The Television Series
Presenter
Announcer
Writer
Camera/Lighting
Field Audio
Editor
Assistant Editor
Post Production Audio
Culinary Advisor
Graphic Design
Computer Animation
Theme Music

Original Music

Additional Footage

Official Hotel
Special Thanks to:

Public Relations
Closing Sequence
Assistant to the
   Executive Producer
Associate Producer
Producer/Director
Executive Producer

Great Chefs Television
Mary Lou Conroy
Andres Calandria
John Beyer
Dave Landry
Charles C. Sainz
George Matulik
Maria D. Estevez
Andres Calandria
Chan Patterson
Escudier & Richard
Imagetech
Performed by
Bobby Short
Written by
Joy & Gary Anderson
Charlie Byrd Trio
   Charlie Byrd
   Rick Whitehead
   Jeff Meyerriecks
PVS, Washington, D.C.
WHYY-TV, Philadelphia, PA
ITT Sheraton Corp.
Embassy Square Hotel, Washington, D.C.
Williamsburg Inn, Williamsburg, VA
Linda Anne Nix
André Renard, Les Célébrités, New York, NY

Cybil W. Curtis
Charles C. Sainz
John Beyer
John Shoup

Index

Chefs' biographies in bold-face type

NOTES